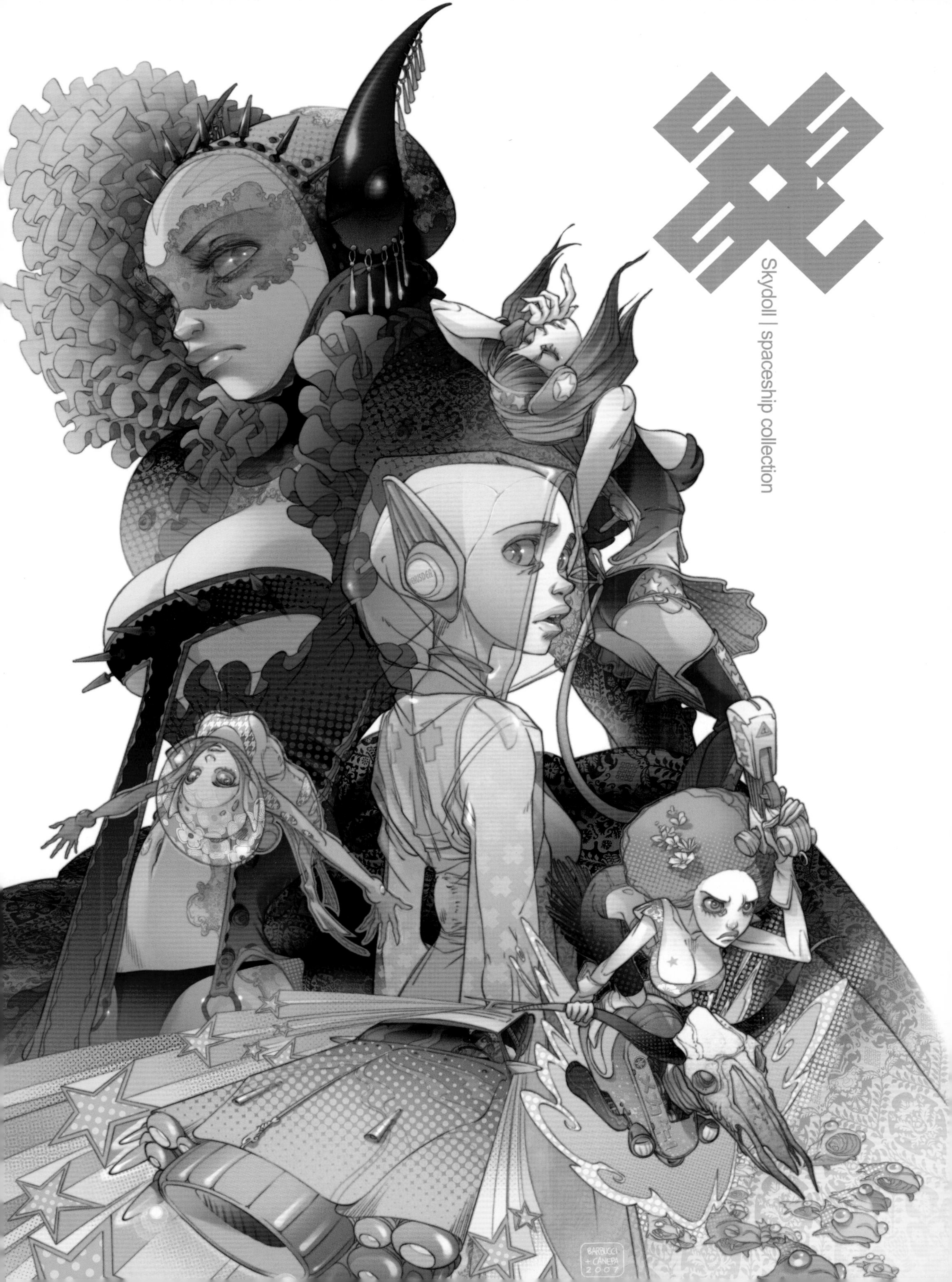
BARBUCCI
+ CANEPA
2007

Skydoll | spaceship collection

SDSSC

Skydoll Spaceship Collection

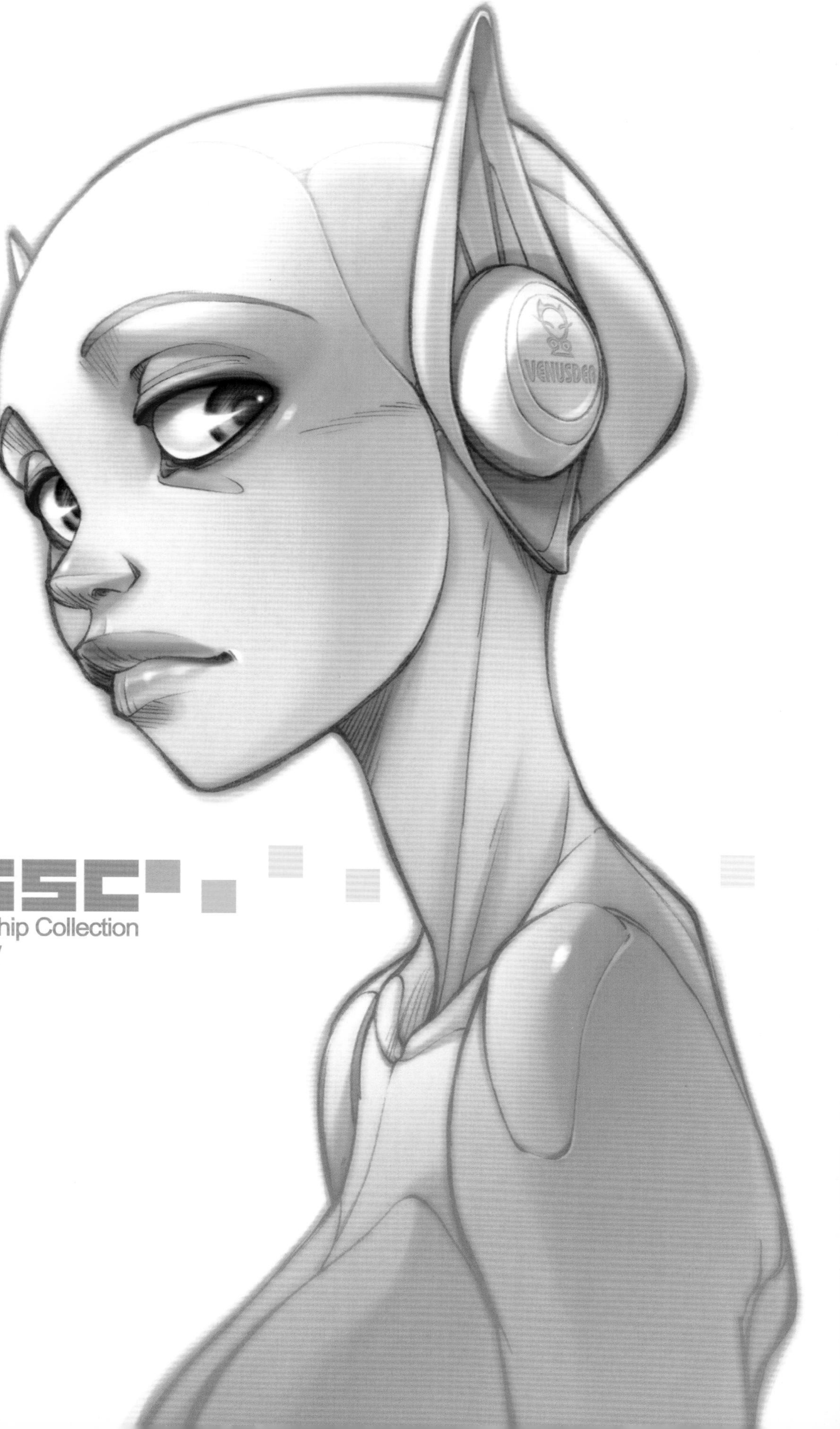
VENUSDEA

ALESSANDRO BARBUCCI

sky-doll

BARBARA CANEPA

skydoll spaceship colle

collection skydoll

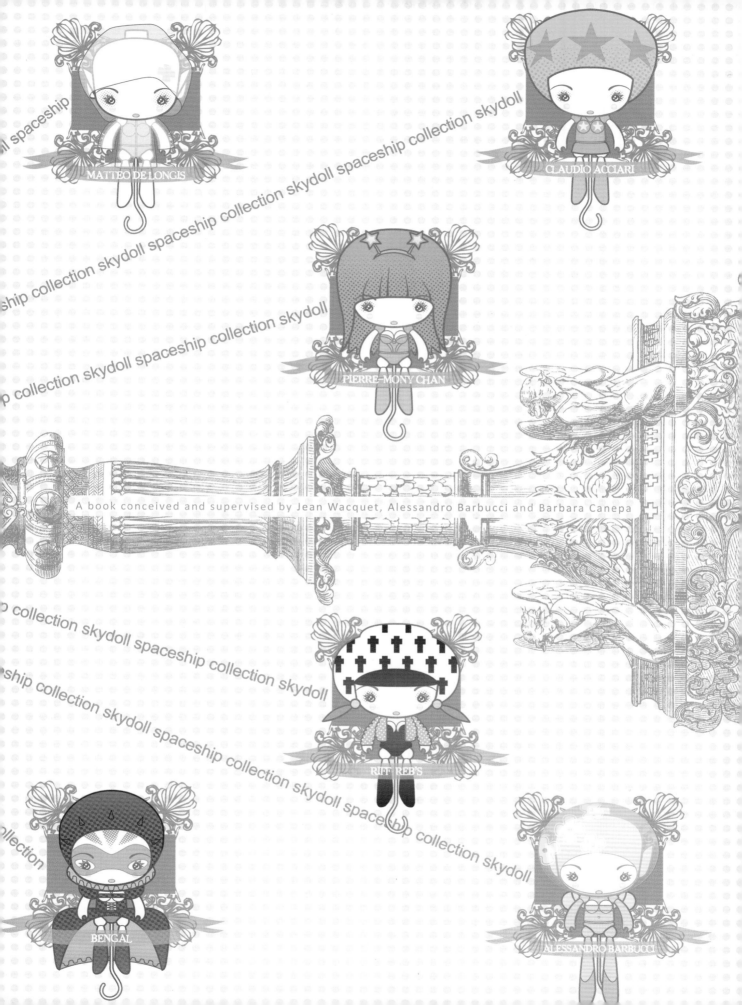

MATTEO DE LONGIS

CLAUDIO ACCIARI

PIERRE-MONY CHAN

A book conceived and supervised by Jean Wacquet, Alessandro Barbucci and Barbara Canepa

RIFF REB'S

BENGAL

ALESSANDRO BARBUCCI

SKYDOLL SPACESHIP COLLECTION

Venusdea industries

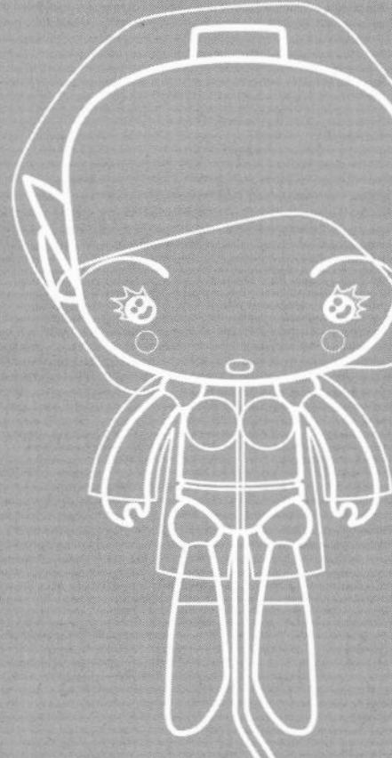

Warning! This track contains:

"But am I running away from him?
No! It can't be! He loves me."

(Sky Doll: Decade, Volume 0, page 168)

- Unripe beauties
- Gauzy lace
- Synthetic clinic

track01: 05~13

La Bambola

Matteo De Longis | Italy

story | Canepa

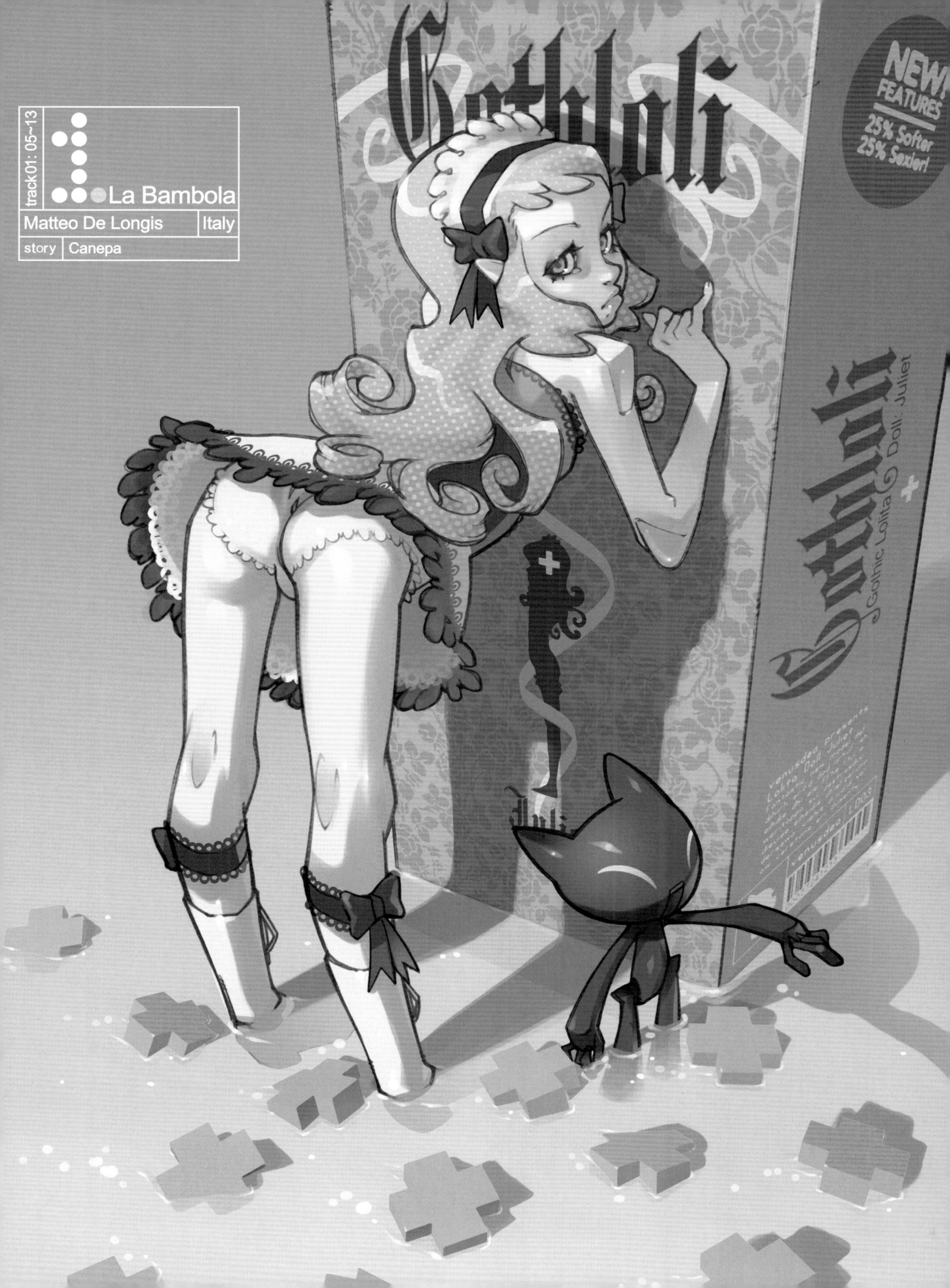
Gothloli
NEW! FEATURES
25% Softer
25% Sexier!
Gothloli
Gothic Lolita Doll: Juliet

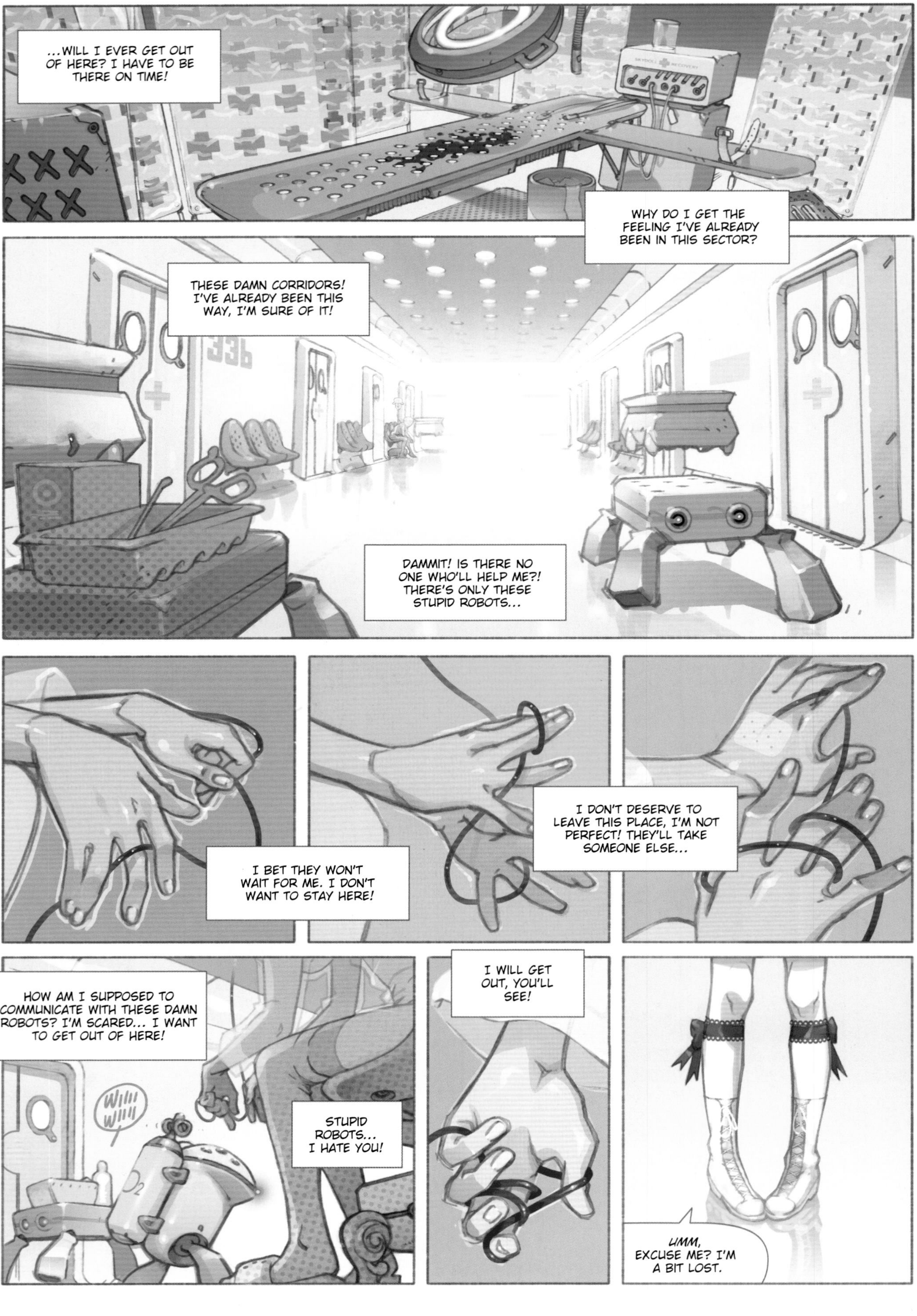
...WILL I EVER GET OUT OF HERE? I HAVE TO BE THERE ON TIME!
WHY DO I GET THE FEELING I'VE ALREADY BEEN IN THIS SECTOR?
THESE DAMN CORRIDORS! I'VE ALREADY BEEN THIS WAY, I'M SURE OF IT!
336
DAMMIT! IS THERE NO ONE WHO'LL HELP ME?! THERE'S ONLY THESE STUPID ROBOTS...
I BET THEY WON'T WAIT FOR ME. I DON'T WANT TO STAY HERE!
I DON'T DESERVE TO LEAVE THIS PLACE, I'M NOT PERFECT! THEY'LL TAKE SOMEONE ELSE...
HOW AM I SUPPOSED TO COMMUNICATE WITH THESE DAMN ROBOTS? I'M SCARED... I WANT TO GET OUT OF HERE!
STUPID ROBOTS... I HATE YOU!
I WILL GET OUT, YOU'LL SEE!
UMM, EXCUSE ME? I'M A BIT LOST.

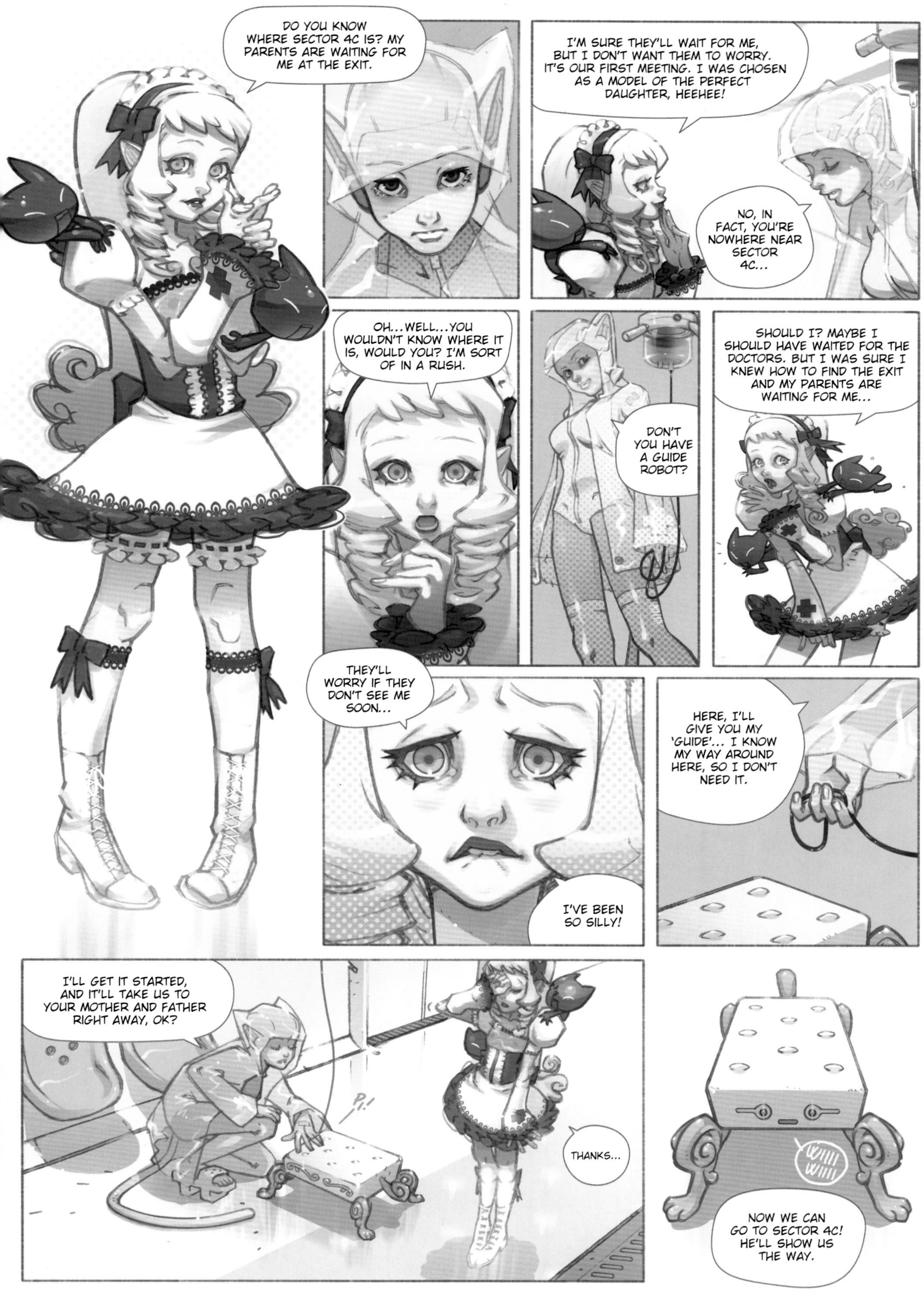
DO YOU KNOW WHERE SECTOR 4C IS? MY PARENTS ARE WAITING FOR ME AT THE EXIT.
I'M SURE THEY'LL WAIT FOR ME, BUT I DON'T WANT THEM TO WORRY. IT'S OUR FIRST MEETING. I WAS CHOSEN AS A MODEL OF THE PERFECT DAUGHTER, HEEHEE!
NO, IN FACT, YOU'RE NOWHERE NEAR SECTOR 4C...
OH...WELL...YOU WOULDN'T KNOW WHERE IT IS, WOULD YOU? I'M SORT OF IN A RUSH.
DON'T YOU HAVE A GUIDE ROBOT?
SHOULD I? MAYBE I SHOULD HAVE WAITED FOR THE DOCTORS. BUT I WAS SURE I KNEW HOW TO FIND THE EXIT AND MY PARENTS ARE WAITING FOR ME...
THEY'LL WORRY IF THEY DON'T SEE ME SOON...
I'VE BEEN SO SILLY!
HERE, I'LL GIVE YOU MY 'GUIDE'... I KNOW MY WAY AROUND HERE, SO I DON'T NEED IT.
I'LL GET IT STARTED, AND IT'LL TAKE US TO YOUR MOTHER AND FATHER RIGHT AWAY, OK?
THANKS...
NOW WE CAN GO TO SECTOR 4C! HE'LL SHOW US THE WAY.

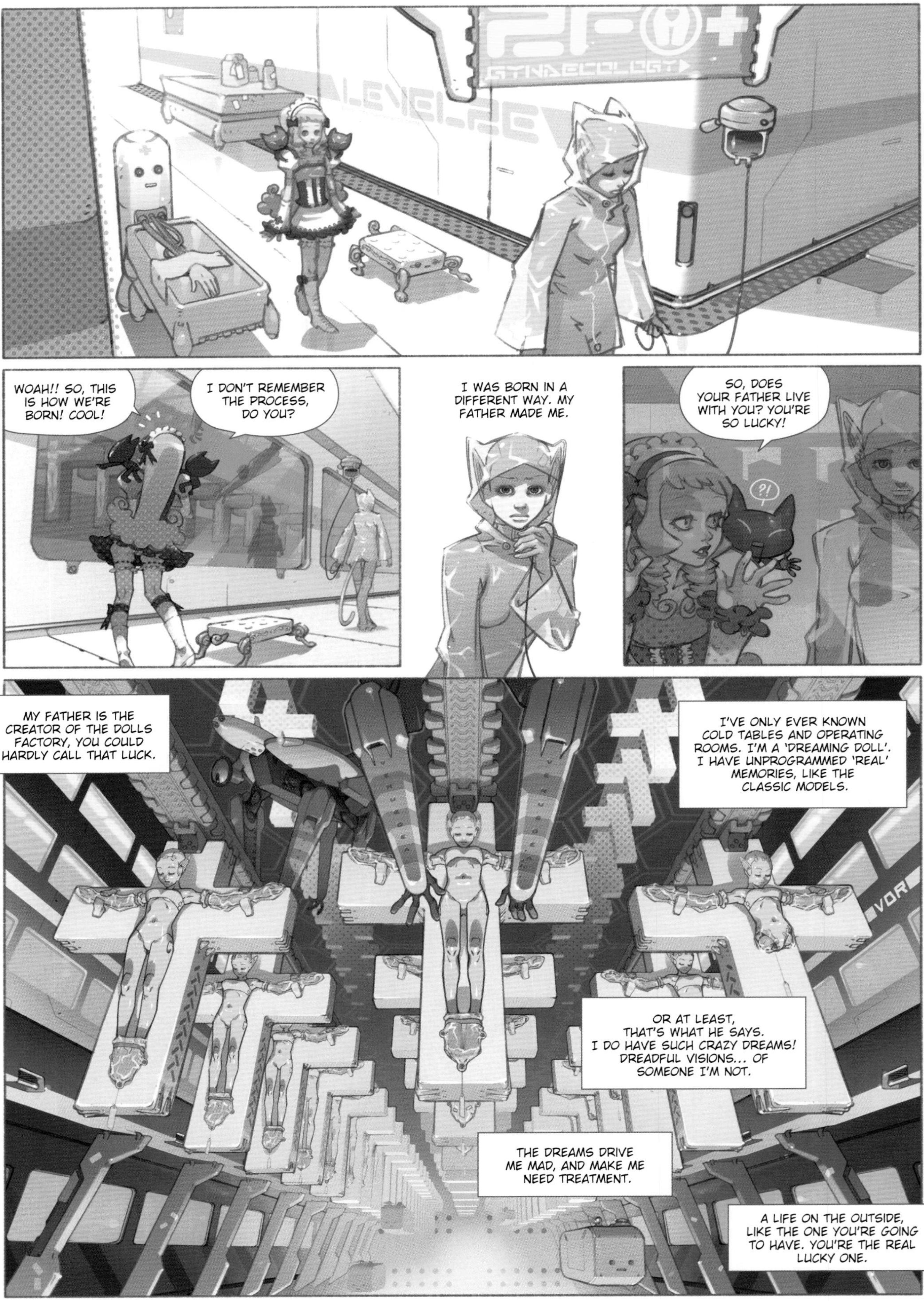
WOAH!! SO, THIS IS HOW WE'RE BORN! COOL!
I DON'T REMEMBER THE PROCESS, DO YOU?
I WAS BORN IN A DIFFERENT WAY. MY FATHER MADE ME.
SO, DOES YOUR FATHER LIVE WITH YOU? YOU'RE SO LUCKY!
?!
MY FATHER IS THE CREATOR OF THE DOLLS FACTORY, YOU COULD HARDLY CALL THAT LUCK.
I'VE ONLY EVER KNOWN COLD TABLES AND OPERATING ROOMS. I'M A 'DREAMING DOLL'. I HAVE UNPROGRAMMED 'REAL' MEMORIES, LIKE THE CLASSIC MODELS.
OR AT LEAST, THAT'S WHAT HE SAYS. I DO HAVE SUCH CRAZY DREAMS! DREADFUL VISIONS... OF SOMEONE I'M NOT.
THE DREAMS DRIVE ME MAD, AND MAKE ME NEED TREATMENT.
A LIFE ON THE OUTSIDE, LIKE THE ONE YOU'RE GOING TO HAVE. YOU'RE THE REAL LUCKY ONE.

I'M SO GLAD I FOUND YOU NOW... I DON'T KNOW WHAT I WOULD HAVE DONE WITHOUT YOUR HELP.

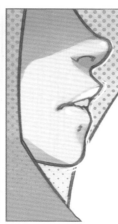

OOPS, MY MISTAKE! IT'S NOT THIS WAY TO SECTOR 4C.

I'M SO FORGETFUL.

AH! OK...

THIS WAY!

!

THIS DOOR?

YES, I REMEMBER NOW! DEFINITELY...

PIIP!

IT'S REALLY DARK INSIDE...

WAIT... WHERE ARE WE?

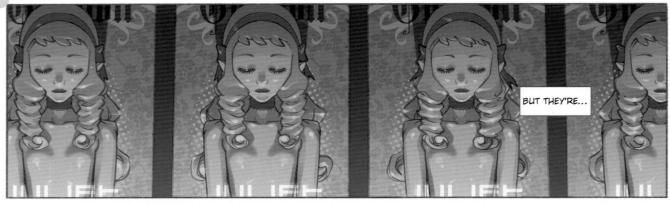

BUT THEY'RE...

THEY'RE JUST LIKE ME!

GOTHLOLI
model: JULIET

1 Sexual purpose doll ◆VIRGIN◆

NEW! sup... pl... d system

2 the ... nd cutest bare... doll!

small tits ... xy - dildo

Galaxy ...
-Realistic feel ...
-Shy lolita mode...
-Ruffled elegant ... ue dress

THIS ONE IS ME.

I'M A SEX MODEL, AREN'T I?

YOU KNEW THE WHOLE TIME!

CLICK

YES!

TO BE PRECISE, YOU'RE A 'GOTHIC LOLITA' MODEL.

WOOOAHHH!

BUT THAT'S AMAZING! I'M A TOY FOR RICH PEOPLE!

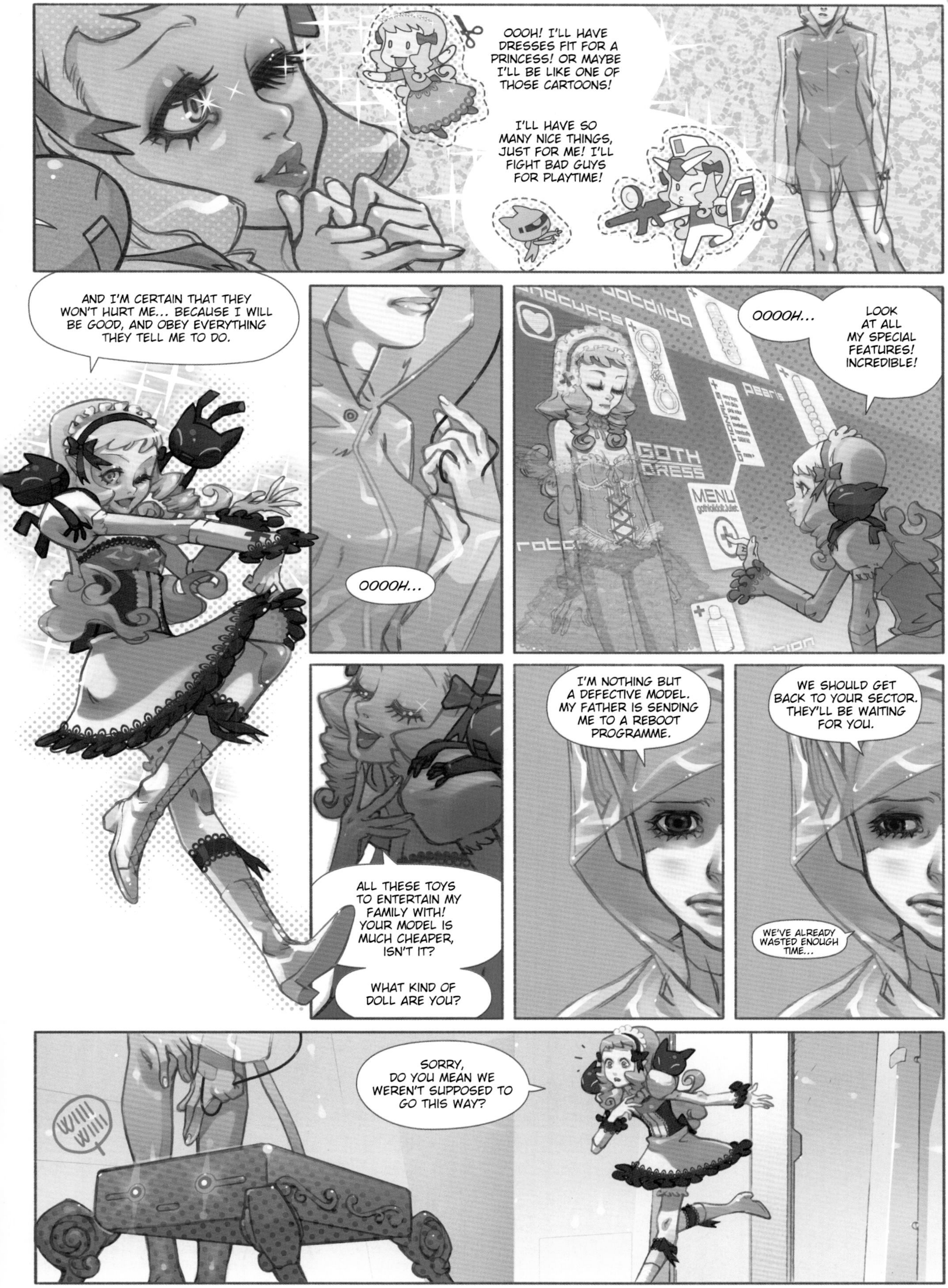
OOOH! I'LL HAVE DRESSES FIT FOR A PRINCESS! OR MAYBE I'LL BE LIKE ONE OF THOSE CARTOONS!
I'LL HAVE SO MANY NICE THINGS, JUST FOR ME! I'LL FIGHT BAD GUYS FOR PLAYTIME!
AND I'M CERTAIN THAT THEY WON'T HURT ME... BECAUSE I WILL BE GOOD, AND OBEY EVERYTHING THEY TELL ME TO DO.
OOOOH...
OOOOH...
LOOK AT ALL MY SPECIAL FEATURES! INCREDIBLE!
GOTH DRESS
MENU
ALL THESE TOYS TO ENTERTAIN MY FAMILY WITH! YOUR MODEL IS MUCH CHEAPER, ISN'T IT?
WHAT KIND OF DOLL ARE YOU?
I'M NOTHING BUT A DEFECTIVE MODEL. MY FATHER IS SENDING ME TO A REBOOT PROGRAMME.
WE SHOULD GET BACK TO YOUR SECTOR. THEY'LL BE WAITING FOR YOU.
WE'VE ALREADY WASTED ENOUGH TIME...
SORRY, DO YOU MEAN WE WEREN'T SUPPOSED TO GO THIS WAY?
WIIII WIIII

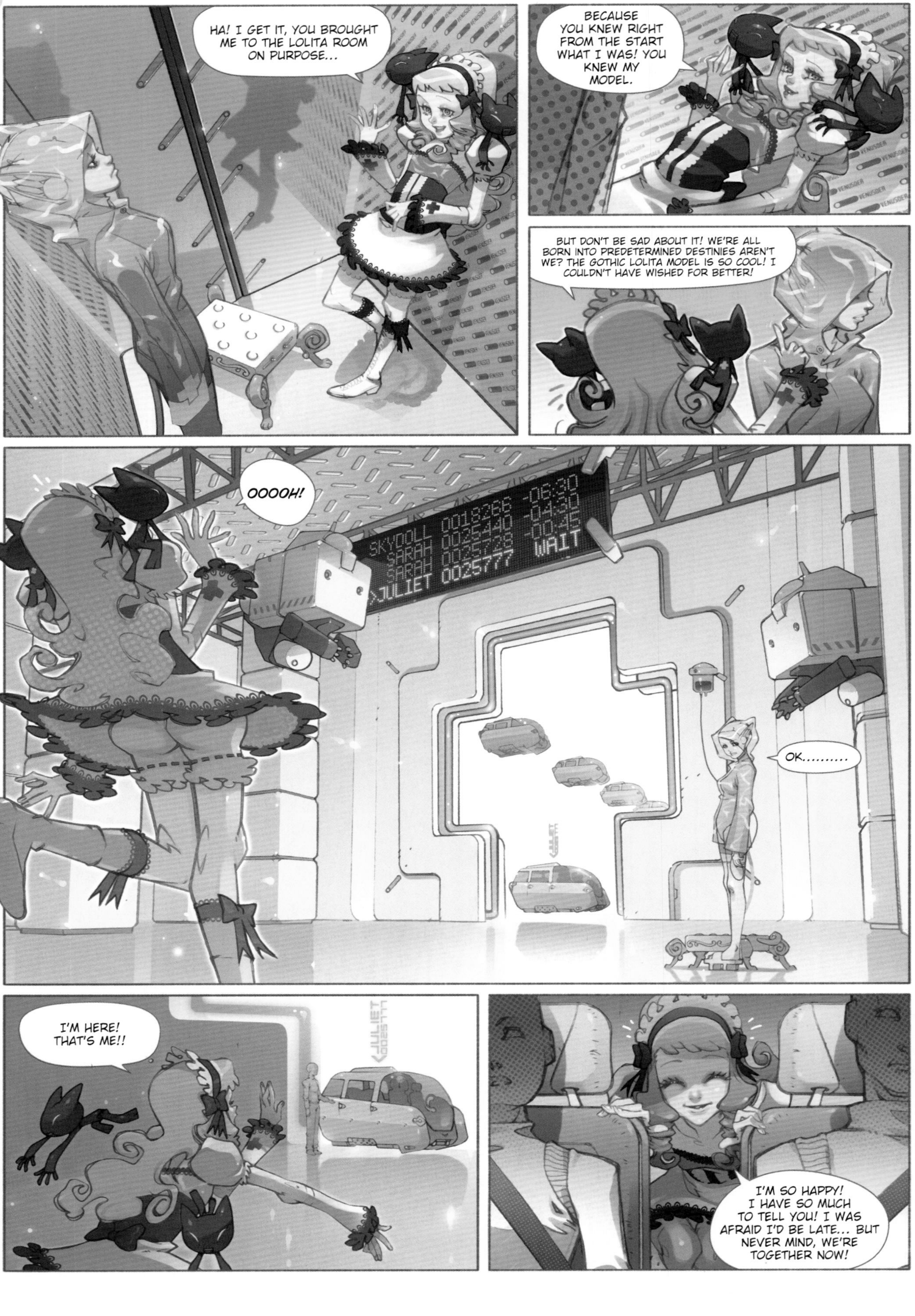
HA! I GET IT, YOU BROUGHT ME TO THE LOLITA ROOM ON PURPOSE...
BECAUSE YOU KNEW RIGHT FROM THE START WHAT I WAS! YOU KNEW MY MODEL.
BUT DON'T BE SAD ABOUT IT! WE'RE ALL BORN INTO PREDETERMINED DESTINIES AREN'T WE? THE GOTHIC LOLITA MODEL IS SO COOL! I COULDN'T HAVE WISHED FOR BETTER!
OOOOH!
SKYDOLL 0018266 -06:30
SARAH 0025440 -04:30
SARAH 0025728 -00:45
>JULIET 0025777 WAIT
OK.........
I'M HERE! THAT'S ME!!
JULIET 0025777
I'M SO HAPPY! I HAVE SO MUCH TO TELL YOU! I WAS AFRAID I'D BE LATE... BUT NEVER MIND, WE'RE TOGETHER NOW!

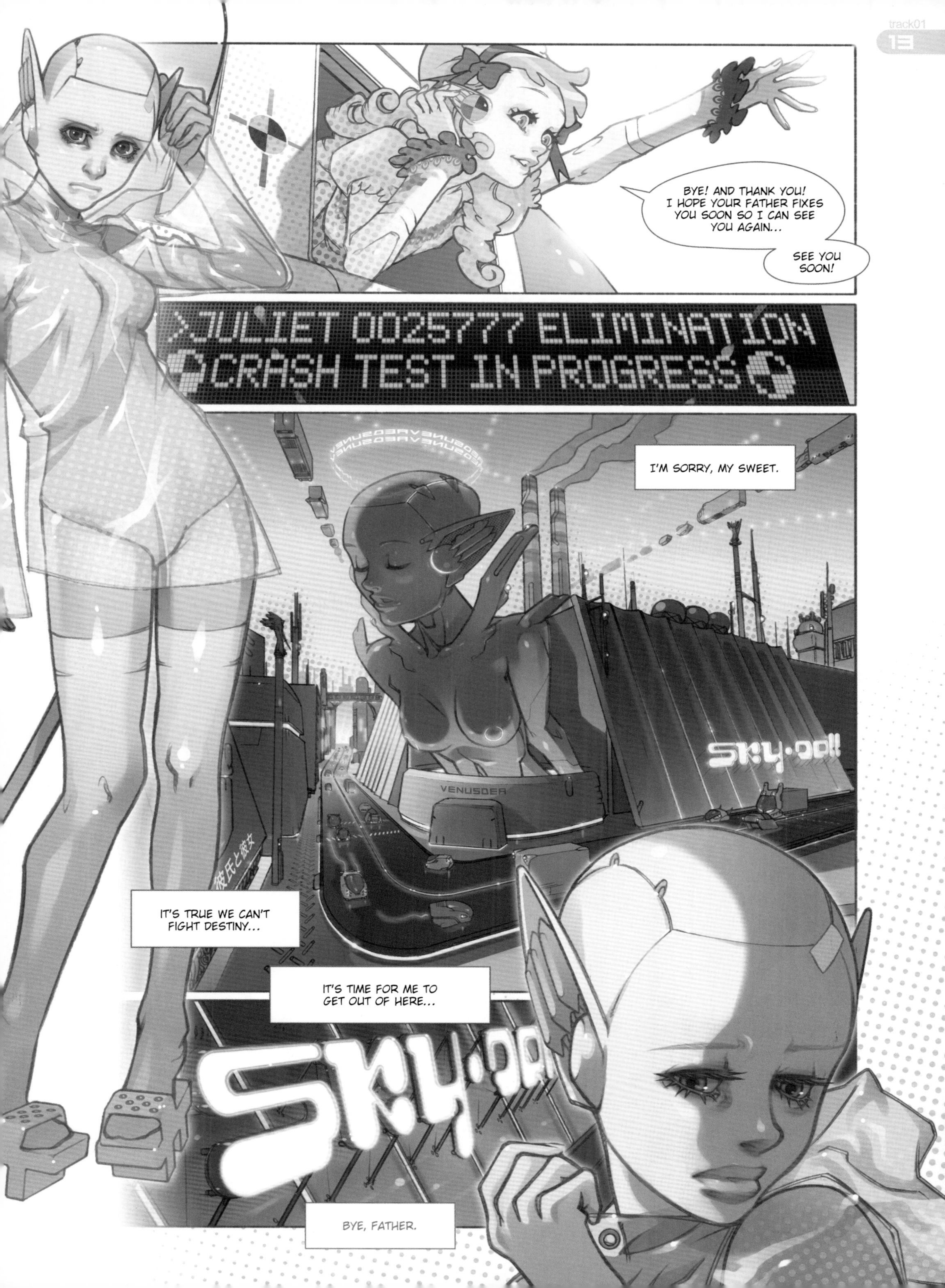
BYE! AND THANK YOU! I HOPE YOUR FATHER FIXES YOU SOON SO I CAN SEE YOU AGAIN...
SEE YOU SOON!
>JULIET 0025777 ELIMINATION
CRASH TEST IN PROGRESS
I'M SORRY, MY SWEET.
VENUSDEA
SKY-DOLL
彼氏と彼女
IT'S TRUE WE CAN'T FIGHT DESTINY...
IT'S TIME FOR ME TO GET OUT OF HERE...
BYE, FATHER.

SKYDOLL SPAACESHIP COLLECTION

Venusdea industries

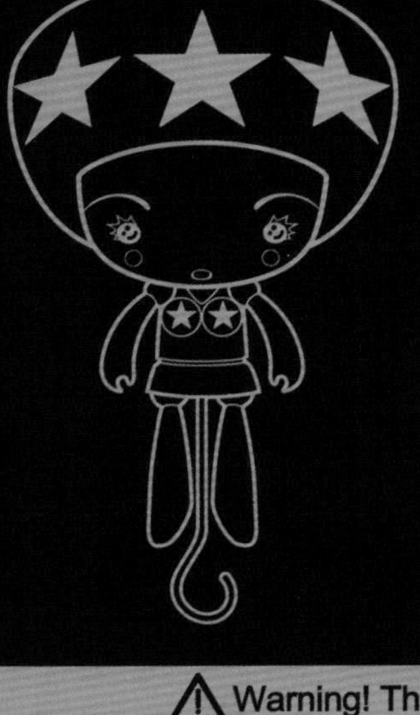

⚠ Warning! This track contains:

"Whoa! Awesome! How'd I learn how to do that?"

(Sky Doll: Decade, Volume 2, page 102)

- Flying bullets
- Dumb cows
- Dangerous girls

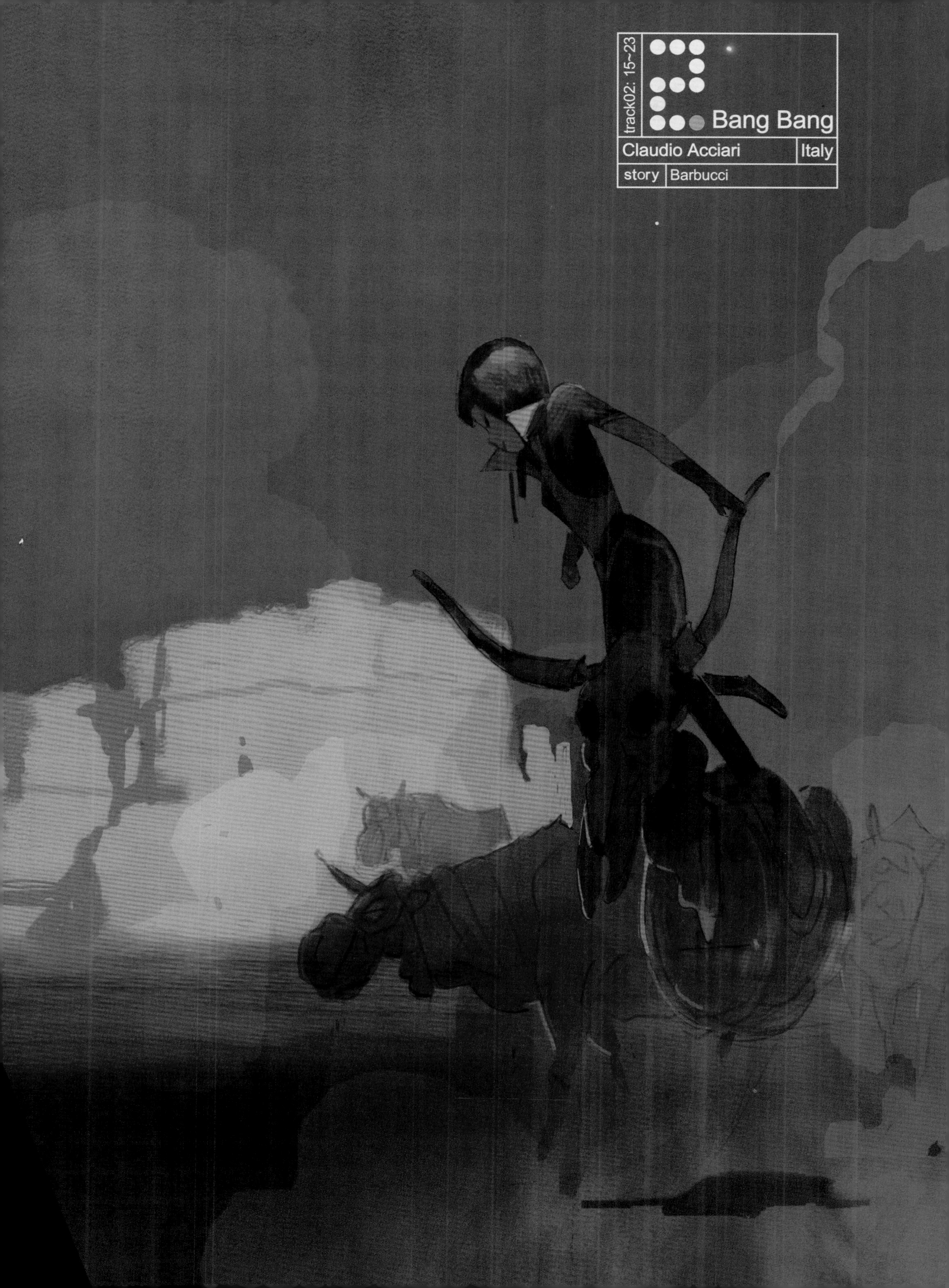
track02: 15~23
Bang Bang
Claudio Acciari
Italy
story
Barbucci

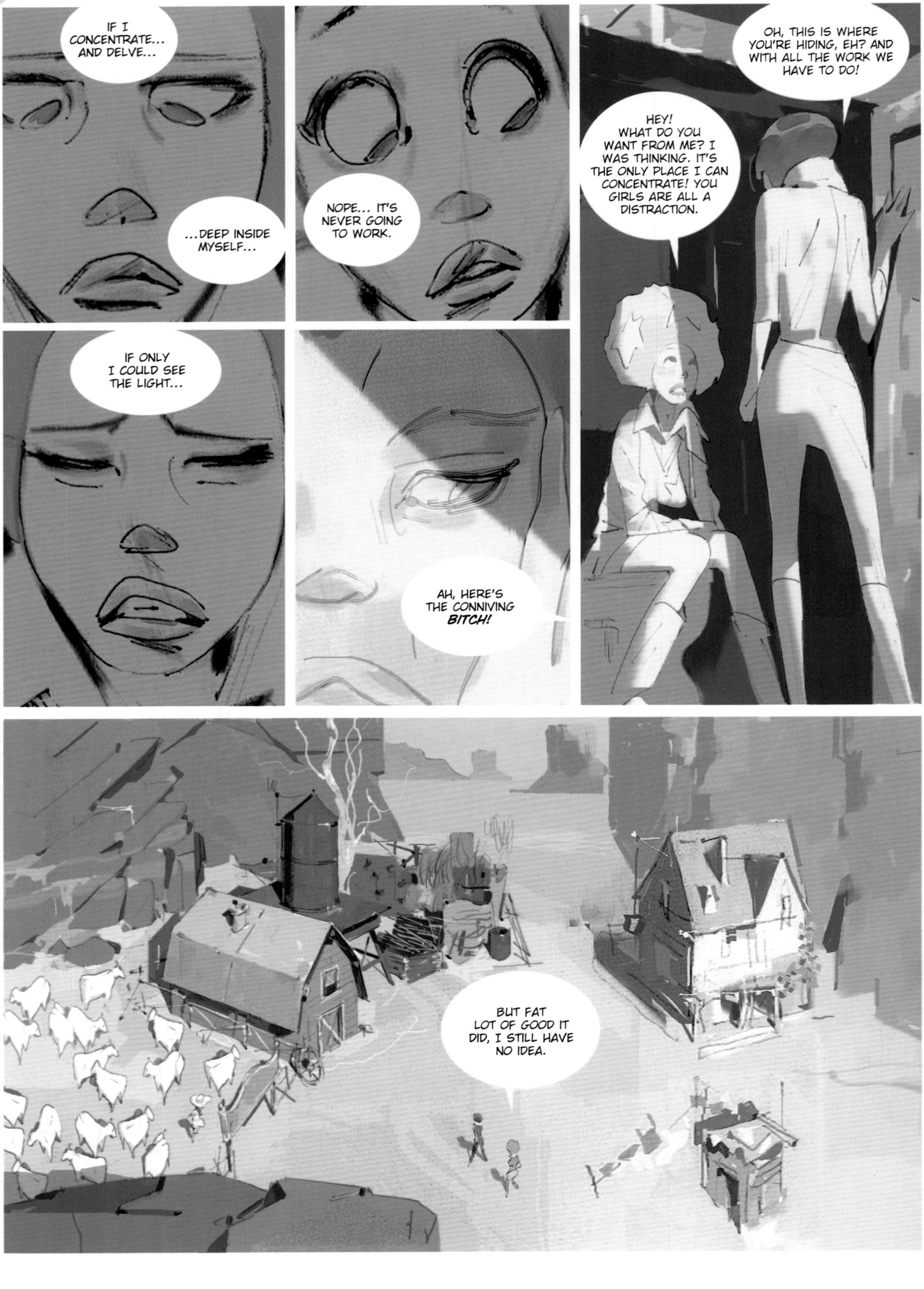
IF I CONCENTRATE... AND DELVE...
...DEEP INSIDE MYSELF...
NOPE... IT'S NEVER GOING TO WORK.
OH, THIS IS WHERE YOU'RE HIDING, EH? AND WITH ALL THE WORK WE HAVE TO DO!
HEY! WHAT DO YOU WANT FROM ME? I WAS THINKING. IT'S THE ONLY PLACE I CAN CONCENTRATE! YOU GIRLS ARE ALL A DISTRACTION.
IF ONLY I COULD SEE THE LIGHT...
AH, HERE'S THE CONNIVING *BITCH!*
BUT FAT LOT OF GOOD IT DID, I STILL HAVE NO IDEA.

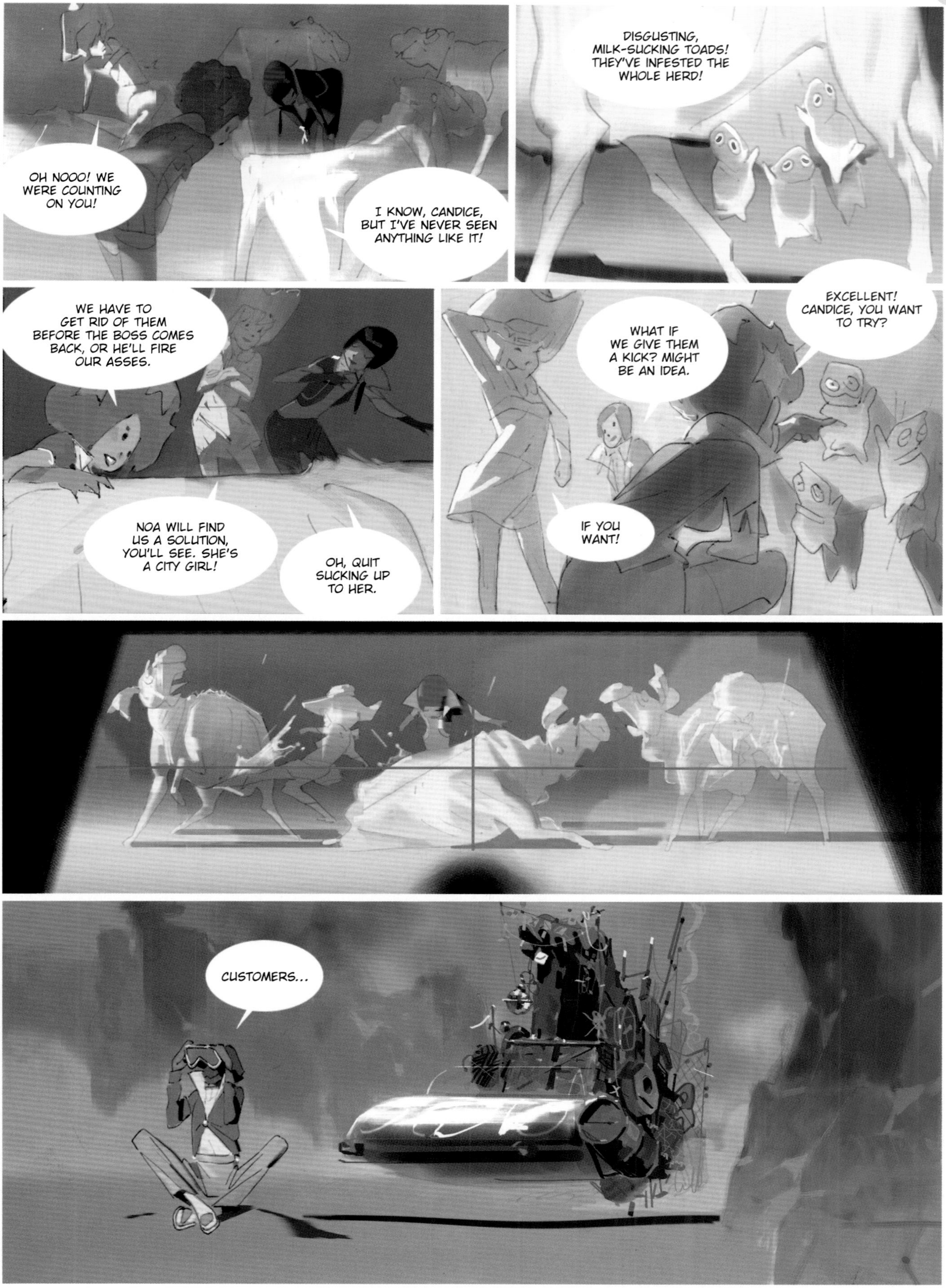
OH NOOO! WE WERE COUNTING ON YOU!
I KNOW, CANDICE, BUT I'VE NEVER SEEN ANYTHING LIKE IT!
DISGUSTING, MILK-SUCKING TOADS! THEY'VE INFESTED THE WHOLE HERD!
WE HAVE TO GET RID OF THEM BEFORE THE BOSS COMES BACK, OR HE'LL FIRE OUR ASSES.
NOA WILL FIND US A SOLUTION, YOU'LL SEE. SHE'S A CITY GIRL!
OH, QUIT SUCKING UP TO HER.
WHAT IF WE GIVE THEM A KICK? MIGHT BE AN IDEA.
IF YOU WANT!
EXCELLENT! CANDICE, YOU WANT TO TRY?
CUSTOMERS...

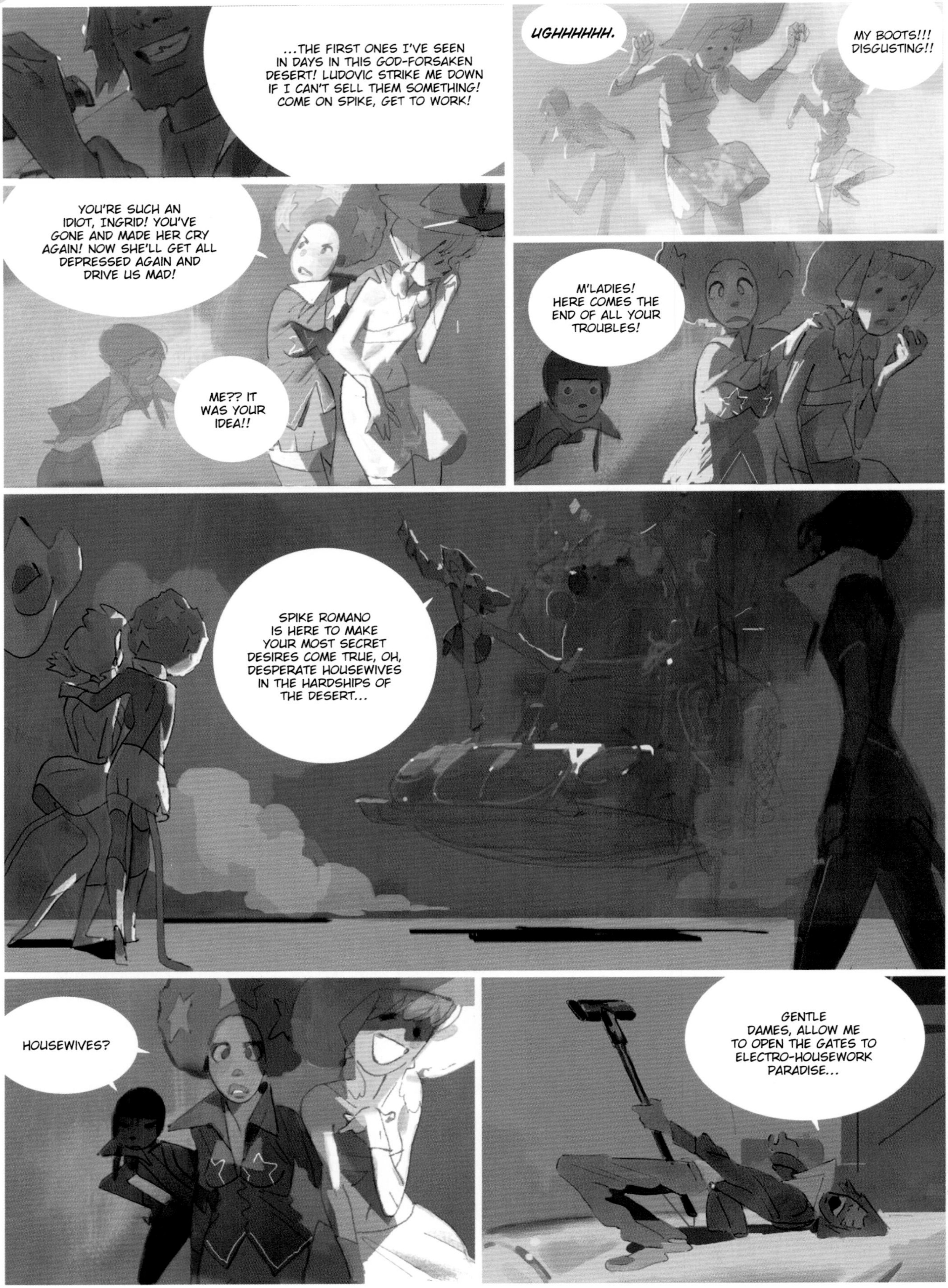
...THE FIRST ONES I'VE SEEN IN DAYS IN THIS GOD-FORSAKEN DESERT! LUDOVIC STRIKE ME DOWN IF I CAN'T SELL THEM SOMETHING! COME ON SPIKE, GET TO WORK!
UGHHHHHH.
MY BOOTS!!! DISGUSTING!!
YOU'RE SUCH AN IDIOT, INGRID! YOU'VE GONE AND MADE HER CRY AGAIN! NOW SHE'LL GET ALL DEPRESSED AGAIN AND DRIVE US MAD!
ME?? IT WAS YOUR IDEA!!
M'LADIES! HERE COMES THE END OF ALL YOUR TROUBLES!
SPIKE ROMANO IS HERE TO MAKE YOUR MOST SECRET DESIRES COME TRUE, OH, DESPERATE HOUSEWIVES IN THE HARDSHIPS OF THE DESERT...
HOUSEWIVES?
GENTLE DAMES, ALLOW ME TO OPEN THE GATES TO ELECTRO-HOUSEWORK PARADISE...

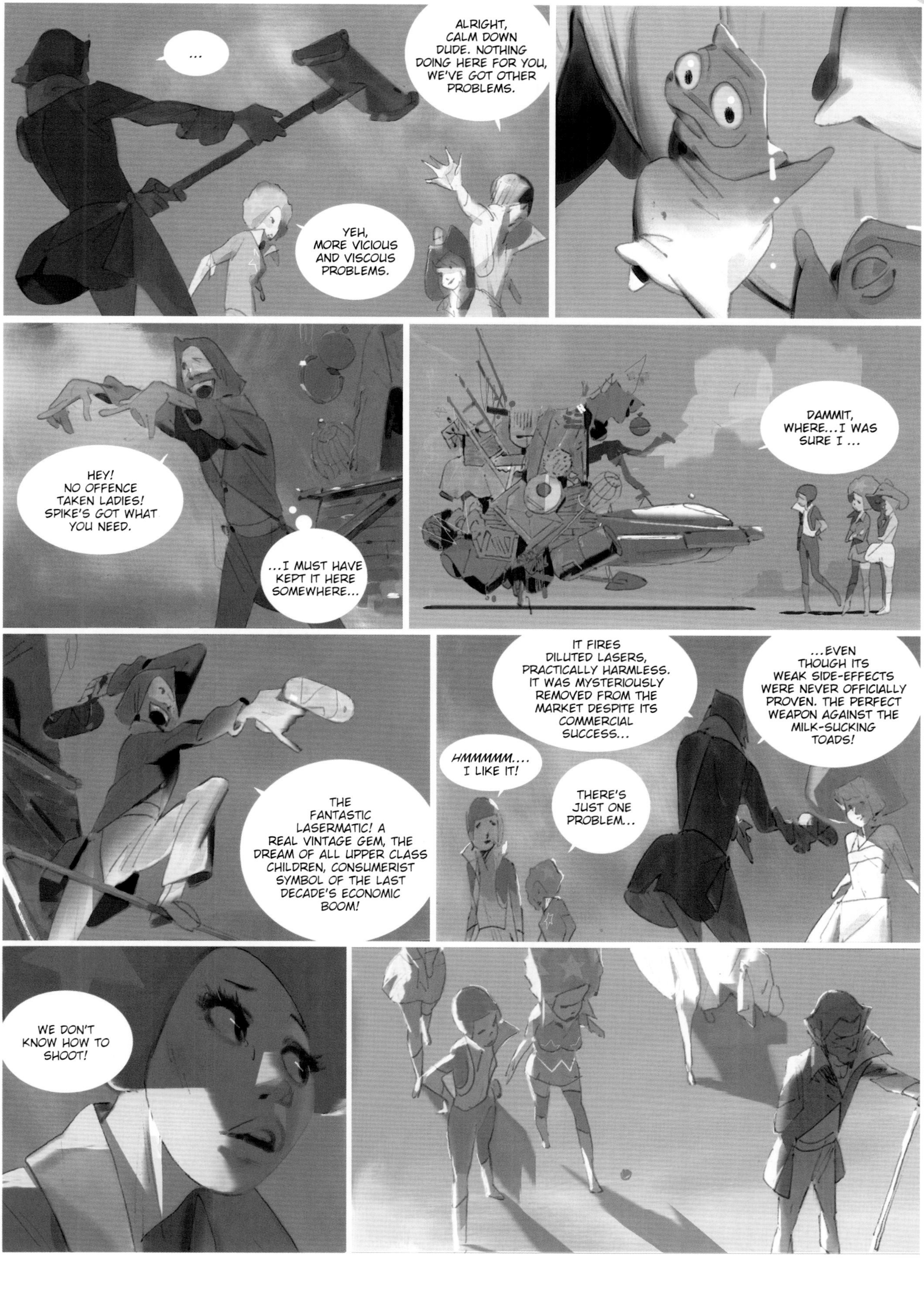
...
ALRIGHT, CALM DOWN DUDE. NOTHING DOING HERE FOR YOU, WE'VE GOT OTHER PROBLEMS.
YEH, MORE VICIOUS AND VISCOUS PROBLEMS.
HEY! NO OFFENCE TAKEN LADIES! SPIKE'S GOT WHAT YOU NEED.
...I MUST HAVE KEPT IT HERE SOMEWHERE...
DAMMIT, WHERE...I WAS SURE I ...
THE FANTASTIC LASERMATIC! A REAL VINTAGE GEM, THE DREAM OF ALL UPPER CLASS CHILDREN, CONSUMERIST SYMBOL OF THE LAST DECADE'S ECONOMIC BOOM!
IT FIRES DILUTED LASERS, PRACTICALLY HARMLESS. IT WAS MYSTERIOUSLY REMOVED FROM THE MARKET DESPITE ITS COMMERCIAL SUCCESS...
...EVEN THOUGH ITS WEAK SIDE-EFFECTS WERE NEVER OFFICIALLY PROVEN. THE PERFECT WEAPON AGAINST THE MILK-SUCKING TOADS!
HMMMMM.... I LIKE IT!
THERE'S JUST ONE PROBLEM...
WE DON'T KNOW HOW TO SHOOT!

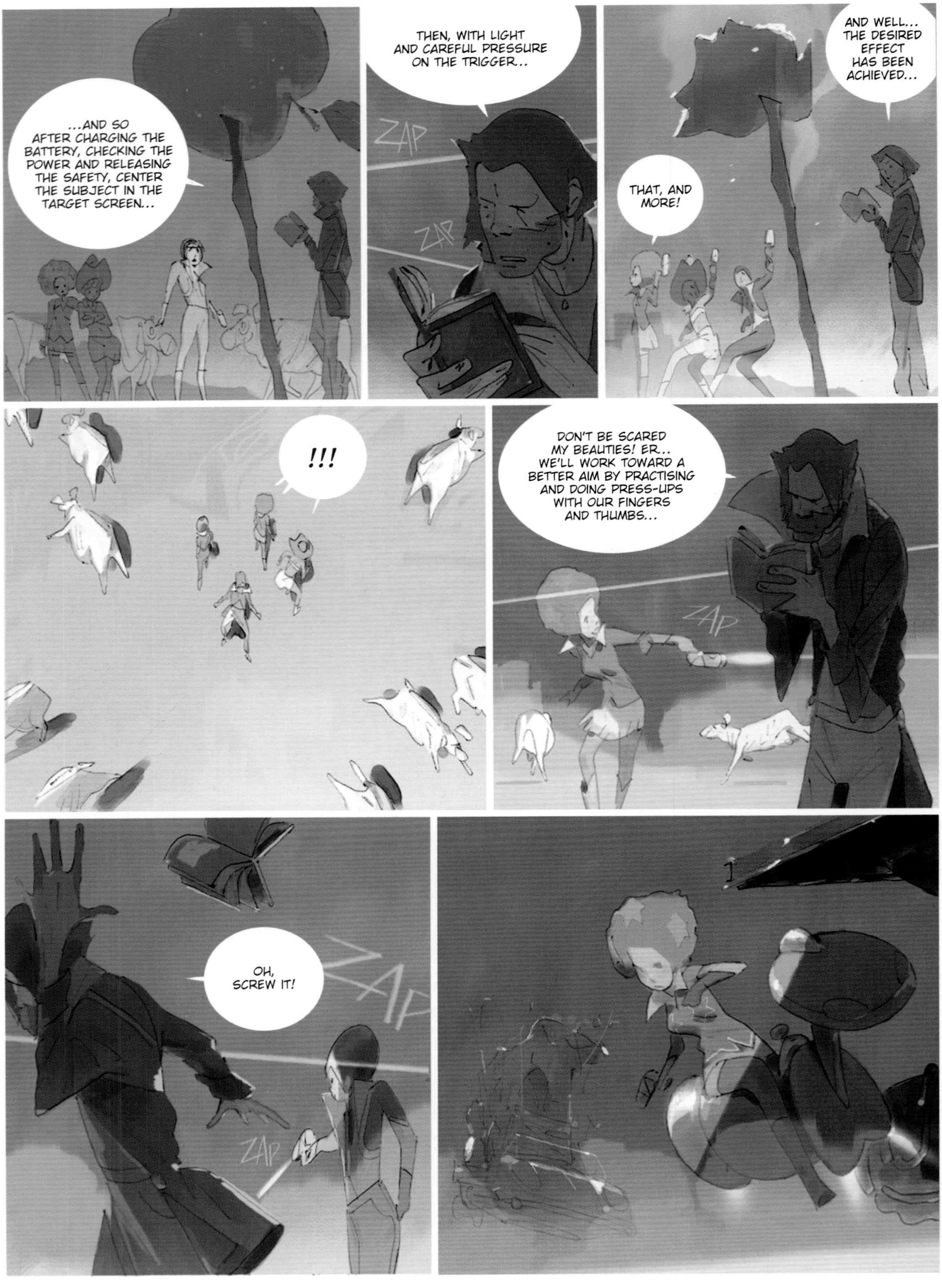
...AND SO AFTER CHARGING THE BATTERY, CHECKING THE POWER AND RELEASING THE SAFETY, CENTER THE SUBJECT IN THE TARGET SCREEN...
THEN, WITH LIGHT AND CAREFUL PRESSURE ON THE TRIGGER...
ZAP
ZAP
AND WELL... THE DESIRED EFFECT HAS BEEN ACHIEVED...
THAT, AND MORE!
!!!
DON'T BE SCARED MY BEAUTIES! ER... WE'LL WORK TOWARD A BETTER AIM BY PRACTISING AND DOING PRESS-UPS WITH OUR FINGERS AND THUMBS...
ZAP
OH, SCREW IT!
ZAP
ZAP

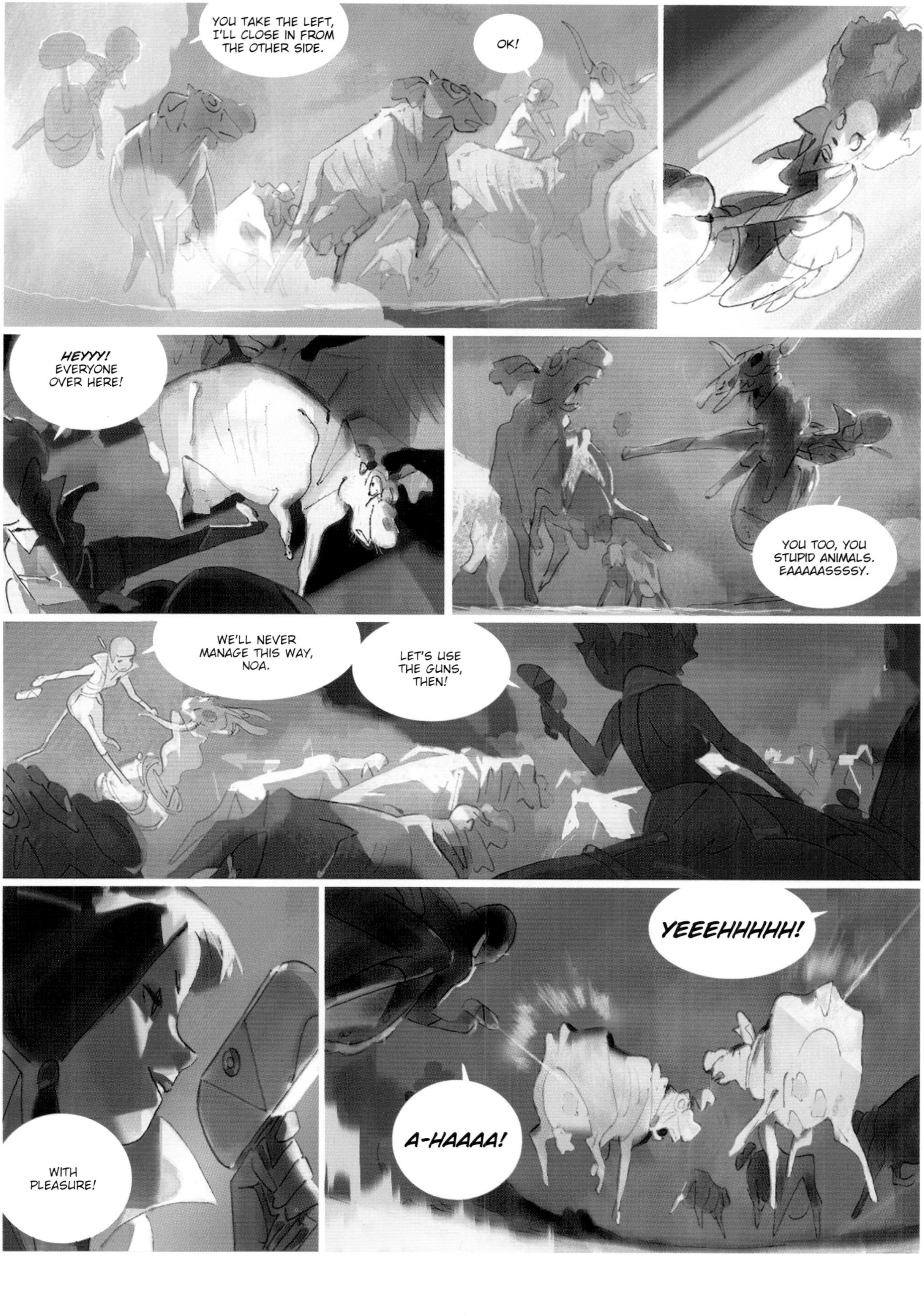
YOU TAKE THE LEFT, I'LL CLOSE IN FROM THE OTHER SIDE.
OK!
HEYYY! EVERYONE OVER HERE!
YOU TOO, YOU STUPID ANIMALS. EAAAAASSSSY.
WE'LL NEVER MANAGE THIS WAY, NOA.
LET'S USE THE GUNS, THEN!
WITH PLEASURE!
YEEEHHHHH!
A-HAAAA!

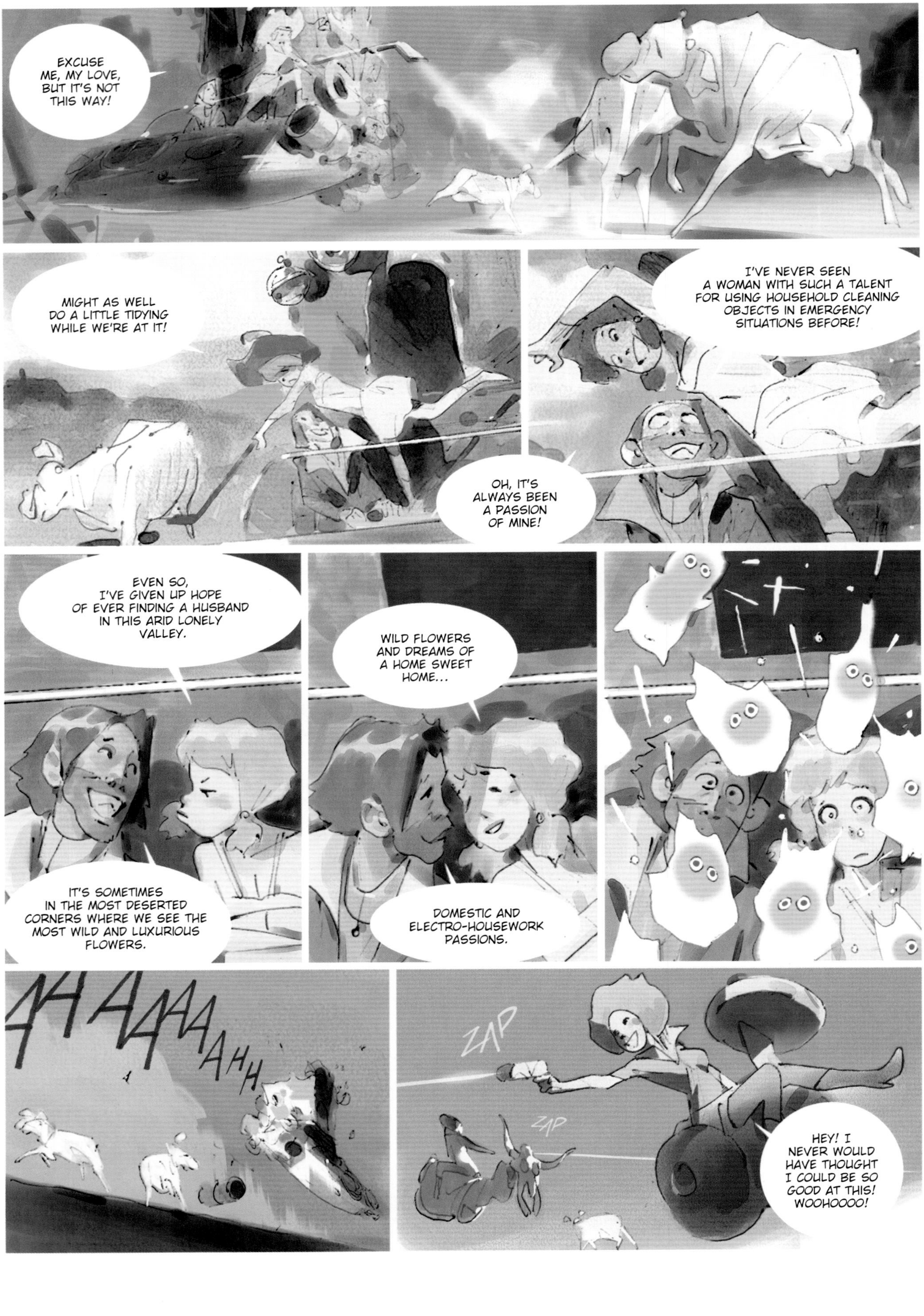
EXCUSE ME, MY LOVE, BUT IT'S NOT THIS WAY!
MIGHT AS WELL DO A LITTLE TIDYING WHILE WE'RE AT IT!
I'VE NEVER SEEN A WOMAN WITH SUCH A TALENT FOR USING HOUSEHOLD CLEANING OBJECTS IN EMERGENCY SITUATIONS BEFORE!
OH, IT'S ALWAYS BEEN A PASSION OF MINE!
EVEN SO, I'VE GIVEN UP HOPE OF EVER FINDING A HUSBAND IN THIS ARID LONELY VALLEY.
IT'S SOMETIMES IN THE MOST DESERTED CORNERS WHERE WE SEE THE MOST WILD AND LUXURIOUS FLOWERS.
WILD FLOWERS AND DREAMS OF A HOME SWEET HOME...
DOMESTIC AND ELECTRO-HOUSEWORK PASSIONS.
AAAAAAAAHH
ZAP
ZAP
HEY! I NEVER WOULD HAVE THOUGHT I COULD BE SO GOOD AT THIS! WOOHOOOO!

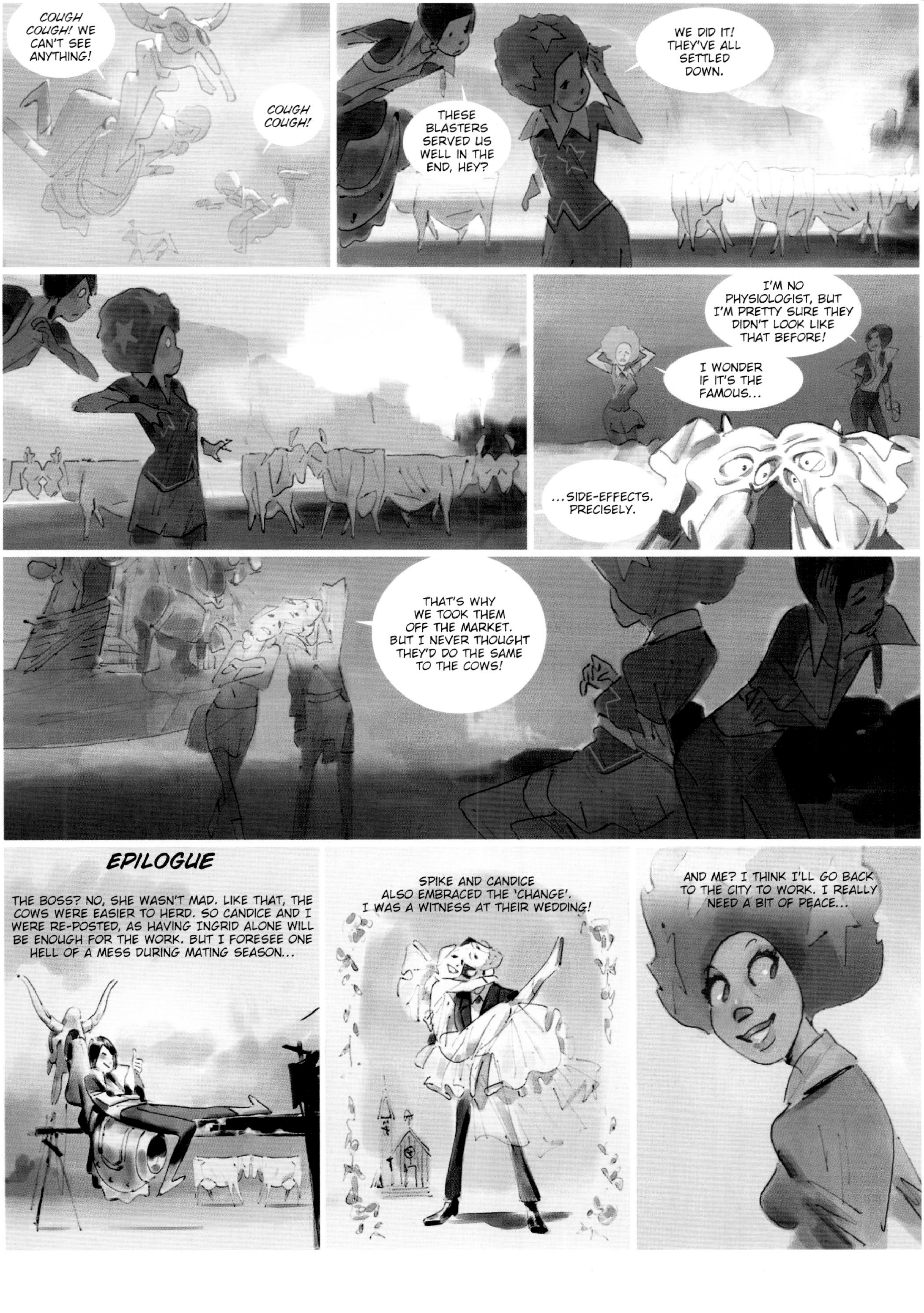
COUGH COUGH! WE CAN'T SEE ANYTHING!
COUGH COUGH!
WE DID IT! THEY'VE ALL SETTLED DOWN.
THESE BLASTERS SERVED US WELL IN THE END, HEY?
I'M NO PHYSIOLOGIST, BUT I'M PRETTY SURE THEY DIDN'T LOOK LIKE THAT BEFORE!
I WONDER IF IT'S THE FAMOUS...
...SIDE-EFFECTS. PRECISELY.
THAT'S WHY WE TOOK THEM OFF THE MARKET. BUT I NEVER THOUGHT THEY'D DO THE SAME TO THE COWS!
EPILOGUE
THE BOSS? NO, SHE WASN'T MAD. LIKE THAT, THE COWS WERE EASIER TO HERD. SO CANDICE AND I WERE RE-POSTED, AS HAVING INGRID ALONE WILL BE ENOUGH FOR THE WORK. BUT I FORESEE ONE HELL OF A MESS DURING MATING SEASON...
SPIKE AND CANDICE ALSO EMBRACED THE 'CHANGE'. I WAS A WITNESS AT THEIR WEDDING!
AND ME? I THINK I'LL GO BACK TO THE CITY TO WORK. I REALLY NEED A BIT OF PEACE...

SKYDOLL SPACESHIP COLLECTION

Venusdea industries ●

⚠ Warning! This track contains:

"I've seen rituals before.
But this…"

(Sky Doll: Volume 4, page **)

 Pierced puppets

 Anime cosplay

 Love on sale

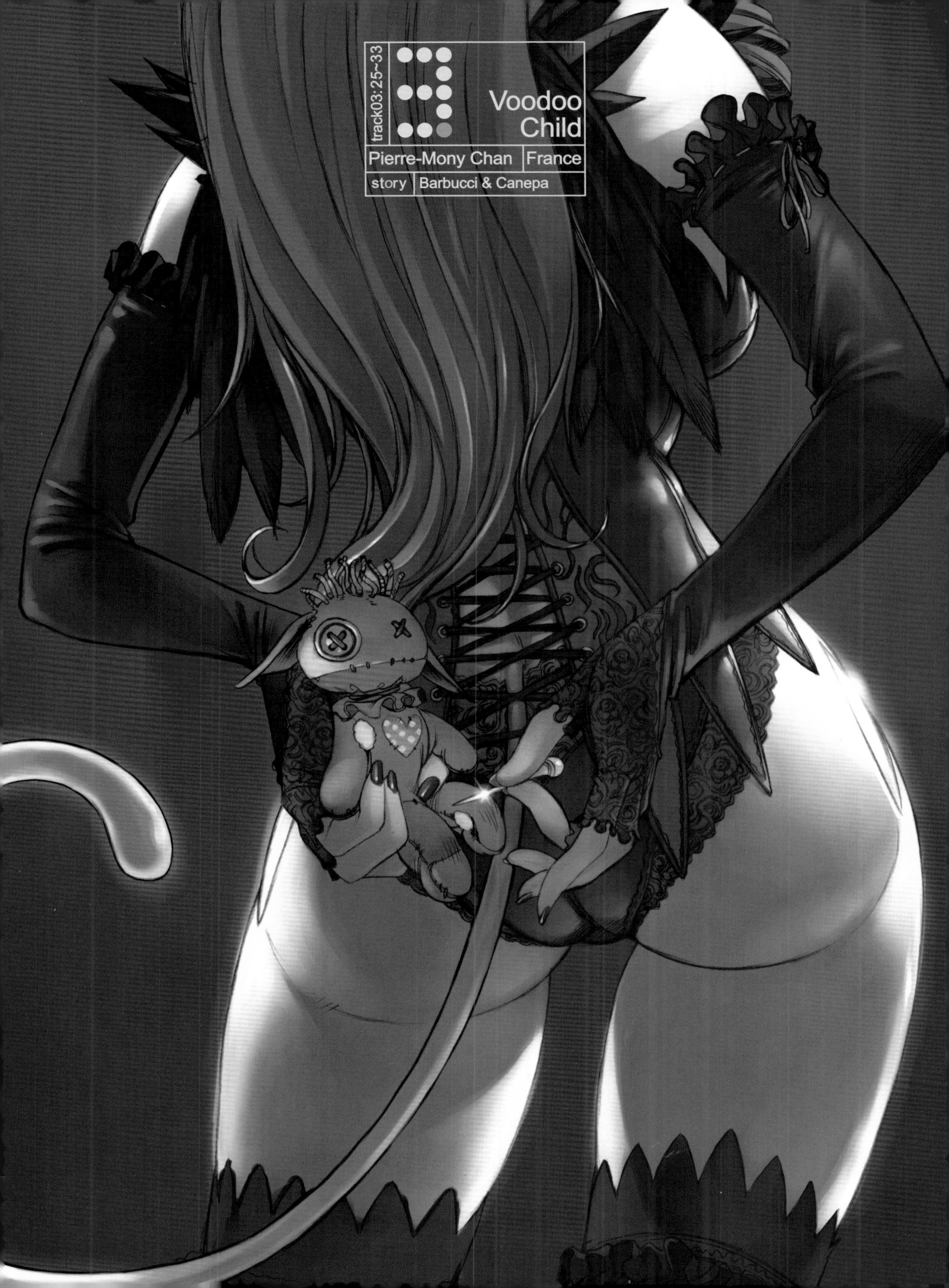
track03:25~33
Voodoo Child
Pierre-Mony Chan
France
story
Barbucci & Canepa

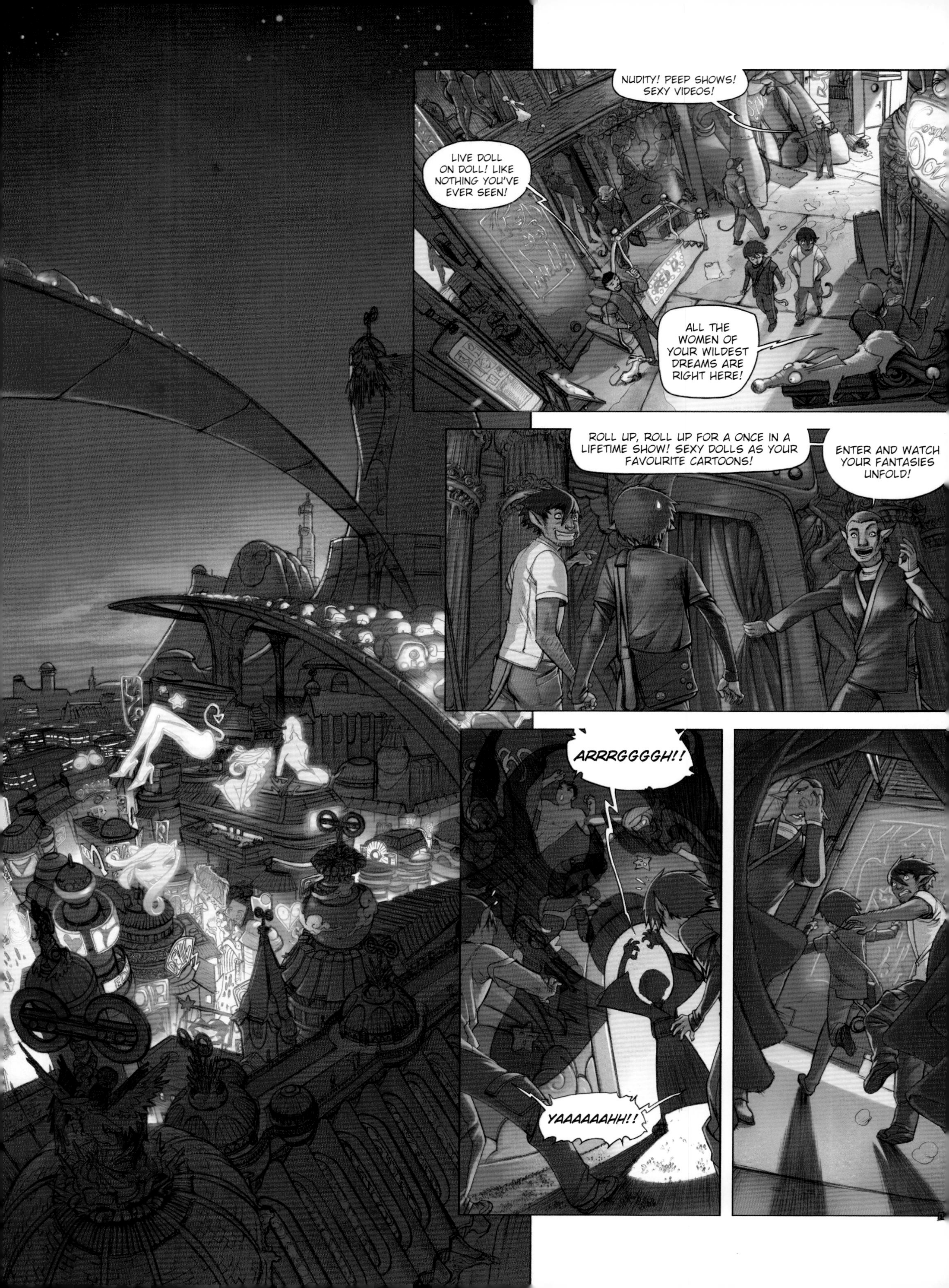
NUDITY! PEEP SHOWS! SEXY VIDEOS!
LIVE DOLL ON DOLL! LIKE NOTHING YOU'VE EVER SEEN!
ALL THE WOMEN OF YOUR WILDEST DREAMS ARE RIGHT HERE!
ROLL UP, ROLL UP FOR A ONCE IN A LIFETIME SHOW! SEXY DOLLS AS YOUR FAVOURITE CARTOONS!
ENTER AND WATCH YOUR FANTASIES UNFOLD!
ARRRGGGGH!!
YAAAAAAHH!!

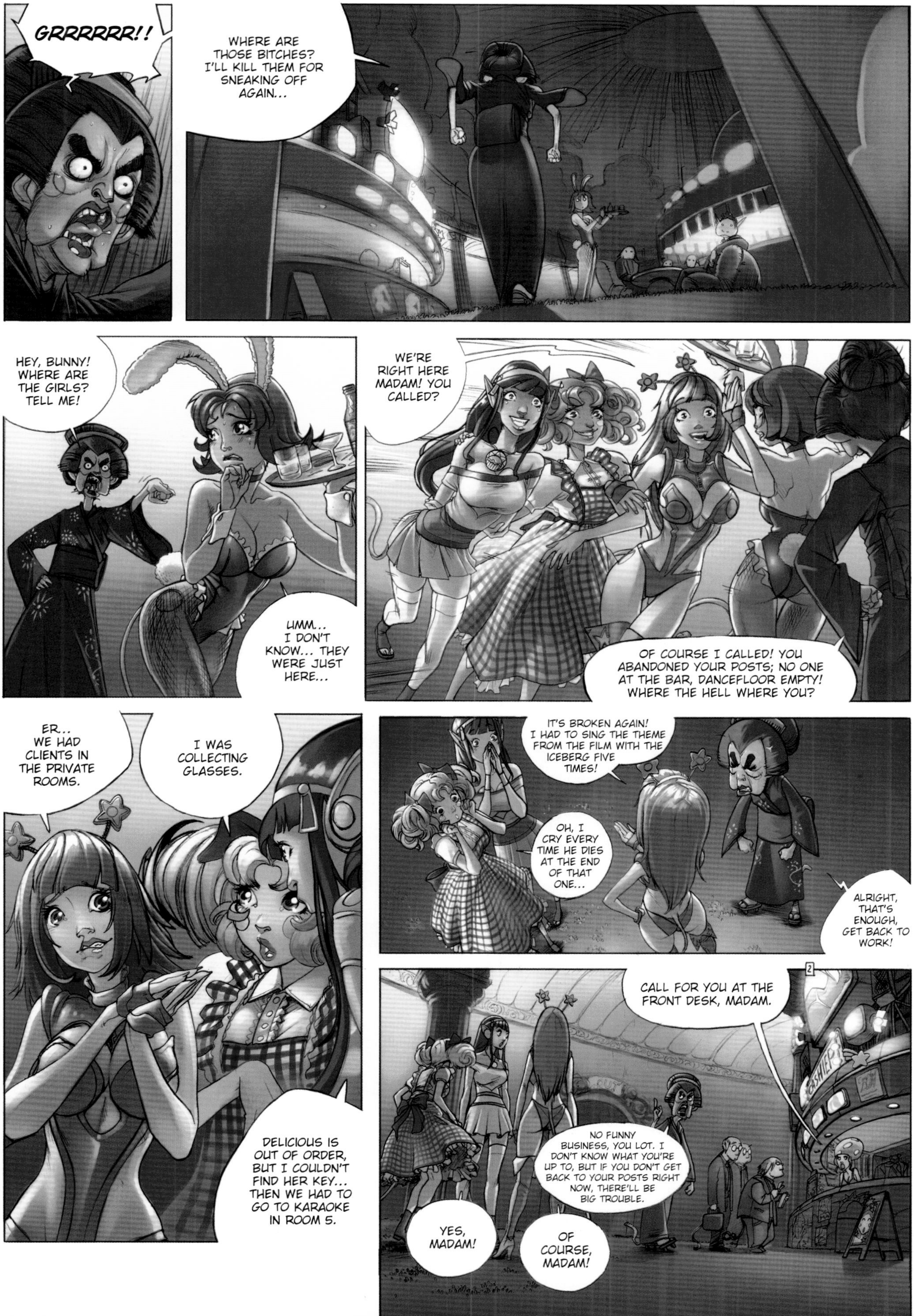
GRRRRRR!!
WHERE ARE THOSE BITCHES? I'LL KILL THEM FOR SNEAKING OFF AGAIN...
HEY, BUNNY! WHERE ARE THE GIRLS? TELL ME!
UMM... I DON'T KNOW... THEY WERE JUST HERE...
WE'RE RIGHT HERE MADAM! YOU CALLED?
OF COURSE I CALLED! YOU ABANDONED YOUR POSTS; NO ONE AT THE BAR, DANCEFLOOR EMPTY! WHERE THE HELL WHERE YOU?
ER... WE HAD CLIENTS IN THE PRIVATE ROOMS.
I WAS COLLECTING GLASSES.
DELICIOUS IS OUT OF ORDER, BUT I COULDN'T FIND HER KEY... THEN WE HAD TO GO TO KARAOKE IN ROOM 5.
IT'S BROKEN AGAIN! I HAD TO SING THE THEME FROM THE FILM WITH THE ICEBERG FIVE TIMES!
OH, I CRY EVERY TIME HE DIES AT THE END OF THAT ONE...
ALRIGHT, THAT'S ENOUGH, GET BACK TO WORK!
CALL FOR YOU AT THE FRONT DESK, MADAM.
NO FUNNY BUSINESS, YOU LOT. I DON'T KNOW WHAT YOU'RE UP TO, BUT IF YOU DON'T GET BACK TO YOUR POSTS RIGHT NOW, THERE'LL BE BIG TROUBLE.
YES, MADAM!
OF COURSE, MADAM!
CASHIER

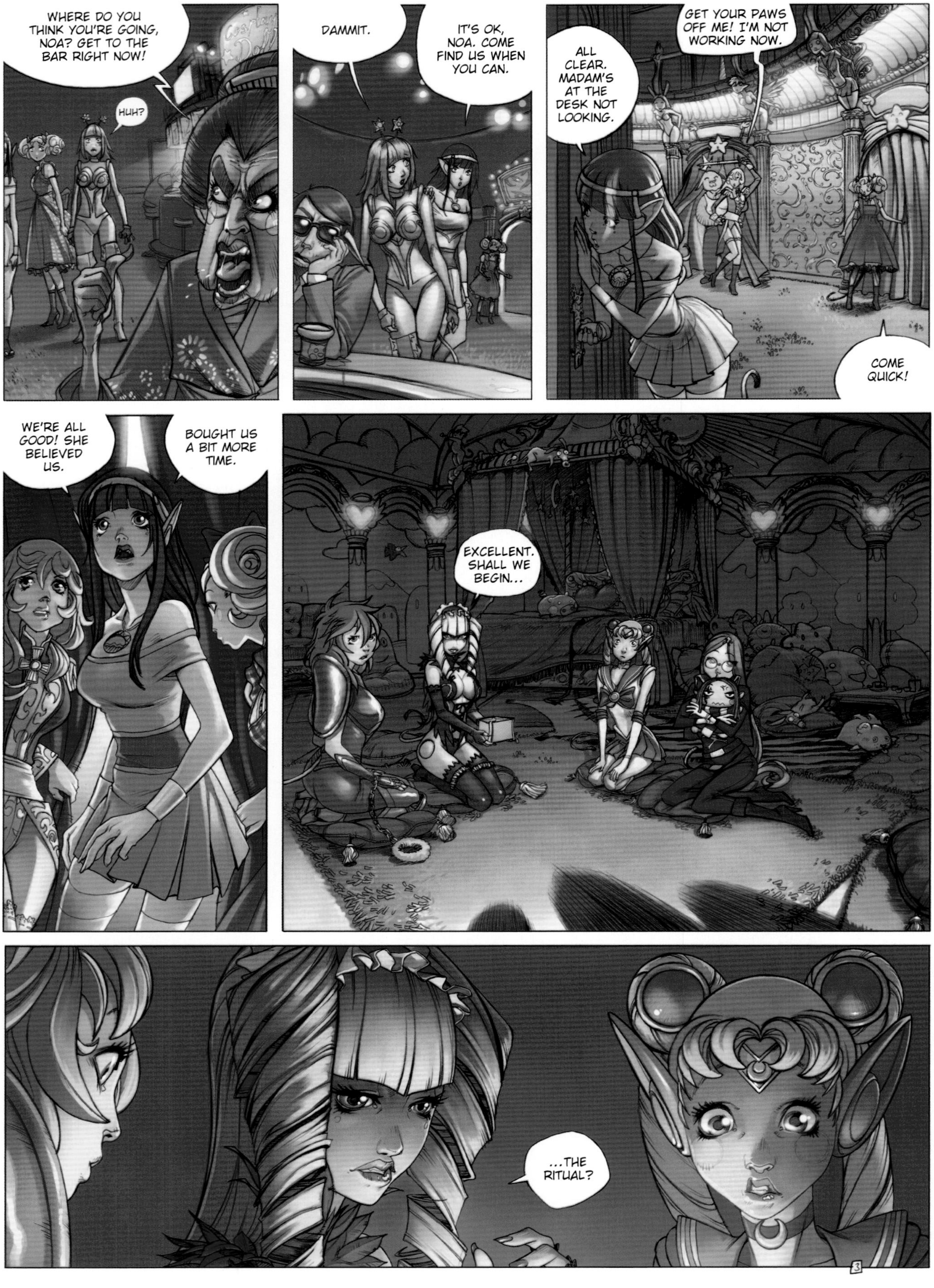
WHERE DO YOU THINK YOU'RE GOING, NOA? GET TO THE BAR RIGHT NOW!
HUH?
DAMMIT.
IT'S OK, NOA. COME FIND US WHEN YOU CAN.
ALL CLEAR. MADAM'S AT THE DESK NOT LOOKING.
GET YOUR PAWS OFF ME! I'M NOT WORKING NOW.
COME QUICK!
WE'RE ALL GOOD! SHE BELIEVED US.
BOUGHT US A BIT MORE TIME.
EXCELLENT. SHALL WE BEGIN...
...THE RITUAL?
3

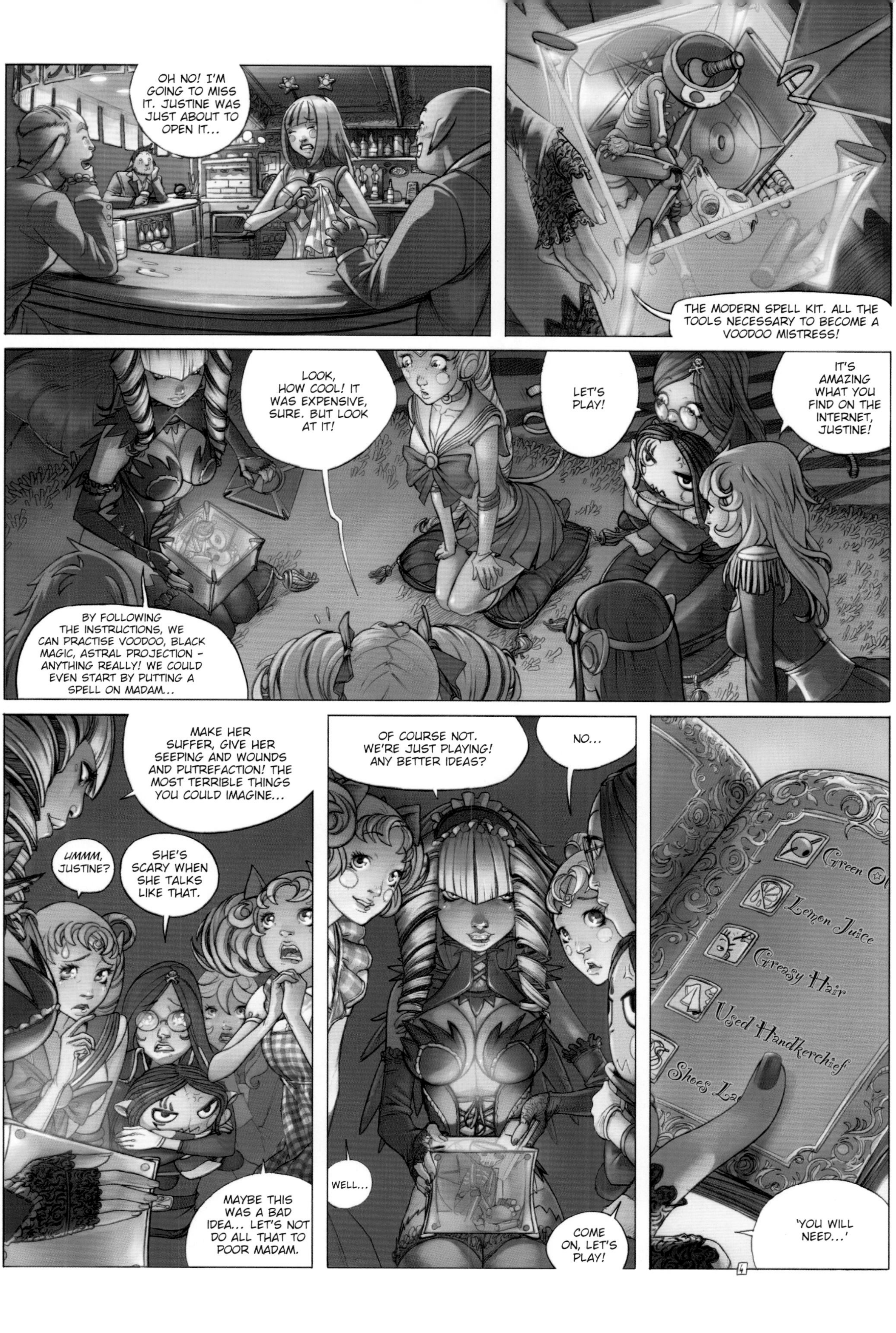
OH NO! I'M GOING TO MISS IT. JUSTINE WAS JUST ABOUT TO OPEN IT...
THE MODERN SPELL KIT. ALL THE TOOLS NECESSARY TO BECOME A VOODOO MISTRESS!
LOOK, HOW COOL! IT WAS EXPENSIVE, SURE. BUT LOOK AT IT!
LET'S PLAY!
IT'S AMAZING WHAT YOU FIND ON THE INTERNET, JUSTINE!
BY FOLLOWING THE INSTRUCTIONS, WE CAN PRACTISE VOODOO, BLACK MAGIC, ASTRAL PROJECTION - ANYTHING REALLY! WE COULD EVEN START BY PUTTING A SPELL ON MADAM...
MAKE HER SUFFER, GIVE HER SEEPING AND WOUNDS AND PUTREFACTION! THE MOST TERRIBLE THINGS YOU COULD IMAGINE...
UMMM, JUSTINE?
SHE'S SCARY WHEN SHE TALKS LIKE THAT.
MAYBE THIS WAS A BAD IDEA... LET'S NOT DO ALL THAT TO POOR MADAM.
OF COURSE NOT. WE'RE JUST PLAYING! ANY BETTER IDEAS?
NO...
WELL...
COME ON, LET'S PLAY!
Green O
Lemon Juice
Greasy Hair
Used Handkerchief
Shoes La
'YOU WILL NEED...'
4

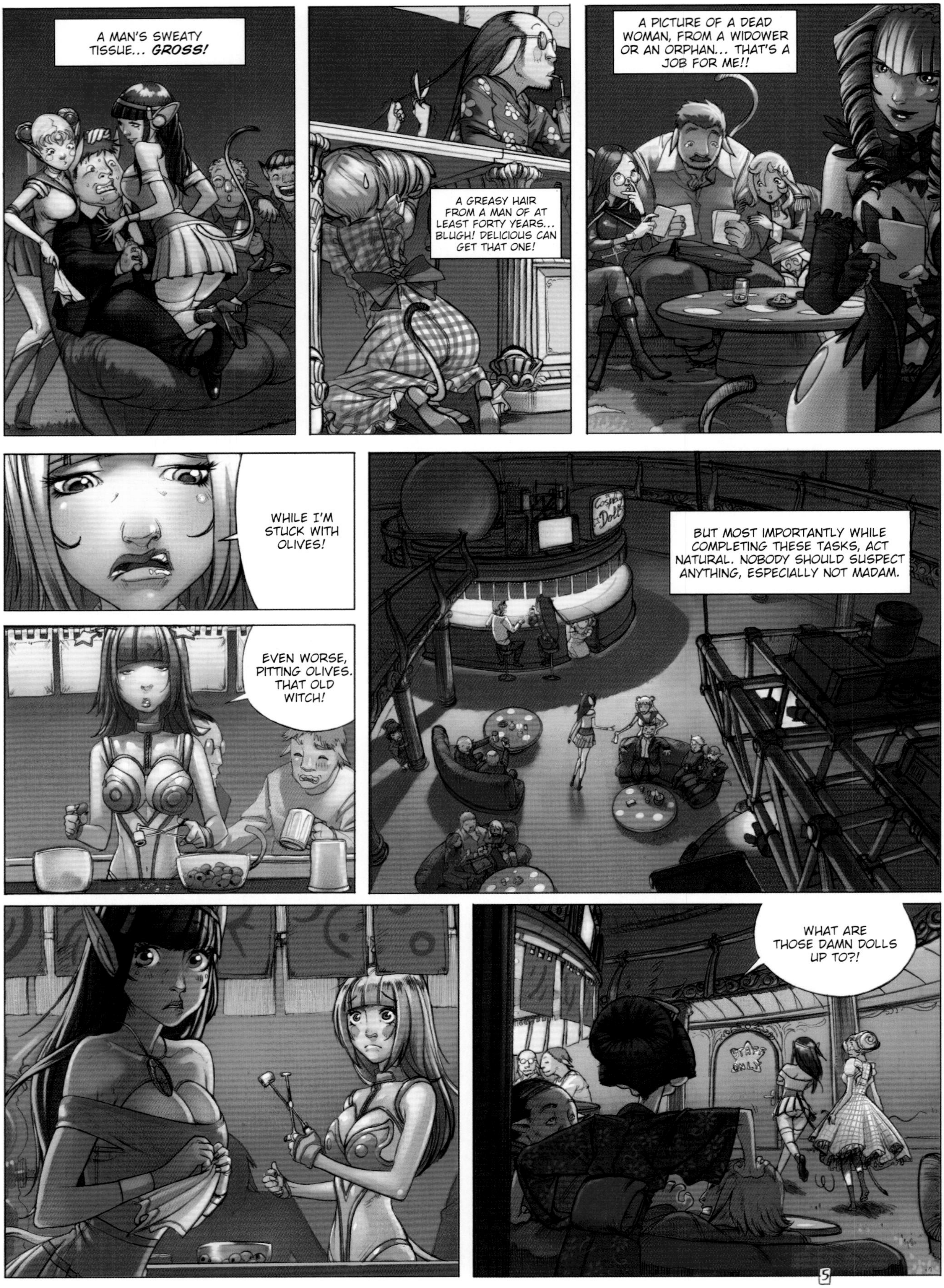
A MAN'S SWEATY TISSUE... GROSS!
A GREASY HAIR FROM A MAN OF AT LEAST FORTY YEARS... BLUGH! DELICIOUS CAN GET THAT ONE!
A PICTURE OF A DEAD WOMAN, FROM A WIDOWER OR AN ORPHAN... THAT'S A JOB FOR ME!!
WHILE I'M STUCK WITH OLIVES!
EVEN WORSE, PITTING OLIVES. THAT OLD WITCH!
BUT MOST IMPORTANTLY WHILE COMPLETING THESE TASKS, ACT NATURAL. NOBODY SHOULD SUSPECT ANYTHING, ESPECIALLY NOT MADAM.
WHAT ARE THOSE DAMN DOLLS UP TO?!
STAFF ONLY

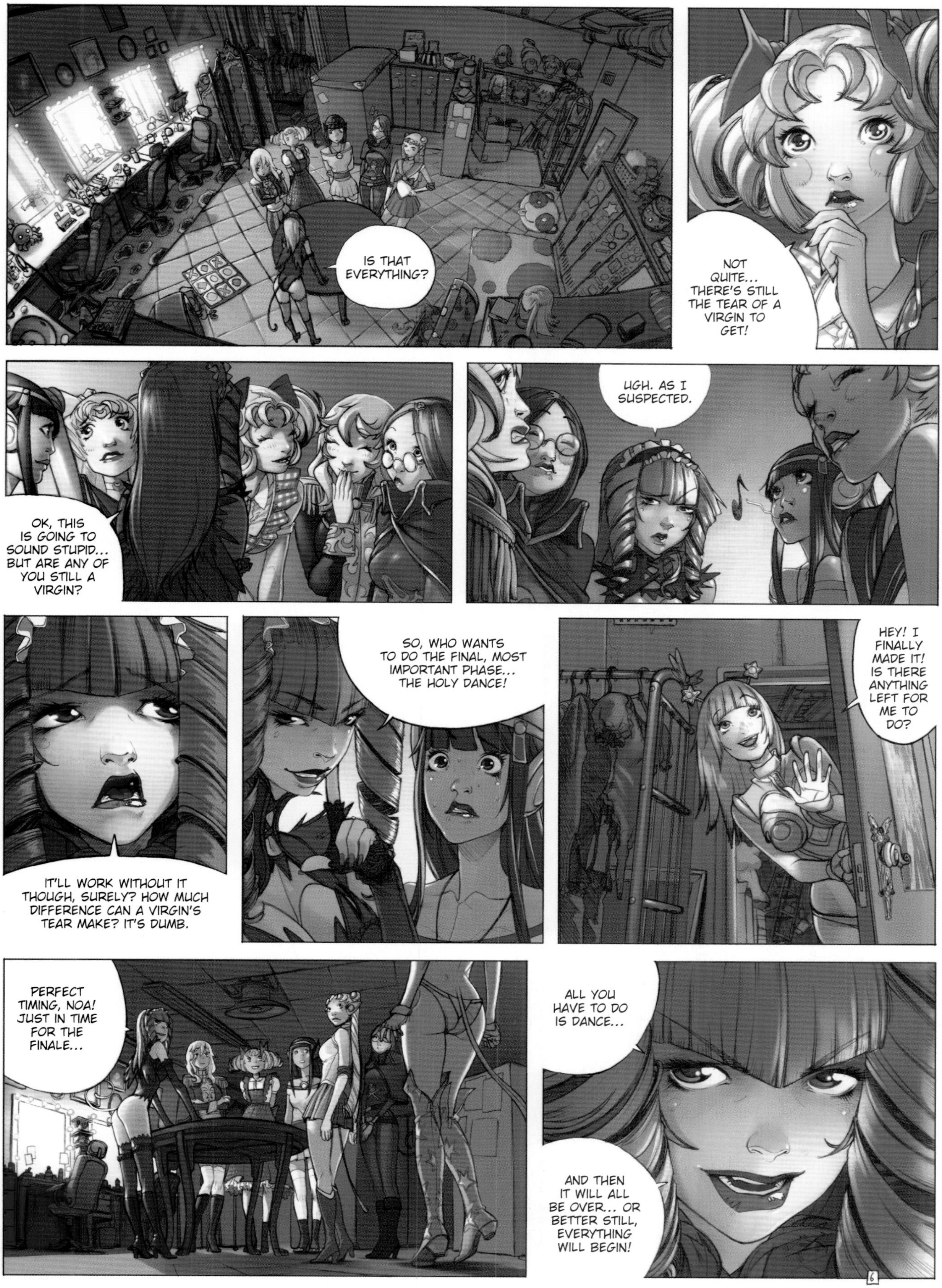
IS THAT EVERYTHING?
NOT QUITE... THERE'S STILL THE TEAR OF A VIRGIN TO GET!
OK, THIS IS GOING TO SOUND STUPID... BUT ARE ANY OF YOU STILL A VIRGIN?
UGH. AS I SUSPECTED.
IT'LL WORK WITHOUT IT THOUGH, SURELY? HOW MUCH DIFFERENCE CAN A VIRGIN'S TEAR MAKE? IT'S DUMB.
SO, WHO WANTS TO DO THE FINAL, MOST IMPORTANT PHASE... THE HOLY DANCE!
HEY! I FINALLY MADE IT! IS THERE ANYTHING LEFT FOR ME TO DO?
PERFECT TIMING, NOA! JUST IN TIME FOR THE FINALE...
ALL YOU HAVE TO DO IS DANCE...
AND THEN IT WILL ALL BE OVER... OR BETTER STILL, EVERYTHING WILL BEGIN!
6

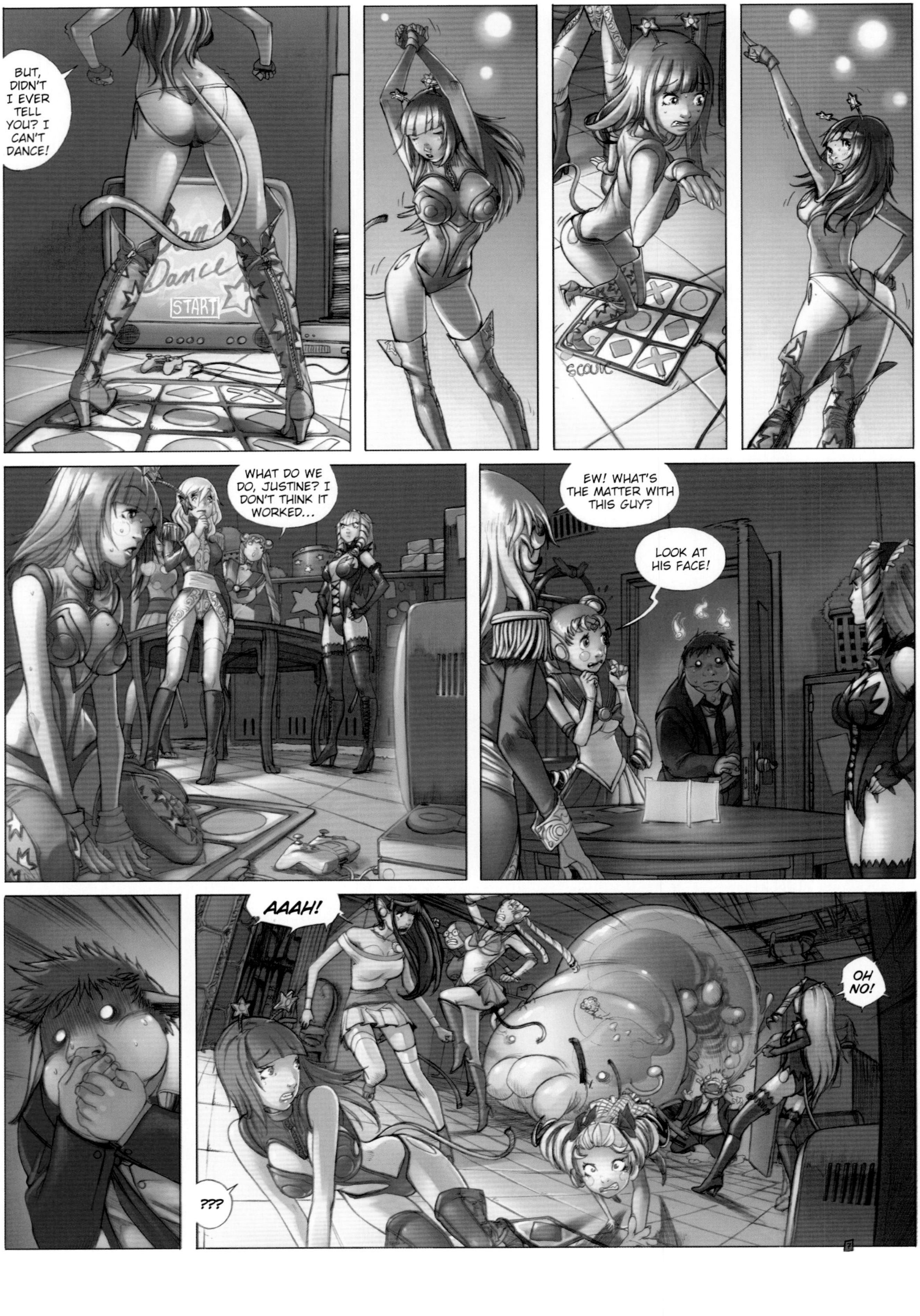
BUT, DIDN'T I EVER TELL YOU? I CAN'T DANCE!
Dance
START
SCOUIC
WHAT DO WE DO, JUSTINE? I DON'T THINK IT WORKED...
EW! WHAT'S THE MATTER WITH THIS GUY?
LOOK AT HIS FACE!
AAAH!
OH NO!
???
7

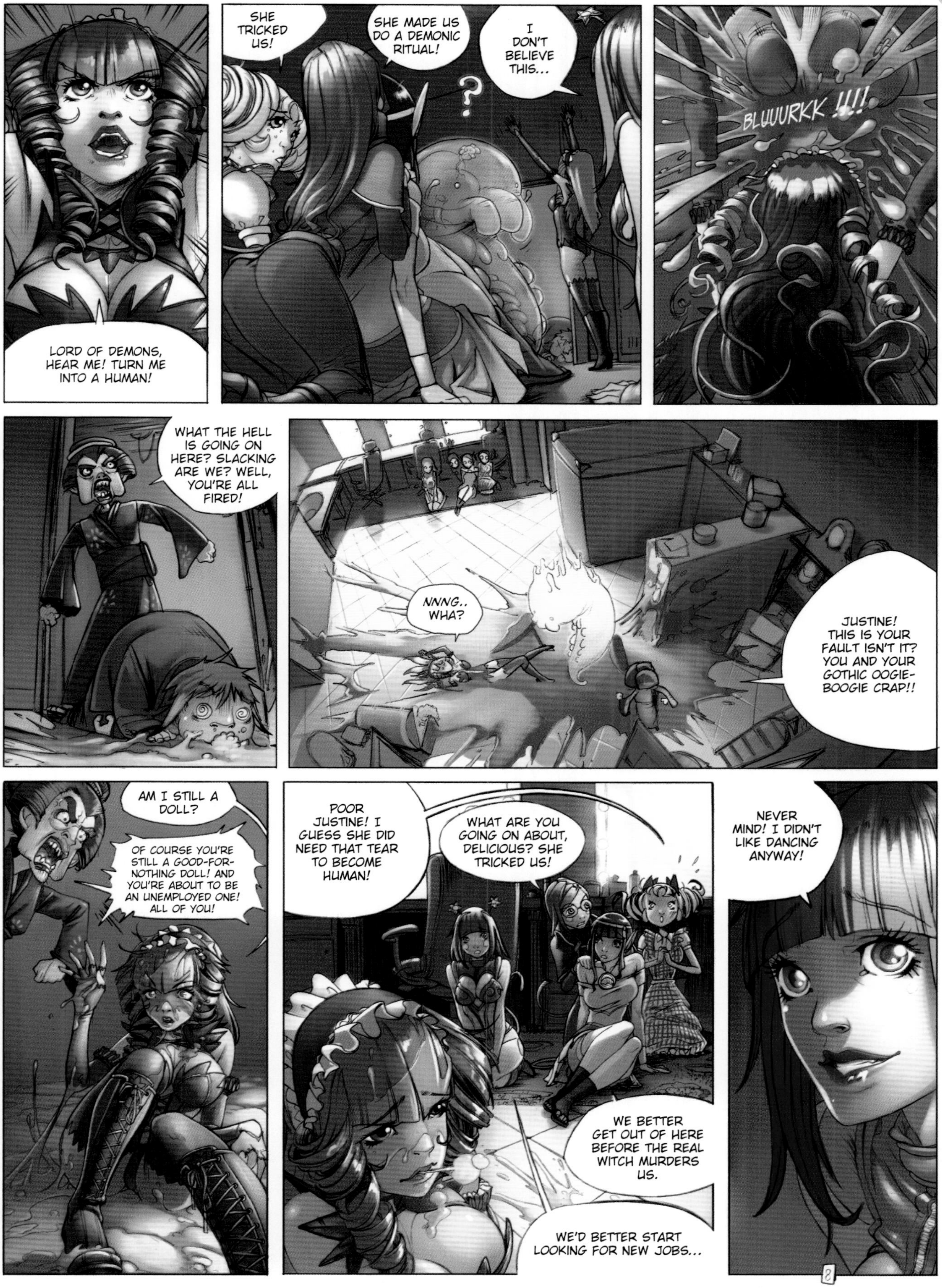
LORD OF DEMONS, HEAR ME! TURN ME INTO A HUMAN!
SHE TRICKED US!
SHE MADE US DO A DEMONIC RITUAL!
?
I DON'T BELIEVE THIS...
BLUUURKK !!!!
WHAT THE HELL IS GOING ON HERE? SLACKING ARE WE? WELL, YOU'RE ALL FIRED!
NNNG.. WHA?
JUSTINE! THIS IS YOUR FAULT ISN'T IT? YOU AND YOUR GOTHIC OOGIE-BOOGIE CRAP!!
AM I STILL A DOLL?
OF COURSE YOU'RE STILL A GOOD-FOR-NOTHING DOLL! AND YOU'RE ABOUT TO BE AN UNEMPLOYED ONE! ALL OF YOU!
POOR JUSTINE! I GUESS SHE DID NEED THAT TEAR TO BECOME HUMAN!
WHAT ARE YOU GOING ON ABOUT, DELICIOUS? SHE TRICKED US!
WE BETTER GET OUT OF HERE BEFORE THE REAL WITCH MURDERS US.
WE'D BETTER START LOOKING FOR NEW JOBS...
NEVER MIND! I DIDN'T LIKE DANCING ANYWAY!
8

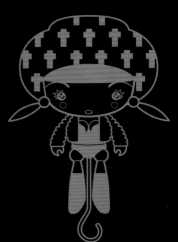

SKYDOLL SPACESHIP COLLECTION

Venusdea industries ●

⚠ Warning! This track contains:

"Things are way worse over
at Vampire Vixens!"

(Sky Doll: Decade, Volume 1, page 16)

 Luxurious limos

 Chic poodles

 Spare parts

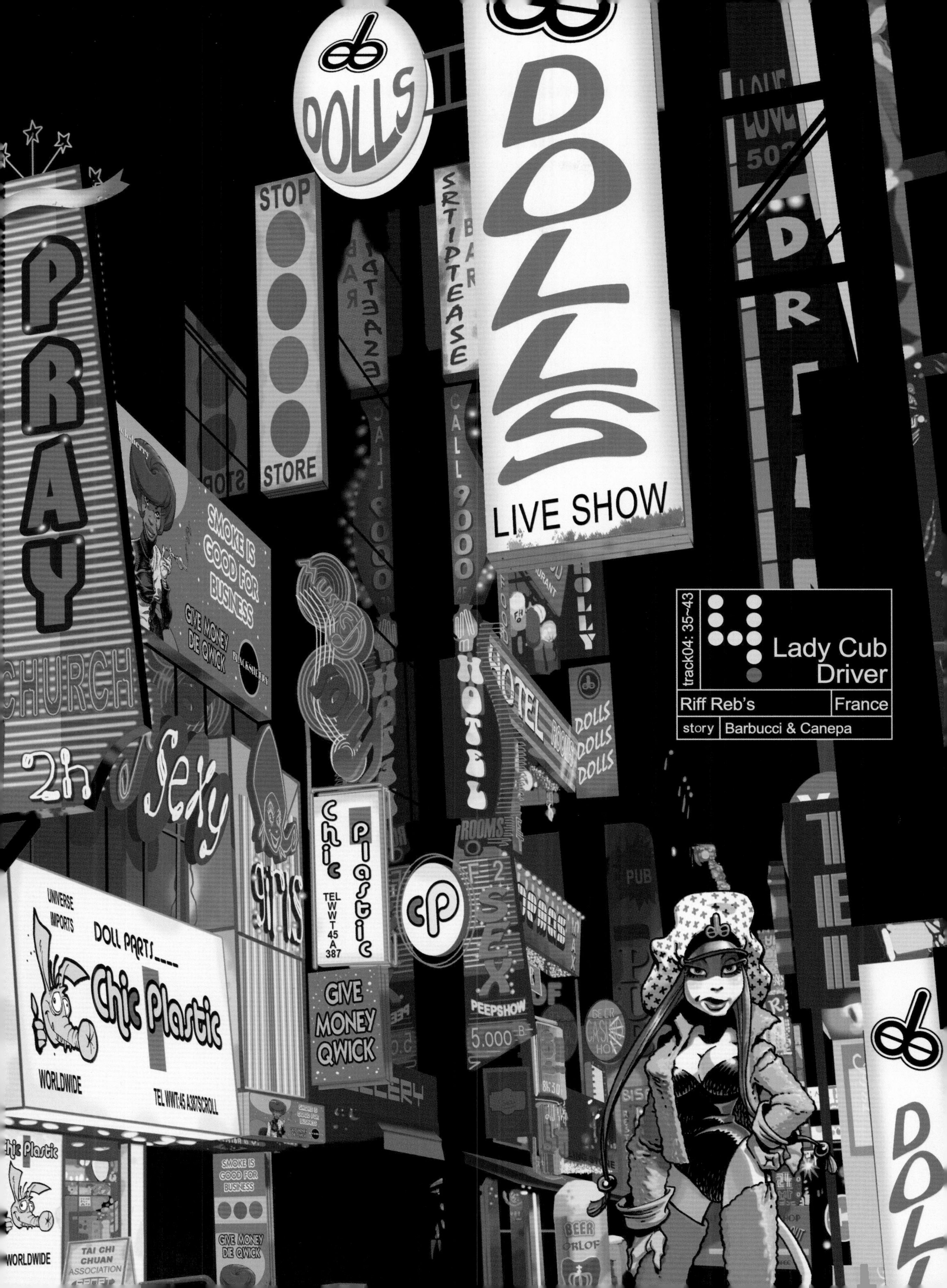
DOLLS
STOP
STORE
SRTIPTEASE
BAR
DOLLS
LIVE SHOW
PRAY
CHURCH
SMOKE IS GOOD FOR BUSINESS
GIVE MONEY DIE QWICK
CALL 9000
2h
Sexy
girls
HOTEL
ROOMS
DOLLS DOLLS DOLLS
Chic Plastic
TEL WWT 45 A 387
UNIVERSE IMPORTS
DOLL PARTS____
Chic Plastic
WORLDWIDE
TEL WWT:45 A387SCROLL
GIVE MONEY QWICK
SEX
PEEPSHOW
5.000 B
PUB
BEER ORLOF
TAI CHI CHUAN ASSOCIATION
Chic Plastic
WORLDWIDE

track04: 35~43

4 Lady Cub Driver

Riff Reb's | France

story | Barbucci & Canepa

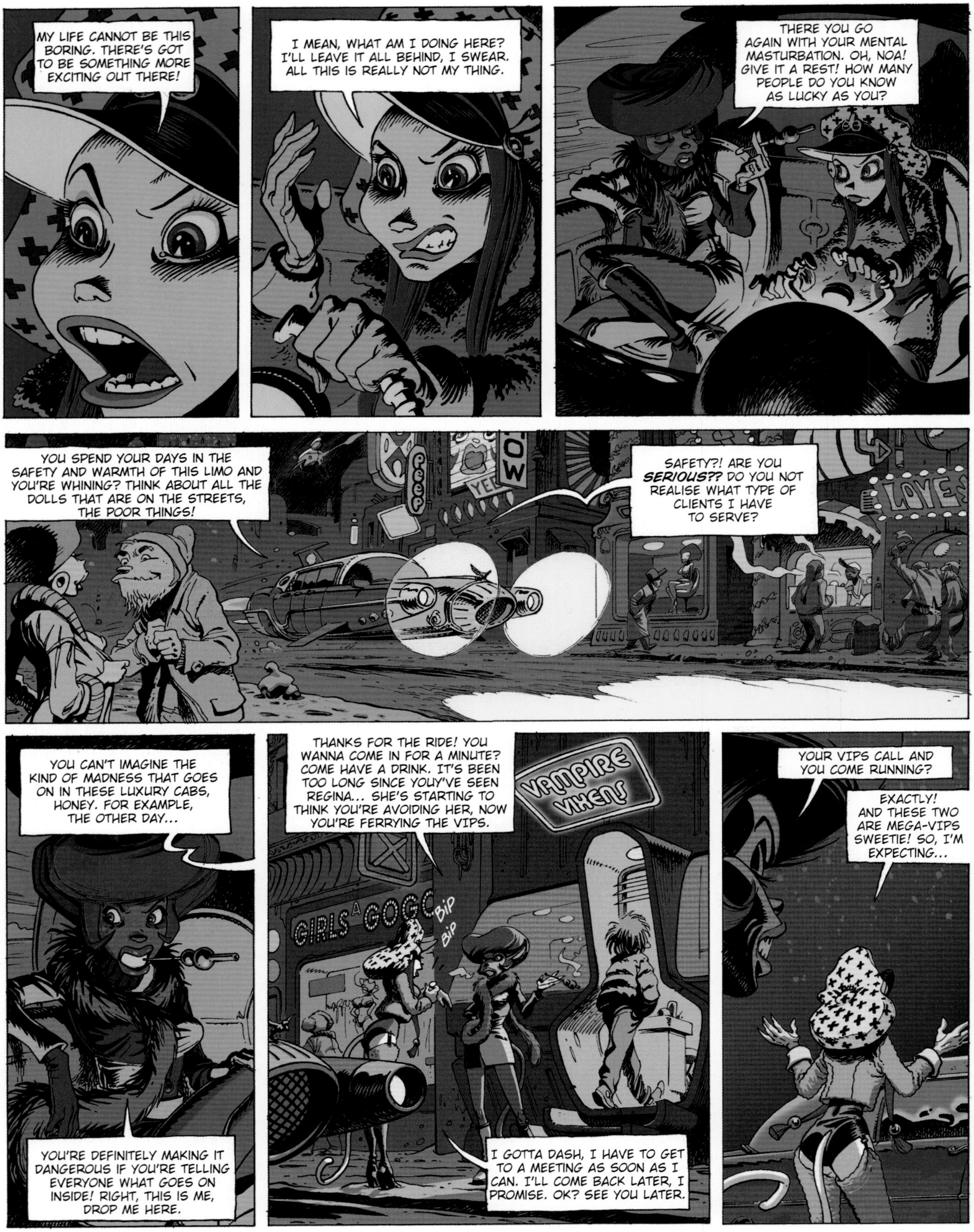
MY LIFE CANNOT BE THIS BORING. THERE'S GOT TO BE SOMETHING MORE EXCITING OUT THERE!
I MEAN, WHAT AM I DOING HERE? I'LL LEAVE IT ALL BEHIND, I SWEAR. ALL THIS IS REALLY NOT MY THING.
THERE YOU GO AGAIN WITH YOUR MENTAL MASTURBATION. OH, NOA! GIVE IT A REST! HOW MANY PEOPLE DO YOU KNOW AS LUCKY AS YOU?
YOU SPEND YOUR DAYS IN THE SAFETY AND WARMTH OF THIS LIMO AND YOU'RE WHINING? THINK ABOUT ALL THE DOLLS THAT ARE ON THE STREETS, THE POOR THINGS!
SAFETY?! ARE YOU SERIOUS?? DO YOU NOT REALISE WHAT TYPE OF CLIENTS I HAVE TO SERVE?
PEEP
LOVE
YOU CAN'T IMAGINE THE KIND OF MADNESS THAT GOES ON IN THESE LUXURY CABS, HONEY. FOR EXAMPLE, THE OTHER DAY...
YOU'RE DEFINITELY MAKING IT DANGEROUS IF YOU'RE TELLING EVERYONE WHAT GOES ON INSIDE! RIGHT, THIS IS ME, DROP ME HERE.
THANKS FOR THE RIDE! YOU WANNA COME IN FOR A MINUTE? COME HAVE A DRINK. IT'S BEEN TOO LONG SINCE YOUY'VE SEEN REGINA... SHE'S STARTING TO THINK YOU'RE AVOIDING HER, NOW YOU'RE FERRYING THE VIPS.
VAMPIRE VIXENS
GIRLS A GOGO
BIP BIP
I GOTTA DASH, I HAVE TO GET TO A MEETING AS SOON AS I CAN. I'LL COME BACK LATER, I PROMISE. OK? SEE YOU LATER.
YOUR VIPS CALL AND YOU COME RUNNING?
EXACTLY! AND THESE TWO ARE MEGA-VIPS SWEETIE! SO, I'M EXPECTING...
1

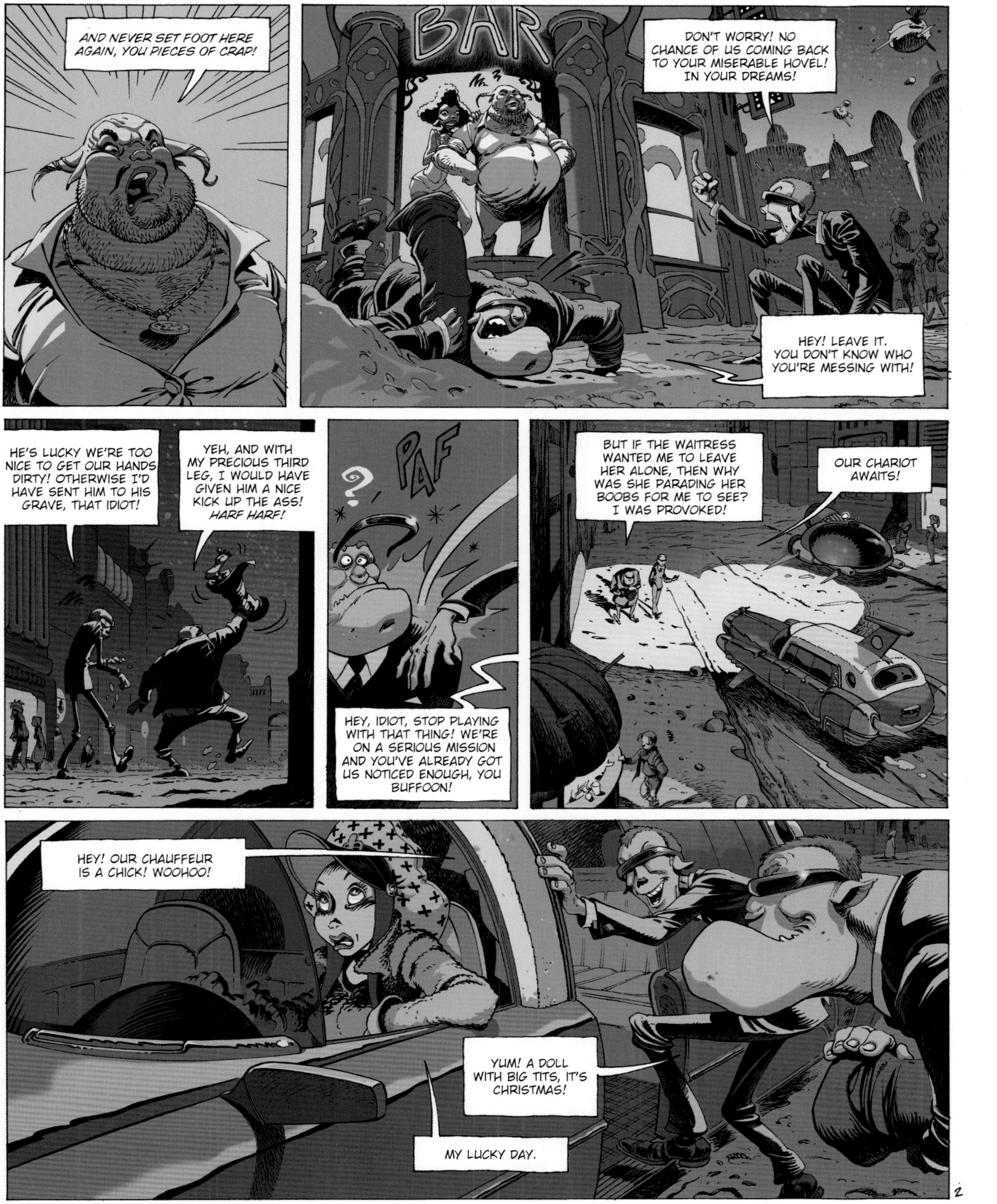
AND NEVER SET FOOT HERE AGAIN, YOU PIECES OF CRAP!
BAR
DON'T WORRY! NO CHANCE OF US COMING BACK TO YOUR MISERABLE HOVEL! IN YOUR DREAMS!
HEY! LEAVE IT. YOU DON'T KNOW WHO YOU'RE MESSING WITH!
HE'S LUCKY WE'RE TOO NICE TO GET OUR HANDS DIRTY! OTHERWISE I'D HAVE SENT HIM TO HIS GRAVE, THAT IDIOT!
YEH, AND WITH MY PRECIOUS THIRD LEG, I WOULD HAVE GIVEN HIM A NICE KICK UP THE ASS! *HARF HARF!*
PAF
?
HEY, IDIOT, STOP PLAYING WITH THAT THING! WE'RE ON A SERIOUS MISSION AND YOU'VE ALREADY GOT US NOTICED ENOUGH, YOU BUFFOON!
BUT IF THE WAITRESS WANTED ME TO LEAVE HER ALONE, THEN WHY WAS SHE PARADING HER BOOBS FOR ME TO SEE? I WAS PROVOKED!
OUR CHARIOT AWAITS!
HEY! OUR CHAUFFEUR IS A CHICK! WOOHOO!
YUM! A DOLL WITH BIG TITS, IT'S CHRISTMAS!
MY LUCKY DAY.
2

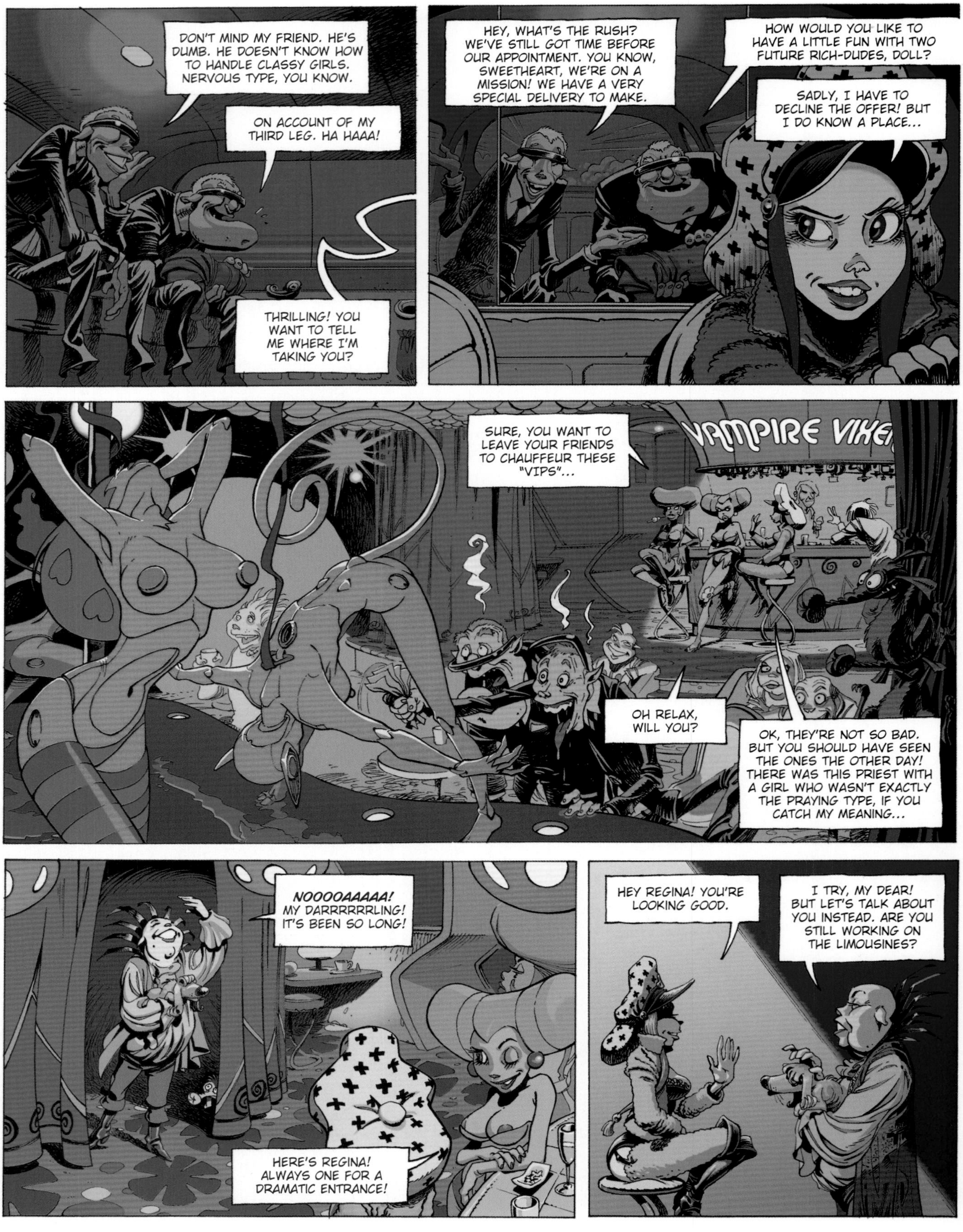
DON'T MIND MY FRIEND. HE'S DUMB. HE DOESN'T KNOW HOW TO HANDLE CLASSY GIRLS. NERVOUS TYPE, YOU KNOW.
ON ACCOUNT OF MY THIRD LEG. HA HAAA!
THRILLING! YOU WANT TO TELL ME WHERE I'M TAKING YOU?
HEY, WHAT'S THE RUSH? WE'VE STILL GOT TIME BEFORE OUR APPOINTMENT. YOU KNOW, SWEETHEART, WE'RE ON A MISSION! WE HAVE A VERY SPECIAL DELIVERY TO MAKE.
HOW WOULD YOU LIKE TO HAVE A LITTLE FUN WITH TWO FUTURE RICH-DUDES, DOLL?
SADLY, I HAVE TO DECLINE THE OFFER! BUT I DO KNOW A PLACE...
SURE, YOU WANT TO LEAVE YOUR FRIENDS TO CHAUFFEUR THESE "VIPS"...
VAMPIRE VIXE
OH RELAX, WILL YOU?
OK, THEY'RE NOT SO BAD. BUT YOU SHOULD HAVE SEEN THE ONES THE OTHER DAY! THERE WAS THIS PRIEST WITH A GIRL WHO WASN'T EXACTLY THE PRAYING TYPE, IF YOU CATCH MY MEANING...
NOOOOAAAAA! MY DARRRRRRLING! IT'S BEEN SO LONG!
HERE'S REGINA! ALWAYS ONE FOR A DRAMATIC ENTRANCE!
HEY REGINA! YOU'RE LOOKING GOOD.
I TRY, MY DEAR! BUT LET'S TALK ABOUT YOU INSTEAD. ARE YOU STILL WORKING ON THE LIMOUSINES?

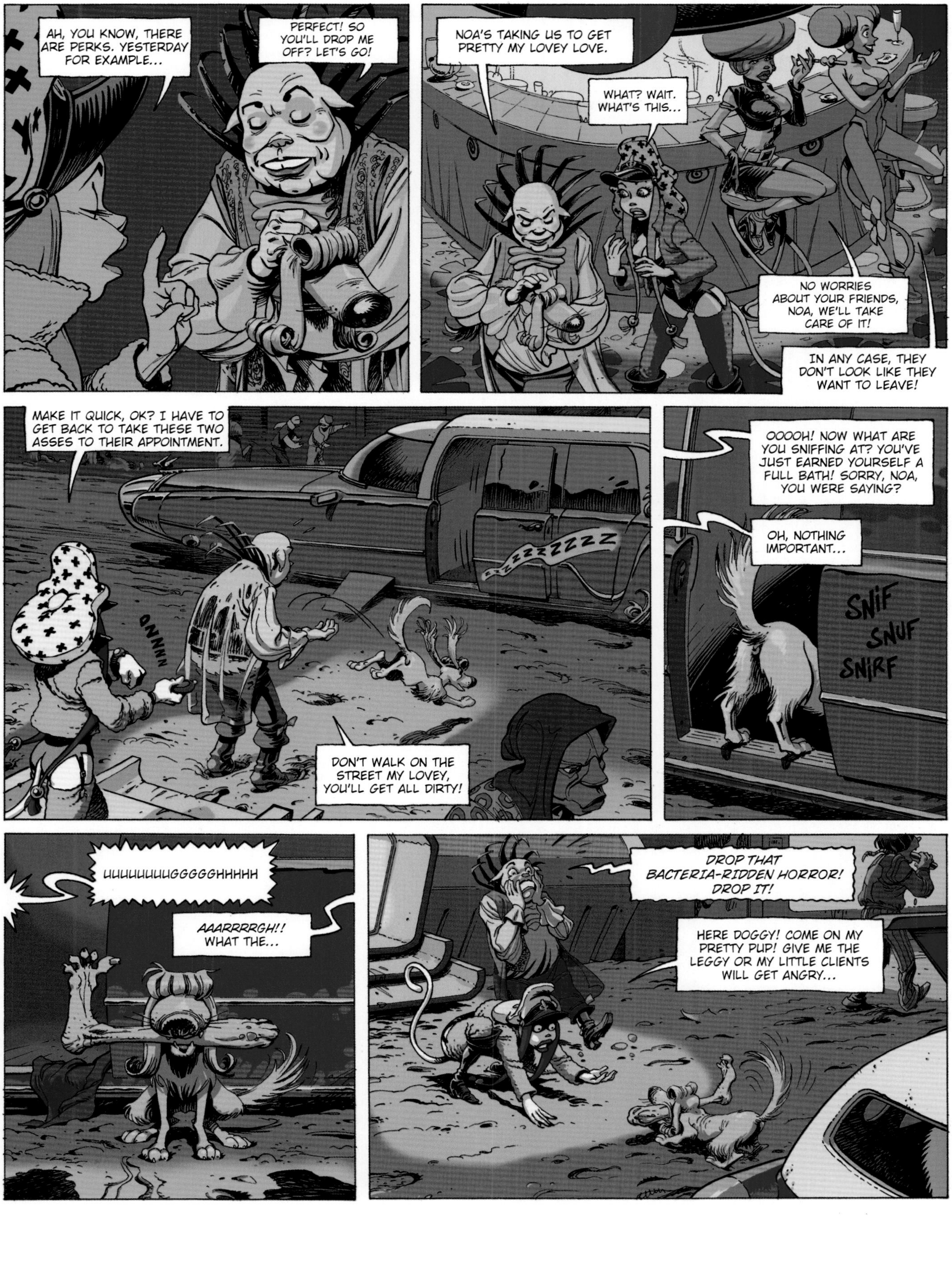
AH, YOU KNOW, THERE ARE PERKS. YESTERDAY FOR EXAMPLE...
PERFECT! SO YOU'LL DROP ME OFF? LET'S GO!
NOA'S TAKING US TO GET PRETTY MY LOVEY LOVE.
WHAT? WAIT. WHAT'S THIS...
NO WORRIES ABOUT YOUR FRIENDS, NOA, WE'LL TAKE CARE OF IT!
IN ANY CASE, THEY DON'T LOOK LIKE THEY WANT TO LEAVE!
MAKE IT QUICK, OK? I HAVE TO GET BACK TO TAKE THESE TWO ASSES TO THEIR APPOINTMENT.
NNNN
ZZZZZZZZ
DON'T WALK ON THE STREET MY LOVEY, YOU'LL GET ALL DIRTY!
OOOOH! NOW WHAT ARE YOU SNIFFING AT? YOU'VE JUST EARNED YOURSELF A FULL BATH! SORRY, NOA, YOU WERE SAYING?
OH, NOTHING IMPORTANT...
SNIF
SNUF
SNIRF
UUUUUUUUGGGGGHHHHH
AAARRRRGH!! WHAT THE...
DROP THAT BACTERIA-RIDDEN HORROR! DROP IT!
HERE DOGGY! COME ON MY PRETTY PUP! GIVE ME THE LEGGY OR MY LITTLE CLIENTS WILL GET ANGRY...
4

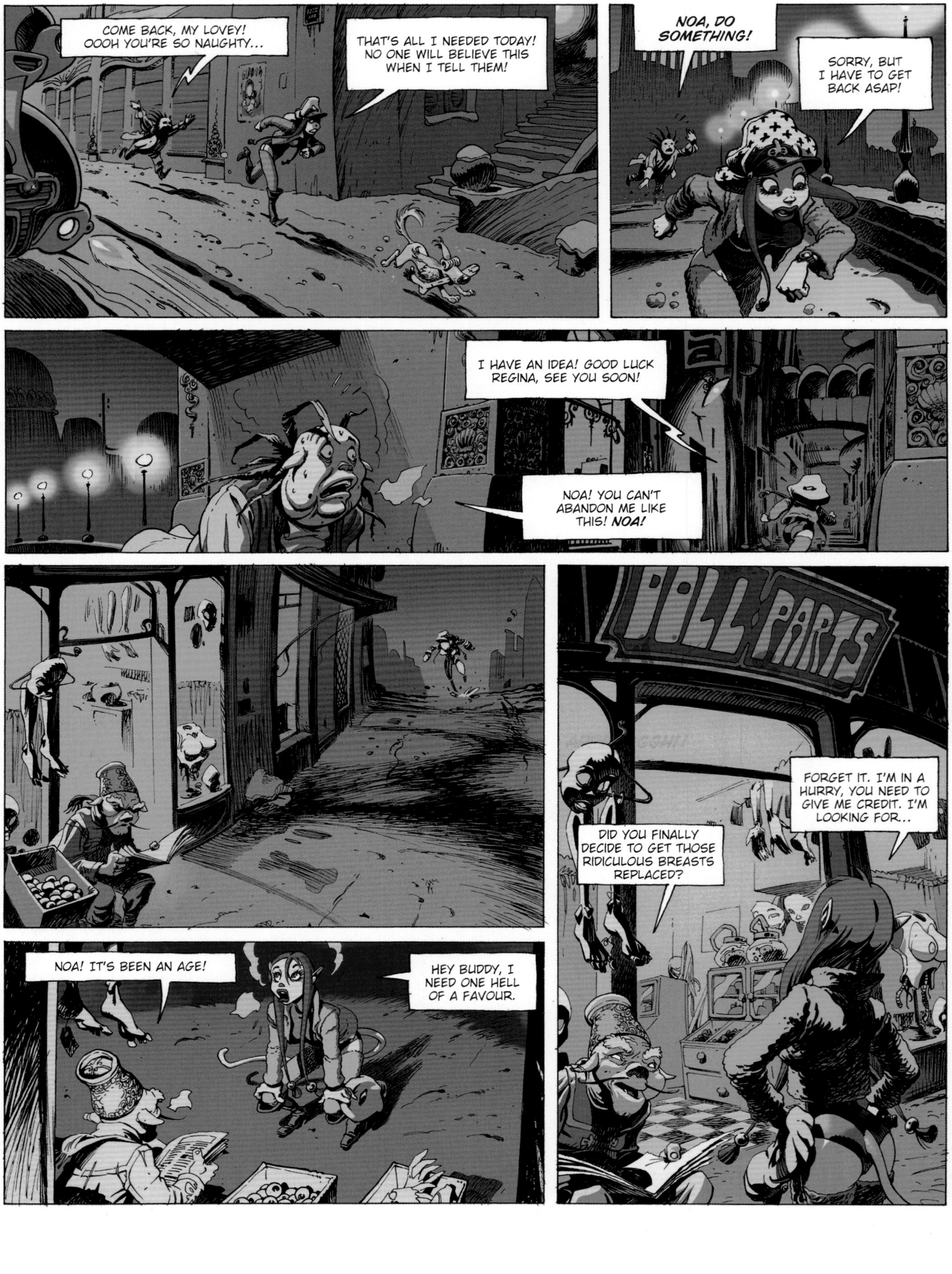
COME BACK, MY LOVEY! OOOH YOU'RE SO NAUGHTY...
THAT'S ALL I NEEDED TODAY! NO ONE WILL BELIEVE THIS WHEN I TELL THEM!
NOA, DO SOMETHING!
SORRY, BUT I HAVE TO GET BACK ASAP!
I HAVE AN IDEA! GOOD LUCK REGINA, SEE YOU SOON!
NOA! YOU CAN'T ABANDON ME LIKE THIS! NOA!
NOA! IT'S BEEN AN AGE!
HEY BUDDY, I NEED ONE HELL OF A FAVOUR.
DOLL PARTS
DID YOU FINALLY DECIDE TO GET THOSE RIDICULOUS BREASTS REPLACED?
FORGET IT. I'M IN A HURRY, YOU NEED TO GIVE ME CREDIT. I'M LOOKING FOR...

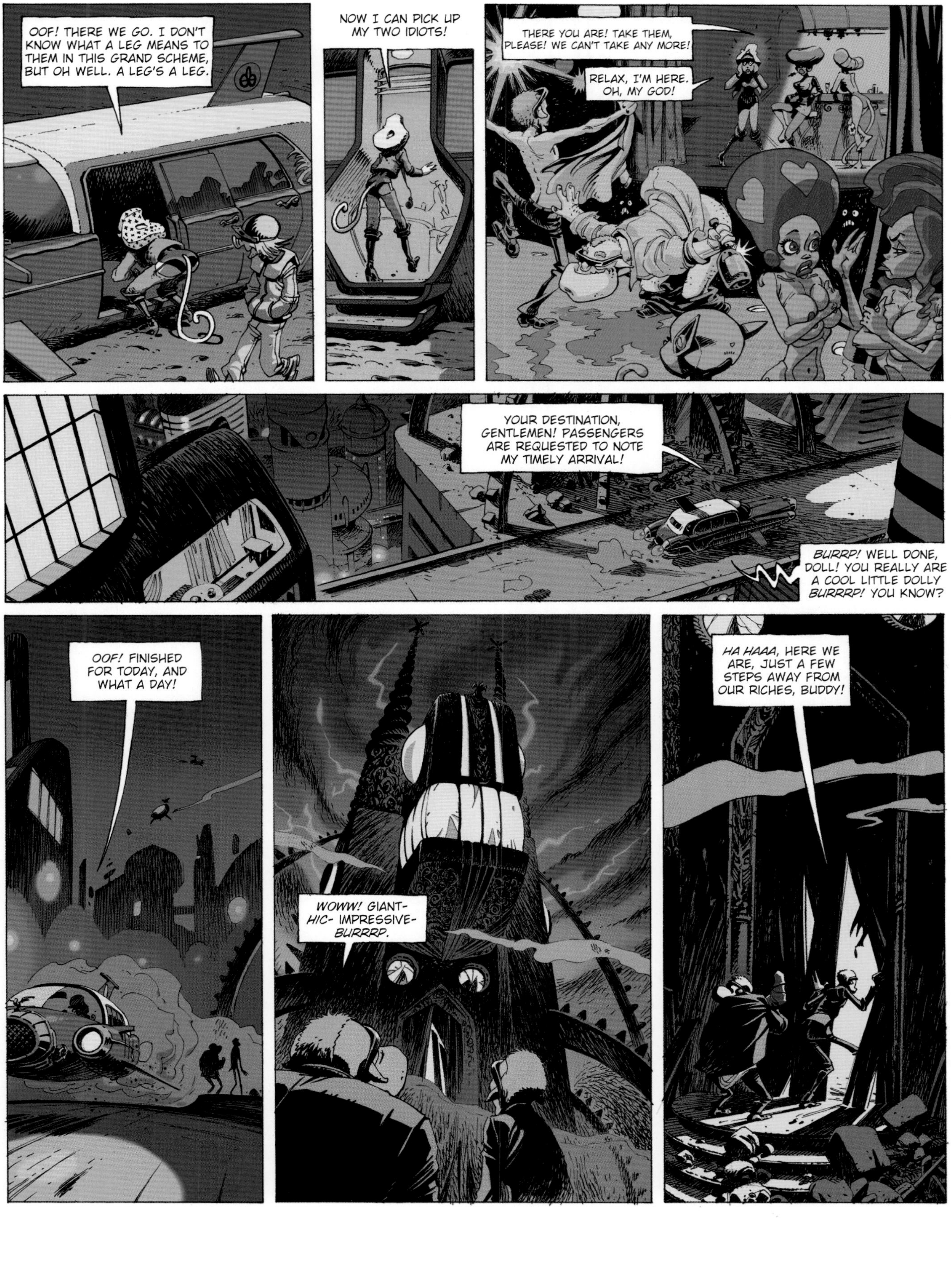
OOF! THERE WE GO. I DON'T KNOW WHAT A LEG MEANS TO THEM IN THIS GRAND SCHEME, BUT OH WELL. A LEG'S A LEG.
NOW I CAN PICK UP MY TWO IDIOTS!
THERE YOU ARE! TAKE THEM, PLEASE! WE CAN'T TAKE ANY MORE!
RELAX, I'M HERE. OH, MY GOD!
YOUR DESTINATION, GENTLEMEN! PASSENGERS ARE REQUESTED TO NOTE MY TIMELY ARRIVAL!
BURRP! WELL DONE, DOLL! YOU REALLY ARE A COOL LITTLE DOLLY BURRRP! YOU KNOW?
OOF! FINISHED FOR TODAY, AND WHAT A DAY!
WOWW! GIANT- HIC- IMPRESSIVE- BURRRP.
HA HAAA, HERE WE ARE, JUST A FEW STEPS AWAY FROM OUR RICHES, BUDDY!
6

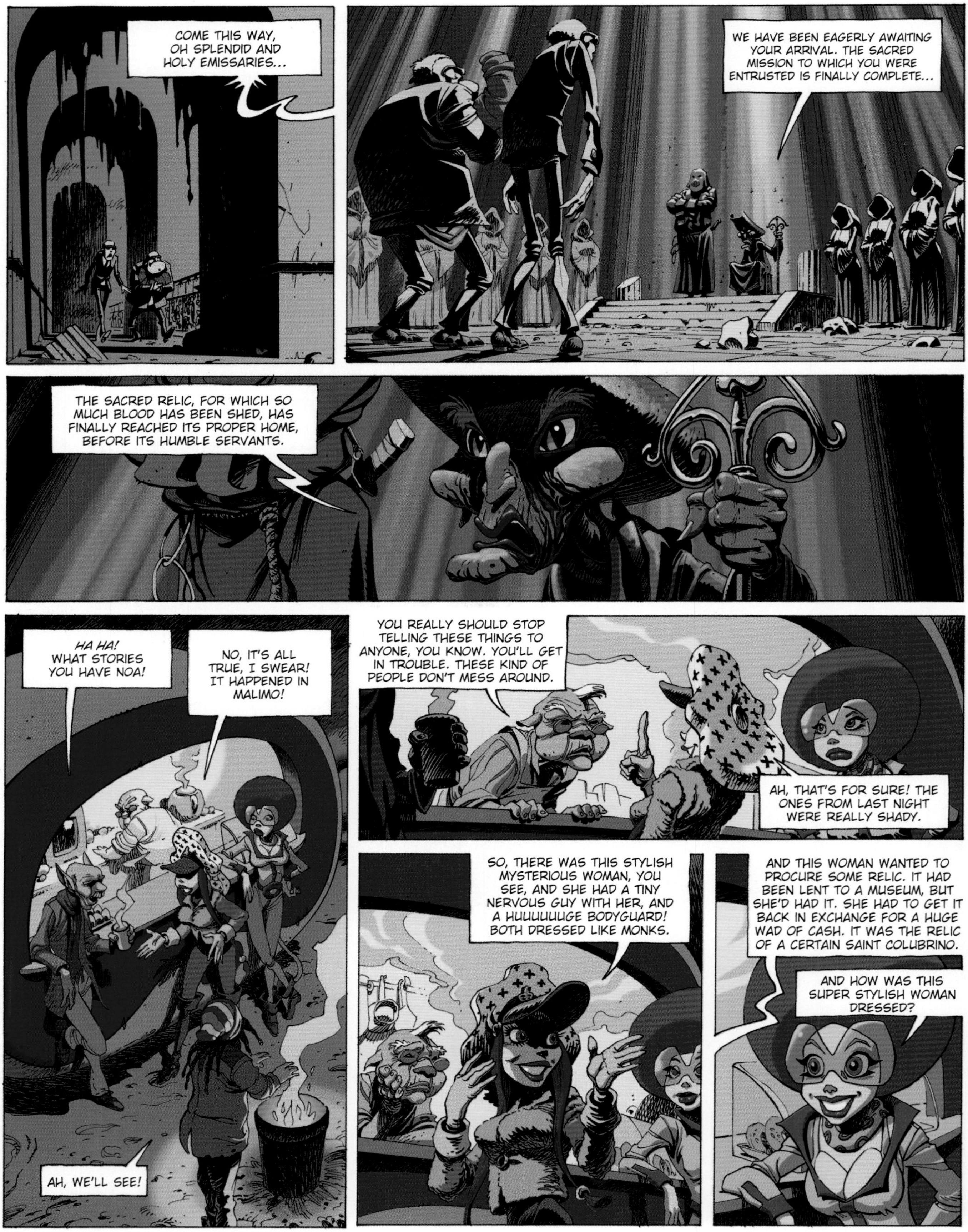
COME THIS WAY, OH SPLENDID AND HOLY EMISSARIES...
WE HAVE BEEN EAGERLY AWAITING YOUR ARRIVAL. THE SACRED MISSION TO WHICH YOU WERE ENTRUSTED IS FINALLY COMPLETE...
THE SACRED RELIC, FOR WHICH SO MUCH BLOOD HAS BEEN SHED, HAS FINALLY REACHED ITS PROPER HOME, BEFORE ITS HUMBLE SERVANTS.
HA HA! WHAT STORIES YOU HAVE NOA!
NO, IT'S ALL TRUE, I SWEAR! IT HAPPENED IN MALIMO!
AH, WE'LL SEE!
YOU REALLY SHOULD STOP TELLING THESE THINGS TO ANYONE, YOU KNOW. YOU'LL GET IN TROUBLE. THESE KIND OF PEOPLE DON'T MESS AROUND.
AH, THAT'S FOR SURE! THE ONES FROM LAST NIGHT WERE REALLY SHADY.
SO, THERE WAS THIS STYLISH MYSTERIOUS WOMAN, YOU SEE, AND SHE HAD A TINY NERVOUS GUY WITH HER, AND A HUUUUUUGE BODYGUARD! BOTH DRESSED LIKE MONKS.
AND THIS WOMAN WANTED TO PROCURE SOME RELIC. IT HAD BEEN LENT TO A MUSEUM, BUT SHE'D HAD IT. SHE HAD TO GET IT BACK IN EXCHANGE FOR A HUGE WAD OF CASH. IT WAS THE RELIC OF A CERTAIN SAINT COLUBRINO.
AND HOW WAS THIS SUPER STYLISH WOMAN DRESSED?

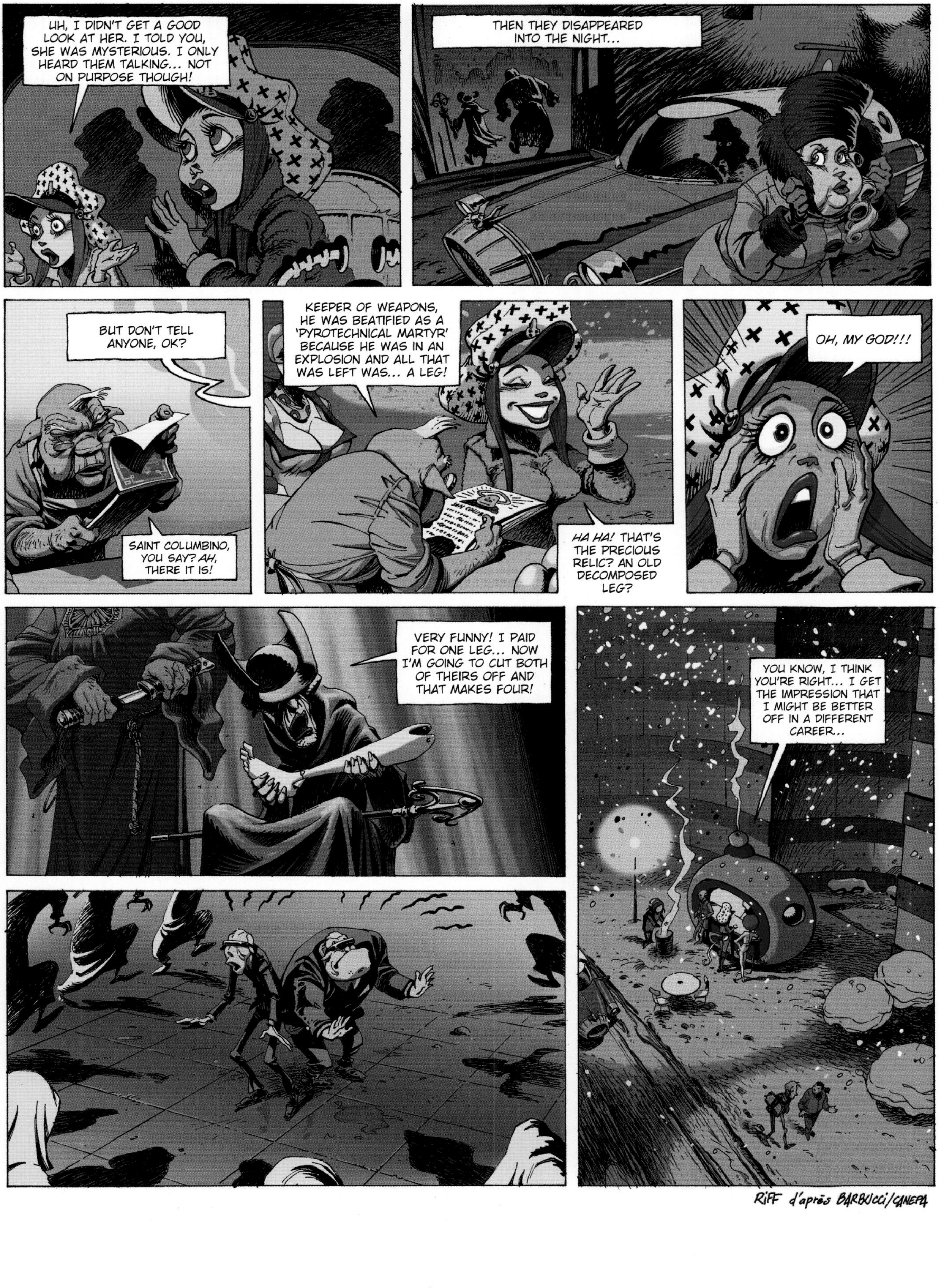
UH, I DIDN'T GET A GOOD LOOK AT HER. I TOLD YOU, SHE WAS MYSTERIOUS. I ONLY HEARD THEM TALKING... NOT ON PURPOSE THOUGH!
THEN THEY DISAPPEARED INTO THE NIGHT...
BUT DON'T TELL ANYONE, OK?
SAINT COLUMBINO, YOU SAY? AH, THERE IT IS!
KEEPER OF WEAPONS, HE WAS BEATIFIED AS A 'PYROTECHNICAL MARTYR' BECAUSE HE WAS IN AN EXPLOSION AND ALL THAT WAS LEFT WAS... A LEG!
HA HA! THAT'S THE PRECIOUS RELIC? AN OLD DECOMPOSED LEG?
OH, MY GOD!!!
VERY FUNNY! I PAID FOR ONE LEG... NOW I'M GOING TO CUT BOTH OF THEIRS OFF AND THAT MAKES FOUR!
YOU KNOW, I THINK YOU'RE RIGHT... I GET THE IMPRESSION THAT I MIGHT BE BETTER OFF IN A DIFFERENT CAREER...
RiFF d'après BARBUCCI/CANEPA

SKYDOLL SPAACESHIP COLLECTION

Venusdea industries

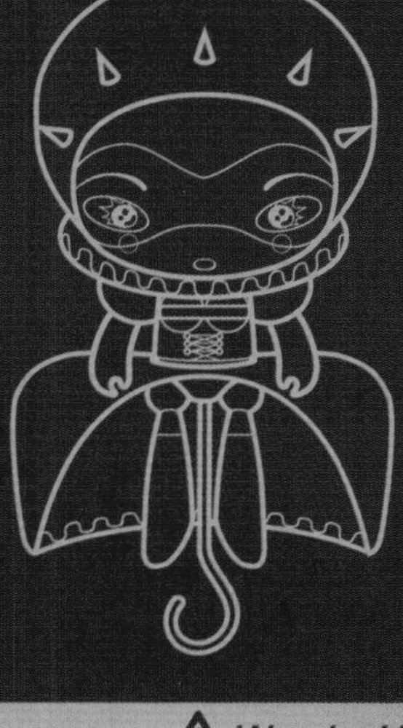

⚠ Warning! This track contains:

"I know... I'm aware that we dolls were invented for kind of a twisted purpose."

(Sky Doll: Decade, Volume 1, page 56)

- Faithful paupers
- Holy mistress
- Sad tunes

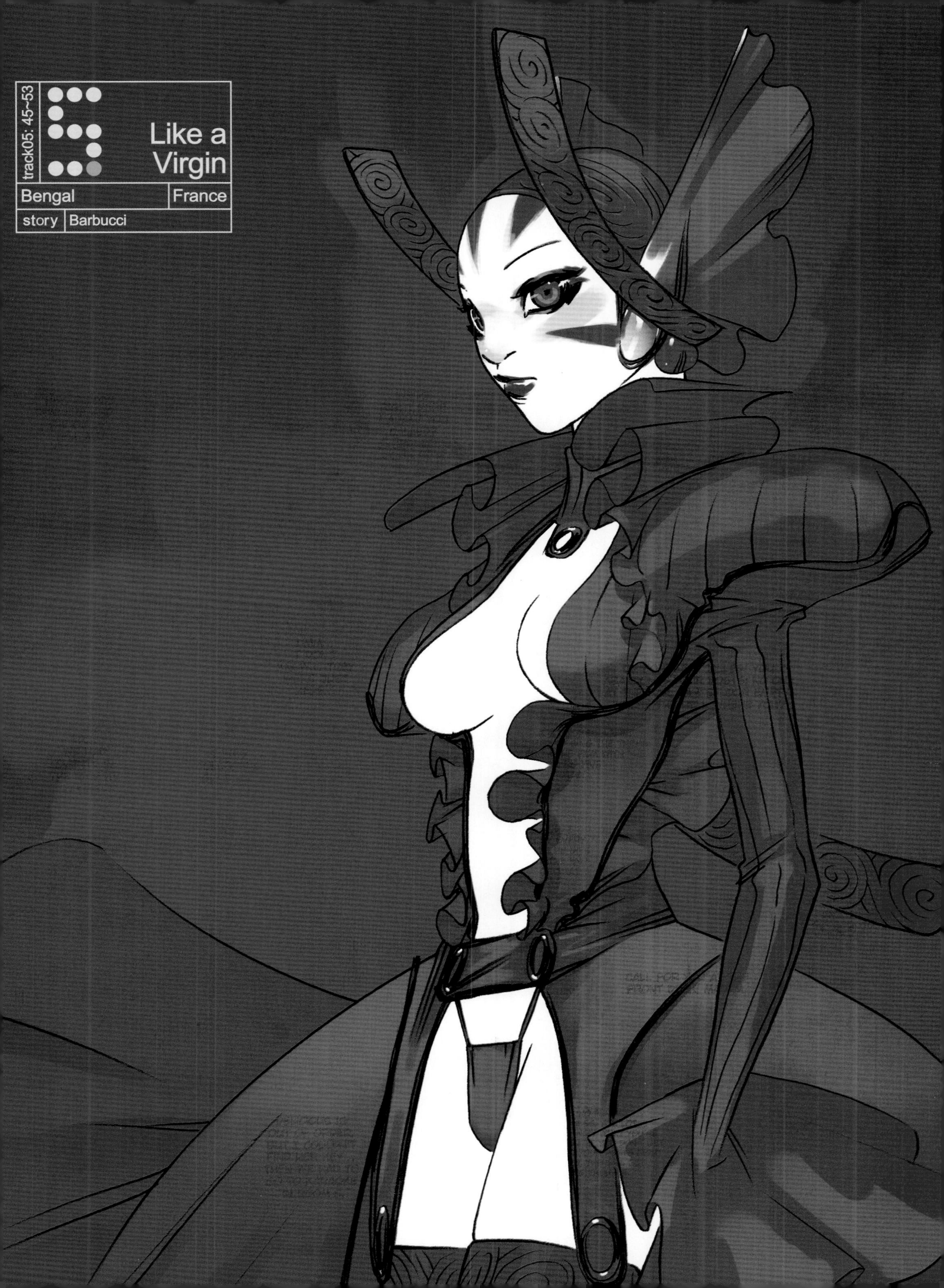
track05: 45~53
5
Like a Virgin
Bengal
France
story Barbucci

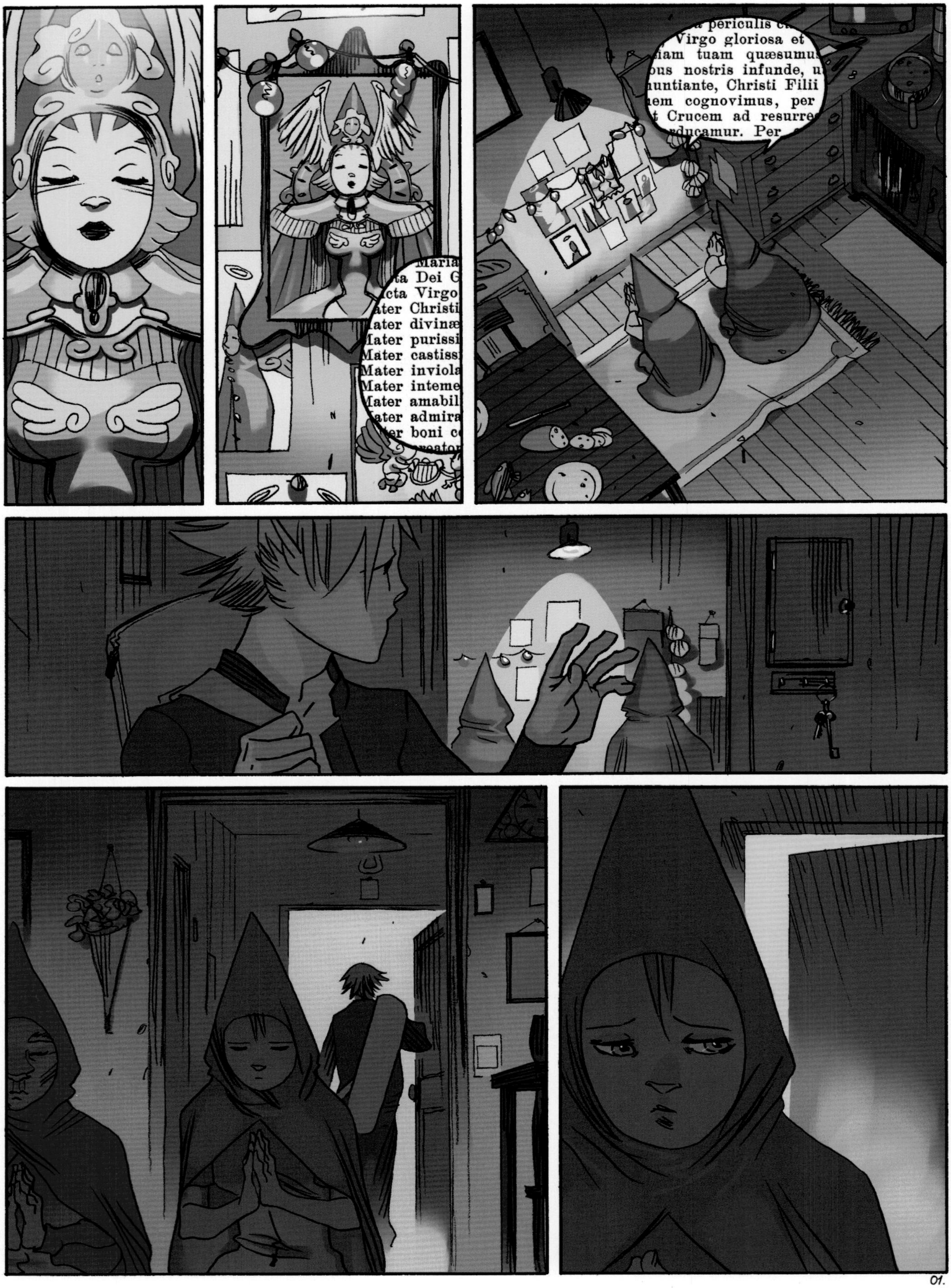
Maria
Dei G
ncta Virgo
ater Christi
ater divinæ
Mater purissi
Mater castiss
Mater inviola
Mater inteme
Mater amabil
ater admira
ter boni c
a periculis c
Virgo gloriosa et
iam tuam quæsumus
ous nostris infunde, u
nuntiante, Christi Filii
em cognovimus, per
t Crucem ad resurre
rducamur. Per

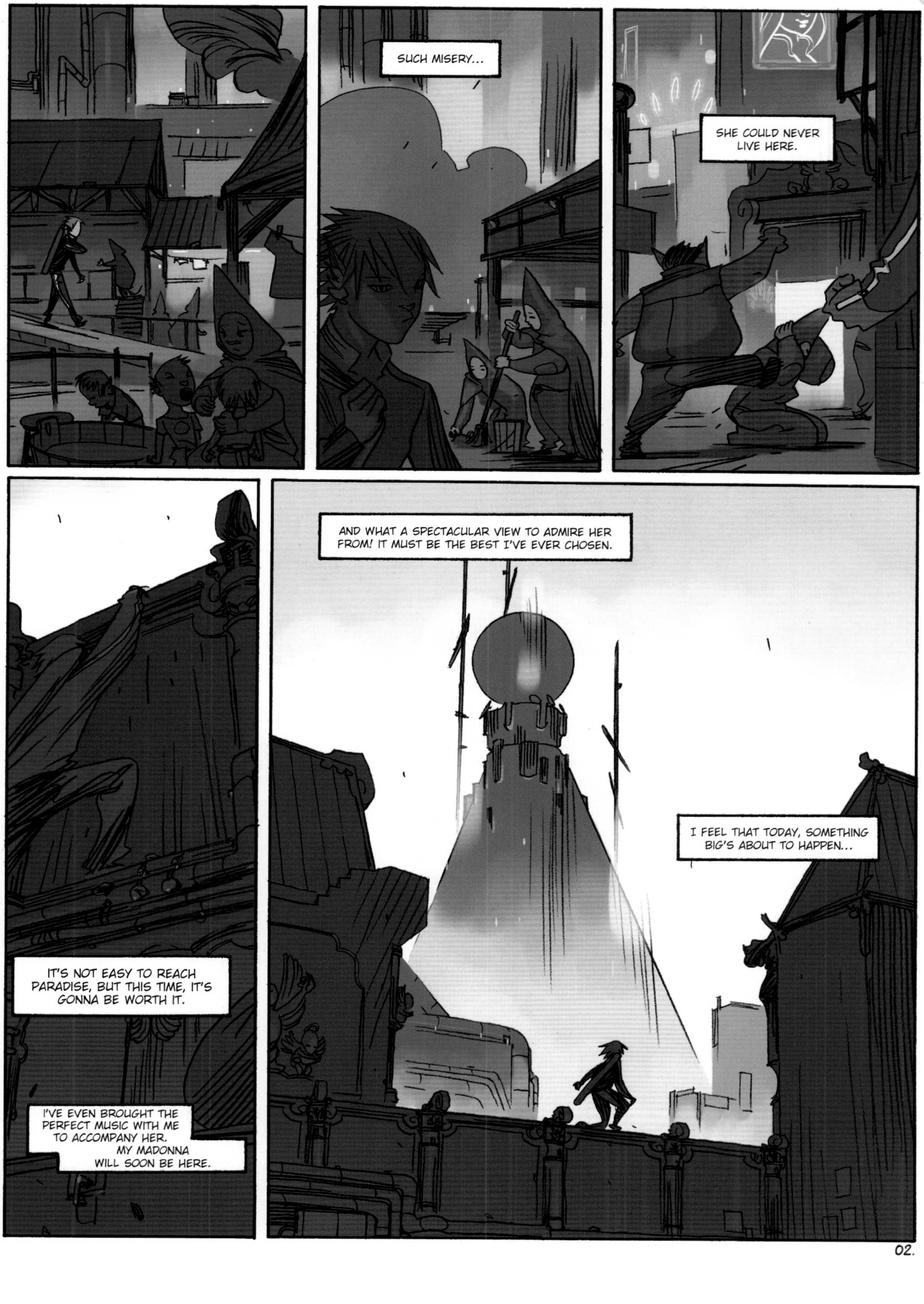
SUCH MISERY...
SHE COULD NEVER LIVE HERE.
IT'S NOT EASY TO REACH PARADISE, BUT THIS TIME, IT'S GONNA BE WORTH IT.
I'VE EVEN BROUGHT THE PERFECT MUSIC WITH ME TO ACCOMPANY HER.
MY MADONNA WILL SOON BE HERE.
AND WHAT A SPECTACULAR VIEW TO ADMIRE HER FROM! IT MUST BE THE BEST I'VE EVER CHOSEN.
I FEEL THAT TODAY, SOMETHING BIG'S ABOUT TO HAPPEN...

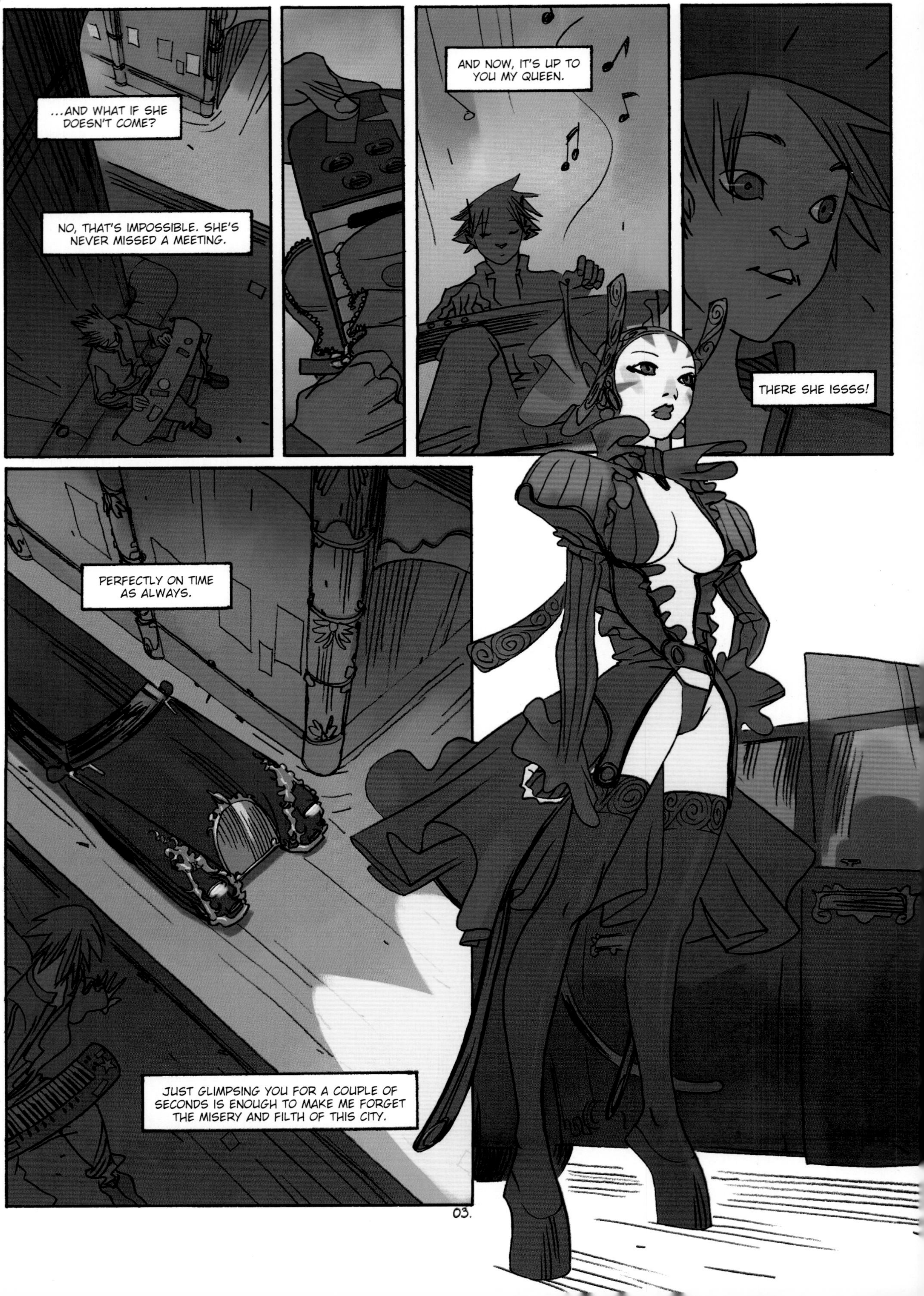
...AND WHAT IF SHE DOESN'T COME?
NO, THAT'S IMPOSSIBLE. SHE'S NEVER MISSED A MEETING.
AND NOW, IT'S UP TO YOU MY QUEEN.
THERE SHE ISSSS!
PERFECTLY ON TIME AS ALWAYS.
JUST GLIMPSING YOU FOR A COUPLE OF SECONDS IS ENOUGH TO MAKE ME FORGET THE MISERY AND FILTH OF THIS CITY.
03.

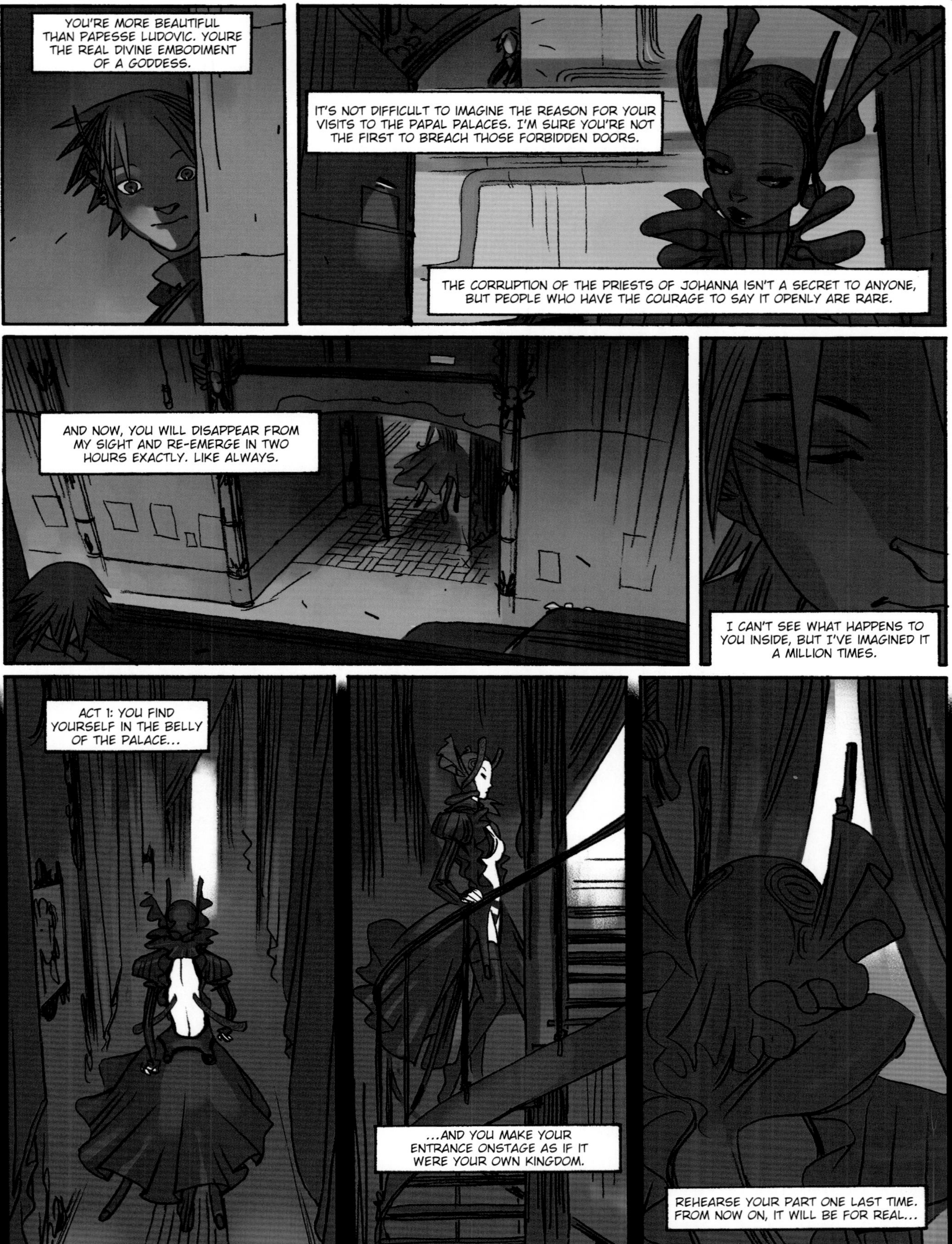
YOU'RE MORE BEAUTIFUL THAN PAPESSE LUDOVIC. YOURE THE REAL DIVINE EMBODIMENT OF A GODDESS.
IT'S NOT DIFFICULT TO IMAGINE THE REASON FOR YOUR VISITS TO THE PAPAL PALACES. I'M SURE YOU'RE NOT THE FIRST TO BREACH THOSE FORBIDDEN DOORS.
THE CORRUPTION OF THE PRIESTS OF JOHANNA ISN'T A SECRET TO ANYONE, BUT PEOPLE WHO HAVE THE COURAGE TO SAY IT OPENLY ARE RARE.
AND NOW, YOU WILL DISAPPEAR FROM MY SIGHT AND RE-EMERGE IN TWO HOURS EXACTLY. LIKE ALWAYS.
I CAN'T SEE WHAT HAPPENS TO YOU INSIDE, BUT I'VE IMAGINED IT A MILLION TIMES.
ACT 1: YOU FIND YOURSELF IN THE BELLY OF THE PALACE...
...AND YOU MAKE YOUR ENTRANCE ONSTAGE AS IF IT WERE YOUR OWN KINGDOM.
REHEARSE YOUR PART ONE LAST TIME. FROM NOW ON, IT WILL BE FOR REAL...

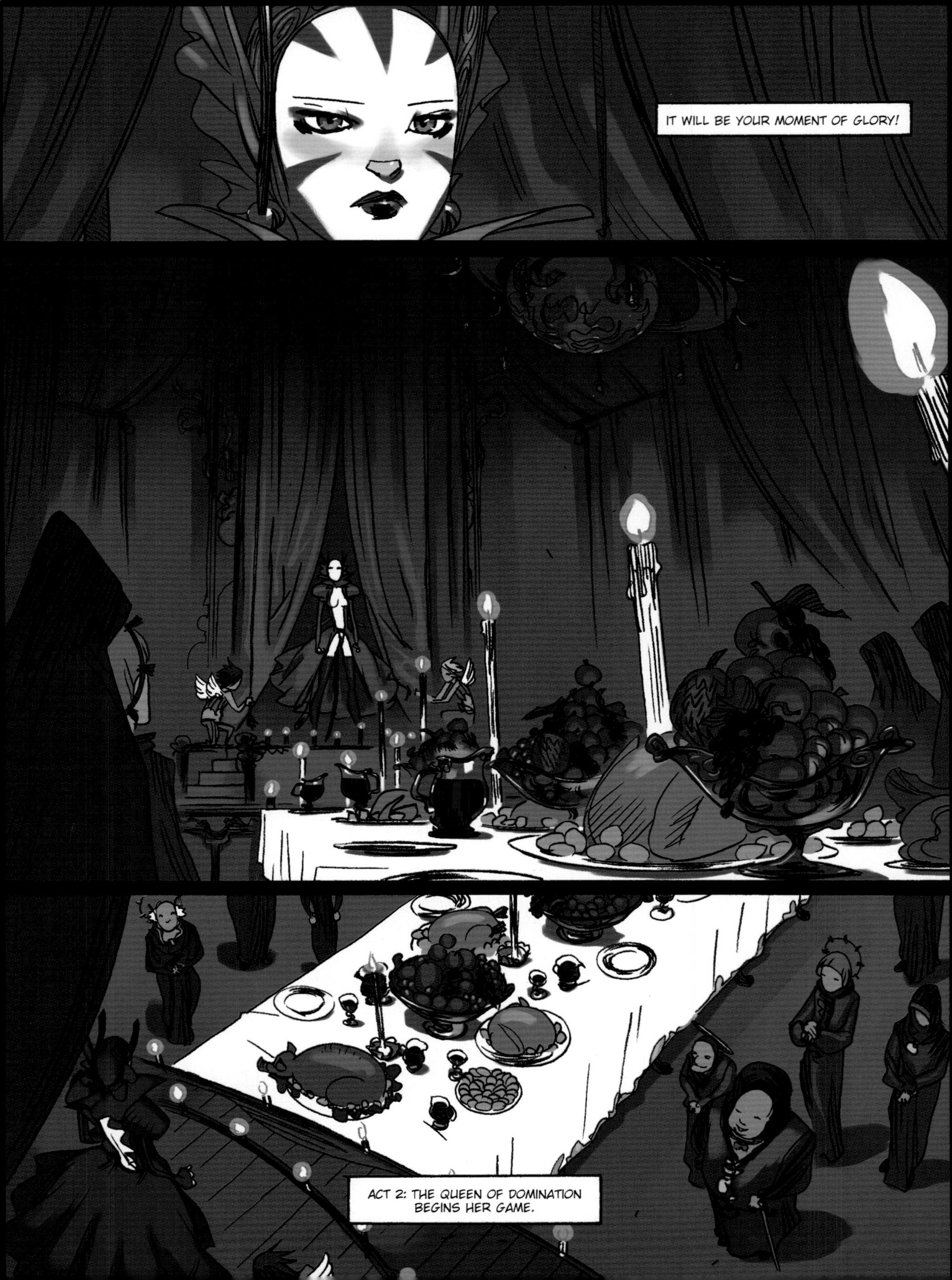
IT WILL BE YOUR MOMENT OF GLORY!
ACT 2: THE QUEEN OF DOMINATION BEGINS HER GAME.

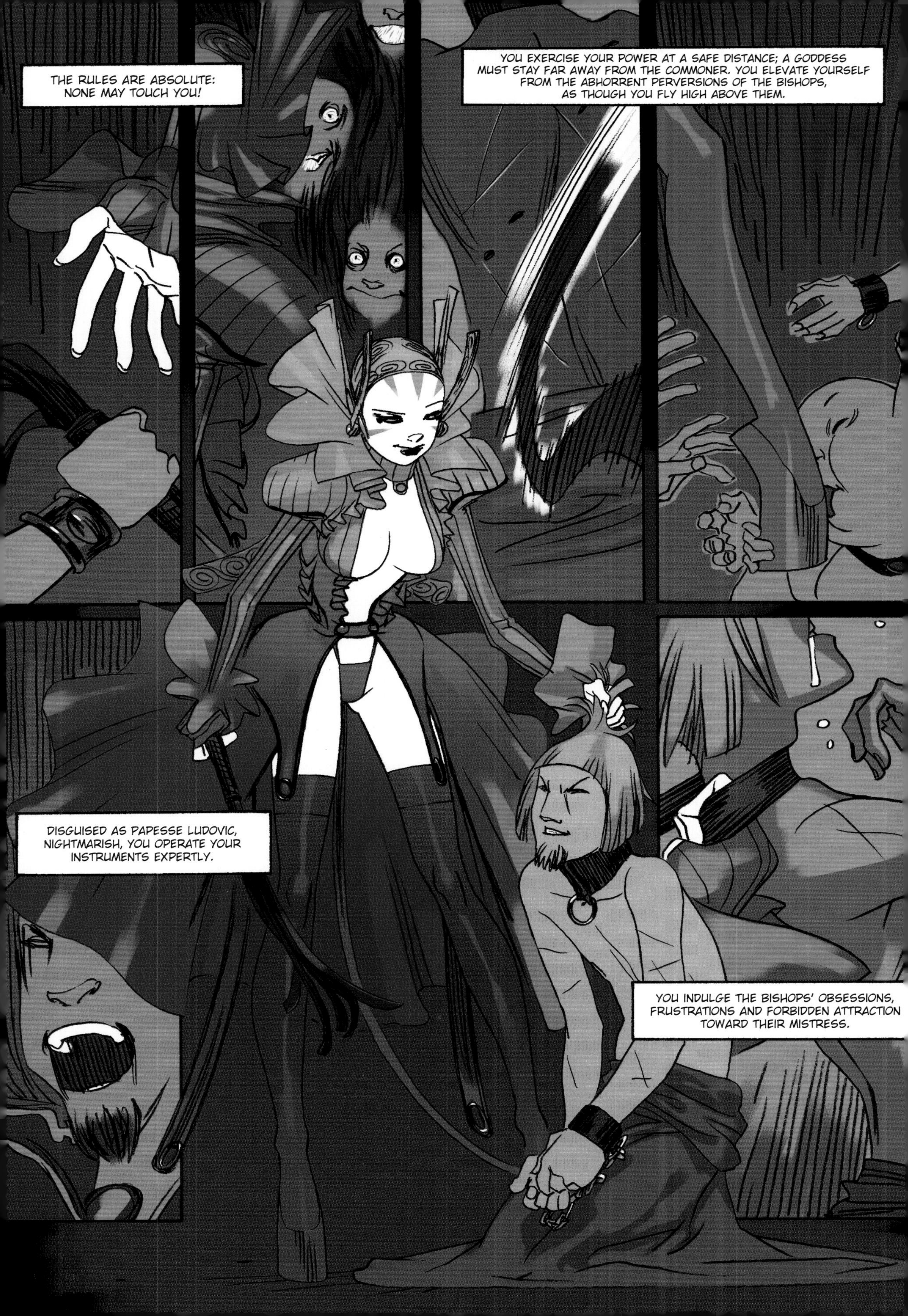
THE RULES ARE ABSOLUTE: NONE MAY TOUCH YOU!
YOU EXERCISE YOUR POWER AT A SAFE DISTANCE; A GODDESS MUST STAY FAR AWAY FROM THE COMMONER. YOU ELEVATE YOURSELF FROM THE ABHORRENT PERVERSIONS OF THE BISHOPS, AS THOUGH YOU FLY HIGH ABOVE THEM.
DISGUISED AS PAPESSE LUDOVIC, NIGHTMARISH, YOU OPERATE YOUR INSTRUMENTS EXPERTLY.
YOU INDULGE THE BISHOPS' OBSESSIONS, FRUSTRATIONS AND FORBIDDEN ATTRACTION TOWARD THEIR MISTRESS.

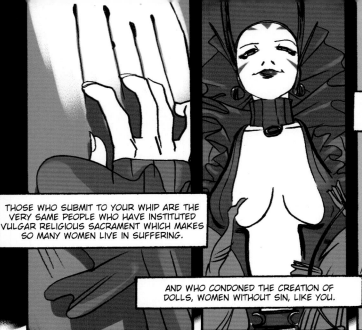

EXERCISING YOUR POWER TAKES ON ANOTHER FORM: VENGEANCE... BUT IF... EVEN AS A DOLL... YOU HAVE A SOUL... IN TAKING PART IN THIS, YOU RISK LOSING IT.

THOSE WHO SUBMIT TO YOUR WHIP ARE THE VERY SAME PEOPLE WHO HAVE INSTITUTED VULGAR RELIGIOUS SACRAMENT WHICH MAKES SO MANY WOMEN LIVE IN SUFFERING.

AND WHO CONDONED THE CREATION OF DOLLS, WOMEN WITHOUT SIN, LIKE YOU.

BECAUSE EVEN IF YOU DON'T WANT TO ADMIT IT, YOU TAKE PLEASURE PARTICIPATING IN THIS SCENE.

07.

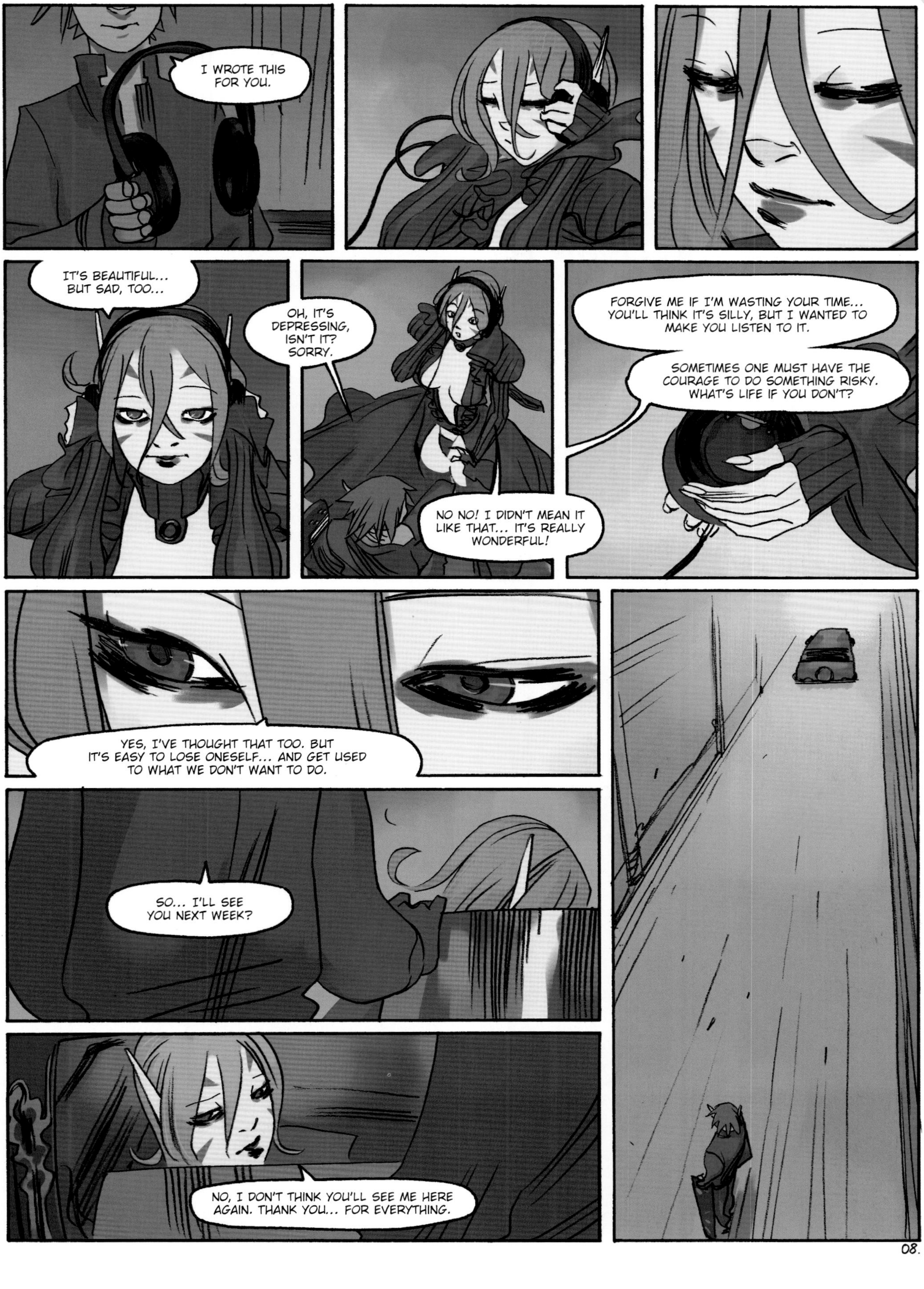
I WROTE THIS FOR YOU.
IT'S BEAUTIFUL... BUT SAD, TOO...
OH, IT'S DEPRESSING, ISN'T IT? SORRY.
NO NO! I DIDN'T MEAN IT LIKE THAT... IT'S REALLY WONDERFUL!
FORGIVE ME IF I'M WASTING YOUR TIME... YOU'LL THINK IT'S SILLY, BUT I WANTED TO MAKE YOU LISTEN TO IT.
SOMETIMES ONE MUST HAVE THE COURAGE TO DO SOMETHING RISKY. WHAT'S LIFE IF YOU DON'T?
YES, I'VE THOUGHT THAT TOO. BUT IT'S EASY TO LOSE ONESELF... AND GET USED TO WHAT WE DON'T WANT TO DO.
SO... I'LL SEE YOU NEXT WEEK?
NO, I DON'T THINK YOU'LL SEE ME HERE AGAIN. THANK YOU... FOR EVERYTHING.

SKYDOLL SPACESHIP COLLECTION

Venusdea Industries ●

⚠ Warning! This track contains:

"But you should know: Your management
style is really pathetic!"

(Sky Doll: Decade, Volume 1, page 14)

 Polychrome phytoplankton

 Voice of God

 Bouncing boobs

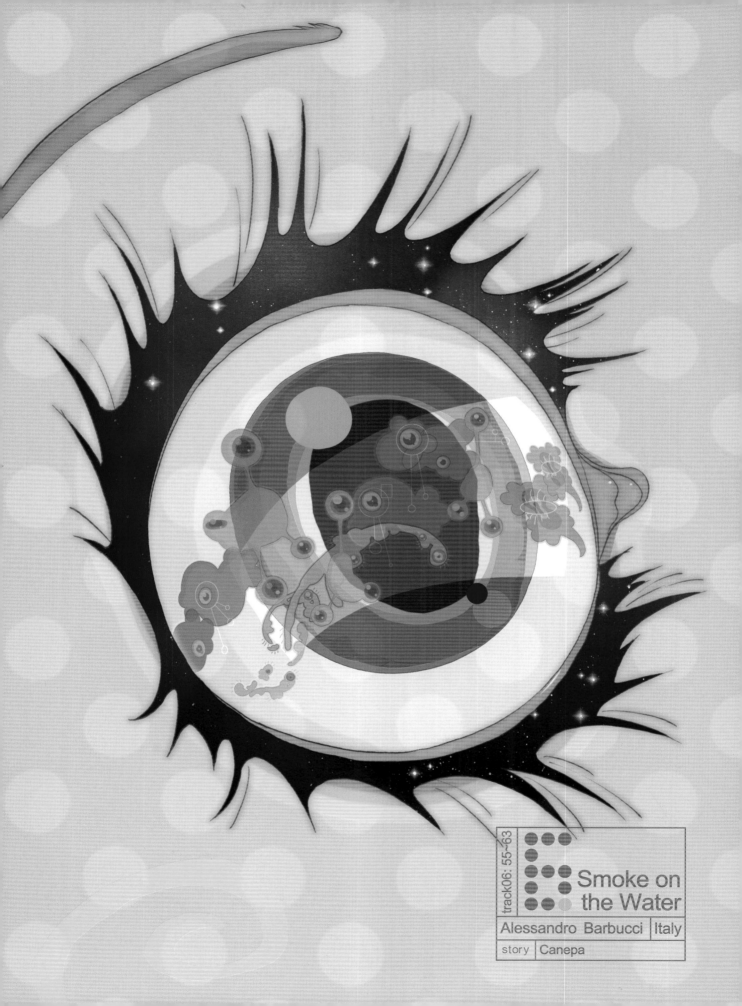

track06: 55–63

Smoke on
the Water

Alessandro Barbucci | Italy

story | Canepa

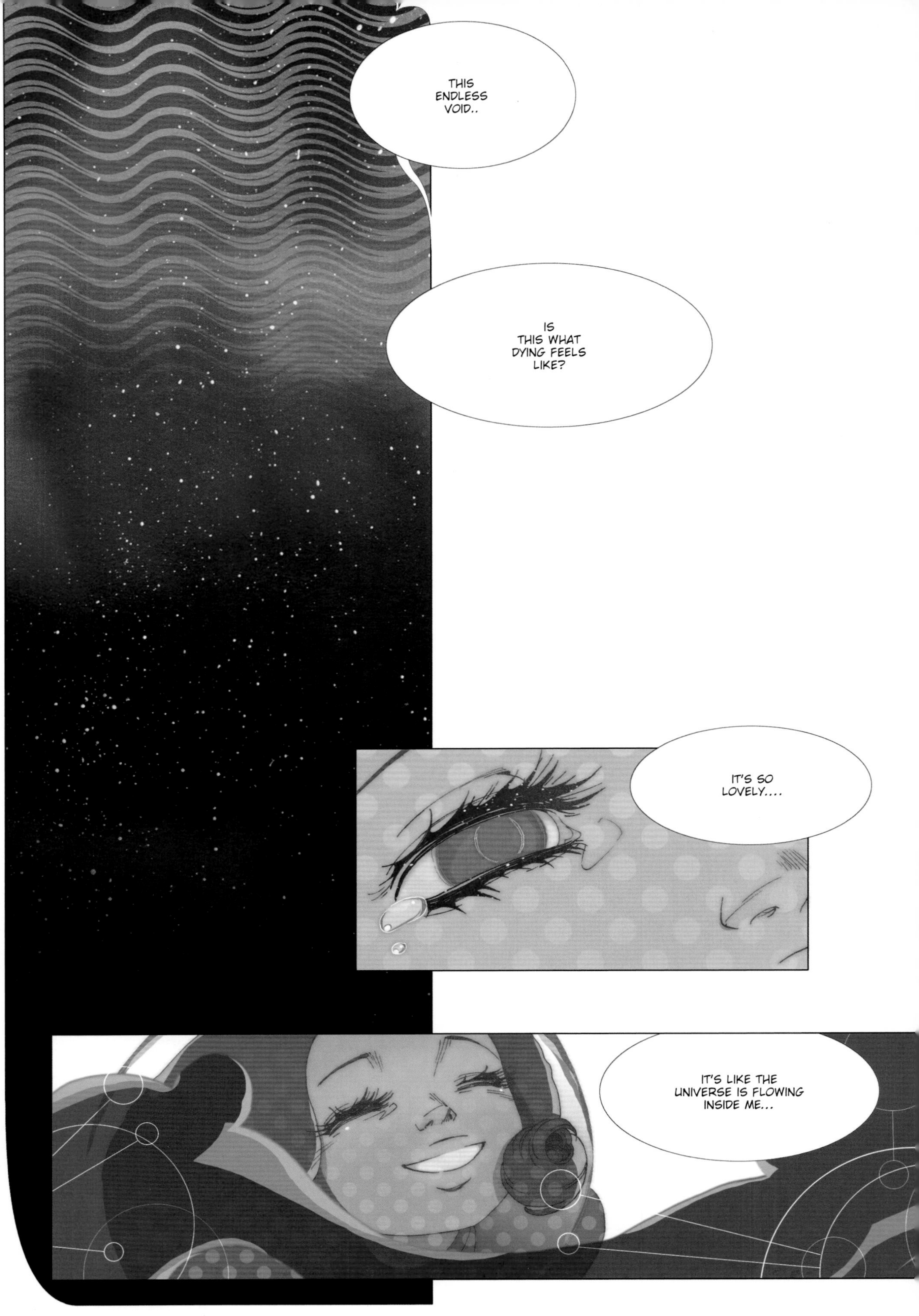
THIS ENDLESS VOID..
IS THIS WHAT DYING FEELS LIKE?
IT'S SO LOVELY....
IT'S LIKE THE UNIVERSE IS FLOWING INSIDE ME...

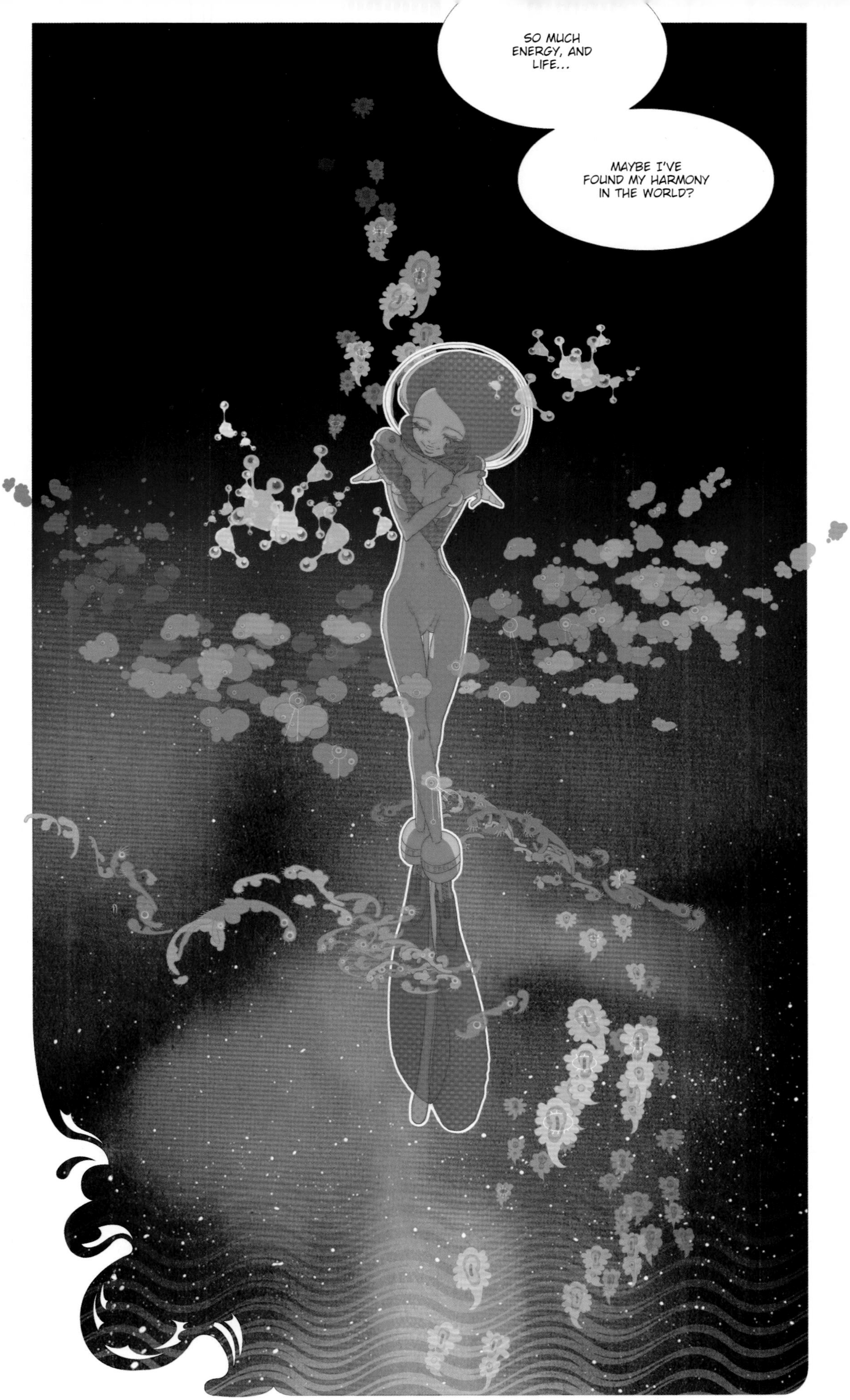
SO MUCH ENERGY, AND LIFE...
MAYBE I'VE FOUND MY HARMONY IN THE WORLD?

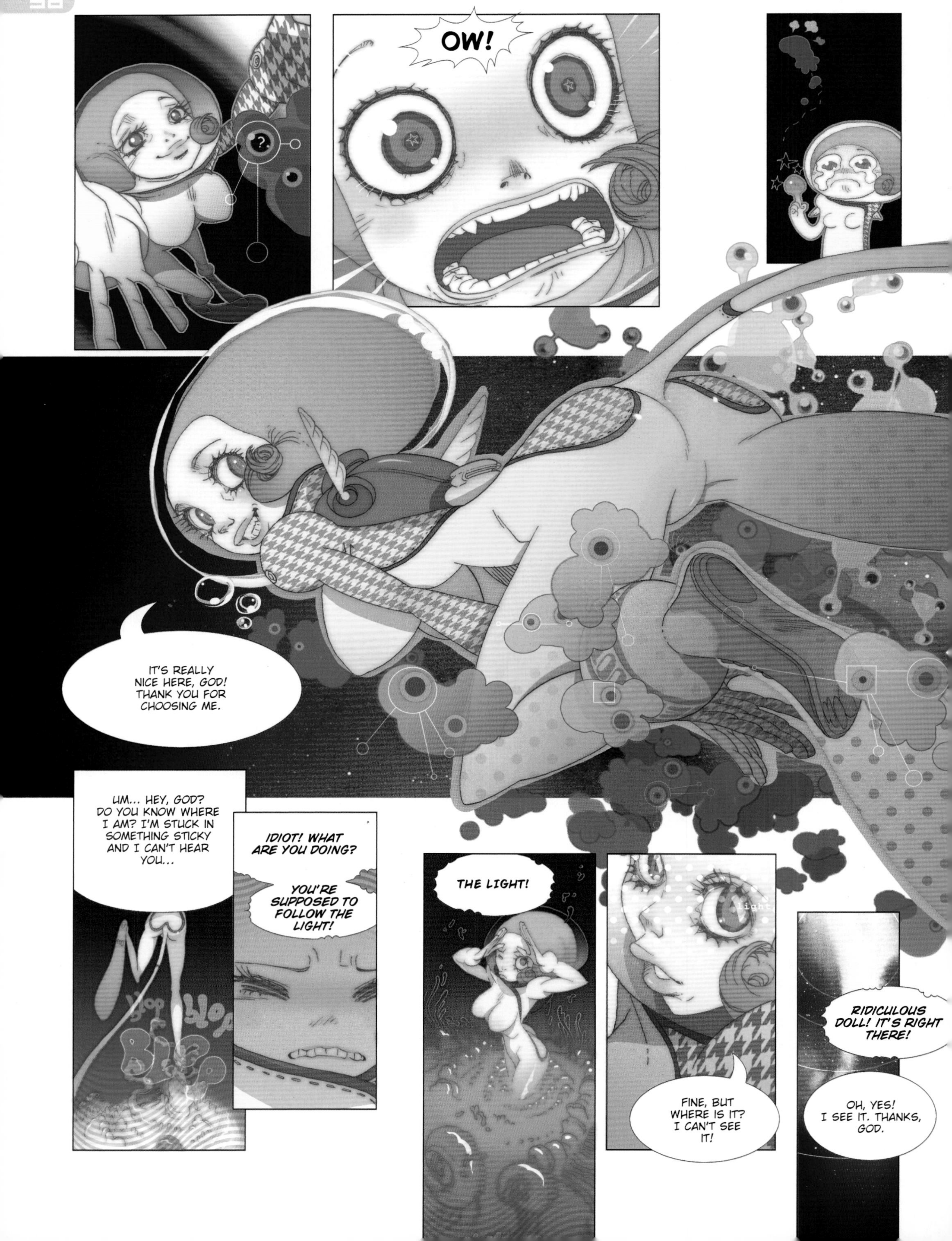
OW!
IT'S REALLY NICE HERE, GOD! THANK YOU FOR CHOOSING ME.
UM... HEY, GOD? DO YOU KNOW WHERE I AM? I'M STUCK IN SOMETHING STICKY AND I CAN'T HEAR YOU...
IDIOT! WHAT ARE YOU DOING?
YOU'RE SUPPOSED TO FOLLOW THE LIGHT!
THE LIGHT!
FINE, BUT WHERE IS IT? I CAN'T SEE IT!
RIDICULOUS DOLL! IT'S RIGHT THERE!
OH, YES! I SEE IT. THANKS, GOD.

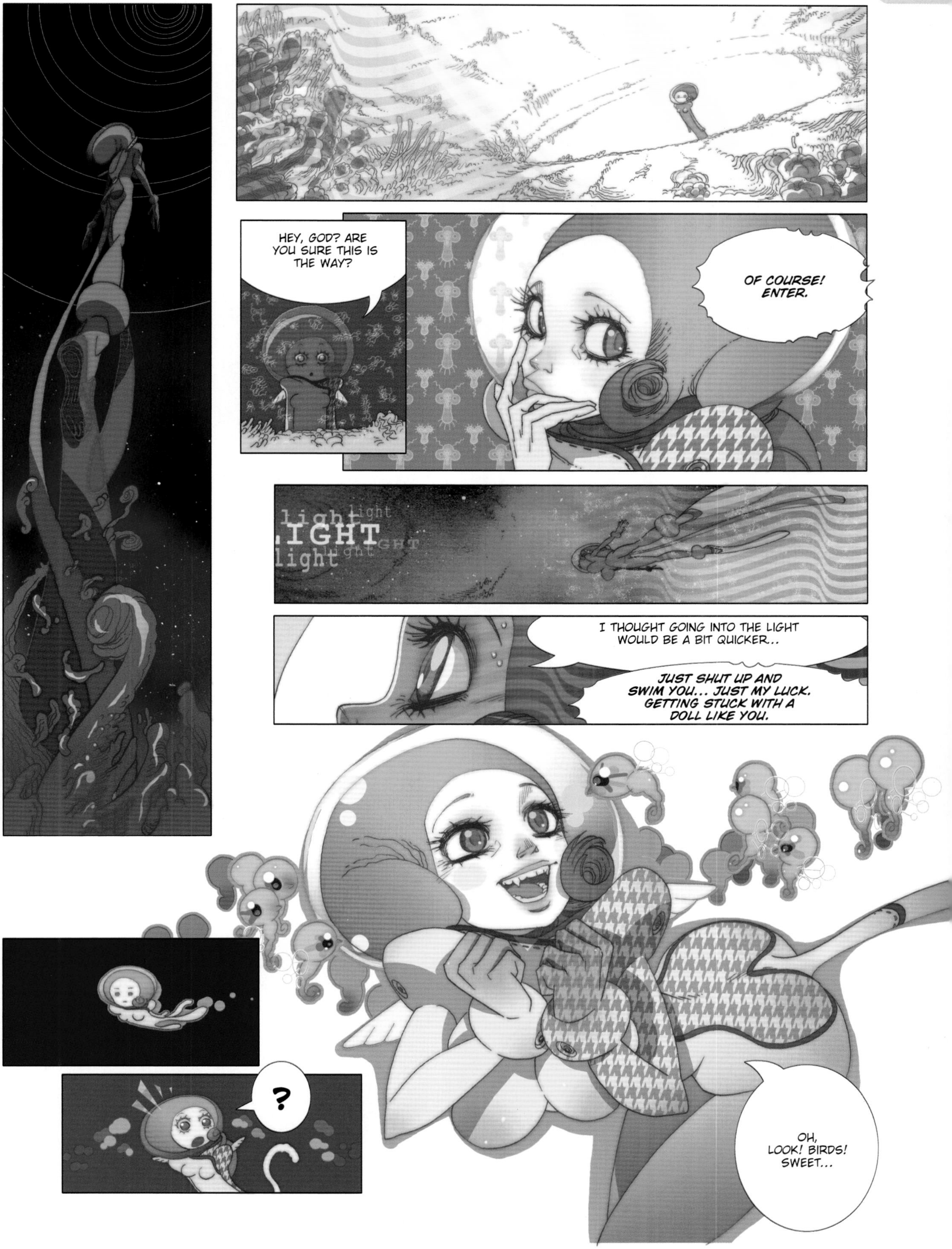
HEY, GOD? ARE YOU SURE THIS IS THE WAY?
OF COURSE! ENTER.
light light LIGHT light light GHT
I THOUGHT GOING INTO THE LIGHT WOULD BE A BIT QUICKER...
JUST SHUT UP AND SWIM YOU... JUST MY LUCK. GETTING STUCK WITH A DOLL LIKE YOU.
?
OH, LOOK! BIRDS! SWEET...

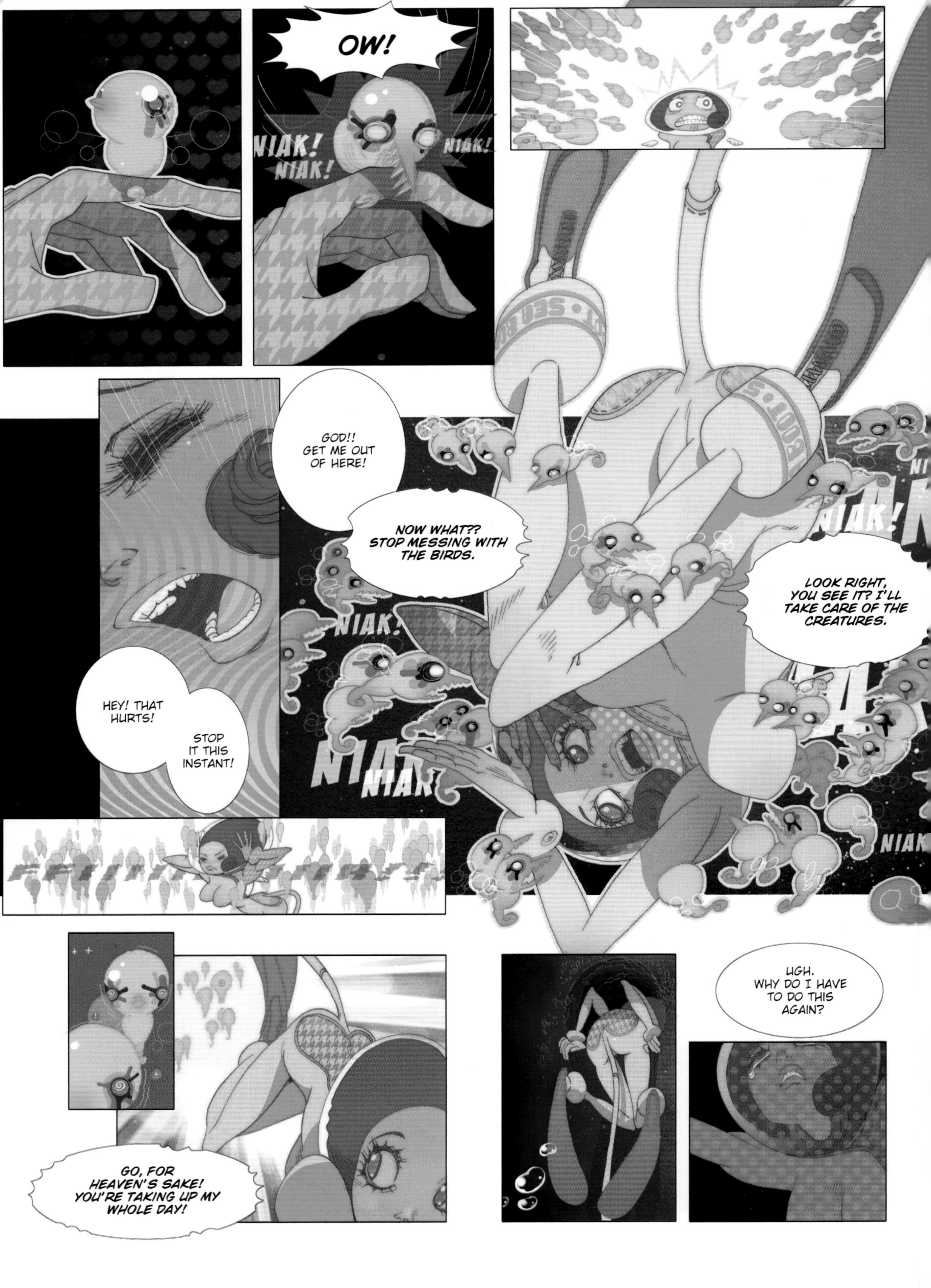
OW!
NIAK! NIAK!
NIAK!
GOD!! GET ME OUT OF HERE!
NOW WHAT?? STOP MESSING WITH THE BIRDS.
HEY! THAT HURTS!
STOP IT THIS INSTANT!
NIAK!
NIAK NIAK
NIAK!
LOOK RIGHT, YOU SEE IT? I'LL TAKE CARE OF THE CREATURES.
GO, FOR HEAVEN'S SAKE! YOU'RE TAKING UP MY WHOLE DAY!
UGH. WHY DO I HAVE TO DO THIS AGAIN?

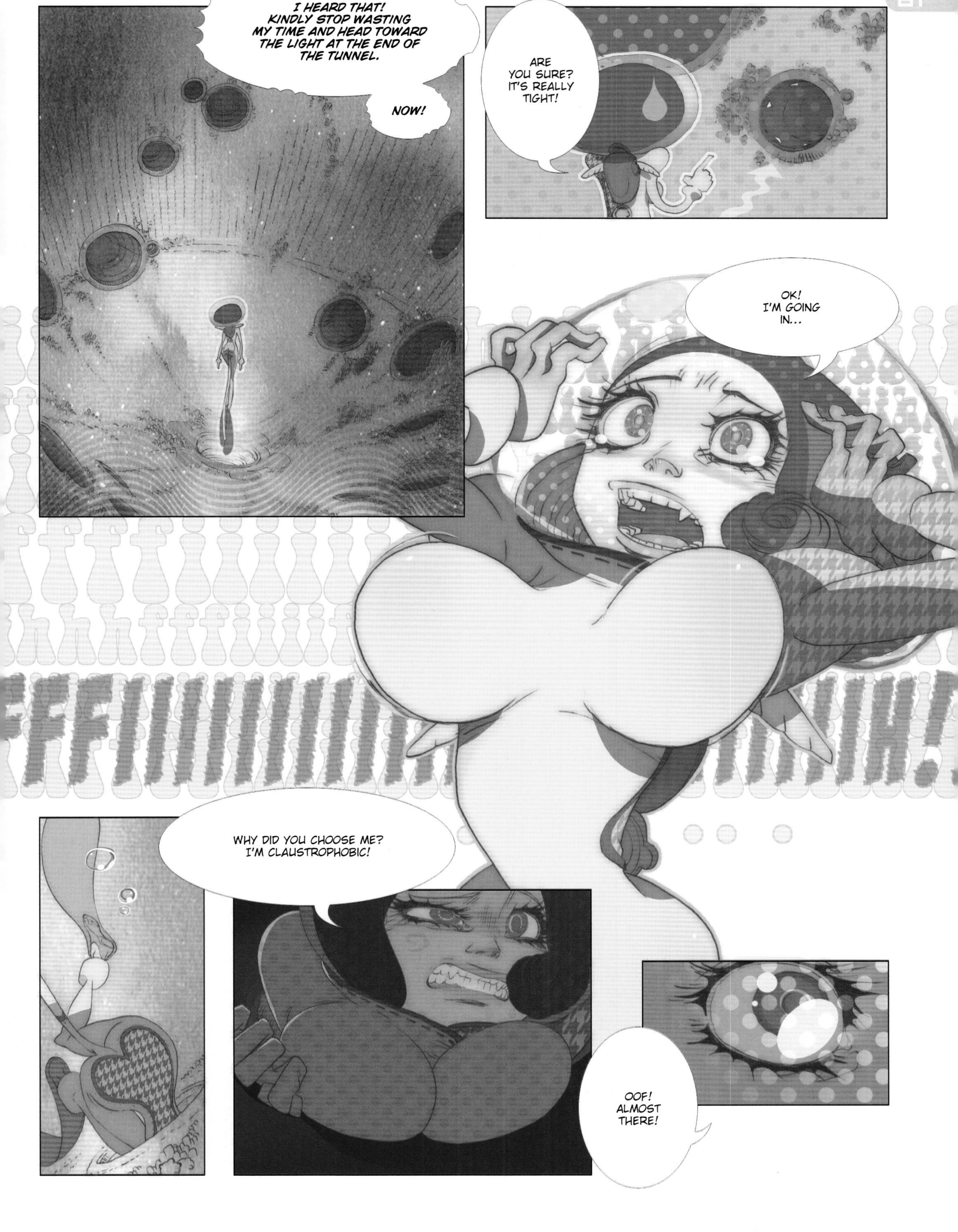
I HEARD THAT! KINDLY STOP WASTING MY TIME AND HEAD TOWARD THE LIGHT AT THE END OF THE TUNNEL.
NOW!
ARE YOU SURE? IT'S REALLY TIGHT!
OK! I'M GOING IN...
WHY DID YOU CHOOSE ME? I'M CLAUSTROPHOBIC!
OOF! ALMOST THERE!

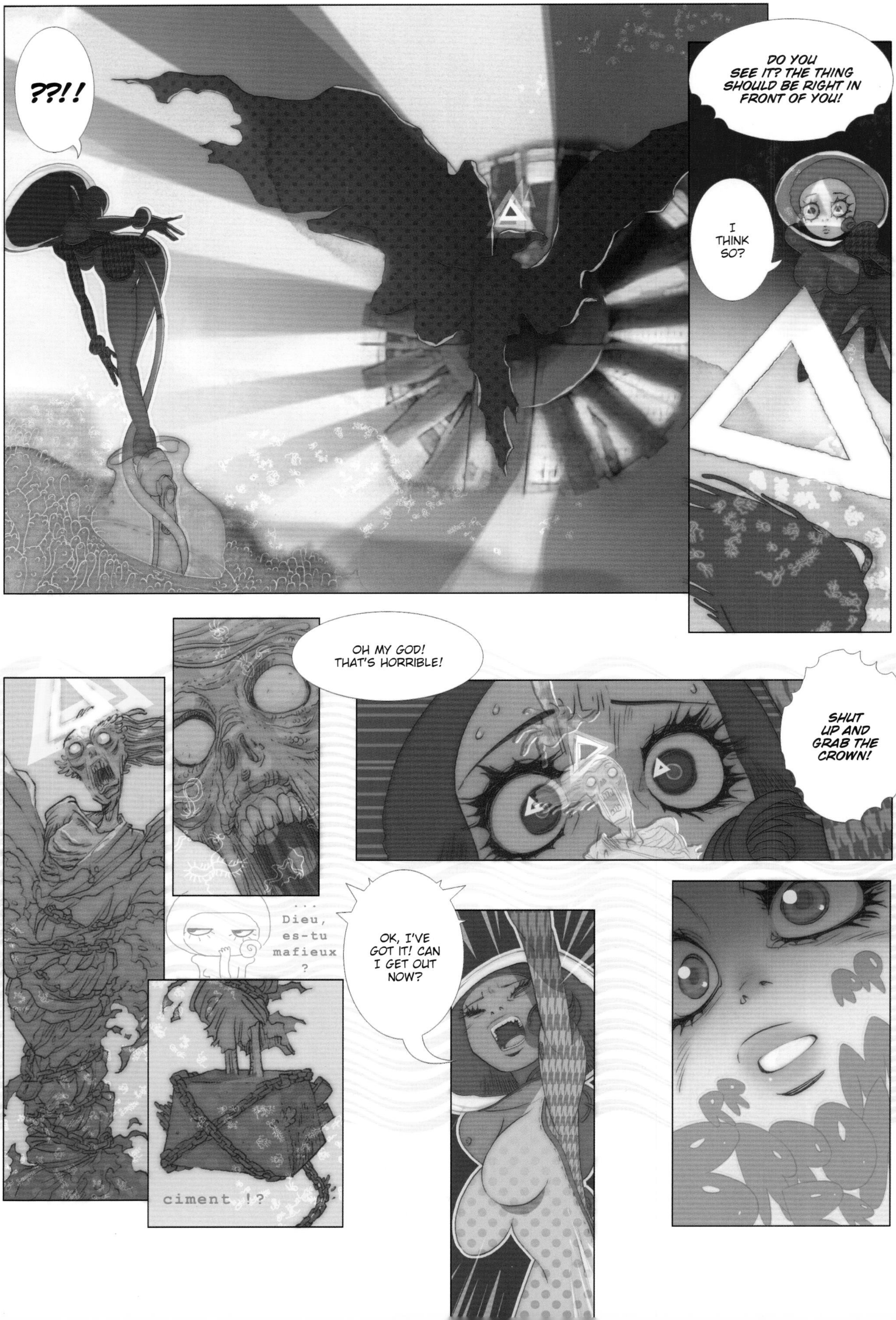
??!!
DO YOU SEE IT? THE THING SHOULD BE RIGHT IN FRONT OF YOU!
I THINK SO?
OH MY GOD! THAT'S HORRIBLE!
SHUT UP AND GRAB THE CROWN!
... Dieu, es-tu mafieux ?
ciment !?
OK, I'VE GOT IT! CAN I GET OUT NOW?

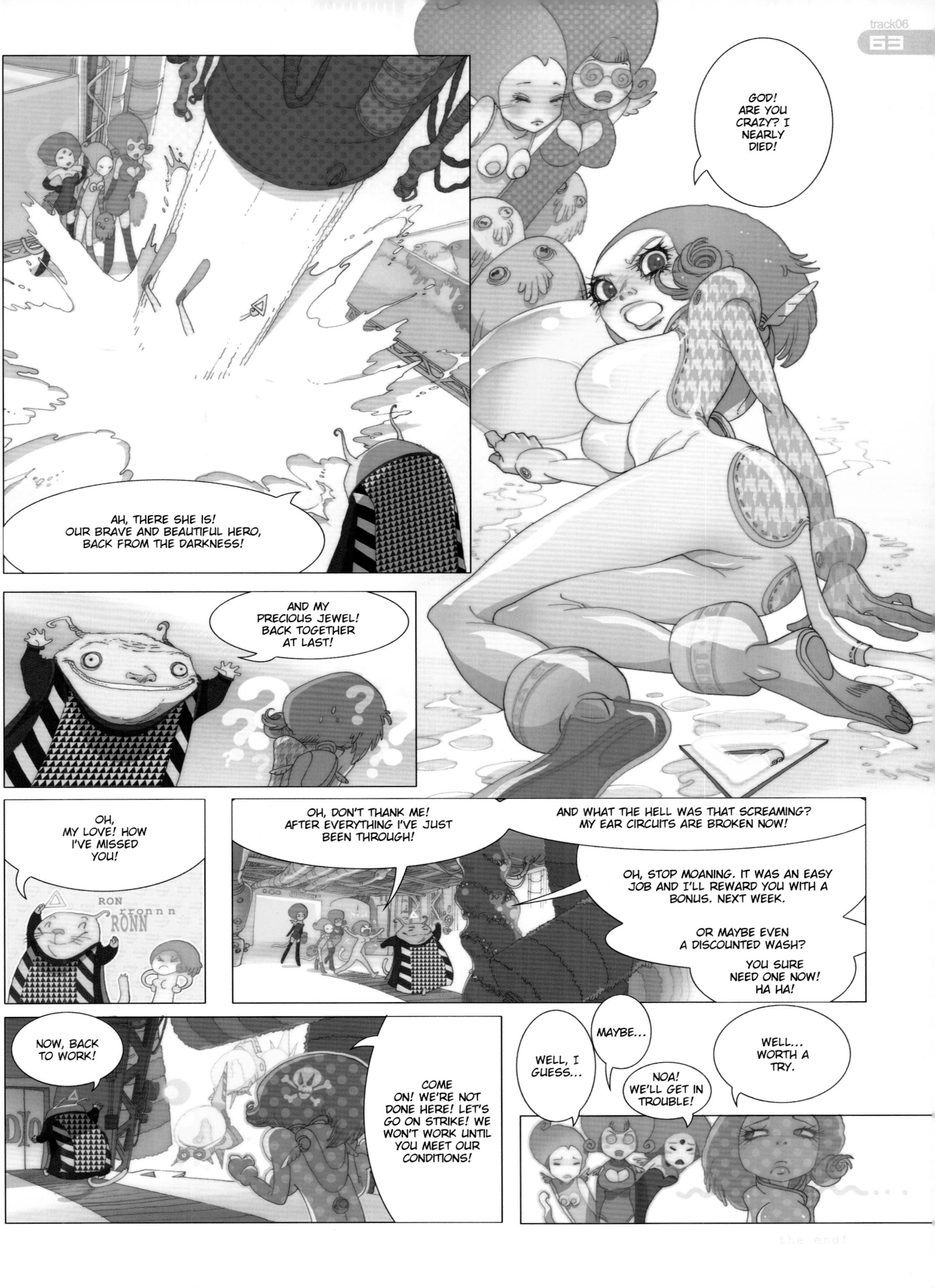
GOD! ARE YOU CRAZY? I NEARLY DIED!
AH, THERE SHE IS! OUR BRAVE AND BEAUTIFUL HERO, BACK FROM THE DARKNESS!
AND MY PRECIOUS JEWEL! BACK TOGETHER AT LAST!
OH, MY LOVE! HOW I'VE MISSED YOU!
RON
rronnn
RONN
OH, DON'T THANK ME! AFTER EVERYTHING I'VE JUST BEEN THROUGH!
AND WHAT THE HELL WAS THAT SCREAMING? MY EAR CIRCUITS ARE BROKEN NOW!
OH, STOP MOANING. IT WAS AN EASY JOB AND I'LL REWARD YOU WITH A BONUS. NEXT WEEK.
OR MAYBE EVEN A DISCOUNTED WASH?
YOU SURE NEED ONE NOW! HA HA!
NOW, BACK TO WORK!
COME ON! WE'RE NOT DONE HERE! LET'S GO ON STRIKE! WE WON'T WORK UNTIL YOU MEET OUR CONDITIONS!
WELL, I GUESS...
MAYBE...
NOA! WE'LL GET IN TROUBLE!
WELL... WORTH A TRY.
the end!

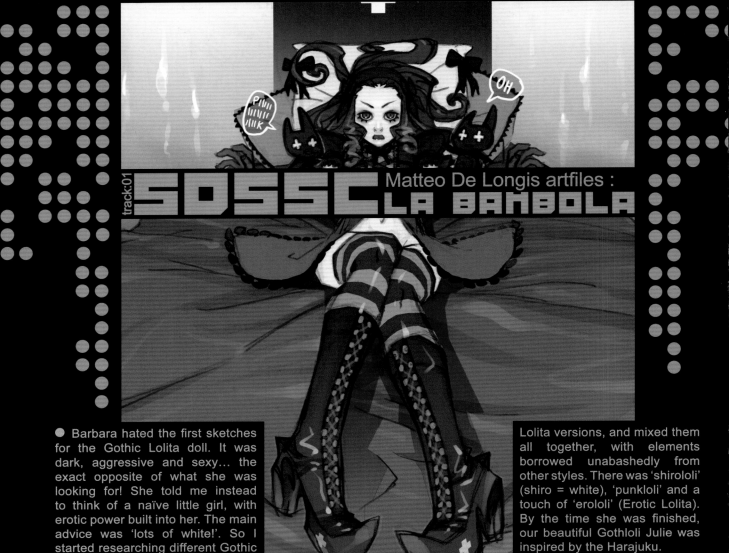

track:01

SDSSC

Matteo De Longis artfiles : LA BAMBOLA

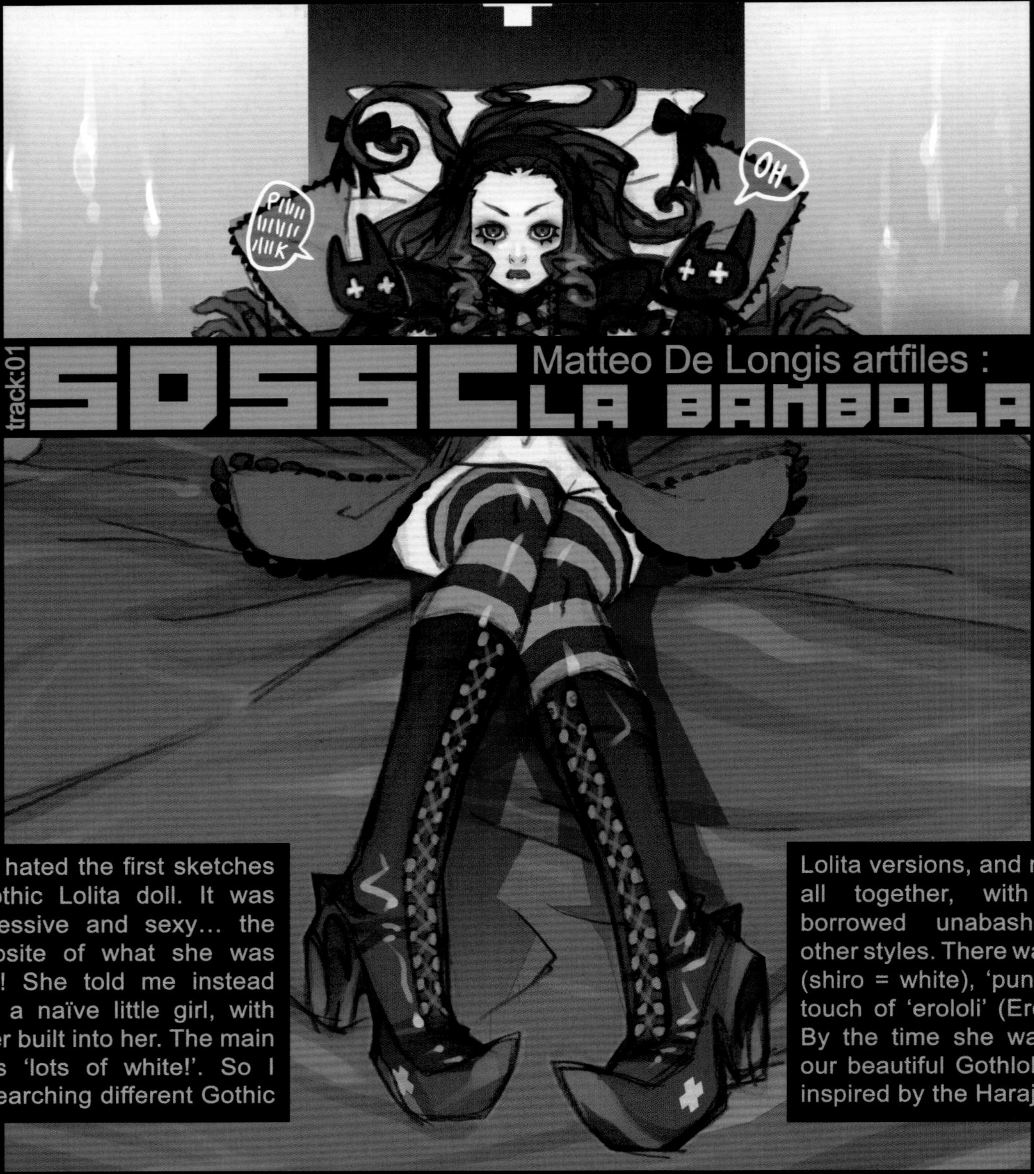
PIIIIIIIIIIIIIK
OH

Barbara hated the first sketches for the Gothic Lolita doll. It was dark, aggressive and sexy… the exact opposite of what she was looking for! She told me instead to think of a naïve little girl, with erotic power built into her. The main advice was 'lots of white!'. So I started researching different Gothic Lolita versions, and mixed them all together, with elements borrowed unabashedly from other styles. There was 'shirololi' (shiro = white), 'punkloli' and a touch of 'eroloii' (Erotic Lolita). By the time she was finished, our beautiful Gothloli Julie was inspired by the Harajuku.

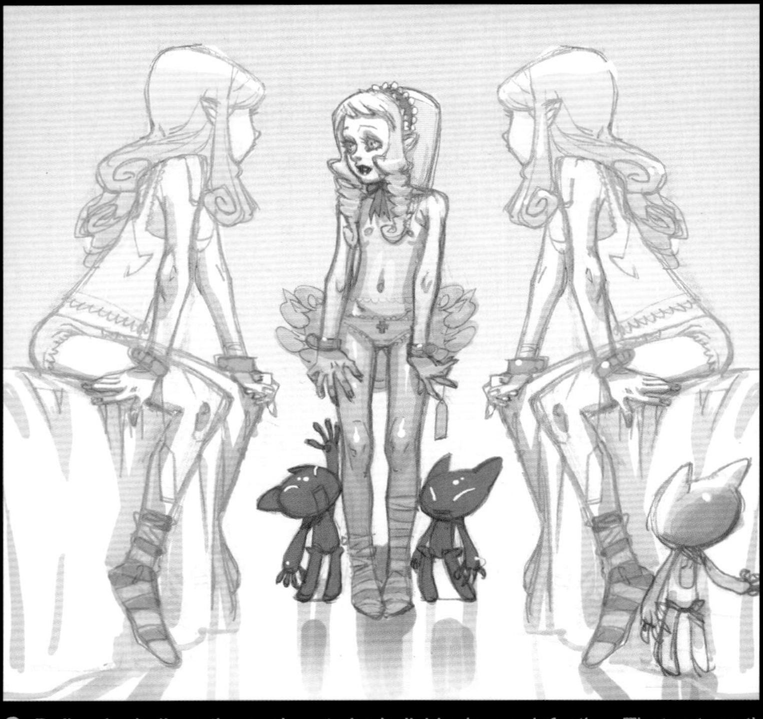

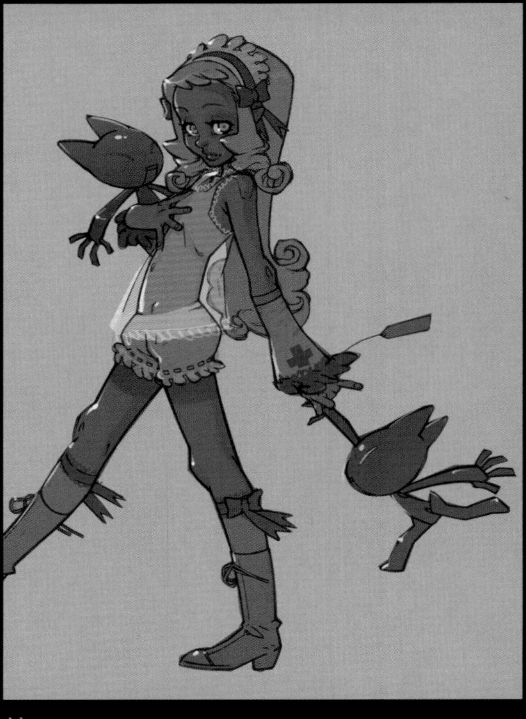

Dolls who believe themselves to be individuals are defective. That got me thinking…

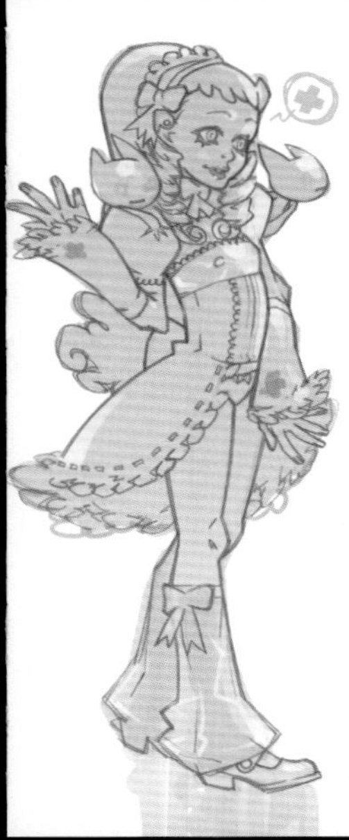

All the beauty and suffering of Noa! She doesn't look like a patient; with red eyelids and white lips she looks more like a model for a makeup advert!

You can probably tell from these early sketches, but I was 'allergic' to Noa's tail and had to force myself to go back through the panels and add it on later.

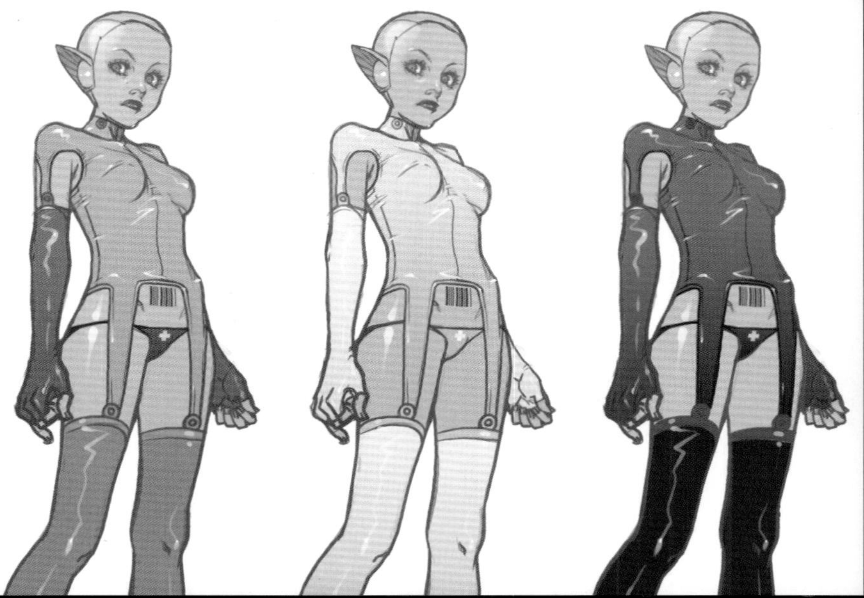

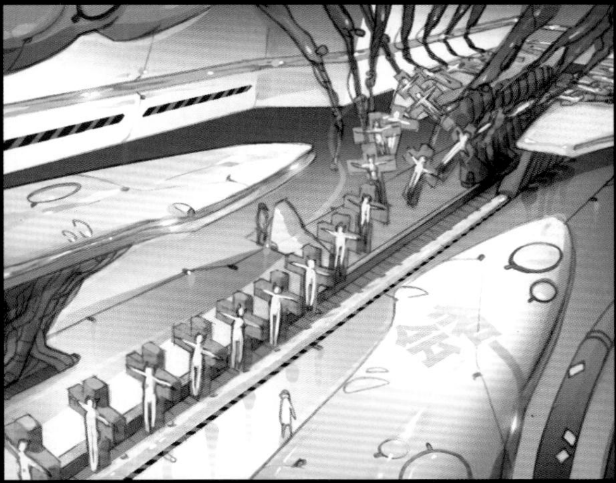

● SkyDoll crucifixes on the production line.

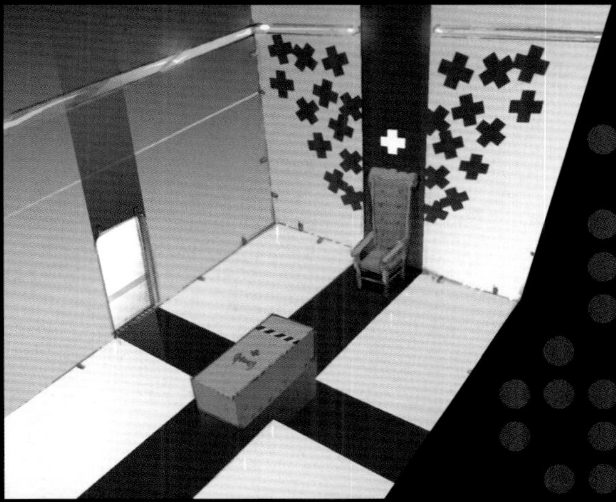

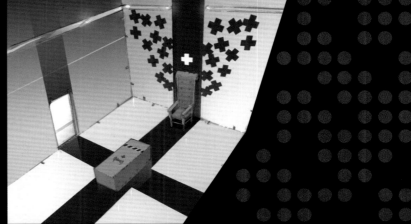

● The equal-sided Greek cross looks like it should be a religious symbol, but it's also a plausible motif you'd find in a hospital. But apart from that, it's a minimalistic shape that I find fascinating, even when you take away its many interpretations.

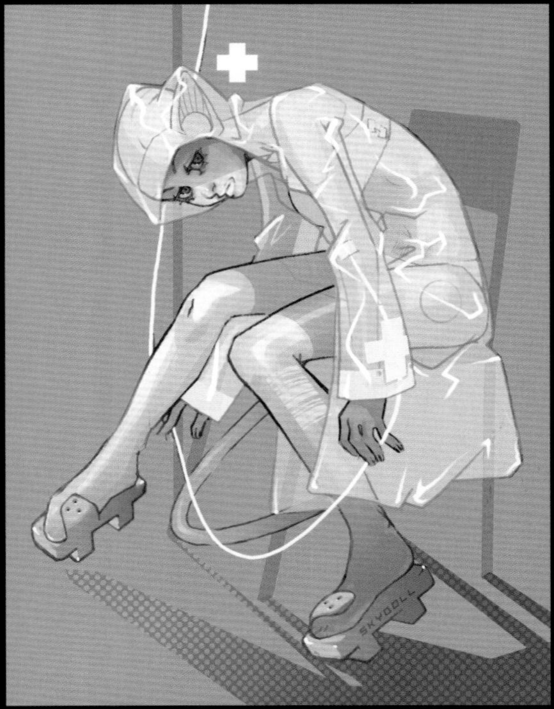

● I love the conflicting use of green and pink together.

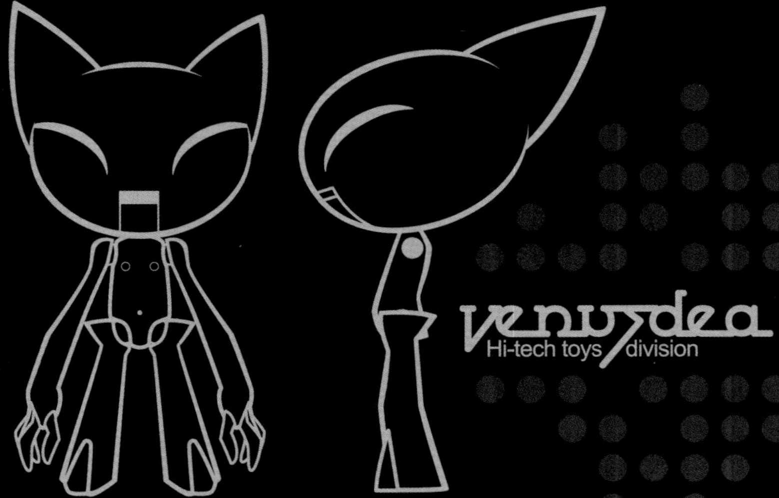
venusdea
Hi-tech toys division

Juliet has two Mekanekos with her: are they just sophisticated toys, or real pet robots? Are all the Gothic Lolita models designed to have these accessories? I don't think so… more likely that she stole them during her break-in to VenusDea industries.
The Mekanekos look more like snobby monkeys than cats.

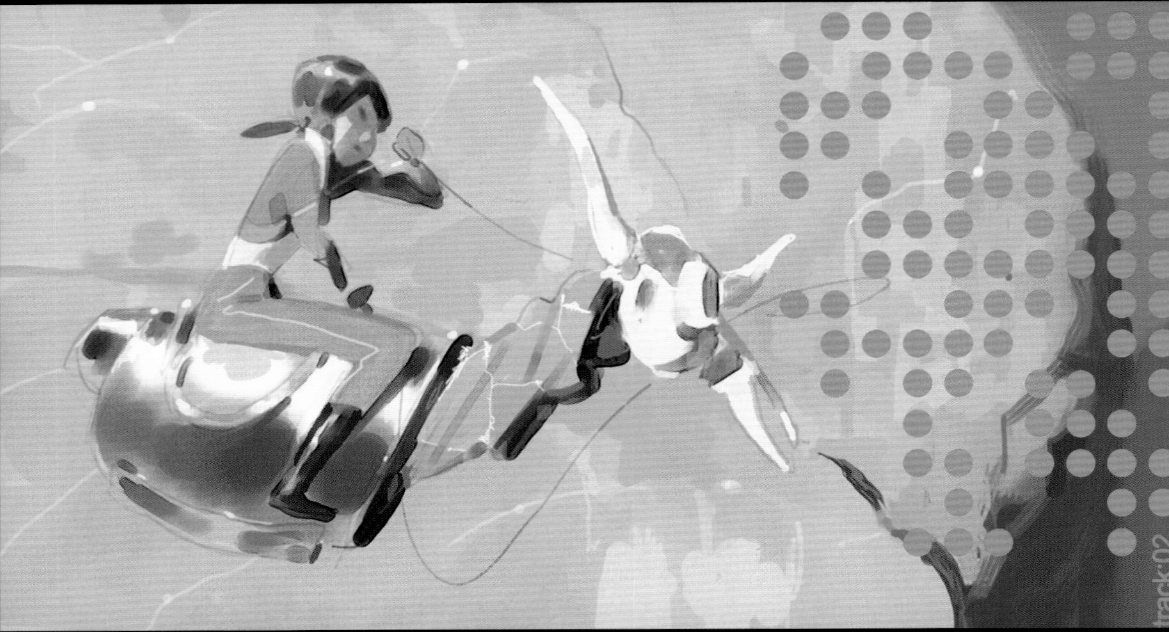

Claudio Acciari artfiles : BANGBANG

track:02

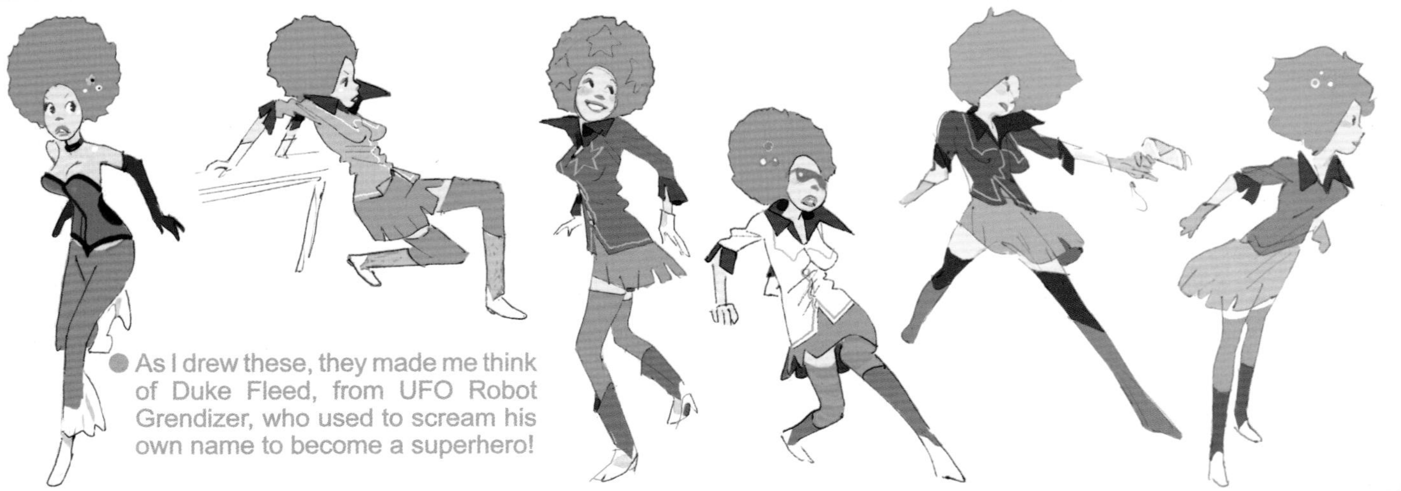

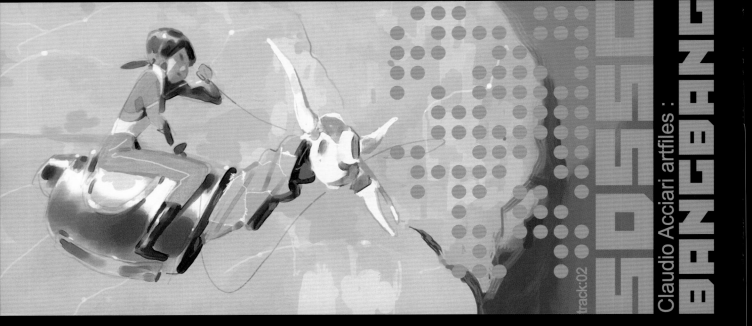

As I drew these, they made me think of Duke Fleed, from UFO Robot Grendizer, who used to scream his own name to become a superhero!

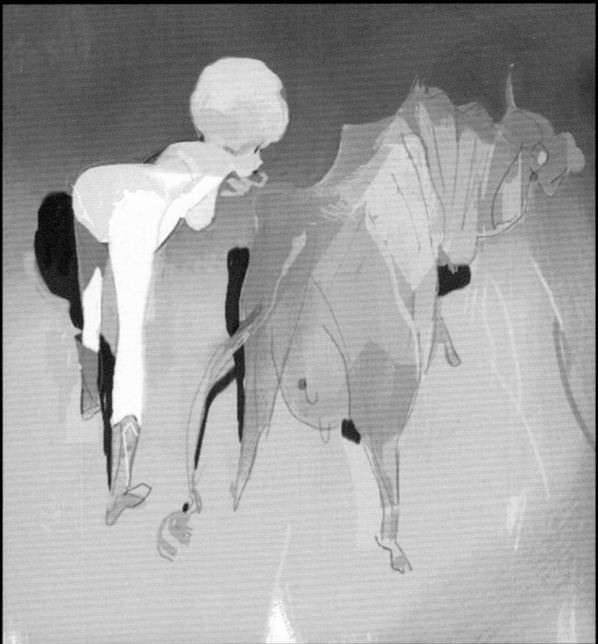

If anyone asked me what color I'd take with me to the Moon, I'd say 'cadmium red!'. I can just see myself on the Moon with this red in my hands…

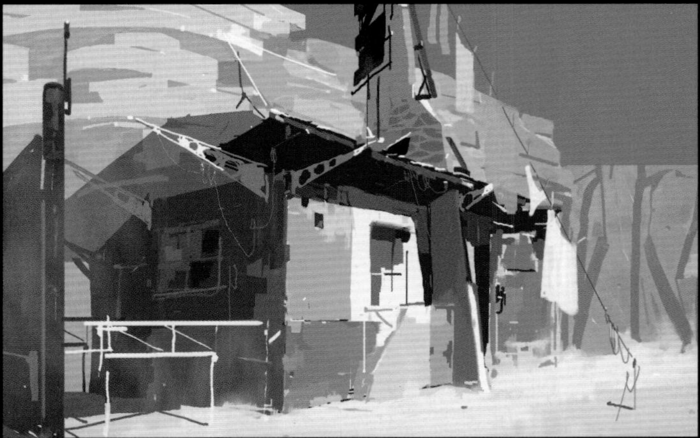

How many udders does a cow have?

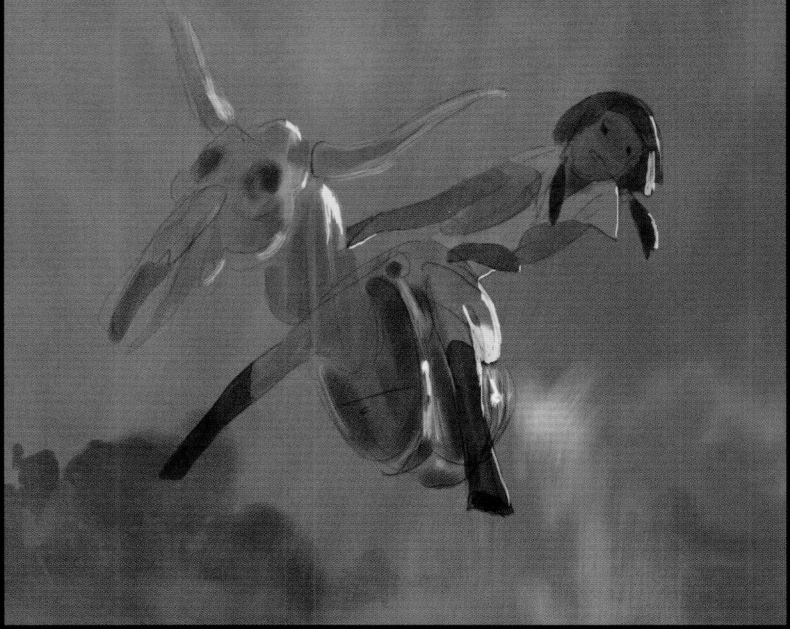

Hey Ingrid, your headlights are out!

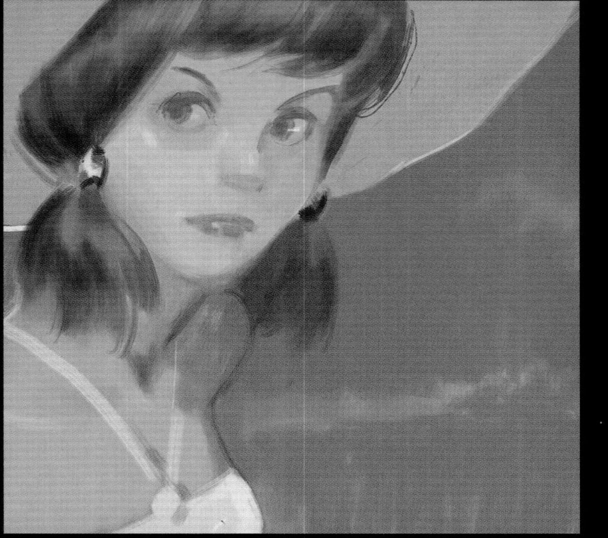

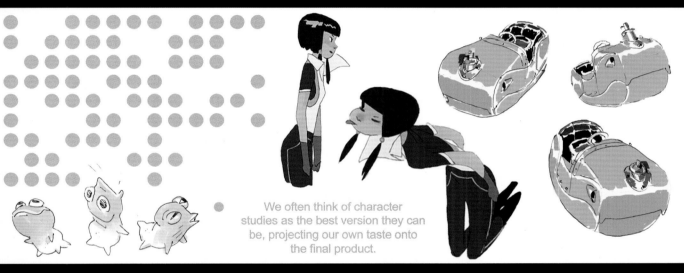

This is Candice's twin sister. She was raised in Japan, and is definitely the more intelligent of the siblings.

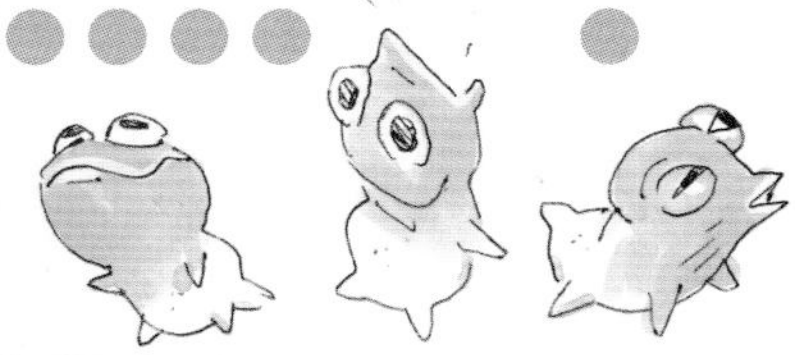

We often think of character studies as the best version they can be, projecting our own taste onto the final product.

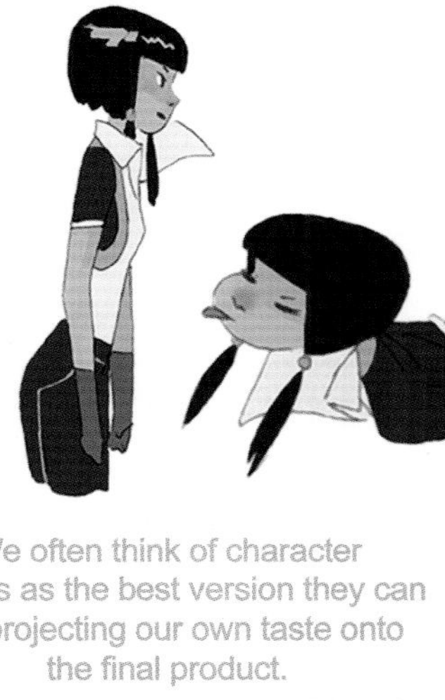

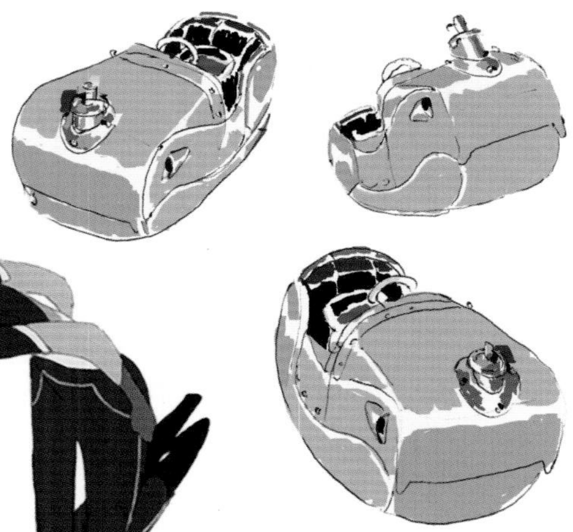

I should have been born in 1800, what am I doing here?

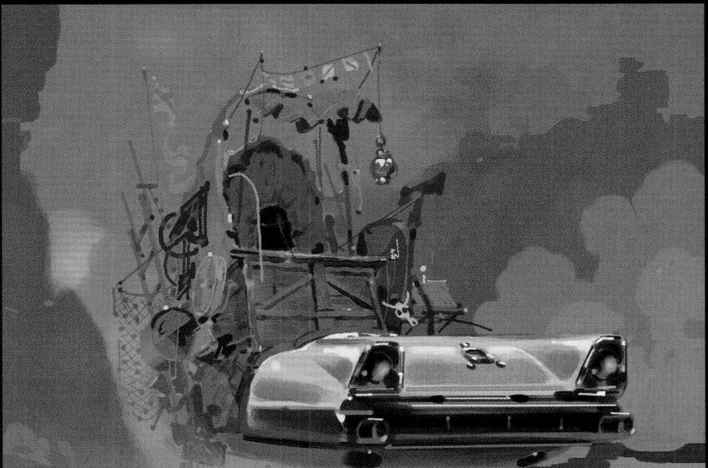

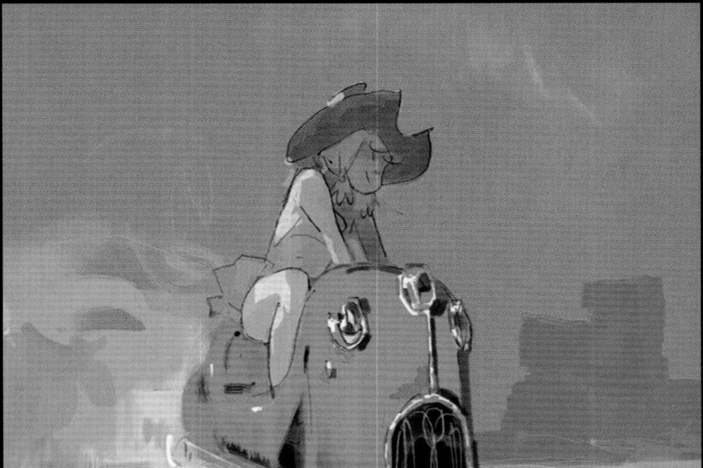

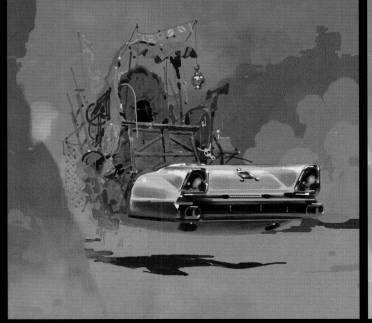

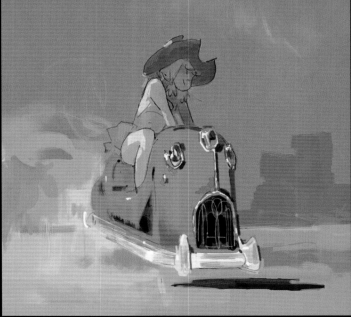

The only thing I remember from the 80s are stables and "Dancing in the Dark."

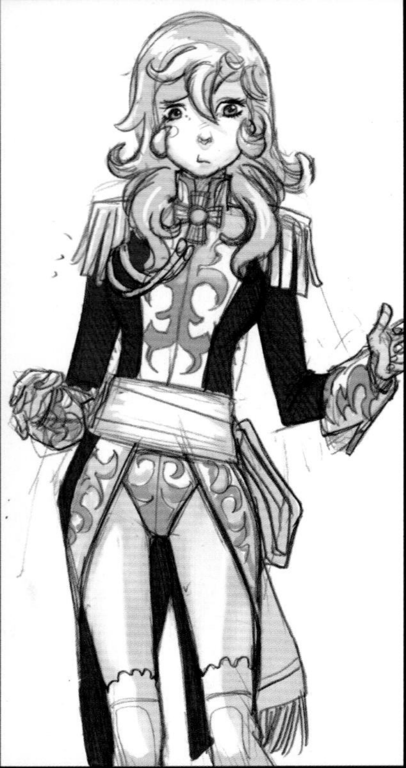
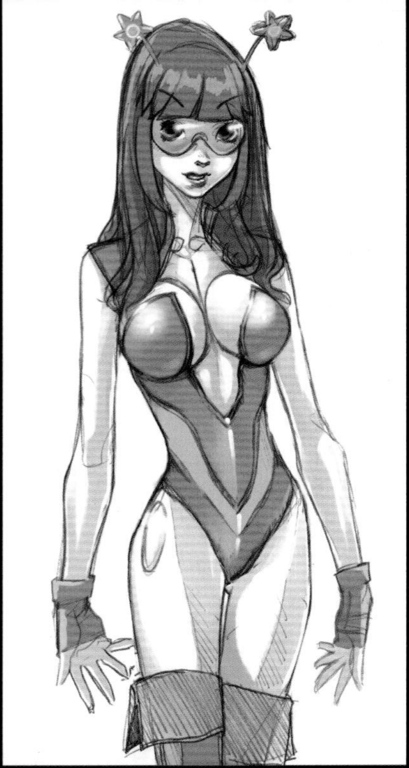
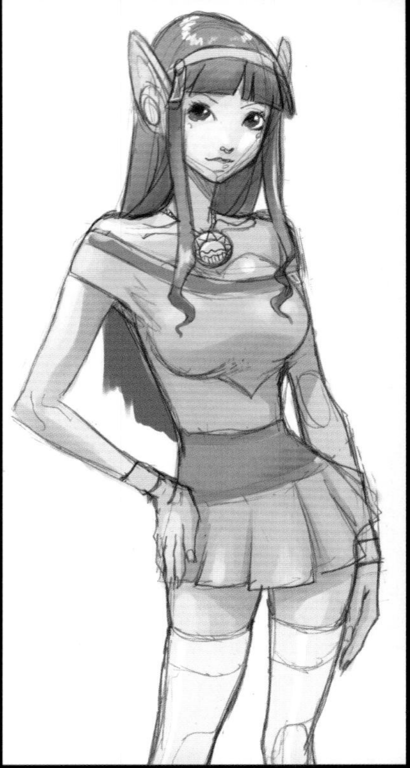

Our beloved Noa practising her Barbarella look! As for the hairband, what can I say? I had one as a kid, and I thought she would look better in it… sniff sniff… all my childhood heroes! It's too much for me! Also interesting here, I drew Chun (from Knights of the Zodiac) as a Doll because like many others, I thought it was a girl… until the character was dubbed in a man's voice, leaving no question as to his virility. Who can resist these pretty things, dressed in lace and looking deep into your soul…

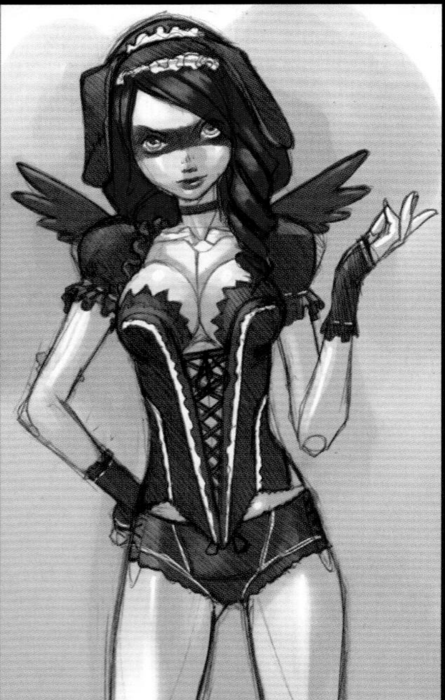
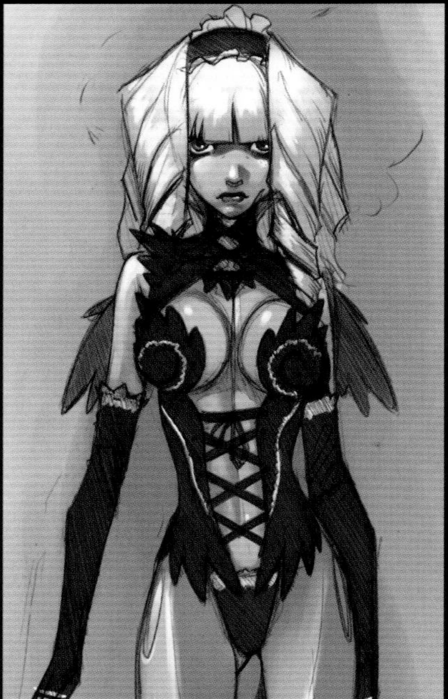
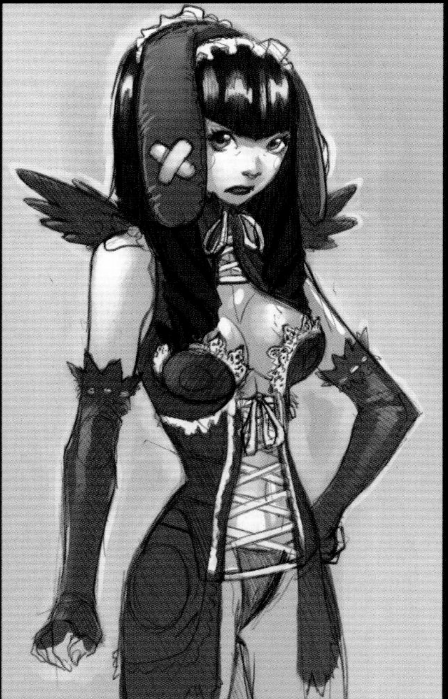

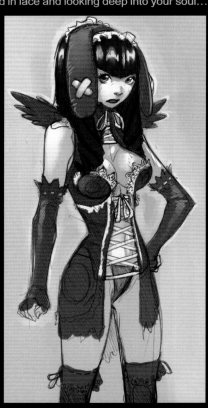

Whoops, I'm getting carried away. In any case, the Justine doll is a mix of lots of aspects of Gothic Lolita costumes, with a hint of sadism and sweet madness thrown in!

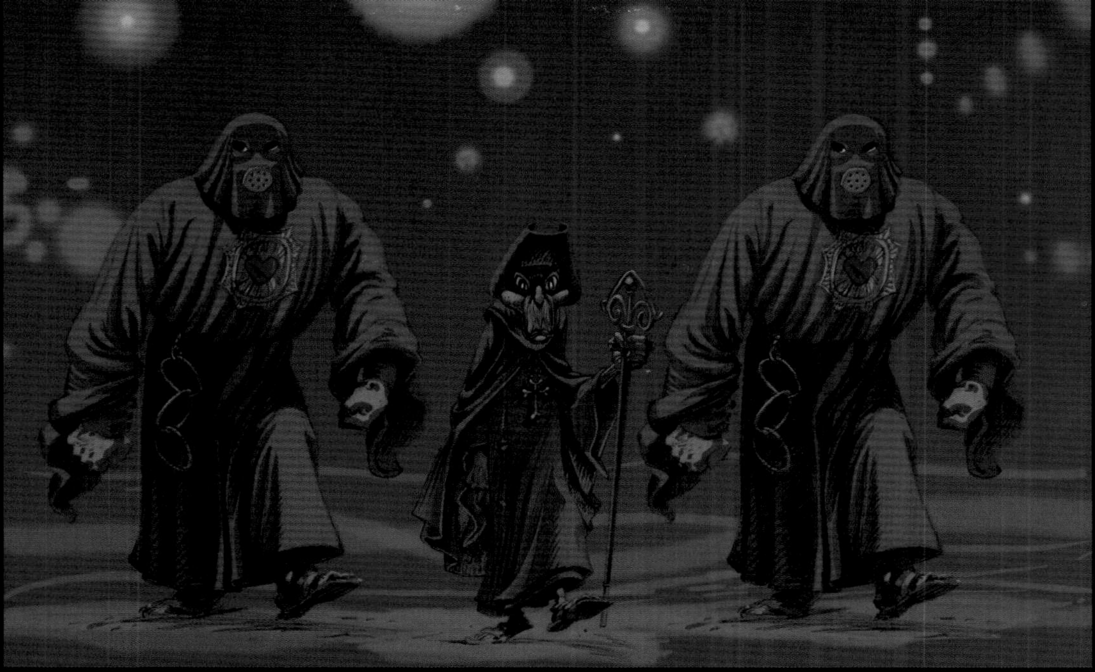

track:04

SOSSC Riff Reb's artfiles : LADY CUB DRIVER

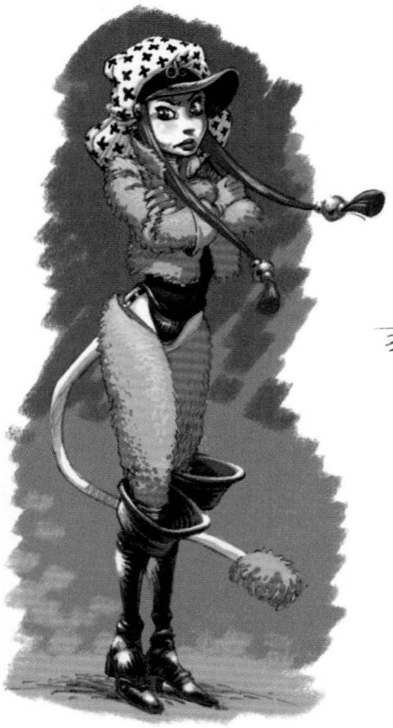

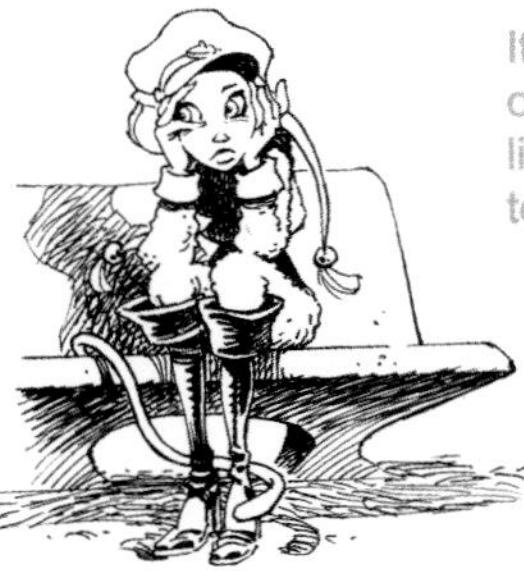

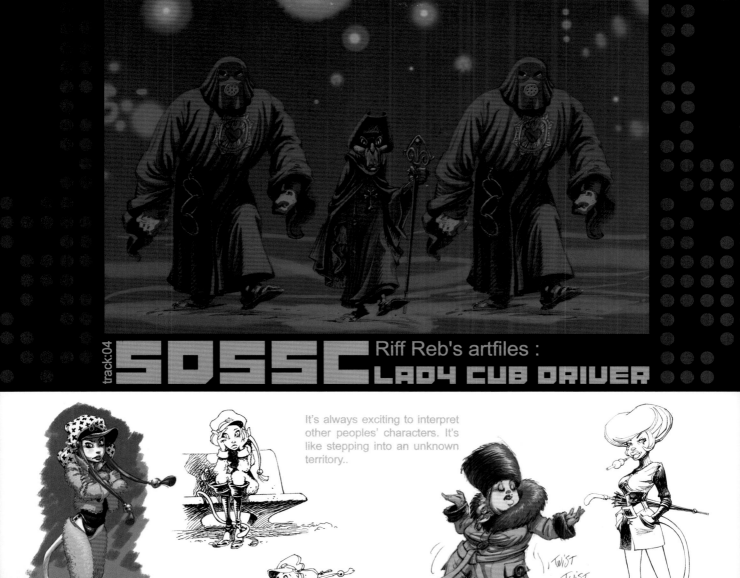

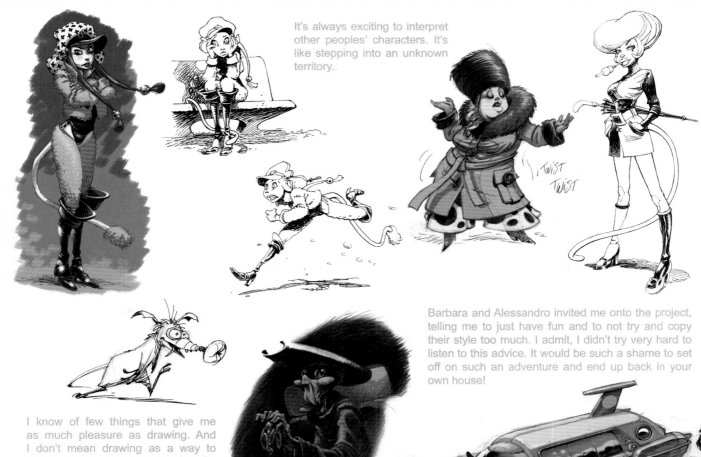

It's always exciting to interpret other peoples' characters. It's like stepping into an unknown territory..

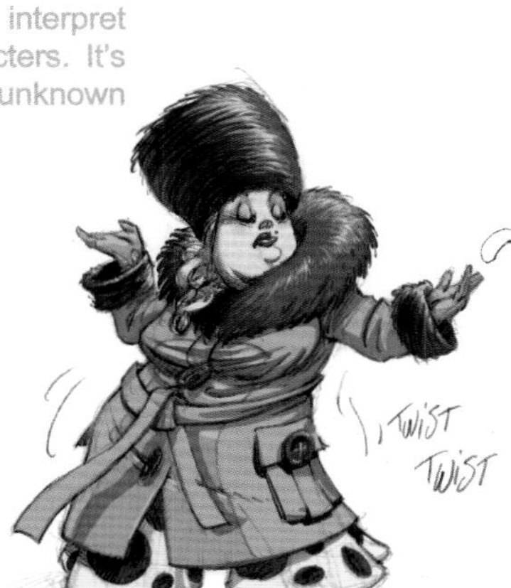
TWIST
TWIST

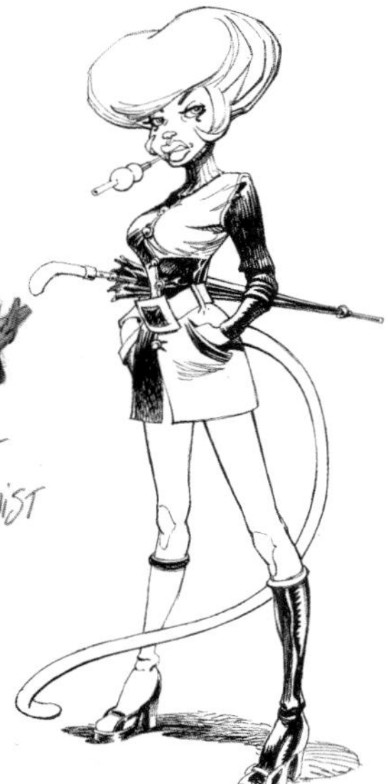

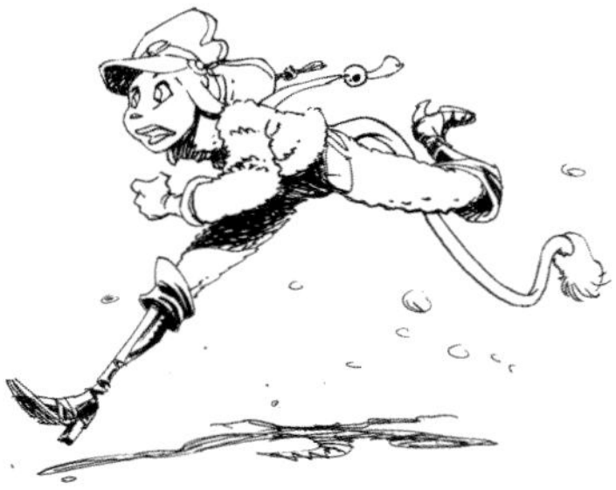

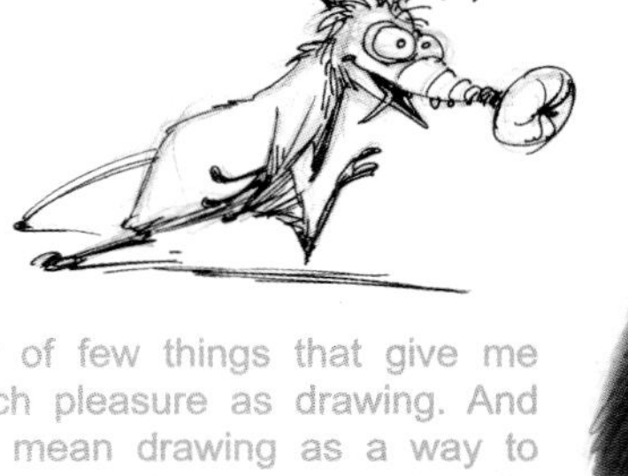

Barbara and Alessandro invited me onto the project, telling me to just have fun and to not try and copy their style too much. I admit, I didn't try very hard to listen to this advice. It would be such a shame to set off on such an adventure and end up back in your own house!

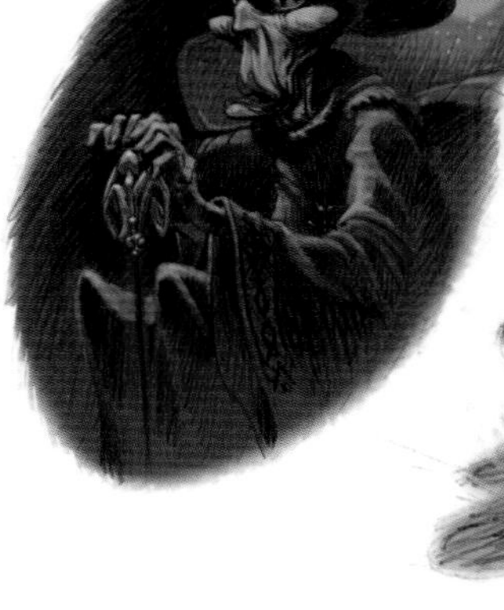

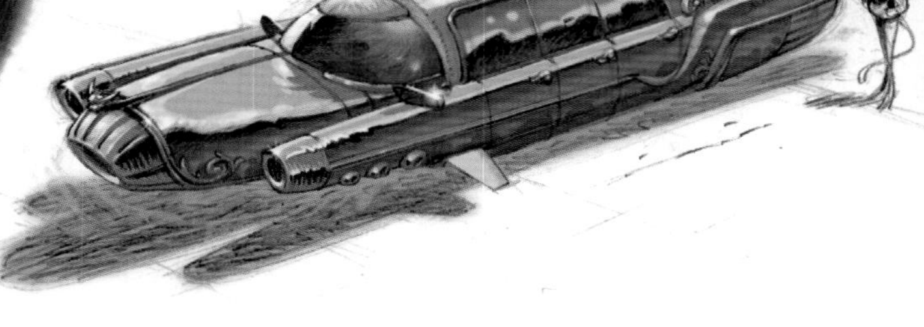

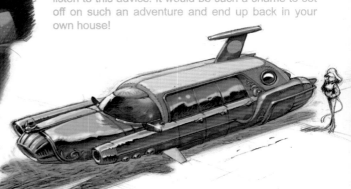

I know of few things that give me as much pleasure as drawing. And I don't mean drawing as a way to make money, but just drawing for the sake of it. Drawing like you're a child at play, creating your own world and breathing life into your creations. Pretending you're God for just a few minutes. Of course, the next day, you end up throwing it away anyway. Maybe God should have done the same…

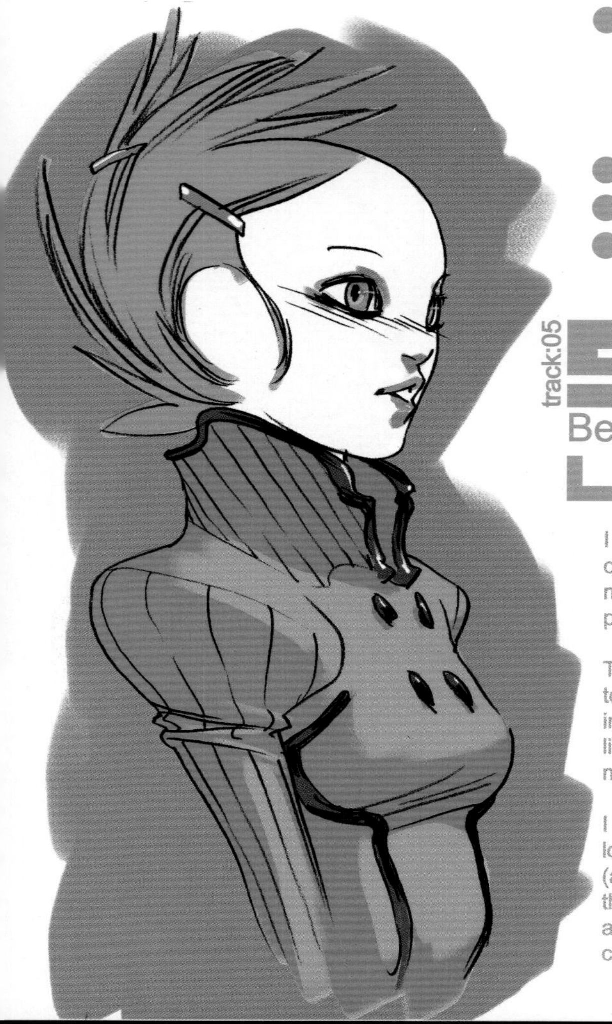

track:05

SOSSC

Bengal artfiles : LIKE A VIRGIN

I really liked the expression on her face I drew here, so I colored it. I wanted to see if pure white skin would work for my story, and with all the reds that would come into play, hey presto! Ok, it was for my own pleasure too…

This was my first attempt at recreating Noa, so I was trying to understand this face, and that fantastic hair-do she had in Volume 1! Of course, I wouldn't know how to draw her like Alessandro, but I wanted to try and capture her face in my own way.

I also wanted to try out a couple of different bizarre looks. Noa is so changeable that she can (and indeed, is supposed to) become the incarnation of many different women, according to the story. I pencilled whatever came into my head for my own entertainment.

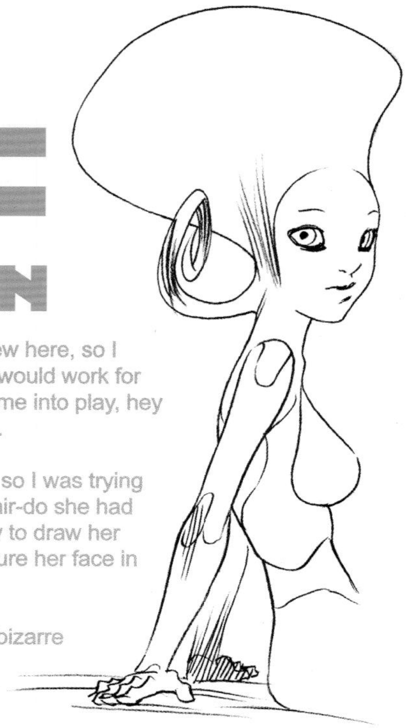

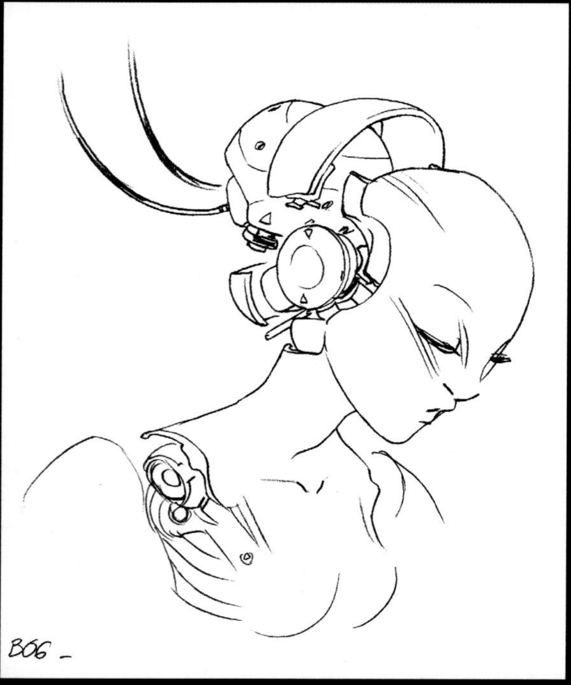
BOG -

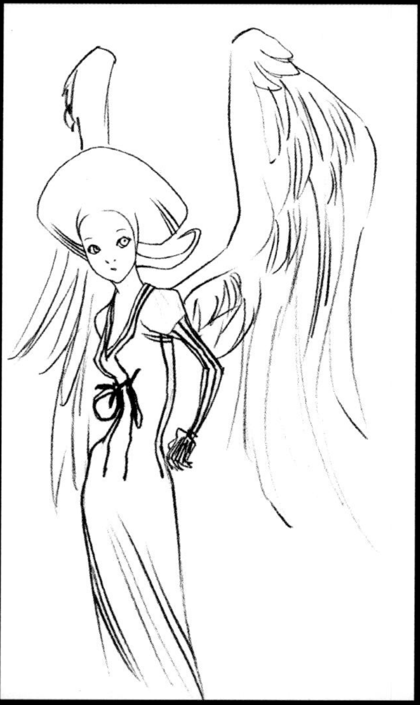

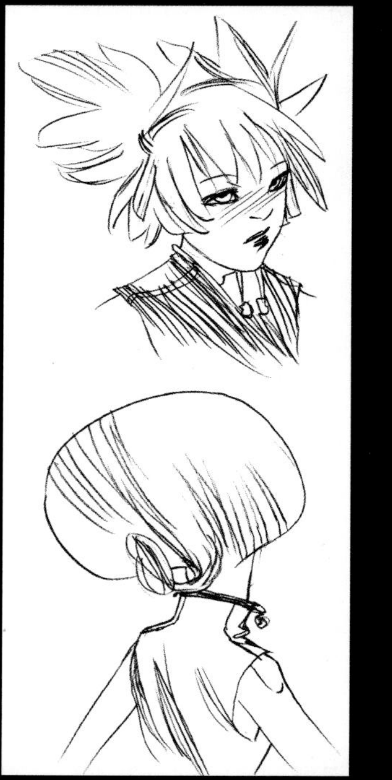

Just as with *Ghost in the Shell*, our heroine is a synthetic human; I really love this relationship between man and machine, and I'm always intrigued to delve into what could form a synthetic creature. It might seem a little strange, but I find a lot of sensuality in the way

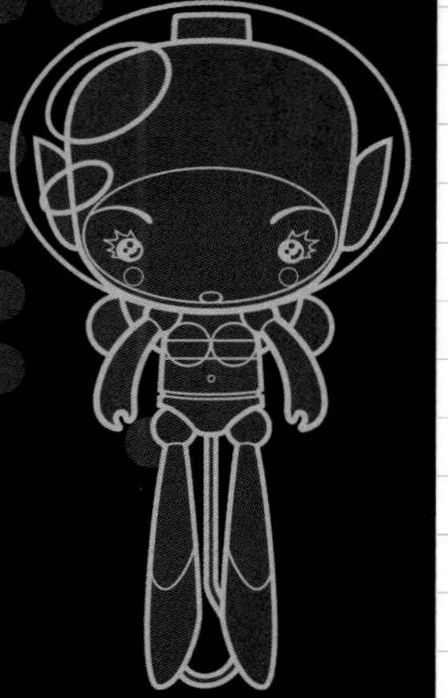

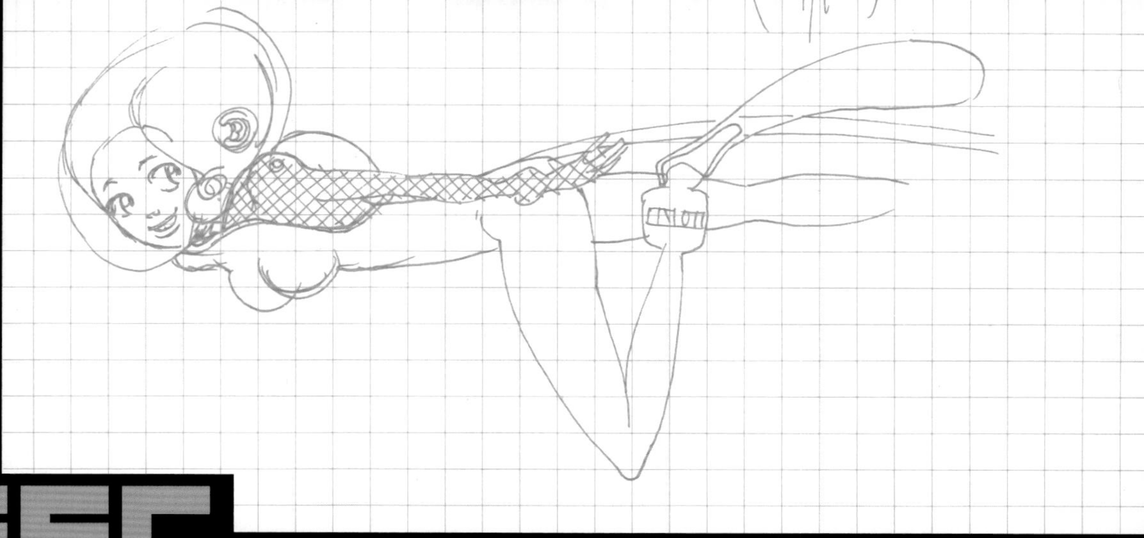

track:06

SDSSC

Alessandro Barbucci artfiles : SMOKE ON THE WATER

A new adventure needs a new outfit!

And for this special occasion, Noa is wearing a jumpsuit with pneumatic shoulders, harking back to they style of the 80s, with undeniable visual motifs from the 70s! Luckily for her, on Papathea, all helmets are designed to accommodate such bouffante and inventive hairstyles!

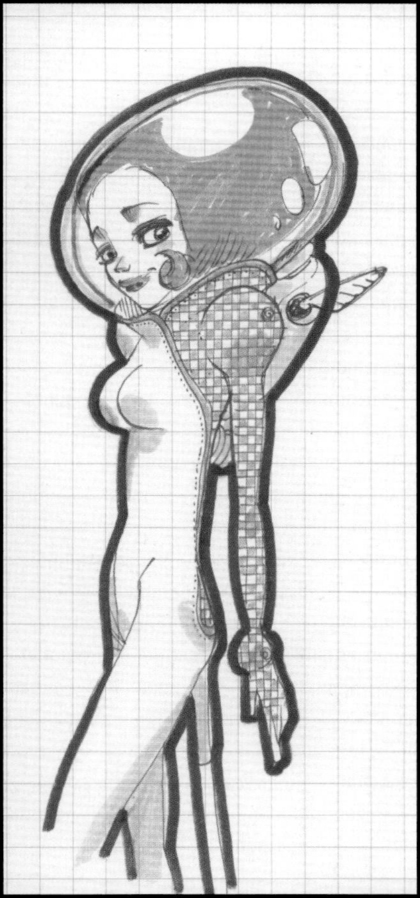

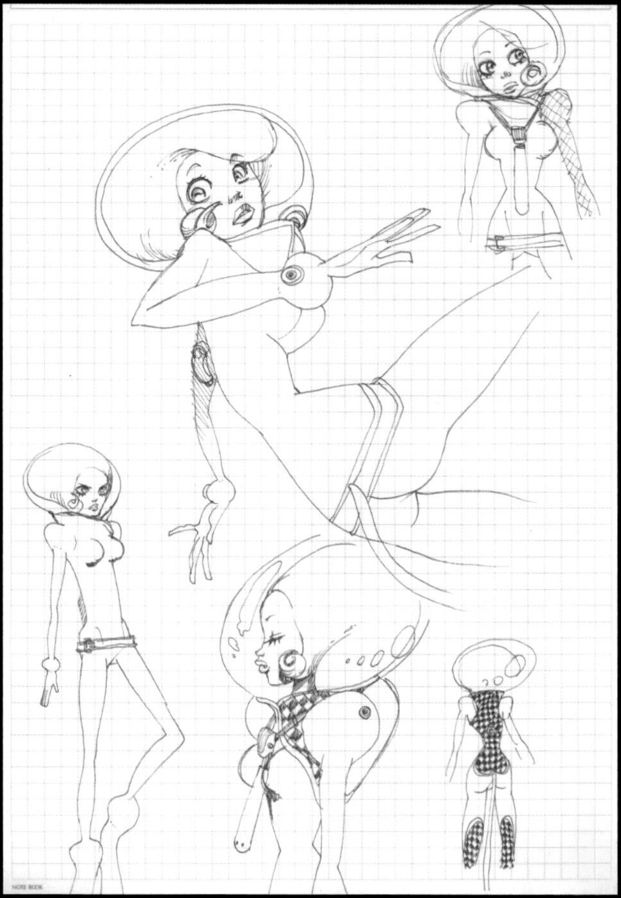

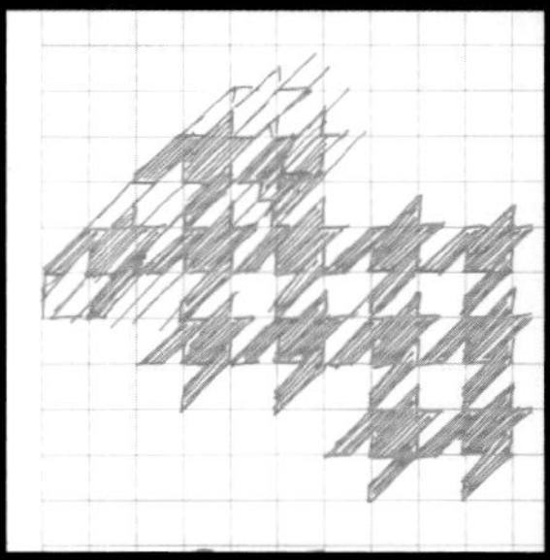

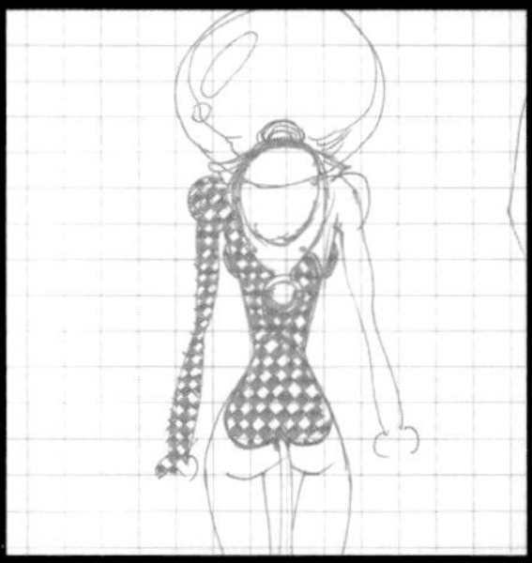

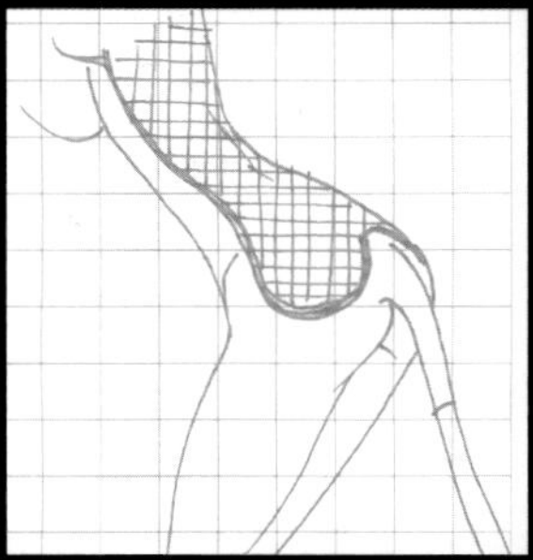

Unfortunately, the vessel's communication cable had to be scrapped on account of our heroine's huge breasts (Julie Andrews also experienced this problem). So, as not to be left behind by my protégés, I used an incredible technique; cheap marker pens!

That's all for now.
See you next time!

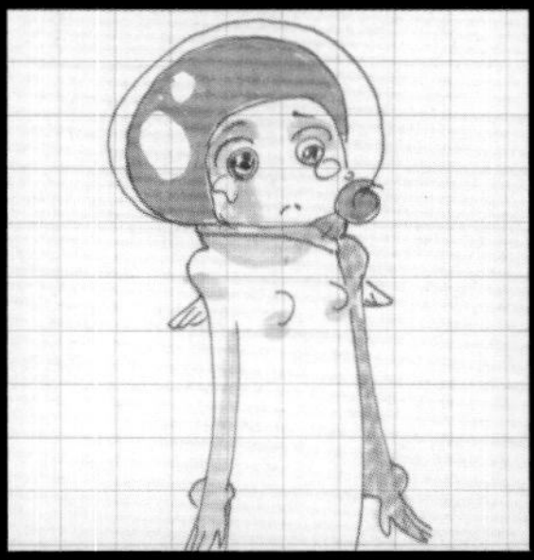

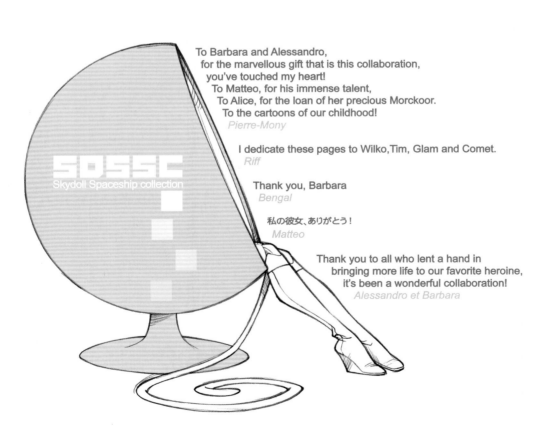

To Barbara and Alessandro,
for the marvellous gift that is this collaboration,
you've touched my heart!
To Matteo, for his immense talent,
To Alice, for the loan of her precious Morckoor.
To the cartoons of our childhood!
Pierre-Mony

I dedicate these pages to Wilko, Tim, Glam and Comet.
Riff

Thank you, Barbara
Bengal

私の彼女、ありがとう！
Matteo

Thank you to all who lent a hand in
bringing more life to our favorite heroine,
it's been a wonderful collaboration!
Alessandro et Barbara

SDSSC
Skydoll Spaceship collection

SKYDOLL LACRIMA CHRISTI COLLECTION |

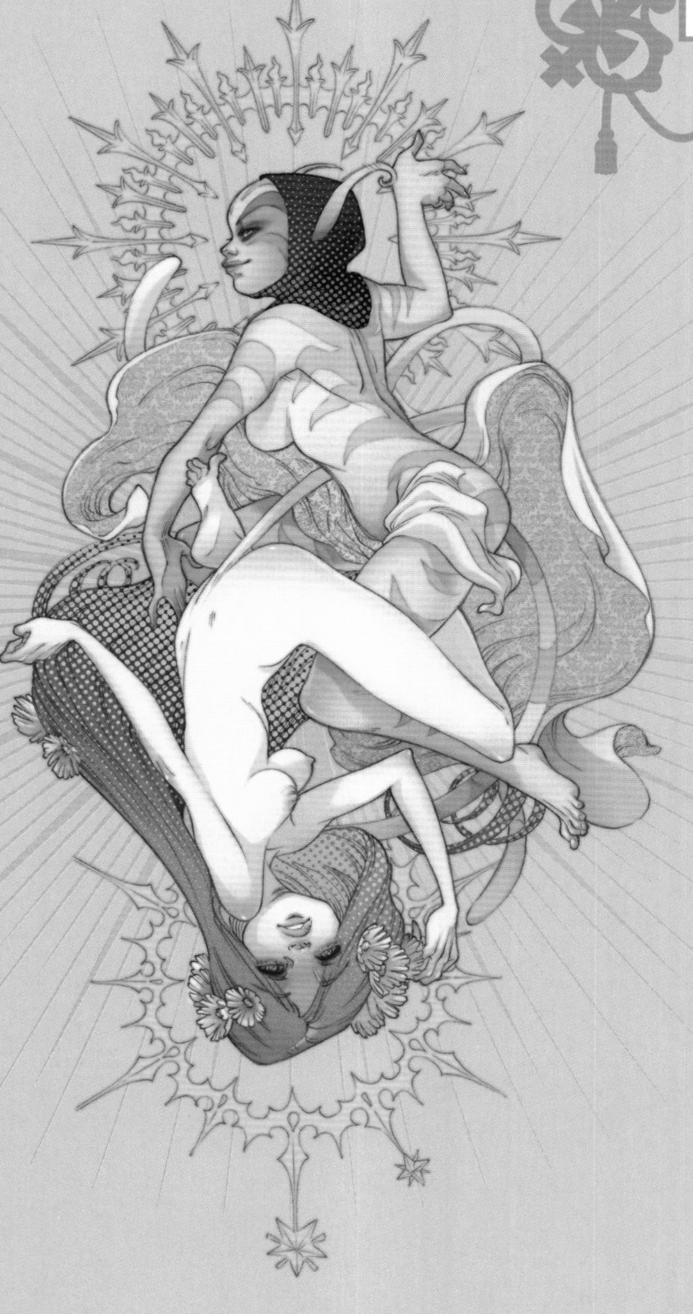

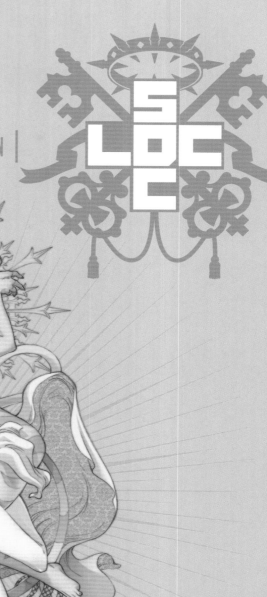

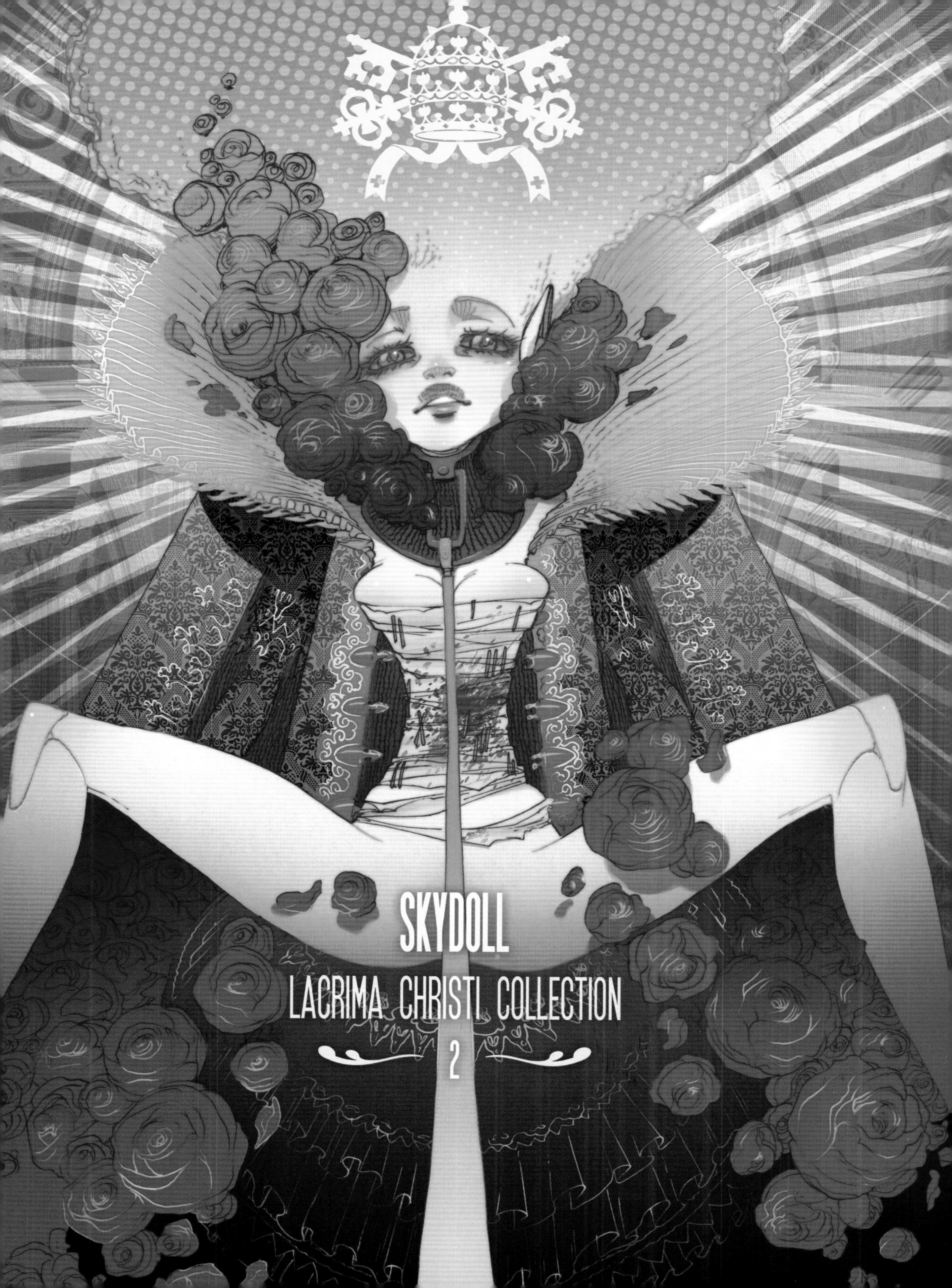
SKYDOLL
LACRIMA CHRISTI COLLECTION
2

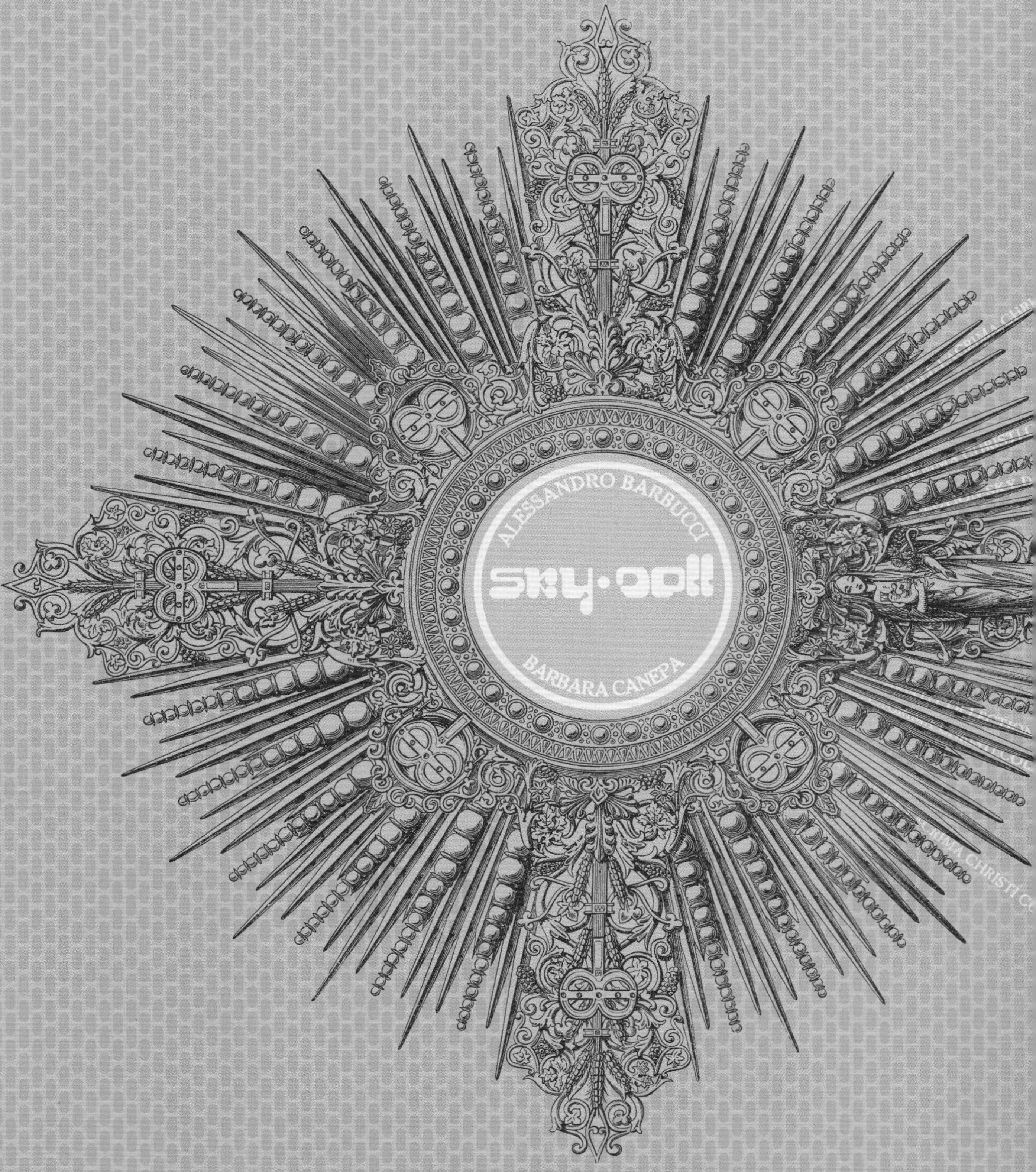
ALESSANDRO BARBUCCI
sky-doll
BARBARA CANEPA

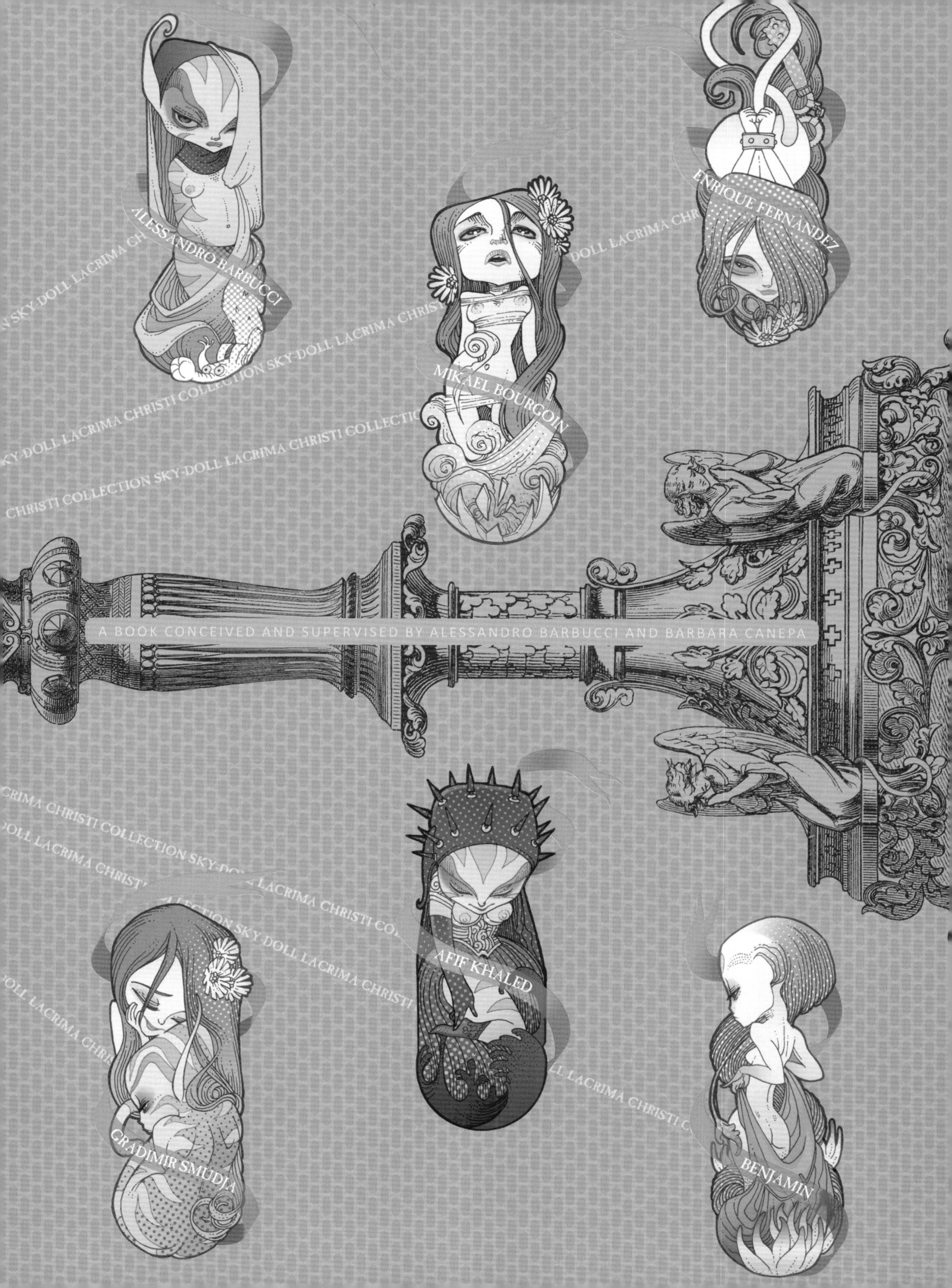
ALESSANDRO BARBUCCI
MIKAEL BOURGOIN
ENRIQUE FERNANDEZ
SKY-DOLL LACRIMA CHRISTI COLLECTION
A BOOK CONCEIVED AND SUPERVISED BY ALESSANDRO BARBUCCI AND BARBARA CANEPA
AFIF KHALED
GRADIMIR SMUDJA
BENJAMIN

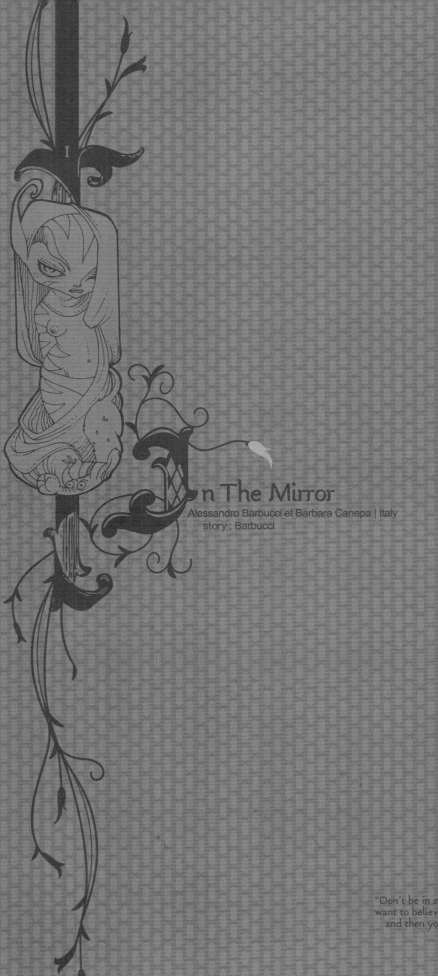

In The Mirror
Alessandro Barbucci et Barbara Canepa | Italy
story : Barbucci

"Don't be in such a hurry to believe next time—I'll tell you why—if yo
want to believe everything, you will tire out the muscles of your min
and then you'll be so weak you won't be able to believe the simples
true things.
Lewis Carro

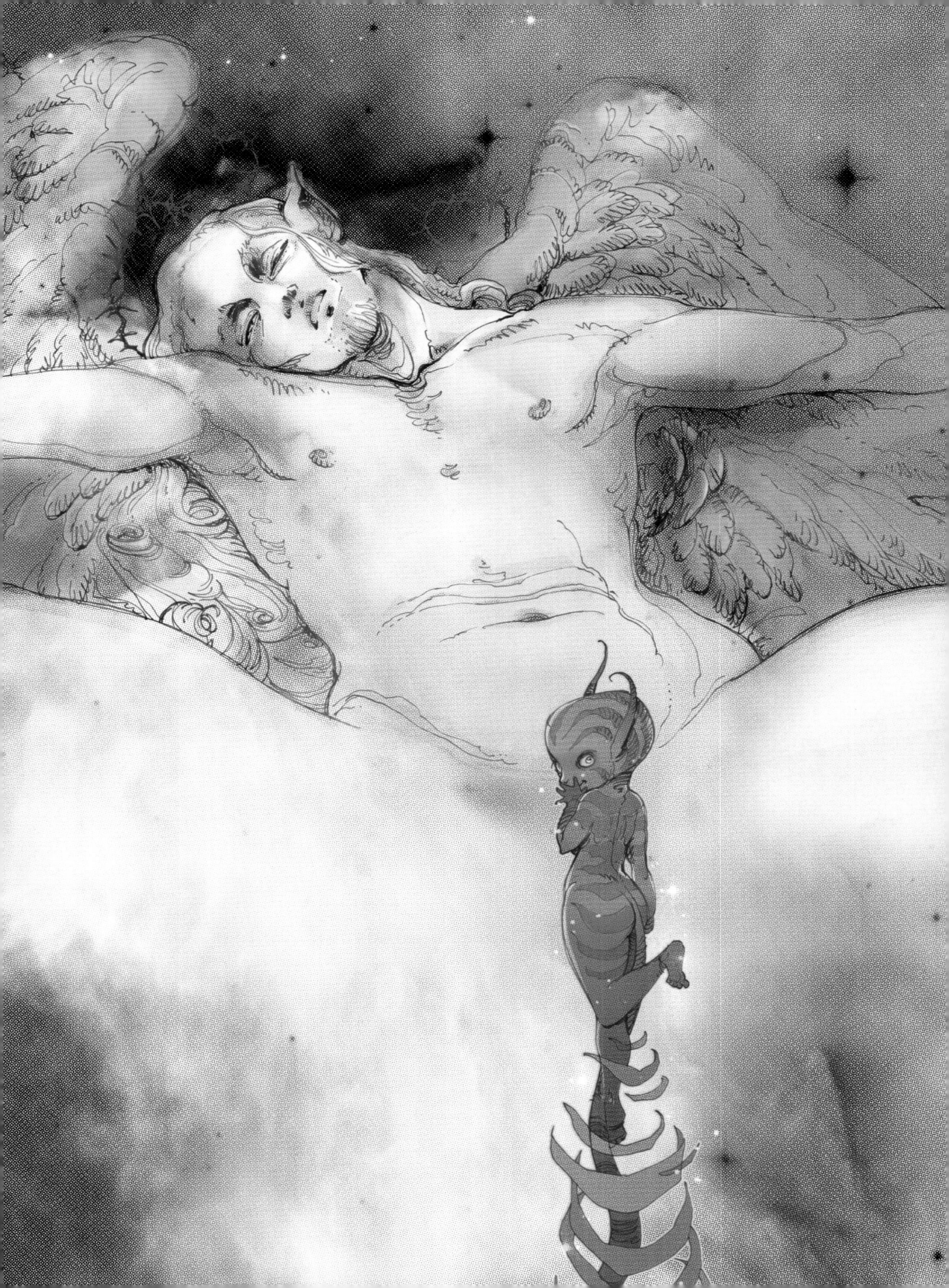

...I KNEW A DRAMATIC TOUCH WOULDN'T DISPLEASE YOU, SO I USED A SPECIAL GLASS. *HEH HEH...*

POP

SUBLIME, AS ALWAYS.

OH, YOU KNOW HOW IT IS! AFTER ALL THESE YEARS, CERTAIN DETAILS COME NATURALLY TO ME.

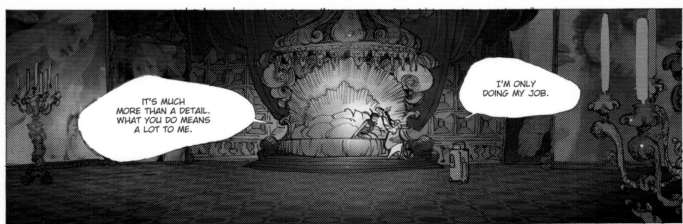

IT'S MUCH MORE THAN A DETAIL. WHAT YOU DO MEANS A LOT TO ME.

I'M ONLY DOING MY JOB.

BUT I MUST ADMIT, OVER TIME I HAVE FAVORED A CERTAIN PATIENT. *HEH HEH.*

I'M UNDER SUCH UNBEARABLE PRESSURE. I FEEL LIKE I'M CONSTANTLY BEING WATCHED, AND JUDGED...

SOMETIMES, THE ONLY THING THAT KEEPS ME GOING IS WAITING FOR OUR NEXT APPOINTMENT.

CALM YOURSELF AND RELAX, NOW. NO NEED TO TALK.

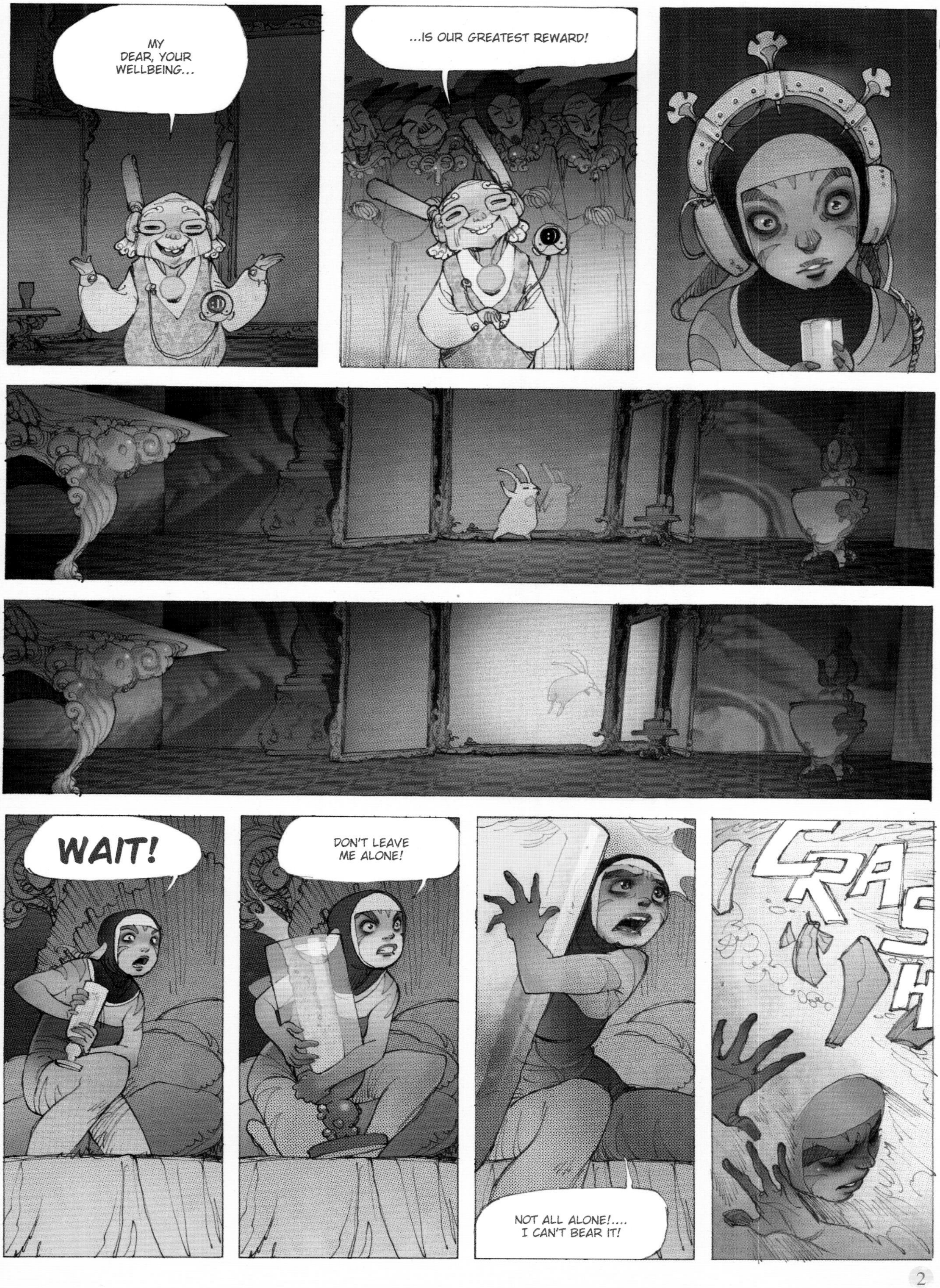
MY DEAR, YOUR WELLBEING...
...IS OUR GREATEST REWARD!
WAIT!
DON'T LEAVE ME ALONE!
NOT ALL ALONE!.... I CAN'T BEAR IT!
CRASH

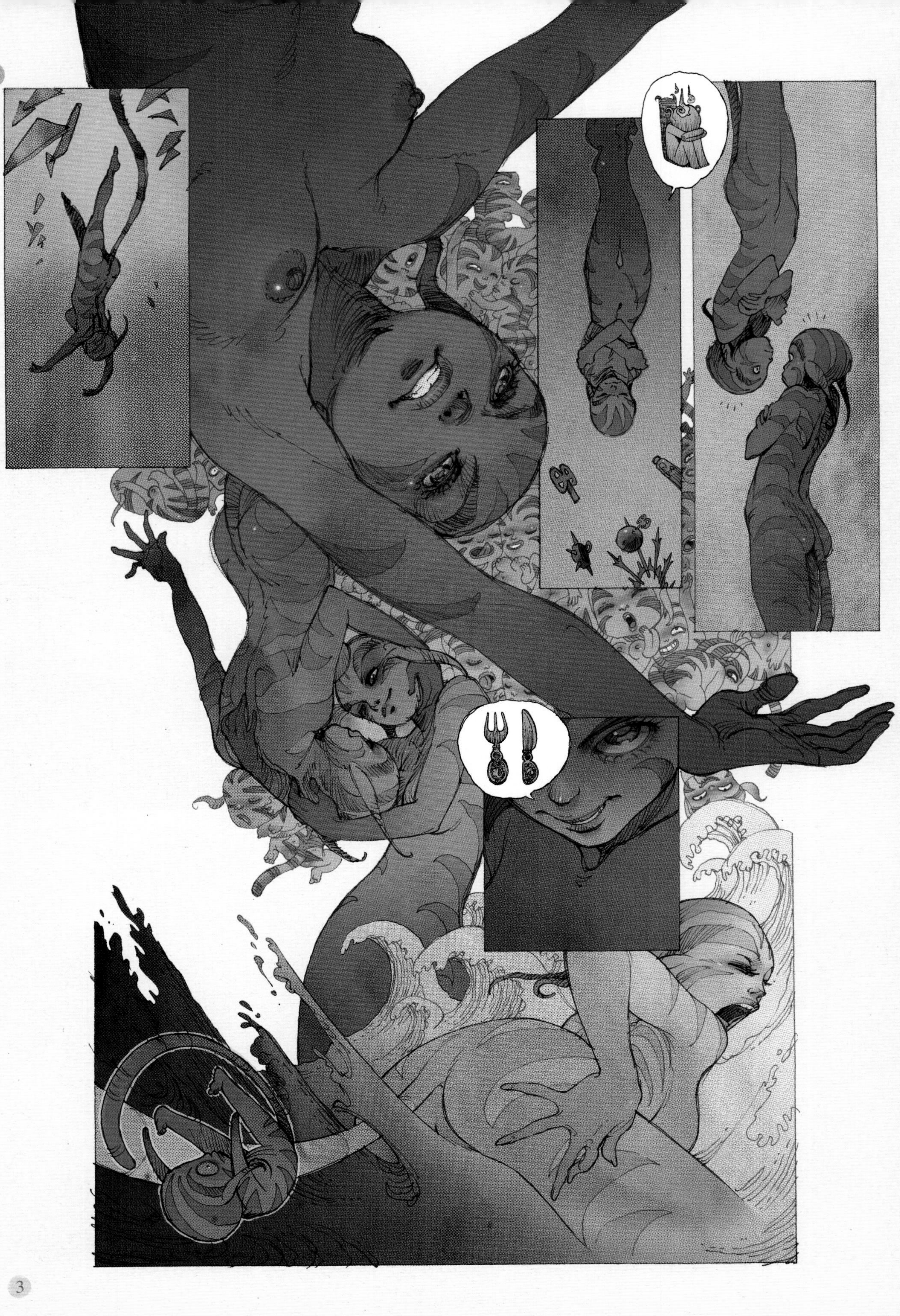

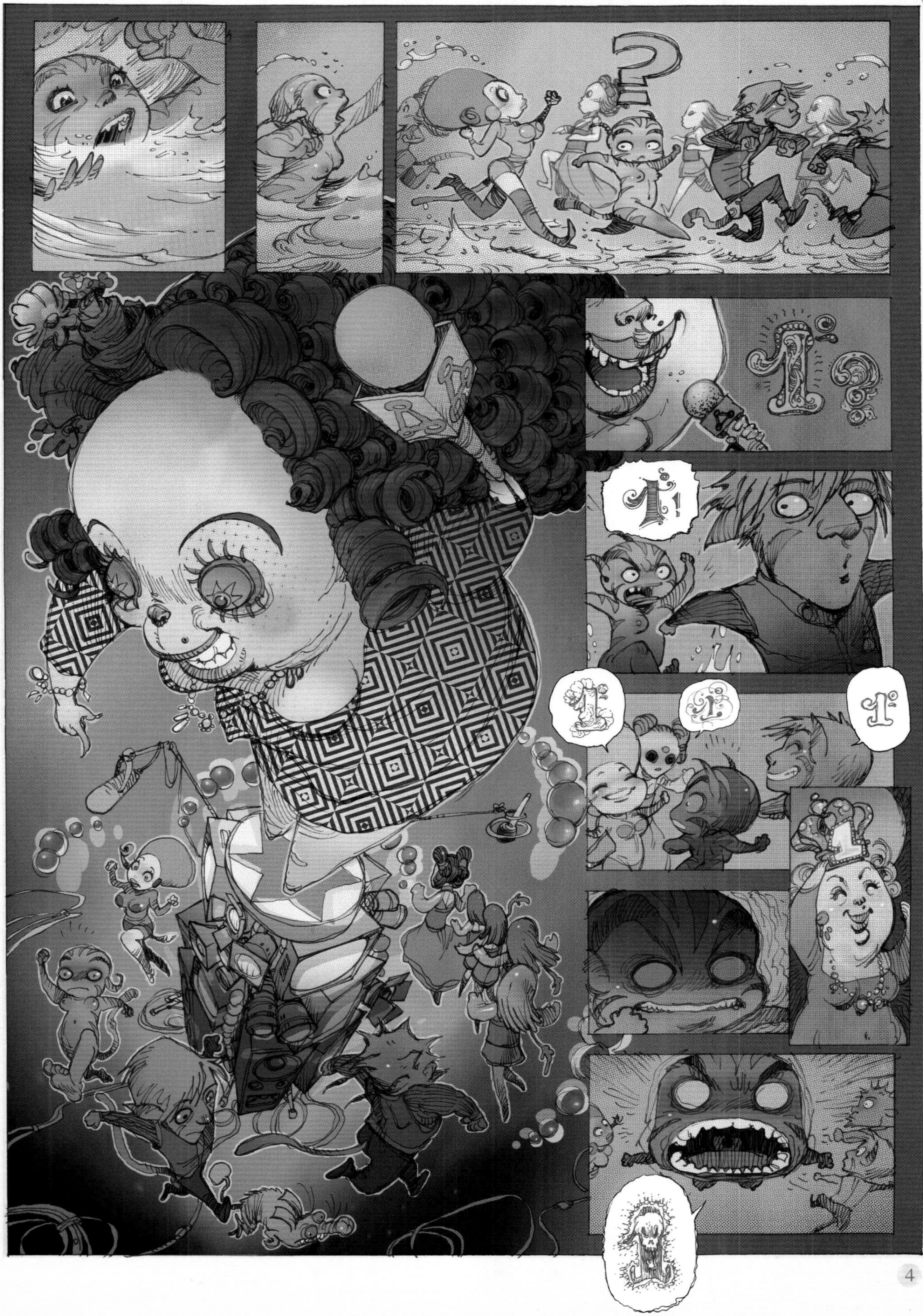
1º?
1º!
1º
1º
1º

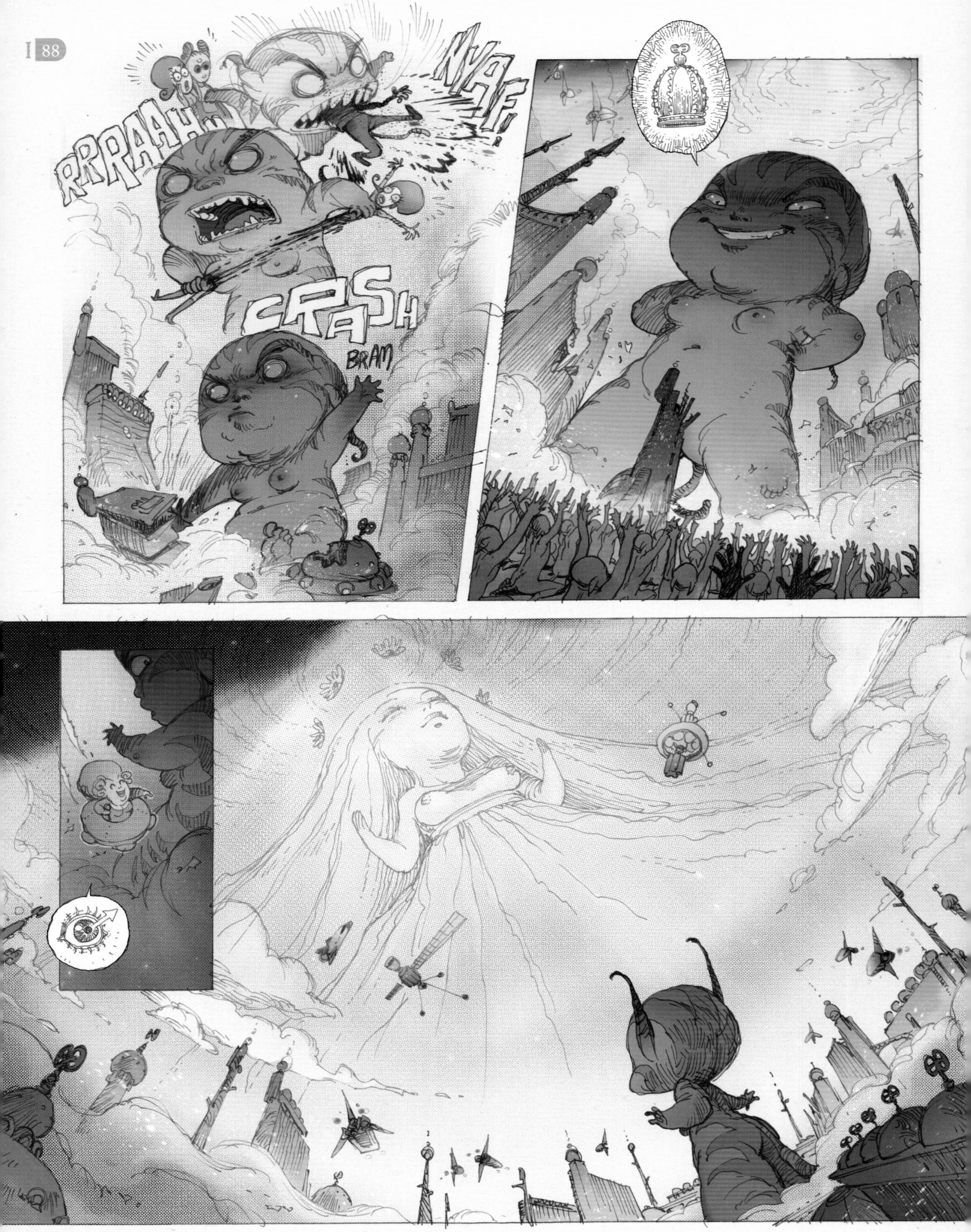
RRRAAAH
NYAF!
CRASH
BRAM

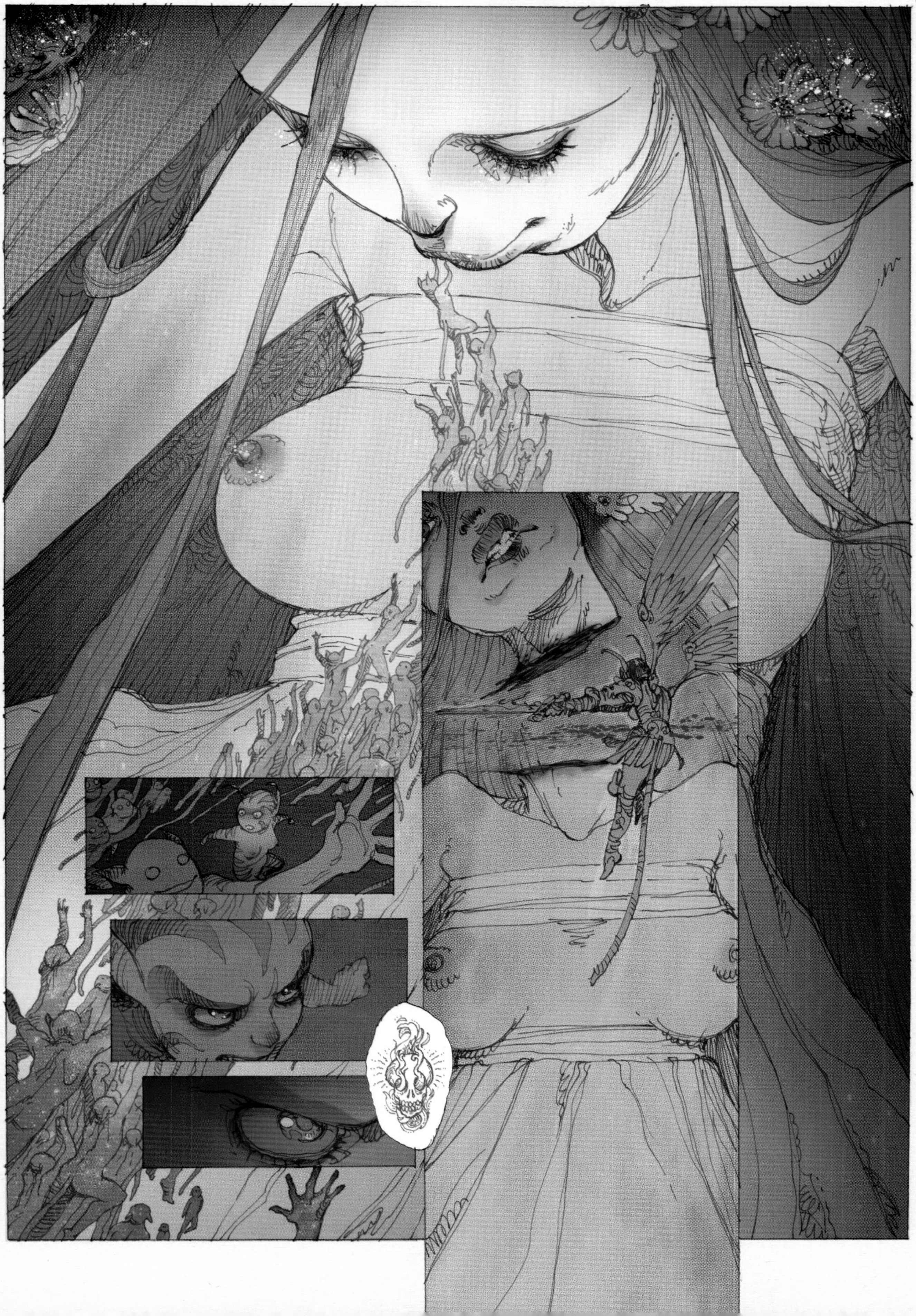

YEEESSSS!!!

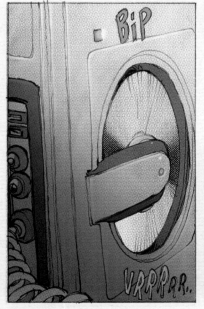

BiP

VRPRRR...

THERE WE ARE, ALL FINISHED. I BET YOU FEEL MUCH BETTER, DON'T YOU?

YES! I FEEL...

COMPLETELY IN CONTROL, AND FREE!

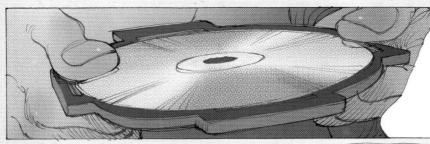

I'M DELIGHTED. *HEH HEH.*
JUST AS WITH OUR PREVIOUS SESSIONS,
THE HALLUCINATORY HYPNOSIS HAS EXPELLED ALL
TERRIBLE DEMONS: FRUSTRATION, FEAR, AND
MEMORIES HIDDEN IN YOUR SUBCONSCIOUS.
IT HAS NOW ALL BEEN DOWNLOADED
ONTO THIS DRIVE...

...WHICH
I WILL FILE
ALONGSIDE THE
OTHERS. THEY'LL
BE SAFE IN MY
IMPENETRABLE
SUPER SECRET
ARCHIVES!
HEH HEH.

OH I KNOW I CAN
TRUST YOU COMPLETELY.
LIKE NO ONE ELSE.

MY CHILD,
YOU ALREADY
KNOW....

YOUR WELLBEING IS MY
GREATEST REWARD!

WE WERE
WAITING FOR YOU.
ANY NEWS?

NOTHING
IMPORTANT. THE
USUAL INFANTILE,
EGOTISTICAL DELUSIONS,
PRENATAL TRAUMAS,
AND STRESSES
CAUSED BY MEDIA
OVEREXPOSURE.

IT'S ALL
IN THERE.

AS ALWAYS,
I INSERTED THE FALSE
MURDER MEMORY AT THE
END. AND NOW I'D LIKE
TO GO TO BED.

ONE
LAST THING...

IF
I MAY...
I WOULD
LIKE TO
KNOW...

WHY DOES THIS
THIS FAKE MEMORY
MEAN SO MUCH
TO YOU?

A FINE
PSYCHOLOGIST
LIKE YOURSELF
SHOULD KNOW...

THERE ARE
SO MANY WAYS
TO MANIPULATE AND
CONTROL A
PERSON...

THE MOST
POWERFUL OF WHICH,
IS THE FEELING
OF GUILT.

SOMETHING
YOU REALLY SHOULD
KNOW ABOUT.

The Saint in a bottle

Mikael Bourgoin | France
story : Barbucci

"For two days Aladdin remained in the dark crying and lamenting. At las
he clasped his hands in prayer, and in doing so rubbed the ring, which the
magician had forgotten to take from him. Immediately an enormous and
frightful genie rose out of the earth, saying 'what wouldst thou with me?
am the Slave of the Ring, and will obey thee in all things.

One Thousand and One Nights

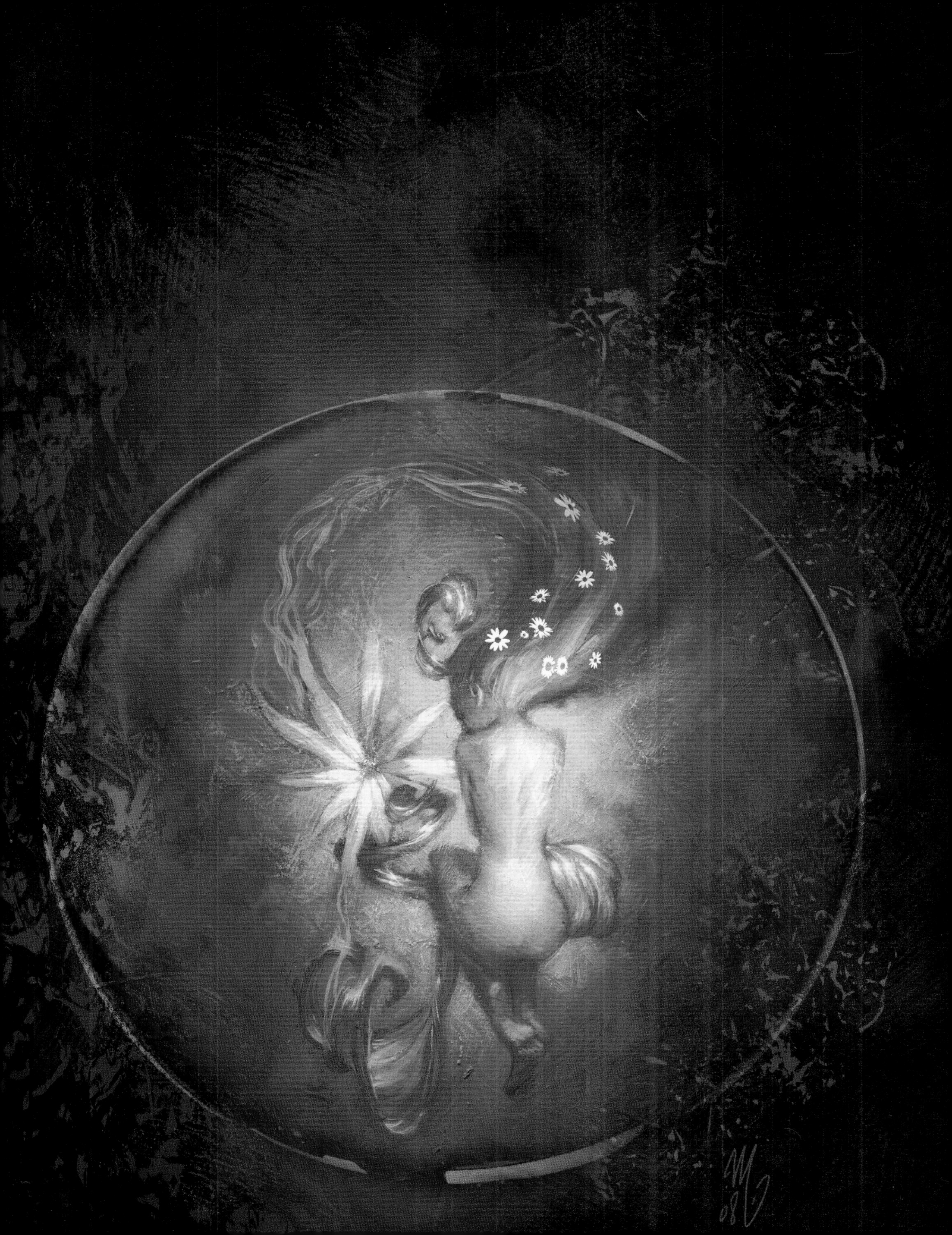

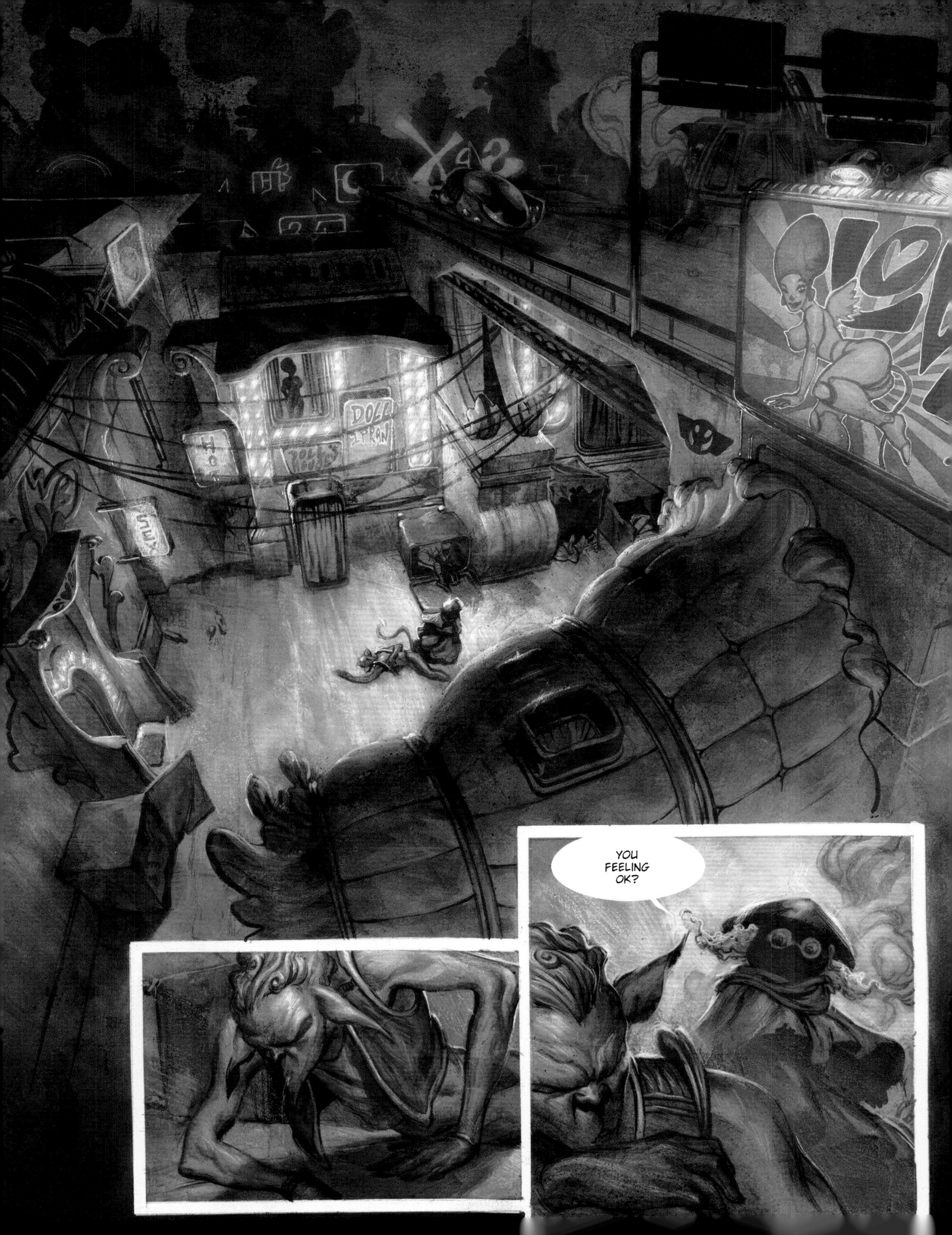
YOU FEELING OK?

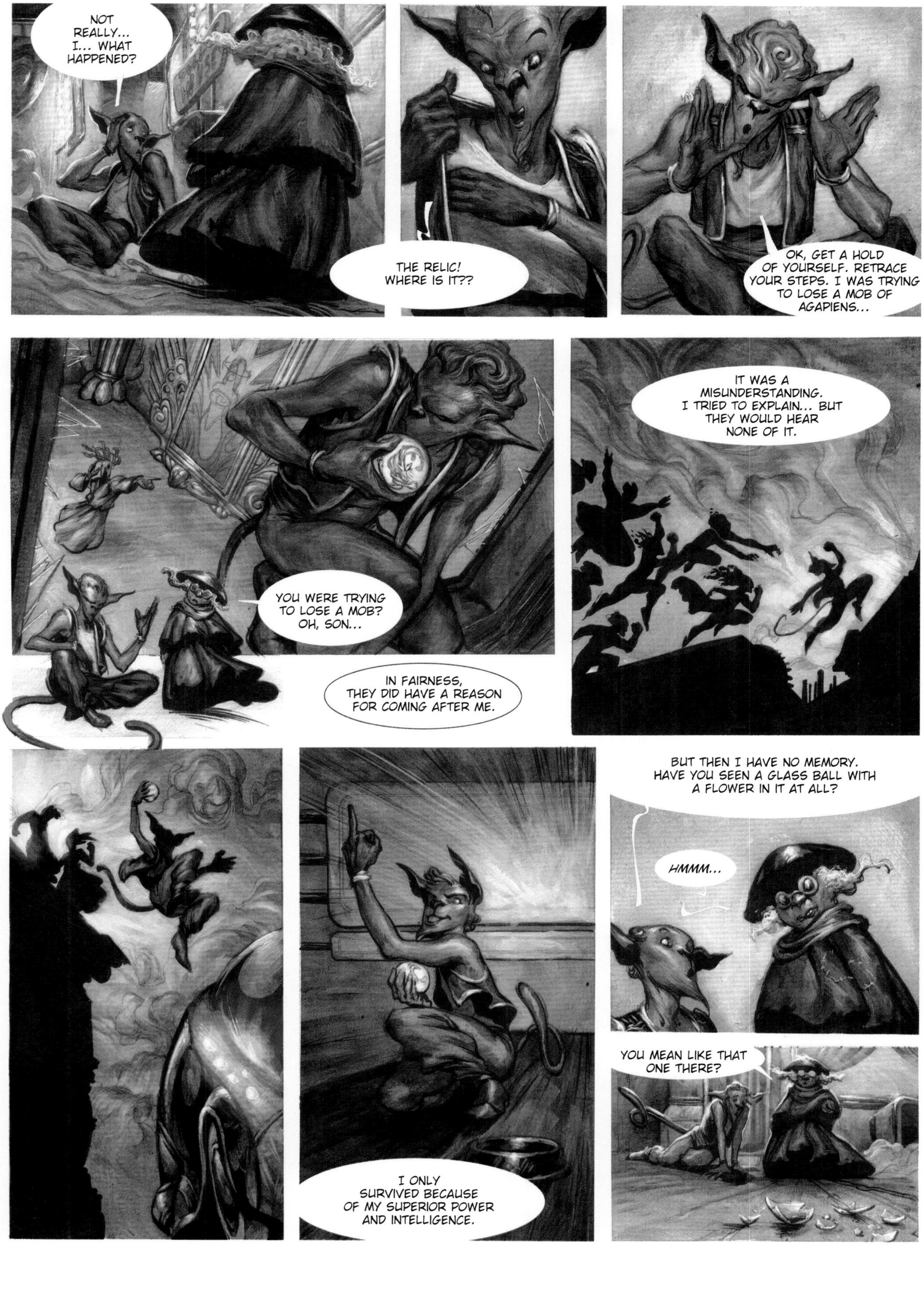
NOT REALLY... I... WHAT HAPPENED?
THE RELIC! WHERE IS IT??
OK, GET A HOLD OF YOURSELF. RETRACE YOUR STEPS. I WAS TRYING TO LOSE A MOB OF AGAPIENS...
YOU WERE TRYING TO LOSE A MOB? OH, SON...
IT WAS A MISUNDERSTANDING. I TRIED TO EXPLAIN... BUT THEY WOULD HEAR NONE OF IT.
IN FAIRNESS, THEY DID HAVE A REASON FOR COMING AFTER ME.
I ONLY SURVIVED BECAUSE OF MY SUPERIOR POWER AND INTELLIGENCE.
BUT THEN I HAVE NO MEMORY. HAVE YOU SEEN A GLASS BALL WITH A FLOWER IN IT AT ALL?
HMMM...
YOU MEAN LIKE THAT ONE THERE?

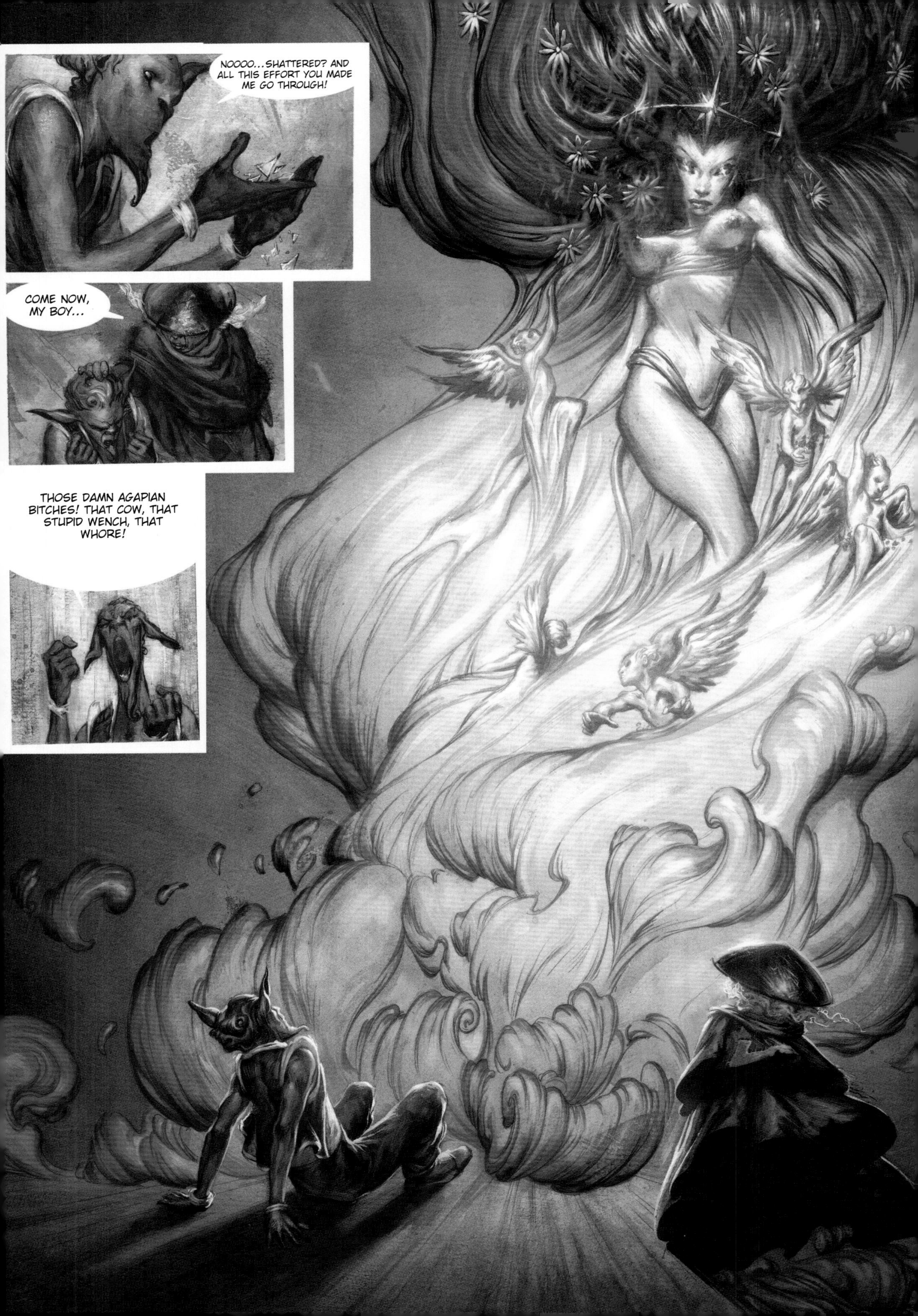
NOOOO...SHATTERED? AND ALL THIS EFFORT YOU MADE ME GO THROUGH!
COME NOW, MY BOY...
THOSE DAMN AGAPIAN BITCHES! THAT COW, THAT STUPID WENCH, THAT WHORE!

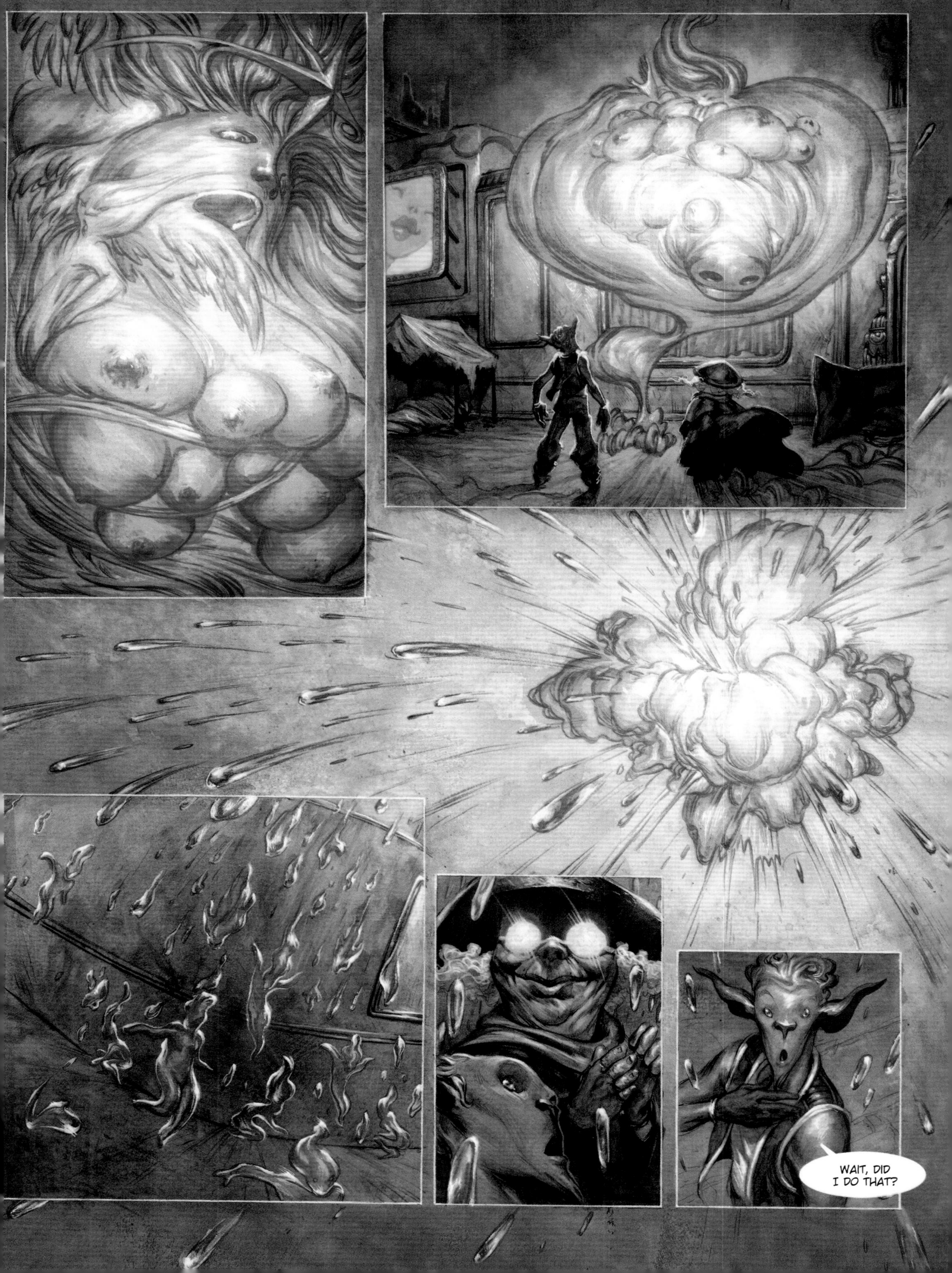
WAIT, DID I DO THAT?

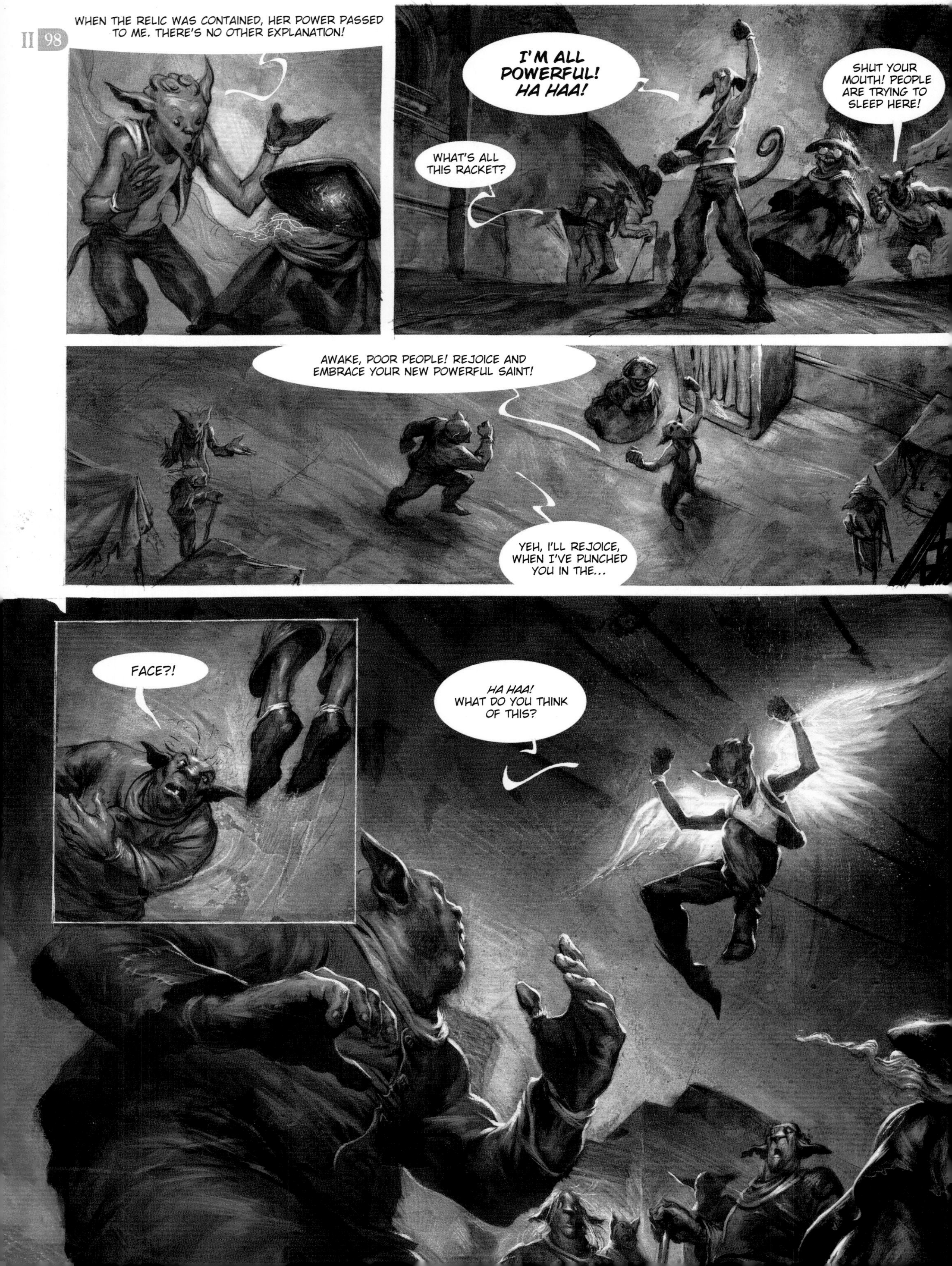
WHEN THE RELIC WAS CONTAINED, HER POWER PASSED TO ME. THERE'S NO OTHER EXPLANATION!
I'M ALL POWERFUL! HA HAA!
WHAT'S ALL THIS RACKET?
SHUT YOUR MOUTH! PEOPLE ARE TRYING TO SLEEP HERE!
AWAKE, POOR PEOPLE! REJOICE AND EMBRACE YOUR NEW POWERFUL SAINT!
YEH, I'LL REJOICE, WHEN I'VE PUNCHED YOU IN THE...
FACE?!
HA HAA! WHAT DO YOU THINK OF THIS?

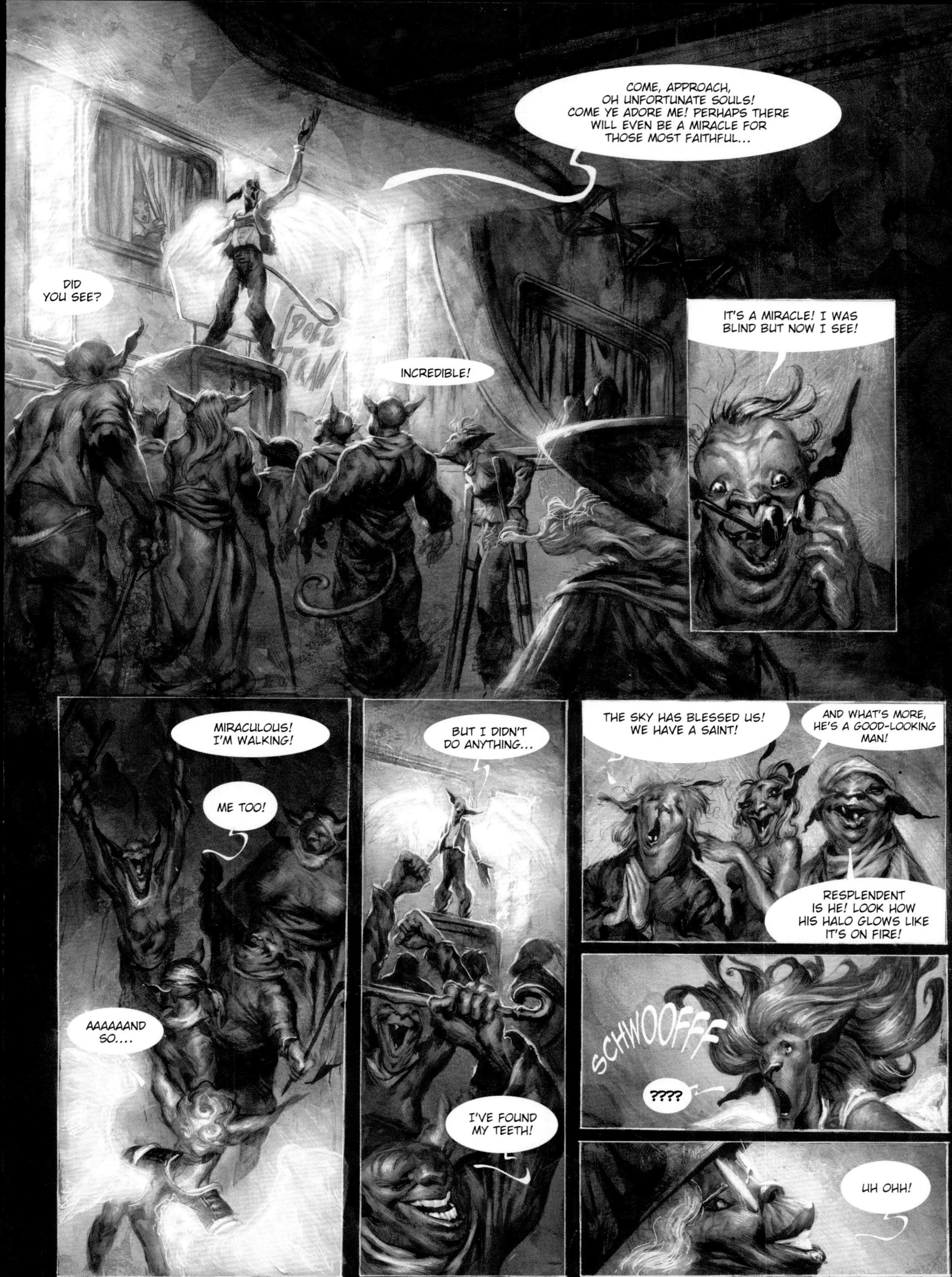
COME, APPROACH, OH UNFORTUNATE SOULS! COME YE ADORE ME! PERHAPS THERE WILL EVEN BE A MIRACLE FOR THOSE MOST FAITHFUL...
DID YOU SEE?
INCREDIBLE!
IT'S A MIRACLE! I WAS BLIND BUT NOW I SEE!
MIRACULOUS! I'M WALKING!
ME TOO!
AAAAAAND SO....
BUT I DIDN'T DO ANYTHING...
I'VE FOUND MY TEETH!
THE SKY HAS BLESSED US! WE HAVE A SAINT!
AND WHAT'S MORE, HE'S A GOOD-LOOKING MAN!
RESPLENDENT IS HE! LOOK HOW HIS HALO GLOWS LIKE IT'S ON FIRE!
SCHWOOFFF
????
UH OHH!

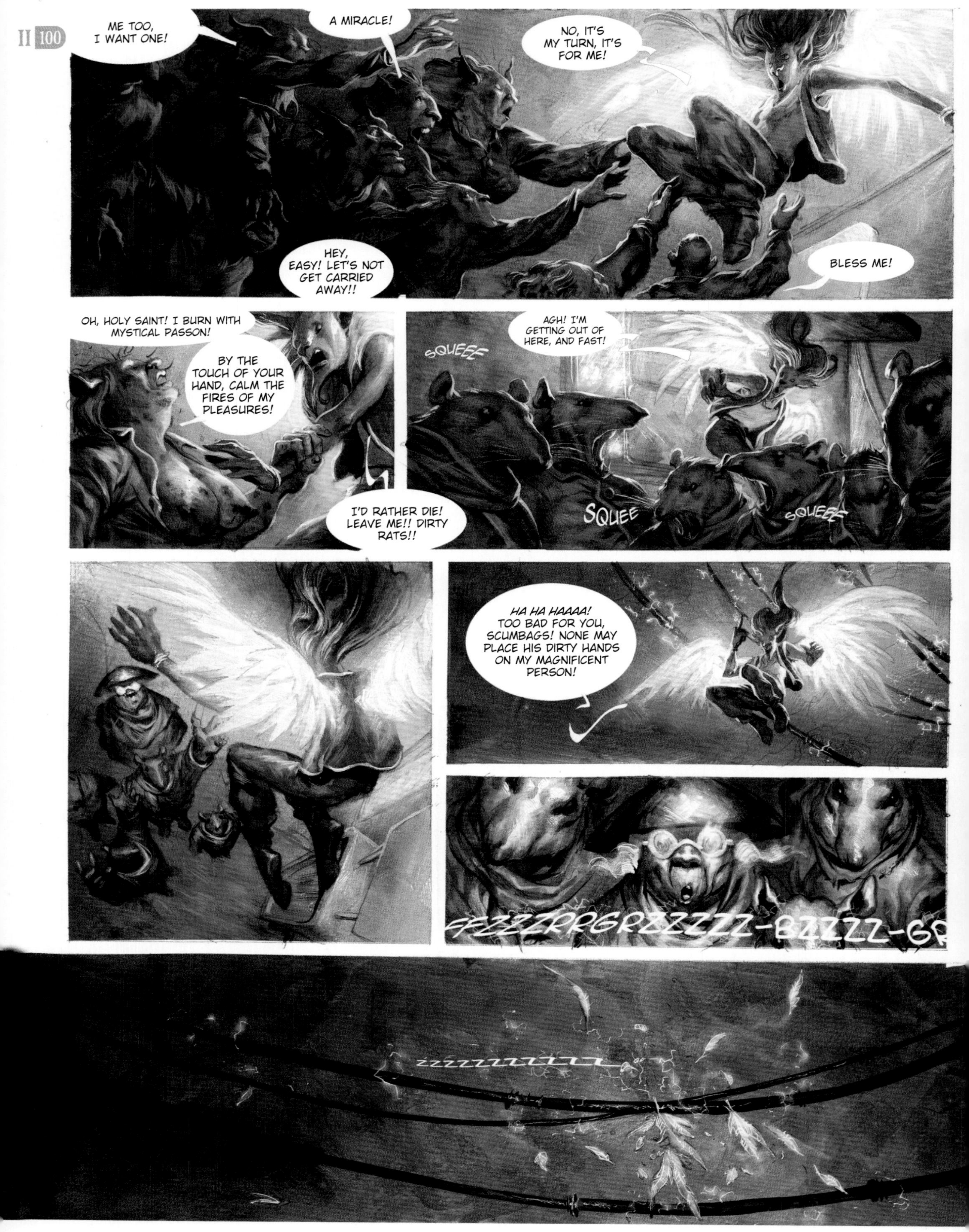
ME TOO, I WANT ONE!
A MIRACLE!
NO, IT'S MY TURN, IT'S FOR ME!
HEY, EASY! LET'S NOT GET CARRIED AWAY!!
BLESS ME!
OH, HOLY SAINT! I BURN WITH MYSTICAL PASSON!
BY THE TOUCH OF YOUR HAND, CALM THE FIRES OF MY PLEASURES!
I'D RATHER DIE! LEAVE ME!! DIRTY RATS!!
AGH! I'M GETTING OUT OF HERE, AND FAST!
SQUEEE
SQUEE
SQUEEE
HA HA HAAAA! TOO BAD FOR YOU, SCUMBAGS! NONE MAY PLACE HIS DIRTY HANDS ON MY MAGNIFICENT PERSON!
FFZZZZRRGRZZZZZZ-BZZZZ-GR
ZZZZZZZZZZZZ

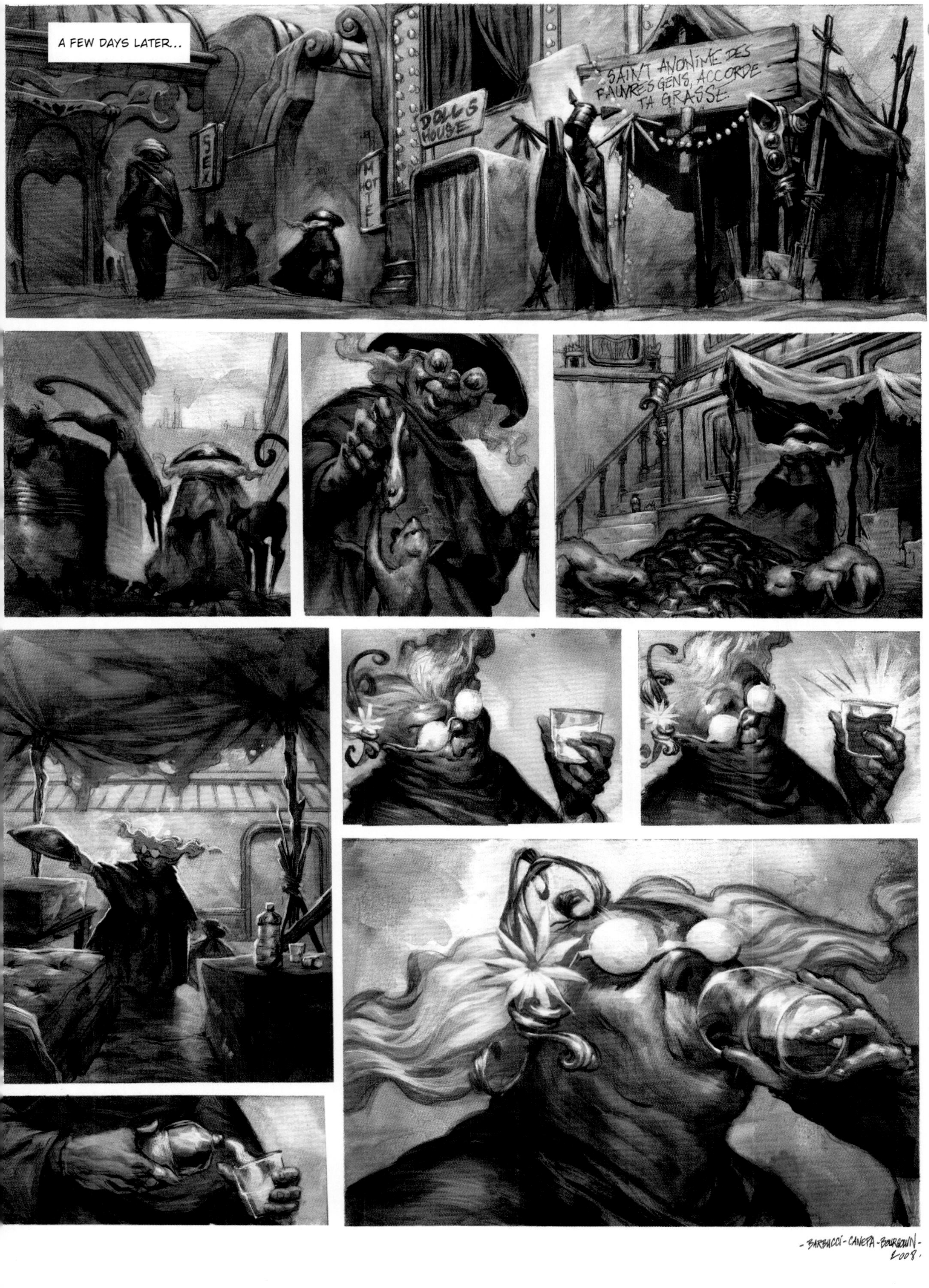
A FEW DAYS LATER...
SEX
MOTEL
DOLLS HOUSE
SAINT ANONIME DES PAUVRES GENS, ACCORDE TA GRASSE.
- BARBUCCÍ - CANEPA - BOURGOUIN -
2008.

VI

Sleeping Dreamer

Benjamin | China
story : Barbucci

"And when the Queen was bathing, a frog crawled out of
the water on to the land, and said to her, 'Your wish shall
be fulfilled; before a year has gone by you shall have a
daughter.'"

The Brothers Grimm

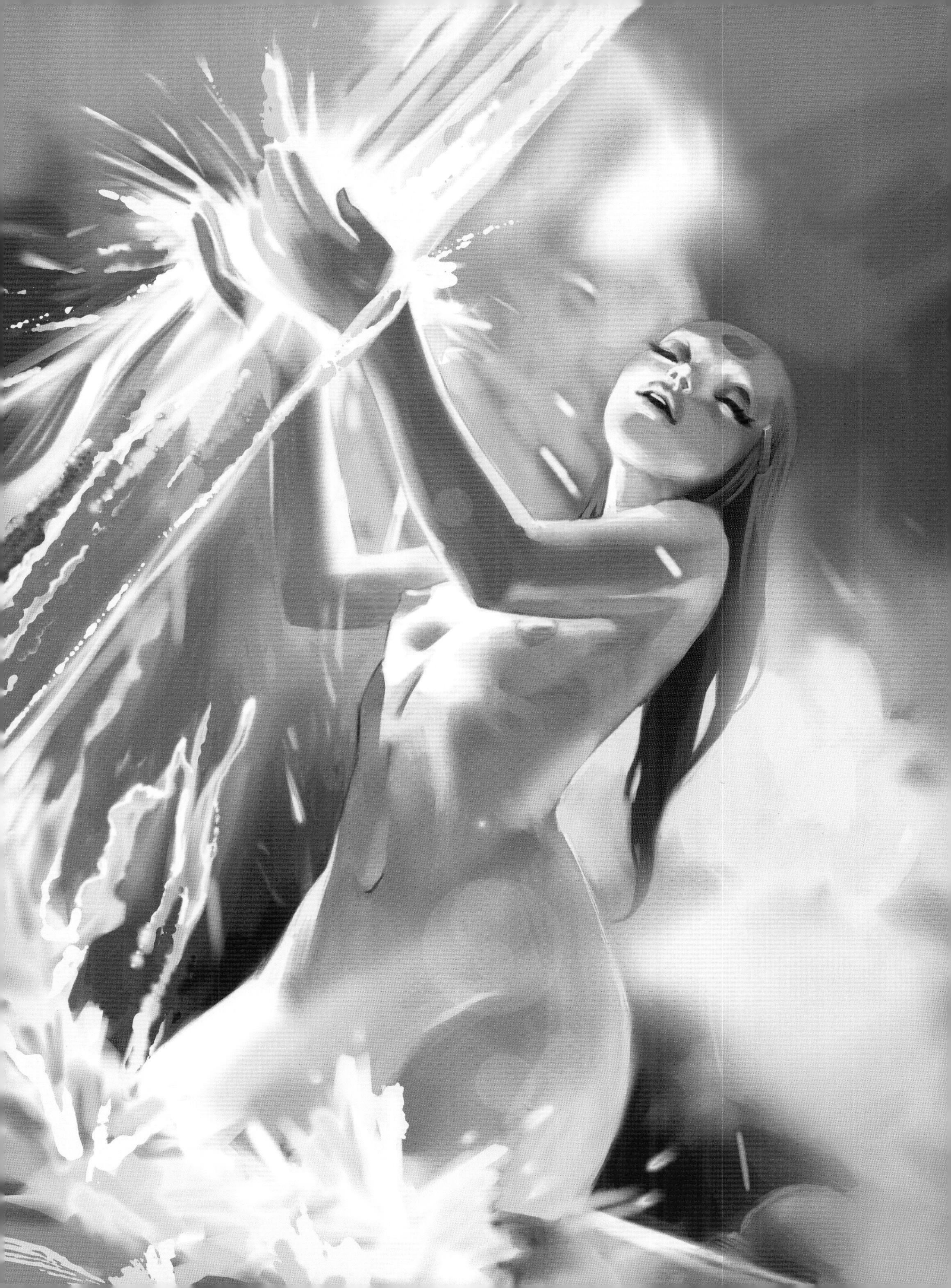

YOUR GOWN, OH MAGNIFICENT SPLENDID ONE...YOUR GOWN, OH MAGNIFICENT...

VRRRRRRR

YOUR GOW... ARGH!

BEEP

VRRRRRRR

SKREEE

GUARD FER-ZEN002! HOW DARE YOU DISTURB THE SERENITY OF THESE HALLS??

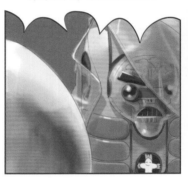

FORGIVE ME, GUARD-CHIEF! I CANNOT HOLD MY EXCITEMENT FOR WHAT'S COMING!

IT DOESN'T PERMIT SUCH BEHAVIOR. THOUGH WONDROUS, IT WILL BE A NECESSARY DUTY.

...AND IN PERFECT HARMONY WITH THE WHOLE OF PLANET AQUA.

VRRRRRR

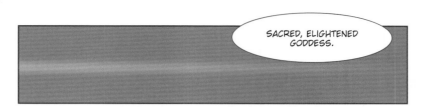

SACRED, ELIGHTENED GODDESS.

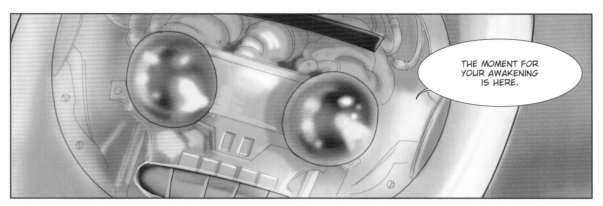

THE MOMENT FOR YOUR AWAKENING IS HERE.

ON BEHALF OF ALL GUARDS, I WISH YOU A PLEASANT MORNING.

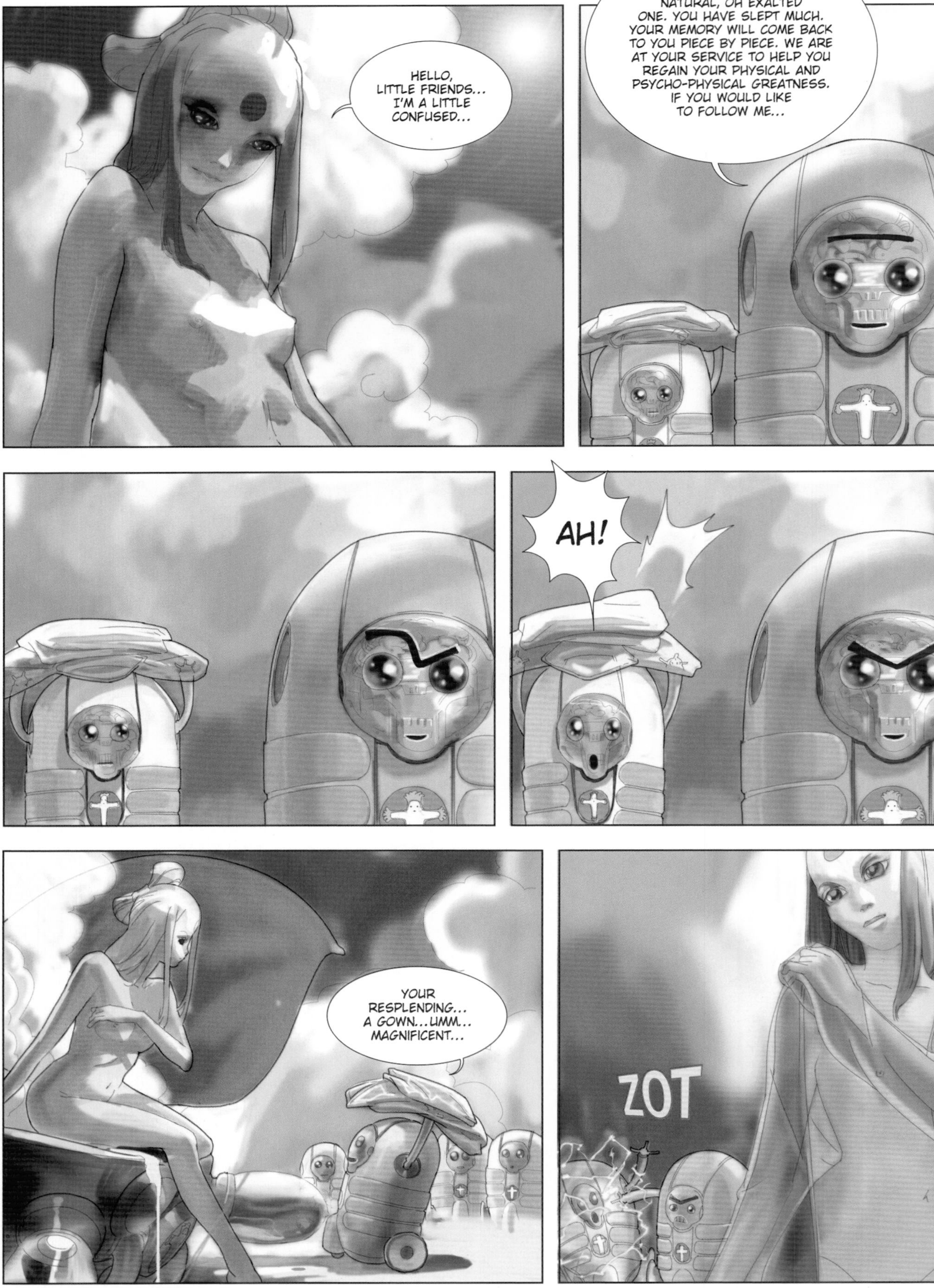
HELLO, LITTLE FRIENDS... I'M A LITTLE CONFUSED...
PERFECTLY NATURAL, OH EXALTED ONE. YOU HAVE SLEPT MUCH. YOUR MEMORY WILL COME BACK TO YOU PIECE BY PIECE. WE ARE AT YOUR SERVICE TO HELP YOU REGAIN YOUR PHYSICAL AND PSYCHO-PHYSICAL GREATNESS. IF YOU WOULD LIKE TO FOLLOW ME...
AH!
YOUR RESPLENDING... A GOWN...UMM... MAGNIFICENT...
ZOT

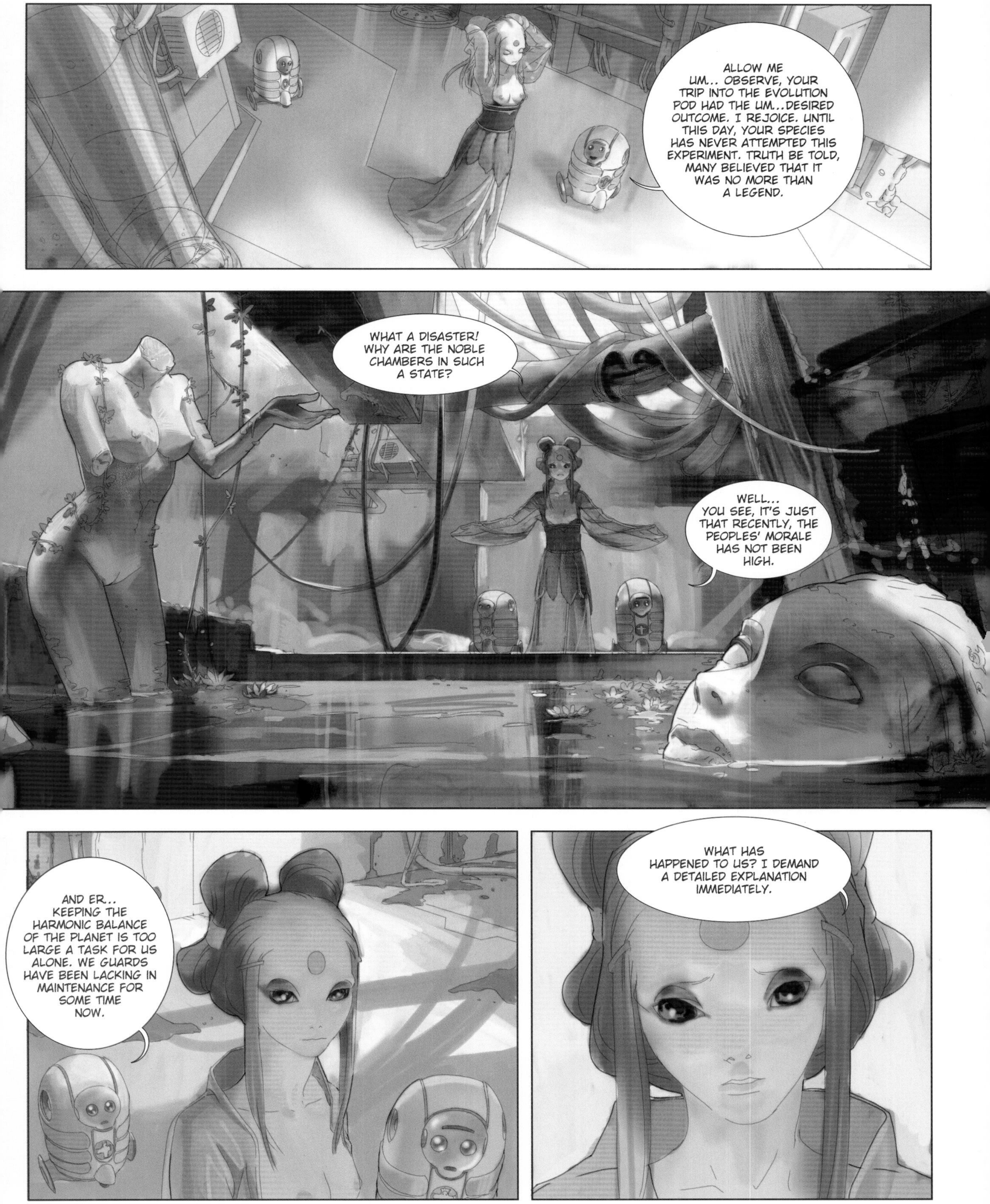
ALLOW ME UM... OBSERVE, YOUR TRIP INTO THE EVOLUTION POD HAD THE UM...DESIRED OUTCOME. I REJOICE. UNTIL THIS DAY, YOUR SPECIES HAS NEVER ATTEMPTED THIS EXPERIMENT. TRUTH BE TOLD, MANY BELIEVED THAT IT WAS NO MORE THAN A LEGEND.
WHAT A DISASTER! WHY ARE THE NOBLE CHAMBERS IN SUCH A STATE?
WELL... YOU SEE, IT'S JUST THAT RECENTLY, THE PEOPLES' MORALE HAS NOT BEEN HIGH.
AND ER... KEEPING THE HARMONIC BALANCE OF THE PLANET IS TOO LARGE A TASK FOR US ALONE. WE GUARDS HAVE BEEN LACKING IN MAINTENANCE FOR SOME TIME NOW.
WHAT HAS HAPPENED TO US? I DEMAND A DETAILED EXPLANATION IMMEDIATELY.

OPENING OUR DOORS TO THE TWO DIPLOMATIC EMISSARIES ROY AND JAHU TURNED OUT TO BE A TERRIBLE MISTAKE. THE TRUE AURA OF THE FIRST WAS NOT ENOUGH TO BALANCE THE INSTABILITY OF THE SECOND.

THE OCCULT PLAN OF PAPESSE LUDOVIC, ANNIHILATION OF THE SACRED FISH WAS THUS ACCOMPLISHED...

...AND THAT BROUGHT ABOUT THE DESTRUCTION OF THE GENETIC ELEMENT CONTAINED WITHIN, THE KEY TO REPRODUCTION BY CLONING THE AQUARIAN PEOPLE, WHO WERE ONCE EXCLUSIVELY FEMALES.

OUR DESIRE FOR EXPANSION TURNED AGAINST US. BY AVIDITÉ WE FORGOT TO TAKE THE NECESSARY PRECAUTIONS TO MAINTAIN SUCH A DELICATE BALANCE. HOW FOOLISH I WAS TO EXPOSE MY PEOPLE TO SUCH DANGER.

WITH ALL DUE RESPECT... YOU HAVE TO ADMIT THEY'VE BEEN REALLY CARELESS.

YOU COULD SEE IT LIKE THAT... UM... BUT WHAT WAS I ABOUT TO SAY? **SHUT UP! SO RUDE!**

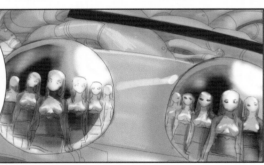

THE GHOST OF EXTINCTION HAS BEEN A HUGE BLOW TO THE PSYCHOLOGICAL BALANCE OF THE PLANET. THERE WERE EVEN DOUBTS AS TO YOUR EXPERIMENT'S CHANCES OF SUCCESS. THE AQUARIANS FEEL LOST AND HAVE LOST ALL MOTIVATION

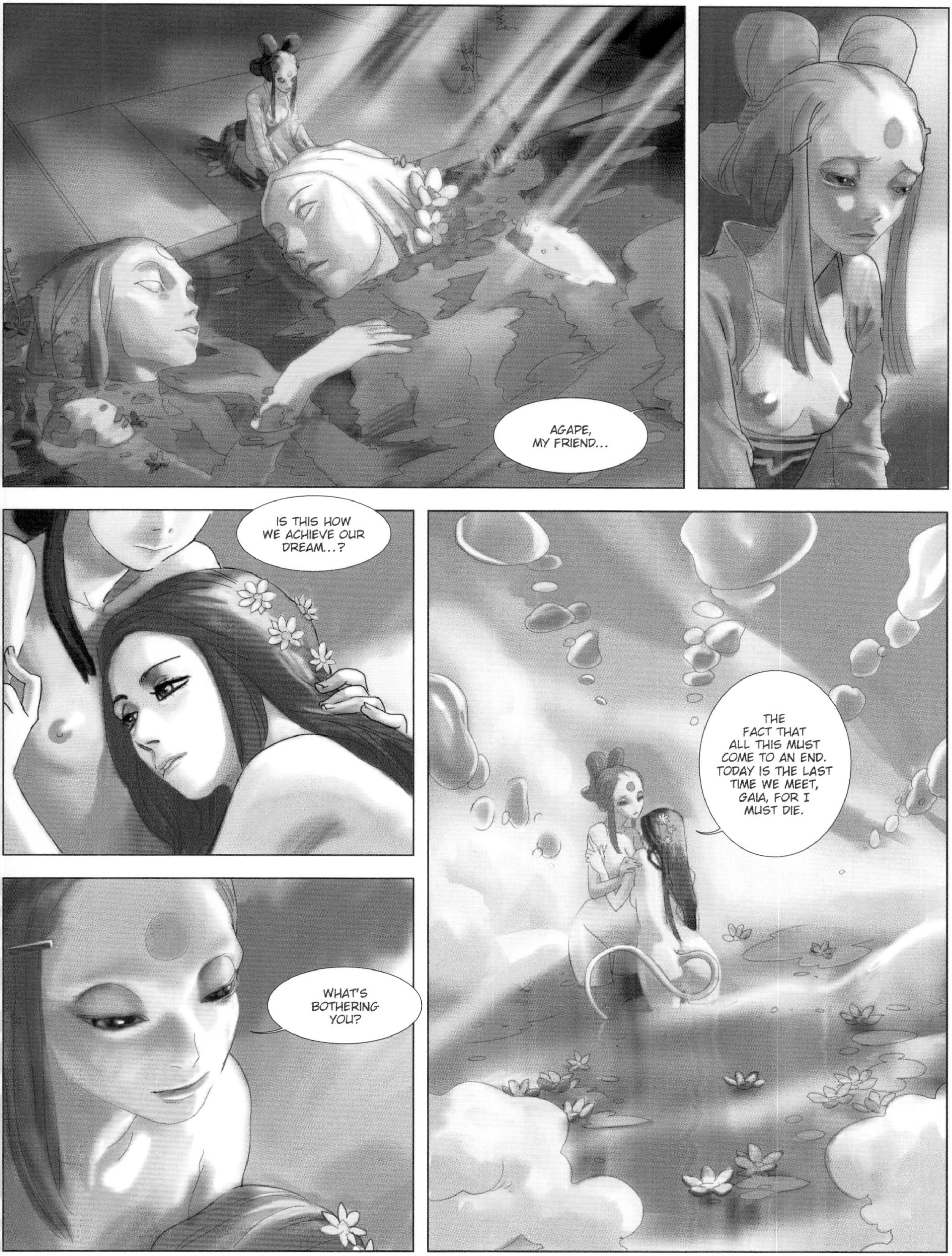
AGAPE, MY FRIEND...
IS THIS HOW WE ACHIEVE OUR DREAM...?
WHAT'S BOTHERING YOU?
THE FACT THAT ALL THIS MUST COME TO AN END. TODAY IS THE LAST TIME WE MEET, GAIA, FOR I MUST DIE.

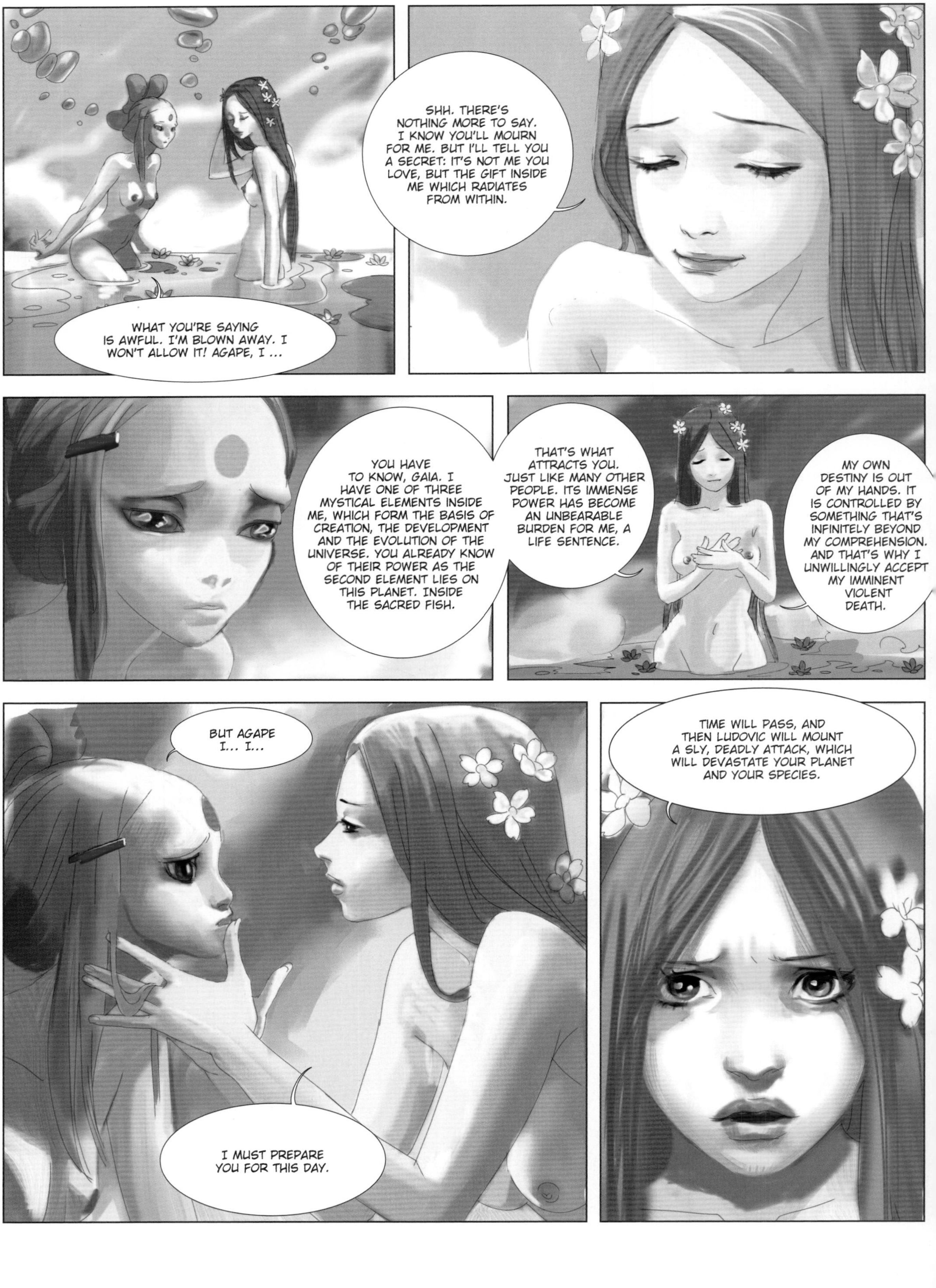
WHAT YOU'RE SAYING IS AWFUL. I'M BLOWN AWAY. I WON'T ALLOW IT! AGAPE, I ...
SHH. THERE'S NOTHING MORE TO SAY. I KNOW YOU'LL MOURN FOR ME. BUT I'LL TELL YOU A SECRET: IT'S NOT ME YOU LOVE, BUT THE GIFT INSIDE ME WHICH RADIATES FROM WITHIN.
YOU HAVE TO KNOW, GAIA. I HAVE ONE OF THREE MYSTICAL ELEMENTS INSIDE ME, WHICH FORM THE BASIS OF CREATION, THE DEVELOPMENT AND THE EVOLUTION OF THE UNIVERSE. YOU ALREADY KNOW OF THEIR POWER AS THE SECOND ELEMENT LIES ON THIS PLANET. INSIDE THE SACRED FISH.
THAT'S WHAT ATTRACTS YOU. JUST LIKE MANY OTHER PEOPLE. ITS IMMENSE POWER HAS BECOME AN UNBEARABLE BURDEN FOR ME, A LIFE SENTENCE.
MY OWN DESTINY IS OUT OF MY HANDS. IT IS CONTROLLED BY SOMETHING THAT'S INFINITELY BEYOND MY COMPREHENSION. AND THAT'S WHY I UNWILLINGLY ACCEPT MY IMMINENT VIOLENT DEATH.
BUT AGAPE I... I...
I MUST PREPARE YOU FOR THIS DAY.
TIME WILL PASS, AND THEN LUDOVIC WILL MOUNT A SLY, DEADLY ATTACK, WHICH WILL DEVASTATE YOUR PLANET AND YOUR SPECIES.

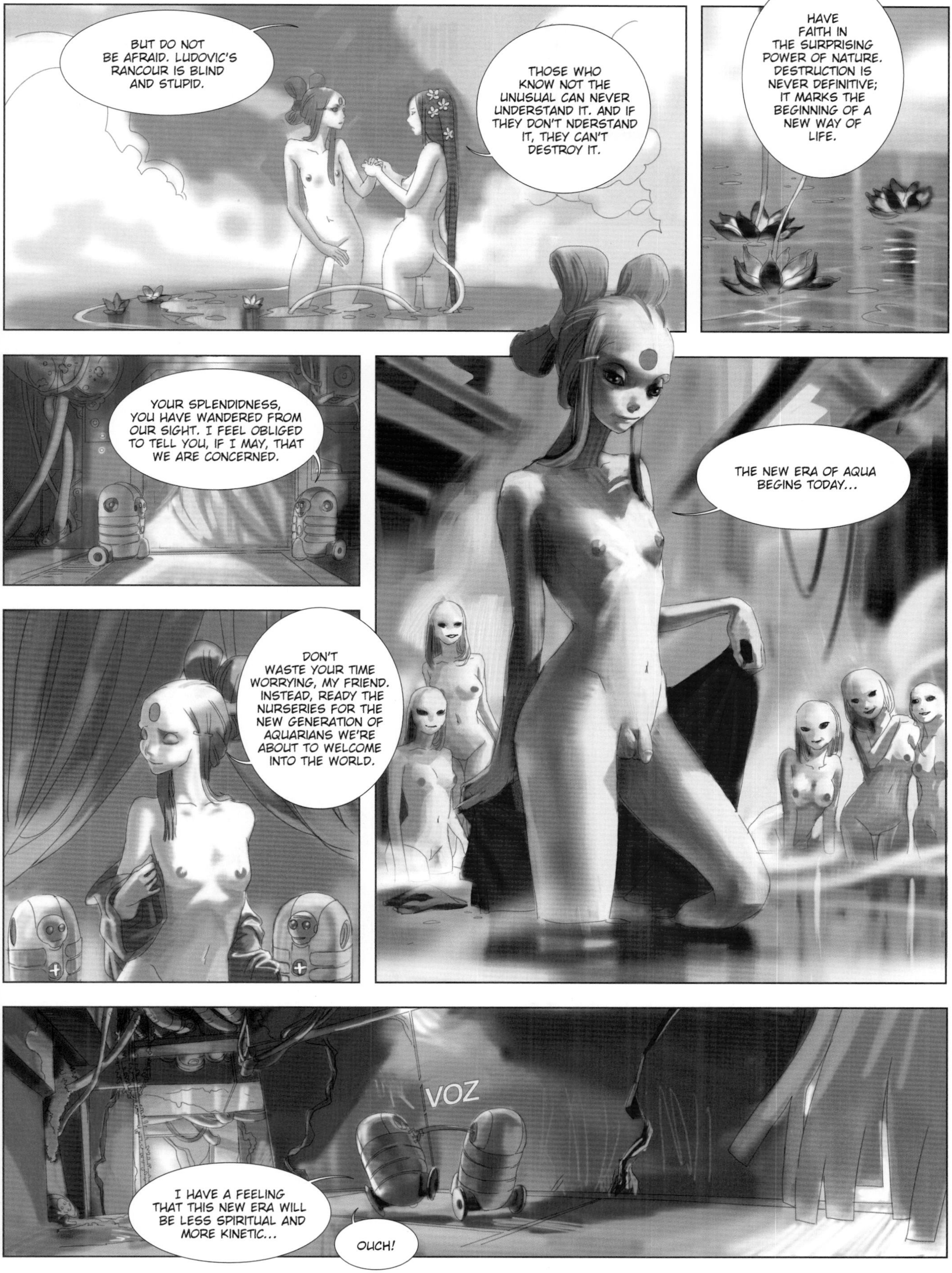
BUT DO NOT BE AFRAID. LUDOVIC'S RANCOUR IS BLIND AND STUPID.
THOSE WHO KNOW NOT THE UNUSUAL CAN NEVER UNDERSTAND IT. AND IF THEY DON'T NDERSTAND IT, THEY CAN'T DESTROY IT.
HAVE FAITH IN THE SURPRISING POWER OF NATURE. DESTRUCTION IS NEVER DEFINITIVE; IT MARKS THE BEGINNING OF A NEW WAY OF LIFE.
YOUR SPLENDIDNESS, YOU HAVE WANDERED FROM OUR SIGHT. I FEEL OBLIGED TO TELL YOU, IF I MAY, THAT WE ARE CONCERNED.
DON'T WASTE YOUR TIME WORRYING, MY FRIEND. INSTEAD, READY THE NURSERIES FOR THE NEW GENERATION OF AQUARIANS WE'RE ABOUT TO WELCOME INTO THE WORLD.
THE NEW ERA OF AQUA BEGINS TODAY...
VOZ
I HAVE A FEELING THAT THIS NEW ERA WILL BE LESS SPIRITUAL AND MORE KINETIC...
OUCH!

IV

The Papess's New Clothes

Gradimir Smudja | Serbia
story : Barbucci - Smudja

"Oh, how splendid are the Emperor's New Clothes. What
magnificent train. How well the clothes fit!" No one dared to adm
that he couldn't see anything, for who would want it to be known tha
he was either stupid or unfit for his post?

H.C. Anderson

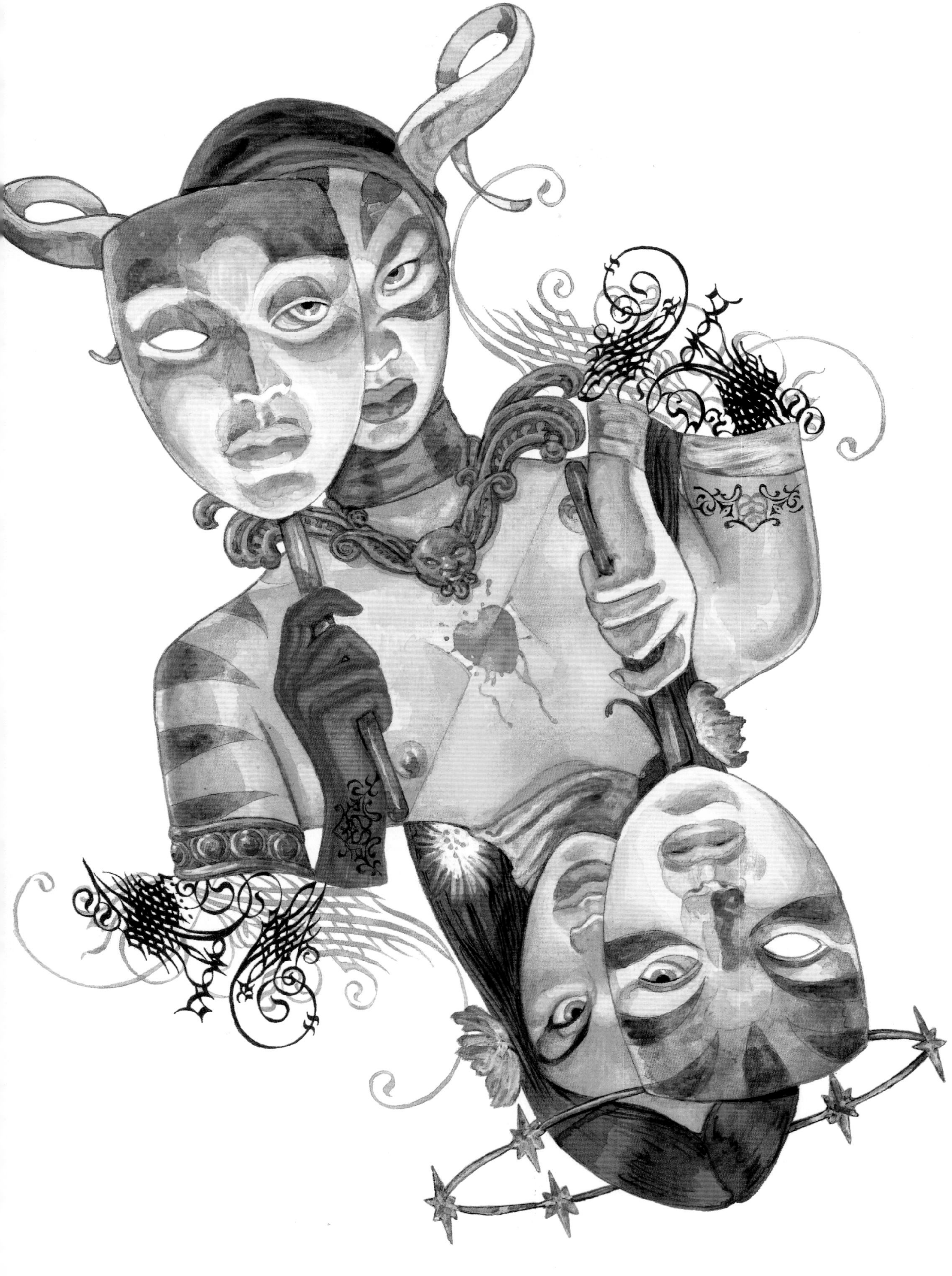

GOLDEN NUGGET
FINALLY!
CAN YOU BELIEVE IT! WATCHING THE OFFICIAL INAUGURATION OF THE NEW PAPPESSES! ITS NOT OFTEN YOU GET TO SEE THAT IN A LIFETIME!
STILL HAPPY! EVEN GIVEN THE PRICE OF THE TICKETS...
GIVEMEE MORE! GIVVVVVVMEEEEEE... GIIIIVEME ONE PAPESSE MORE...

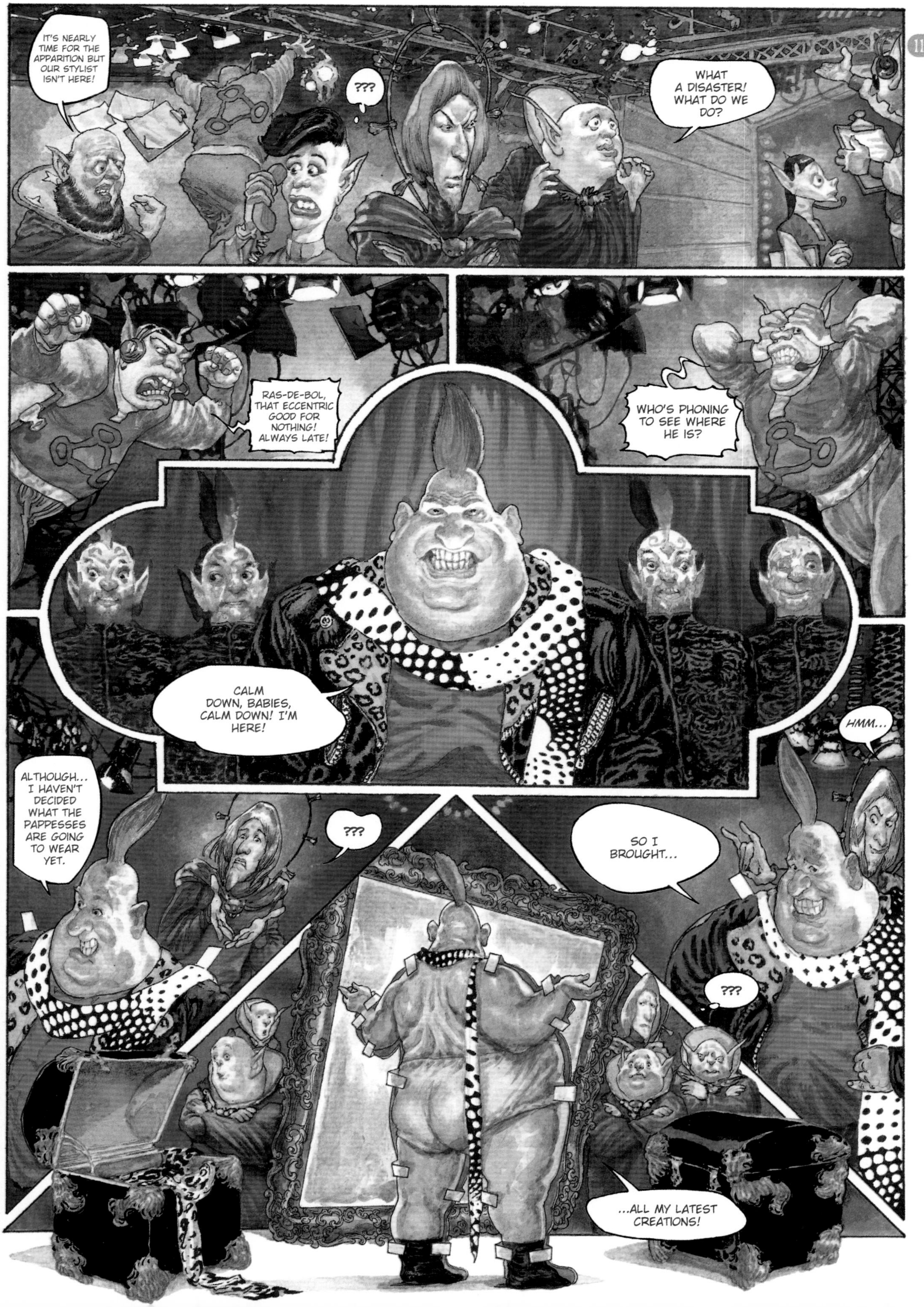
IT'S NEARLY TIME FOR THE APPARITION BUT OUR STYLIST ISN'T HERE!
???
WHAT A DISASTER! WHAT DO WE DO?
RAS-DE-BOL, THAT ECCENTRIC GOOD FOR NOTHING! ALWAYS LATE!
WHO'S PHONING TO SEE WHERE HE IS?
CALM DOWN, BABIES, CALM DOWN! I'M HERE!
HMM...
ALTHOUGH... I HAVEN'T DECIDED WHAT THE PAPPESSES ARE GOING TO WEAR YET.
???
SO I BROUGHT...
???
...ALL MY LATEST CREATIONS!

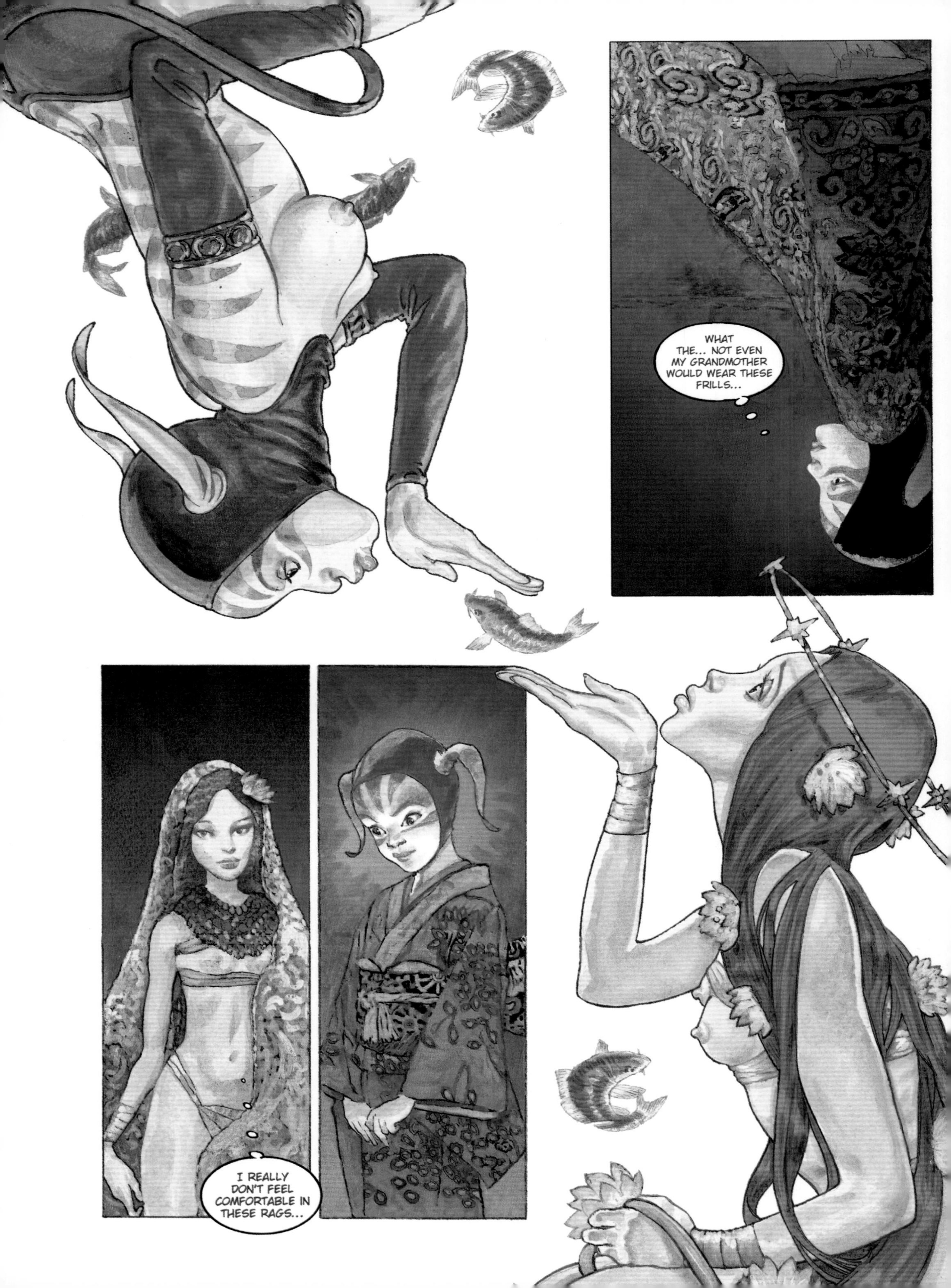
WHAT THE... NOT EVEN MY GRANDMOTHER WOULD WEAR THESE FRILLS...
I REALLY DON'T FEEL COMFORTABLE IN THESE RAGS...

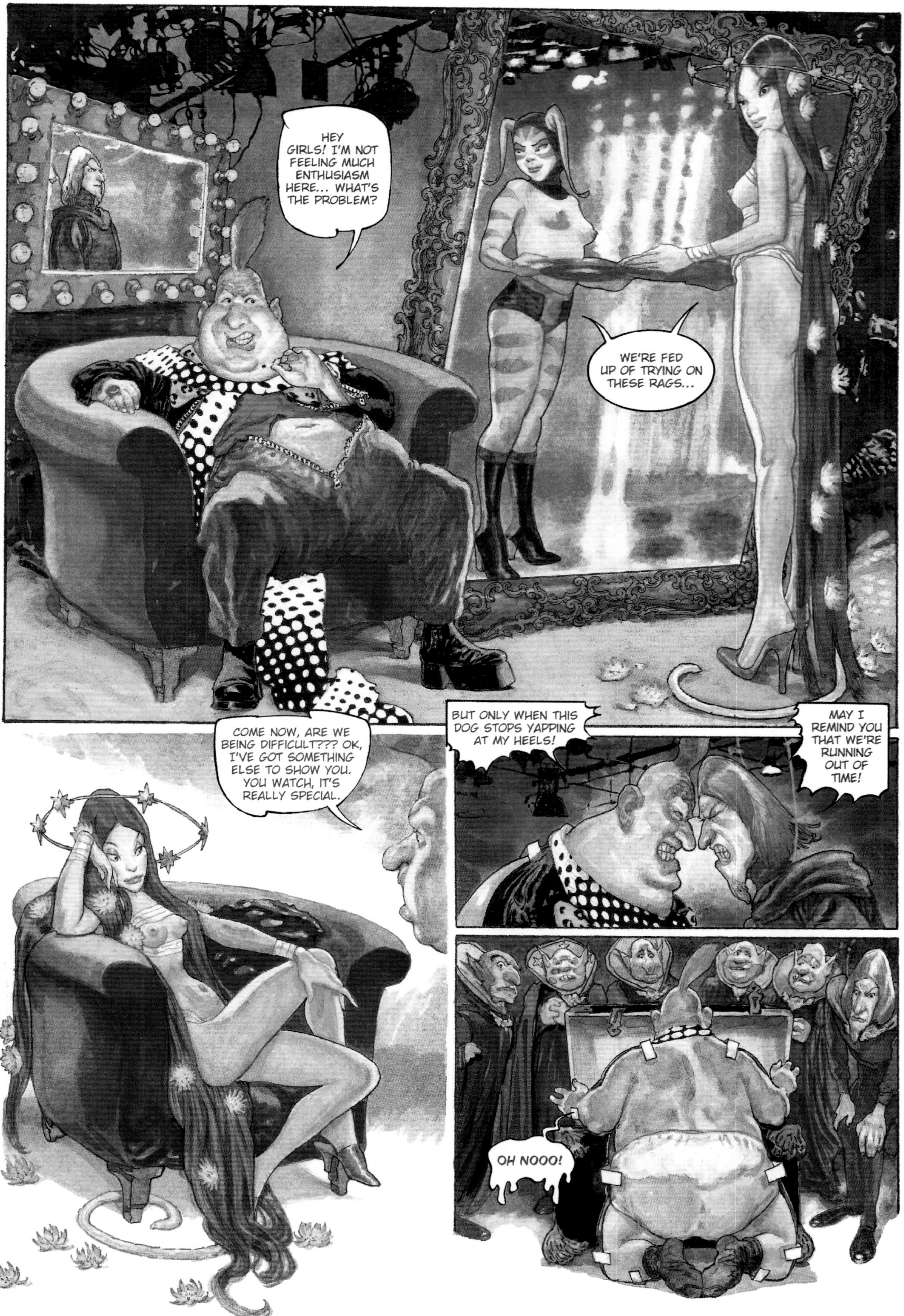
HEY GIRLS! I'M NOT FEELING MUCH ENTHUSIASM HERE... WHAT'S THE PROBLEM?
WE'RE FED UP OF TRYING ON THESE RAGS...
COME NOW, ARE WE BEING DIFFICULT??? OK, I'VE GOT SOMETHING ELSE TO SHOW YOU. YOU WATCH, IT'S REALLY SPECIAL.
BUT ONLY WHEN THIS DOG STOPS YAPPING AT MY HEELS!
MAY I REMIND YOU THAT WE'RE RUNNING OUT OF TIME!
OH NOOO!

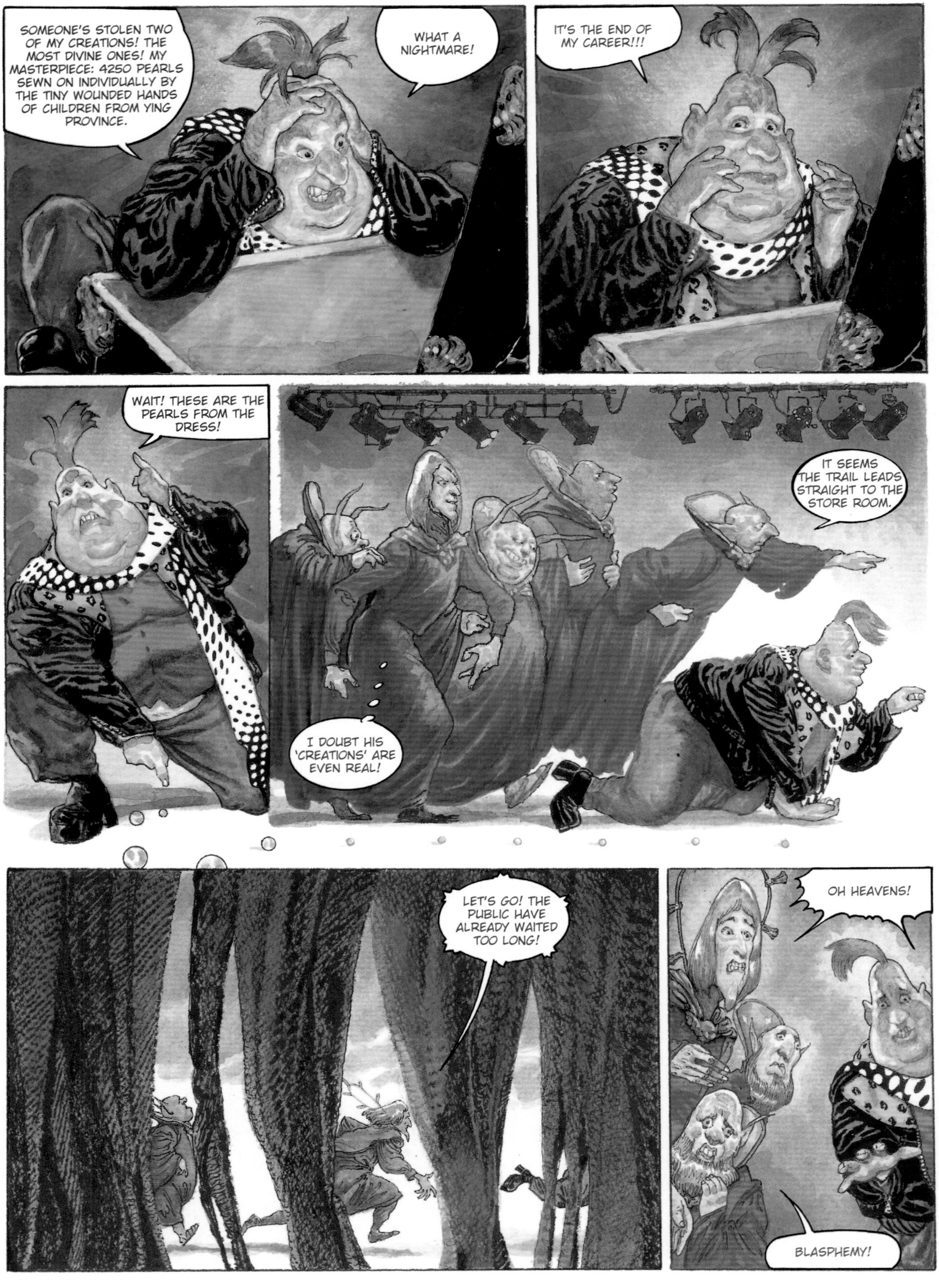
SOMEONE'S STOLEN TWO OF MY CREATIONS! THE MOST DIVINE ONES! MY MASTERPIECE: 4250 PEARLS SEWN ON INDIVIDUALLY BY THE TINY WOUNDED HANDS OF CHILDREN FROM YING PROVINCE.
WHAT A NIGHTMARE!
IT'S THE END OF MY CAREER!!!
WAIT! THESE ARE THE PEARLS FROM THE DRESS!
IT SEEMS THE TRAIL LEADS STRAIGHT TO THE STORE ROOM.
I DOUBT HIS 'CREATIONS' ARE EVEN REAL!
LET'S GO! THE PUBLIC HAVE ALREADY WAITED TOO LONG!
OH HEAVENS!
BLASPHEMY!

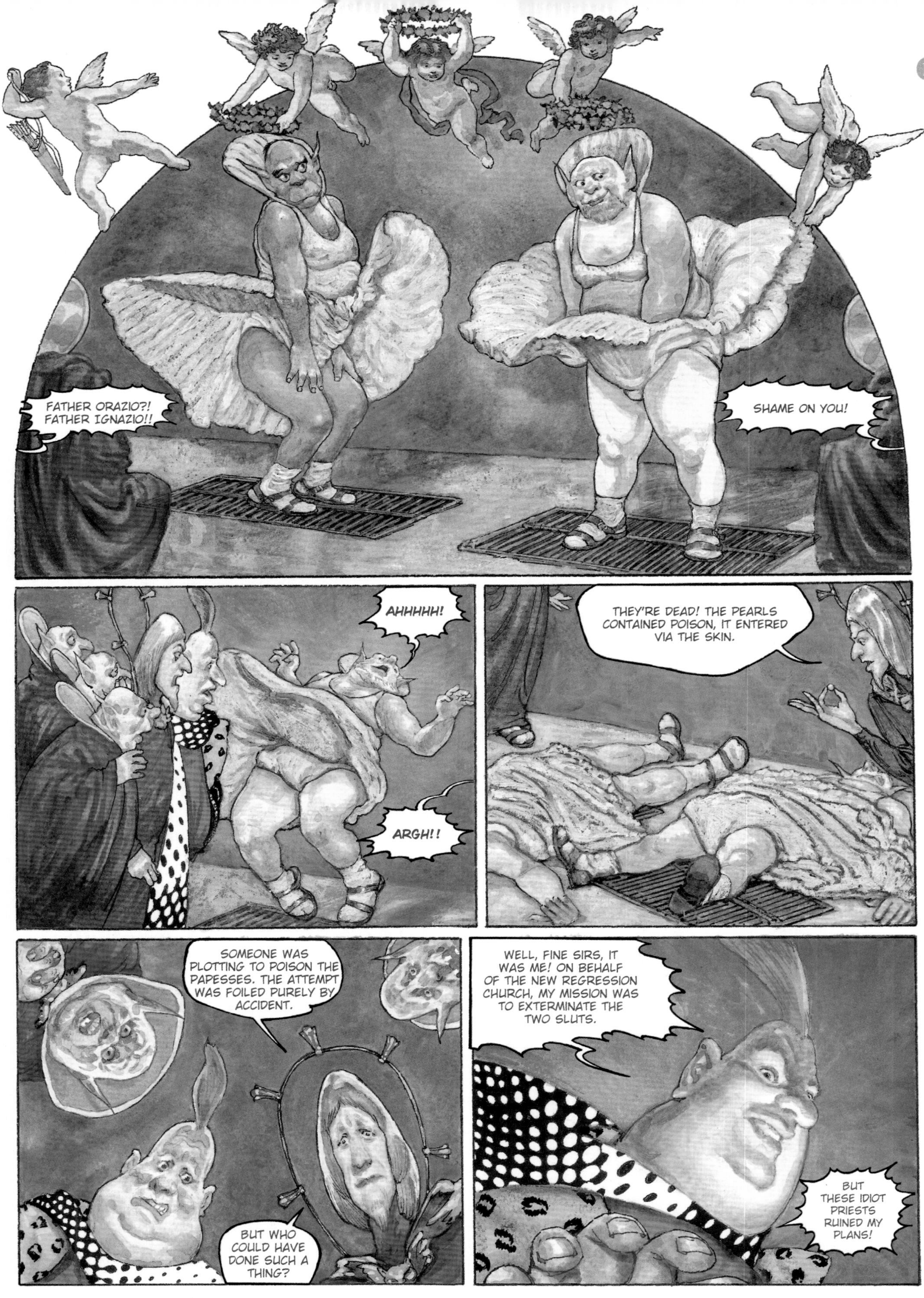
FATHER ORAZIO?! FATHER IGNAZIO!!
SHAME ON YOU!
AHHHHH!
ARGH!!
THEY'RE DEAD! THE PEARLS CONTAINED POISON, IT ENTERED VIA THE SKIN.
SOMEONE WAS PLOTTING TO POISON THE PAPESSES. THE ATTEMPT WAS FOILED PURELY BY ACCIDENT.
BUT WHO COULD HAVE DONE SUCH A THING?
WELL, FINE SIRS, IT WAS ME! ON BEHALF OF THE NEW REGRESSION CHURCH, MY MISSION WAS TO EXTERMINATE THE TWO SLUTS.
BUT THESE IDIOT PRIESTS RUINED MY PLANS!

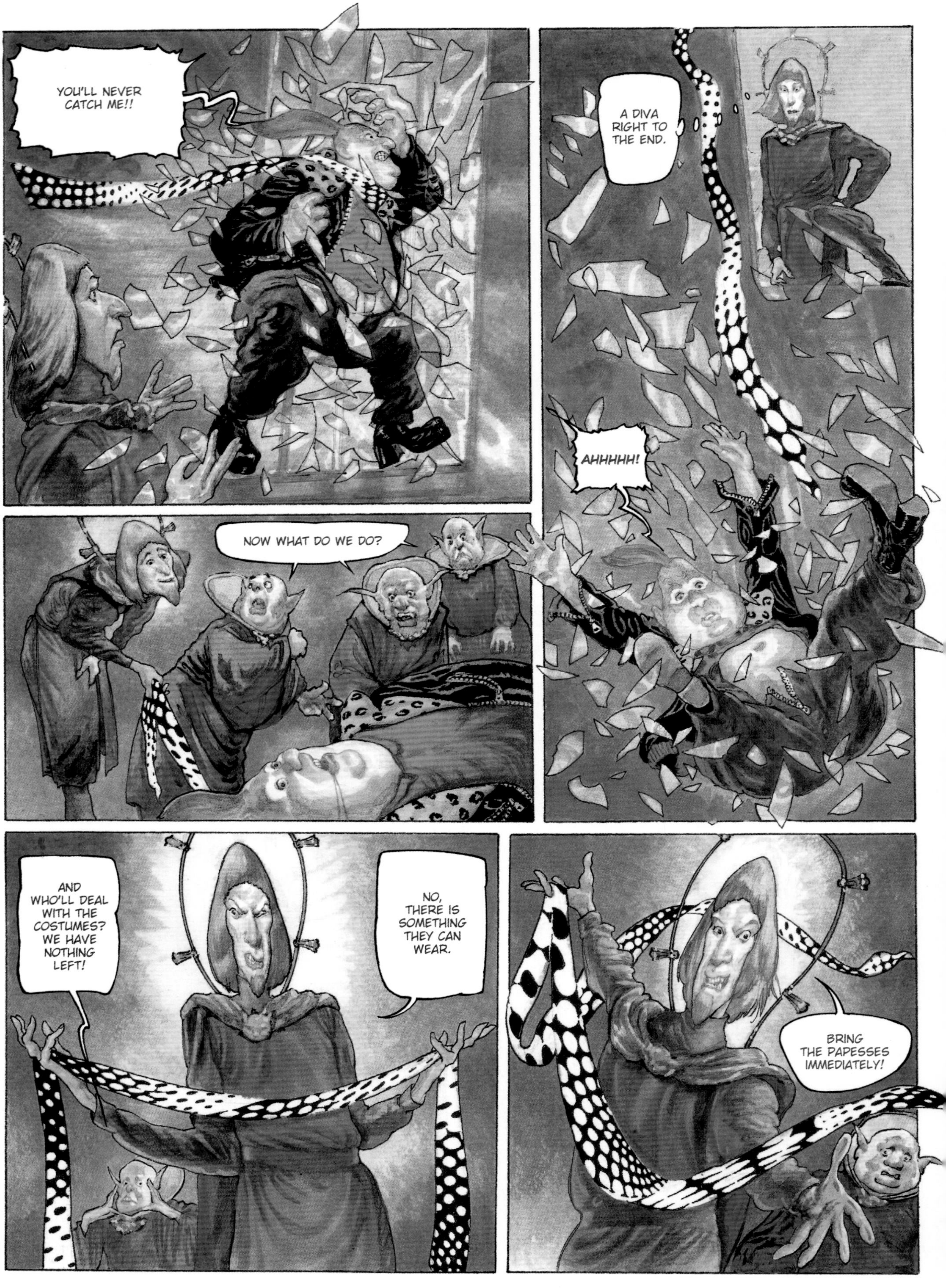
YOU'LL NEVER CATCH ME!!
A DIVA RIGHT TO THE END.
AHHHHH!
NOW WHAT DO WE DO?
AND WHO'LL DEAL WITH THE COSTUMES? WE HAVE NOTHING LEFT!
NO, THERE IS SOMETHING THEY CAN WEAR.
BRING THE PAPESSES IMMEDIATELY!

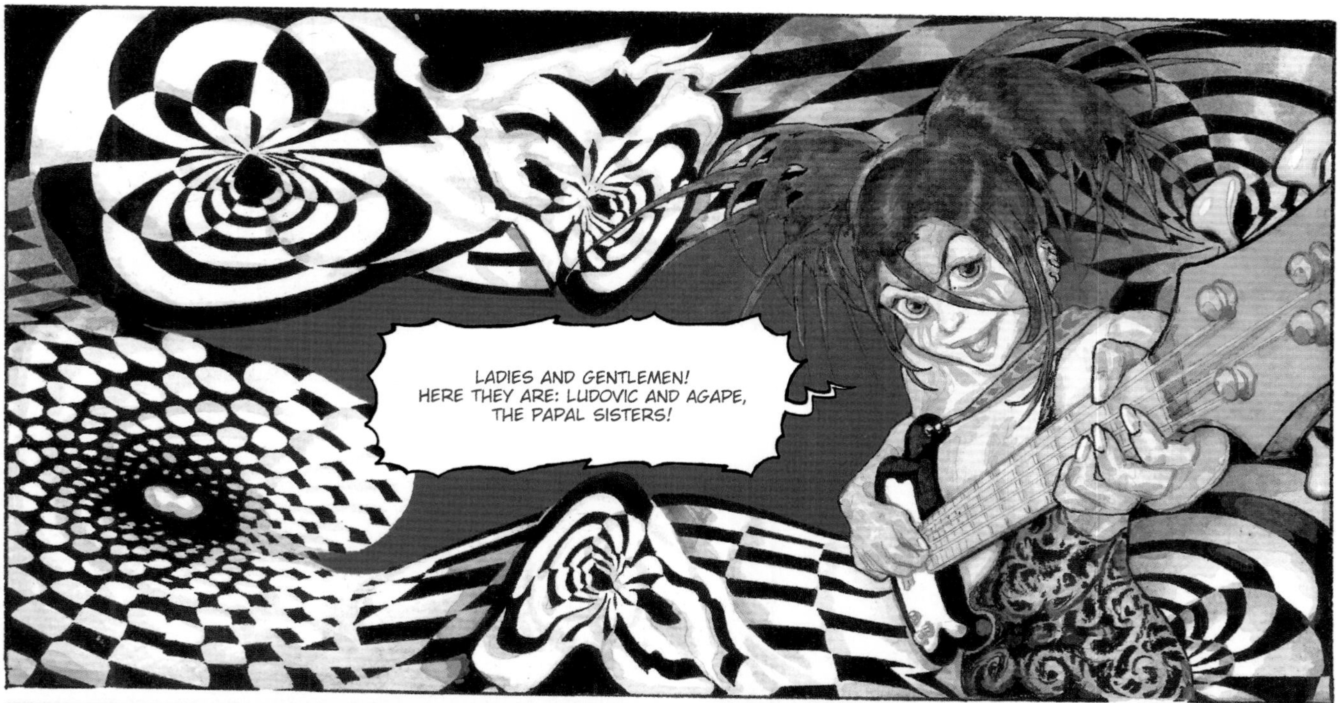
LADIES AND GENTLEMEN!
HERE THEY ARE: LUDOVIC AND AGAPE,
THE PAPAL SISTERS!

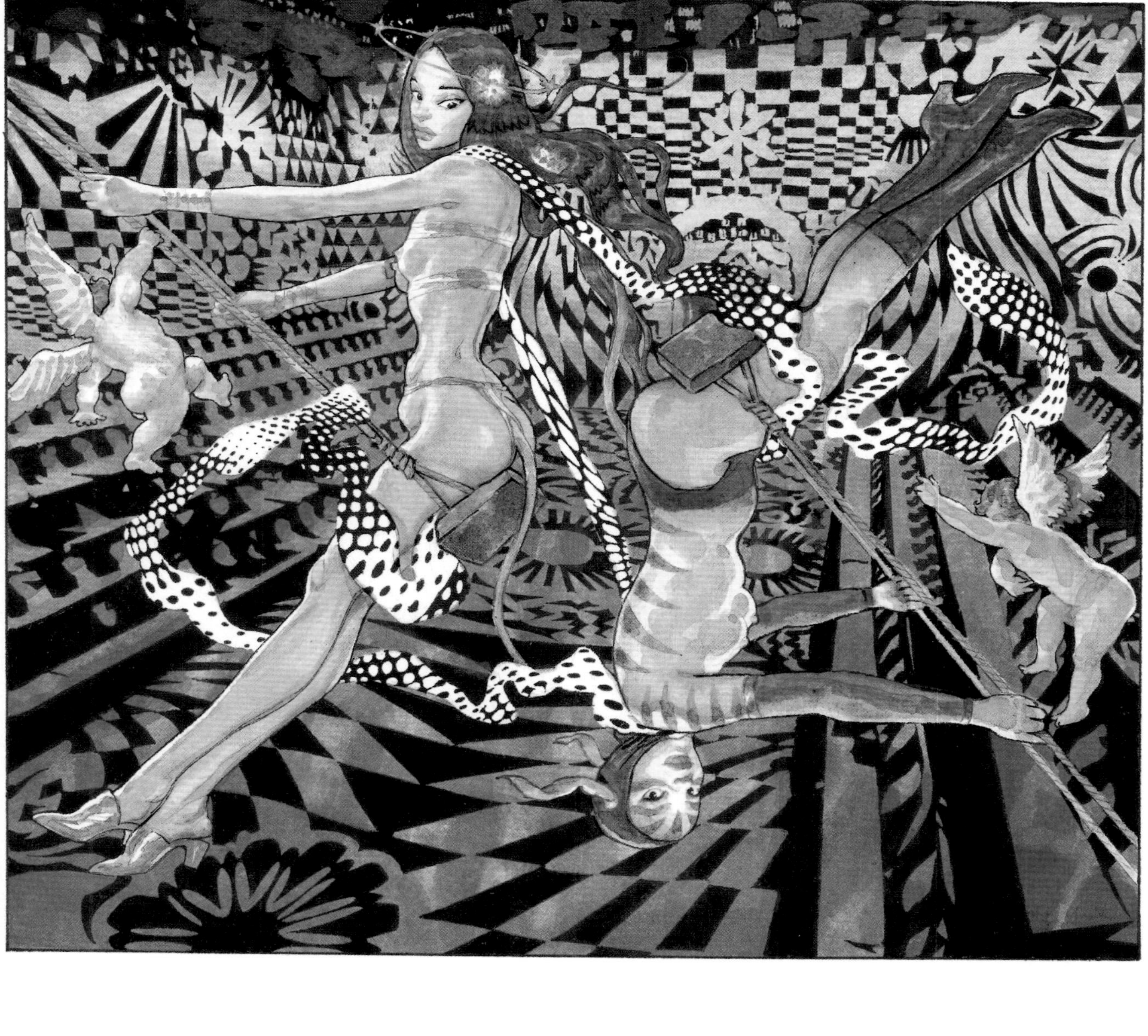

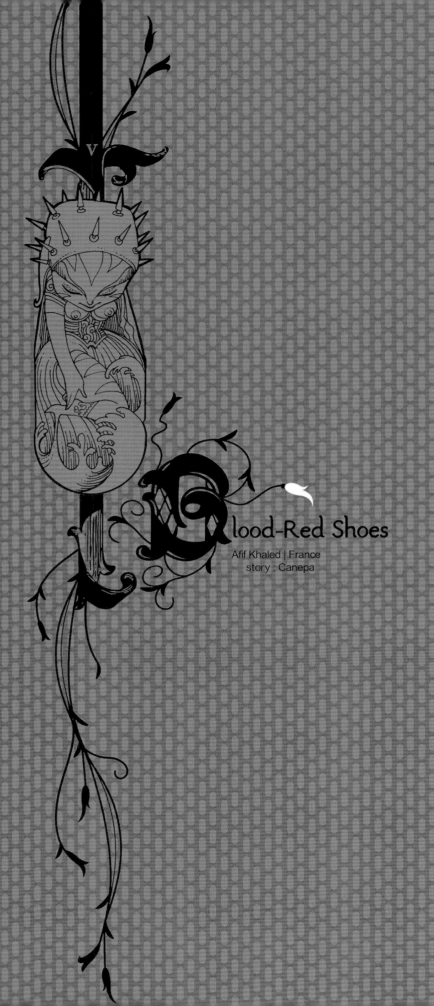

Blood-Red Shoes

Afif Khaled | France
story : Canepa

"Oh it's gonna be the way you always thought it would be
But it's gonna be no illusion
Oh its gonna be the way you always dreamt about it
But it's gonna be really happening to ya.

Kate Bush

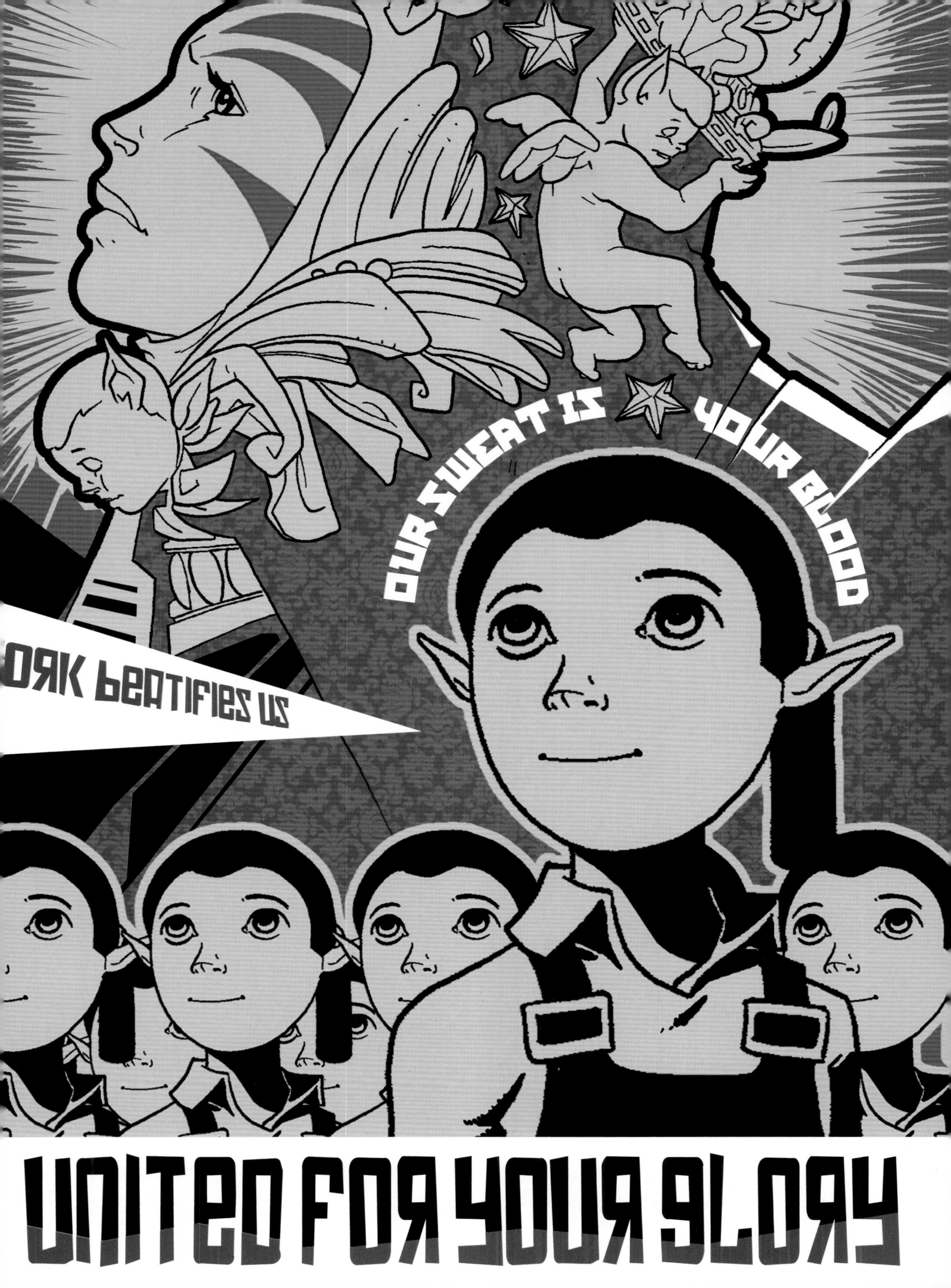
OUR SWEAT IS YOUR BLOOD
ORK BEATIFIES US
UNITED FOR YOUR GLORY

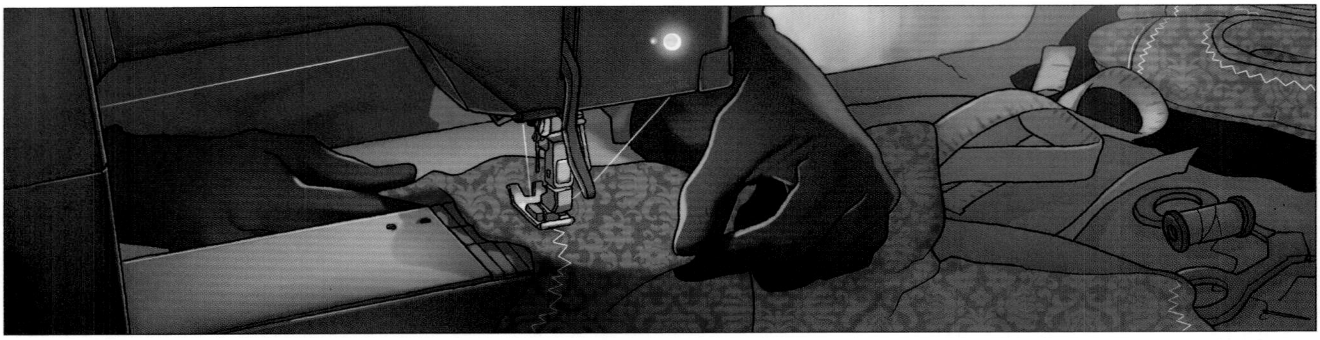

I salute you, oh, Queen.

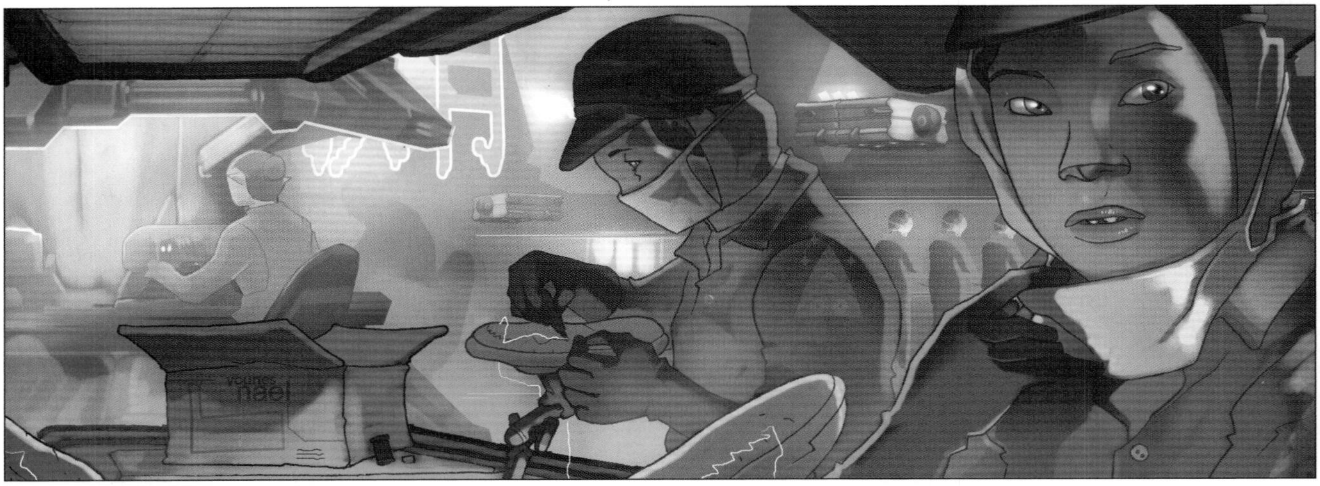

Mother of mercy, our life, our comfort, our hope, hail!

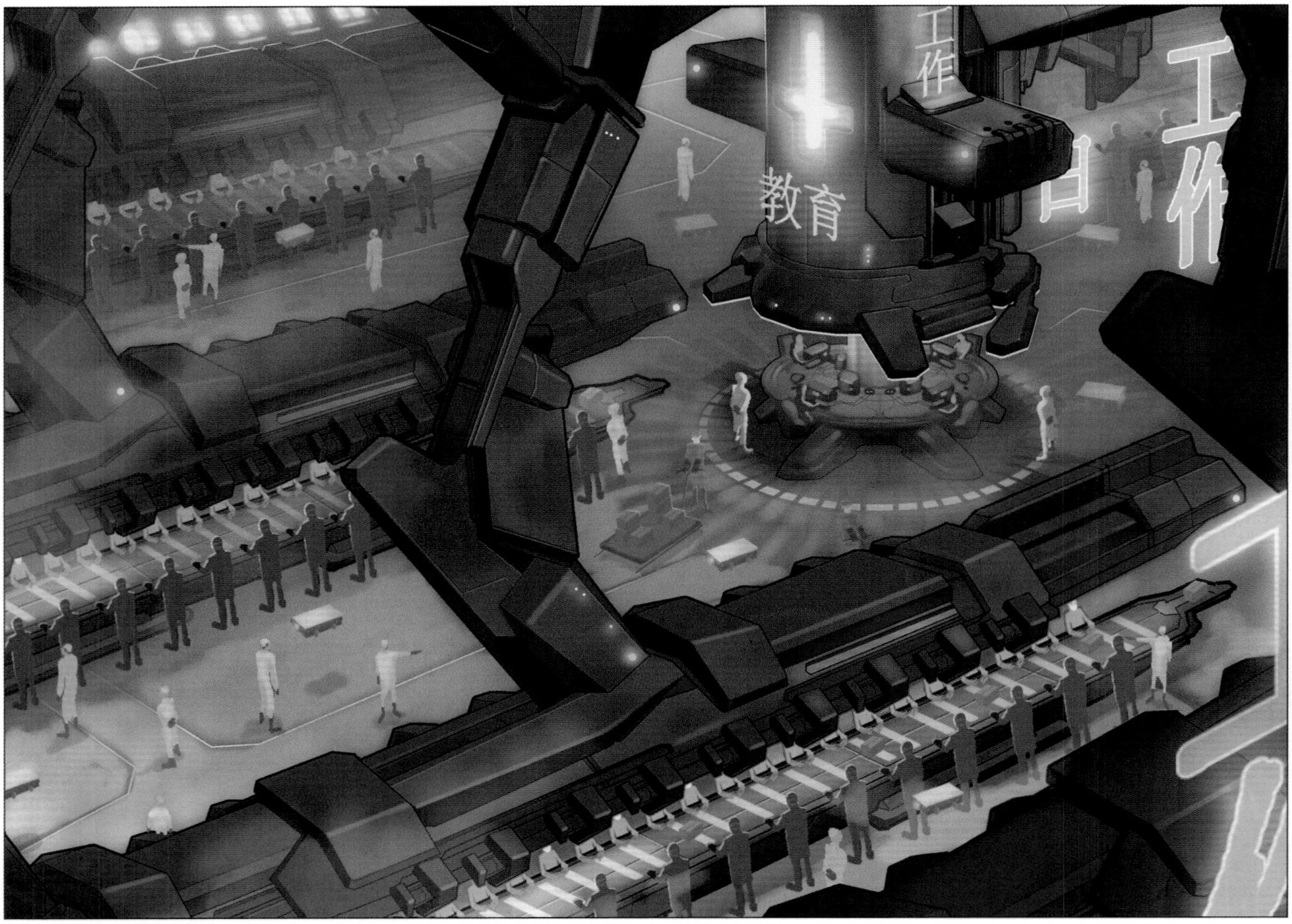
工作
教育
工作

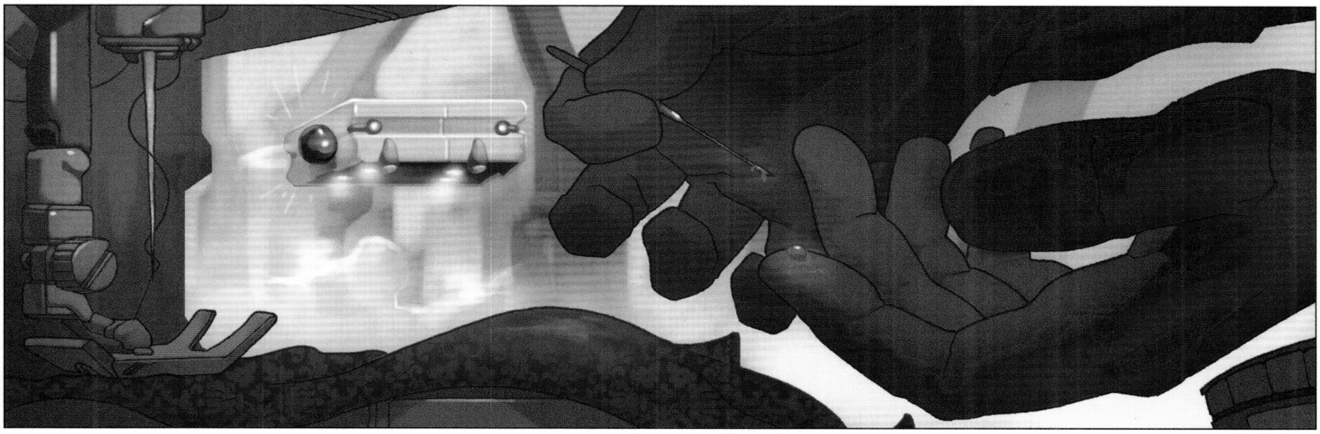

Children of Ludovic, we raise our hopes to you,

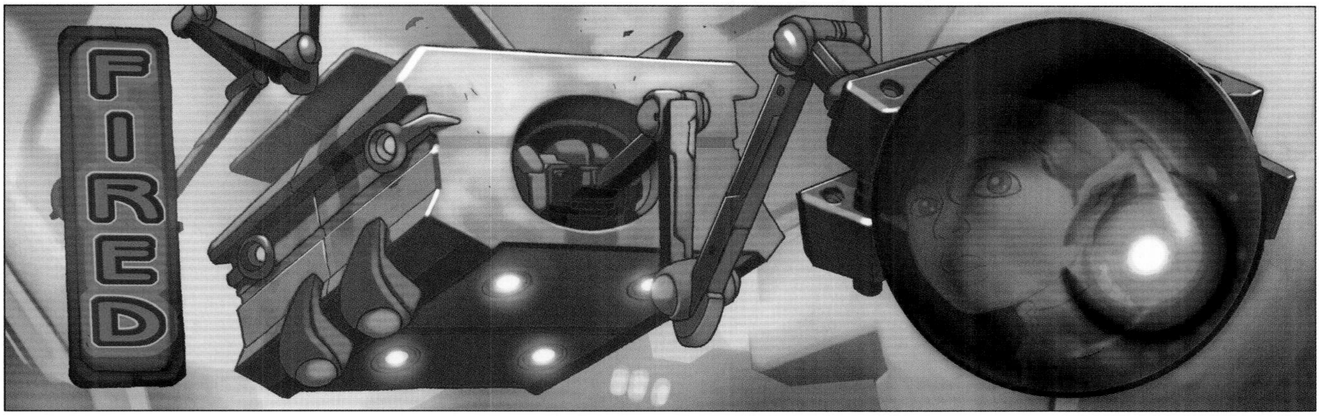
FIRED

we long for you.

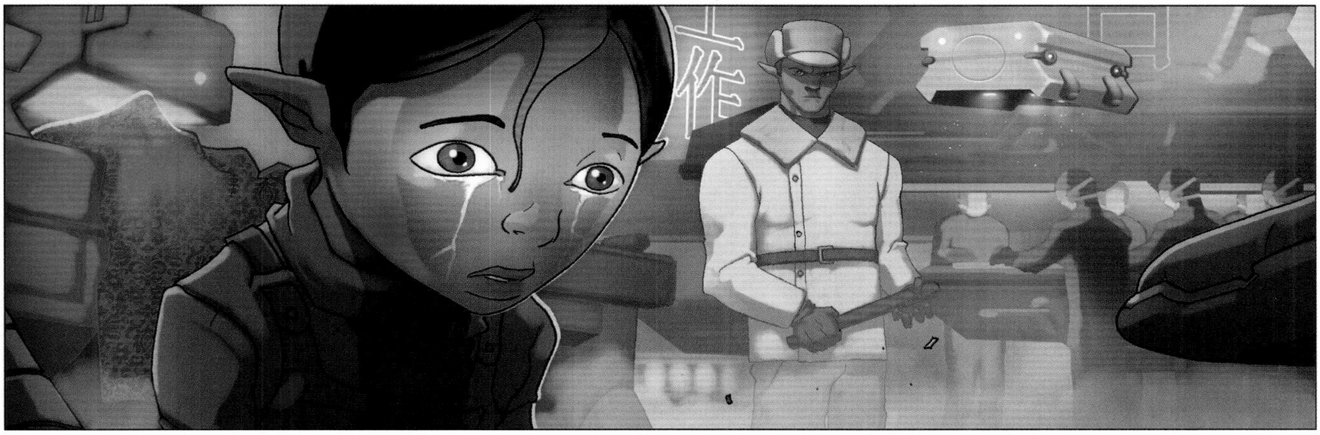
作

Wailing and crying in this valley of tears.

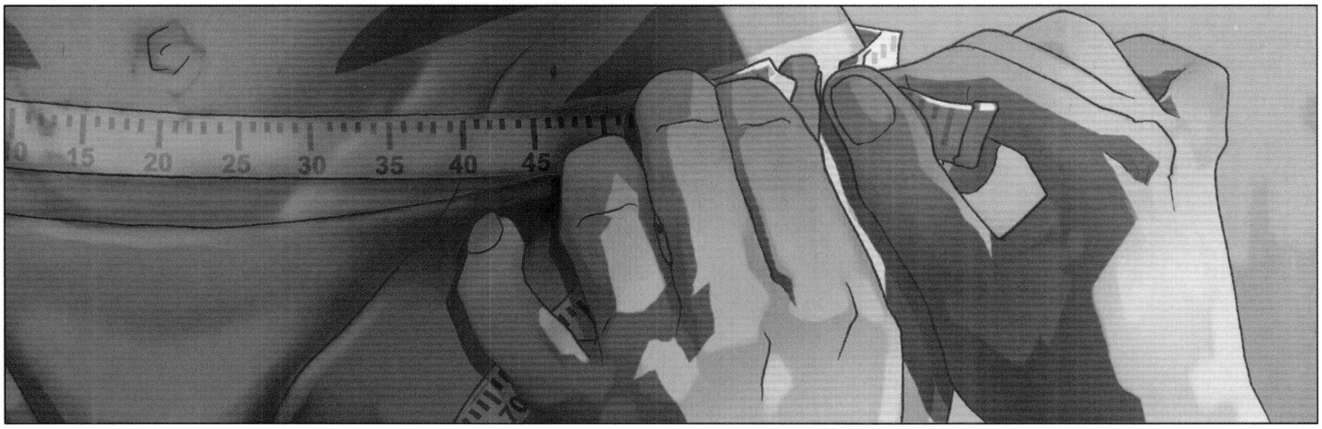
15 20 25 30 35 40 45

Oh, pure soul!

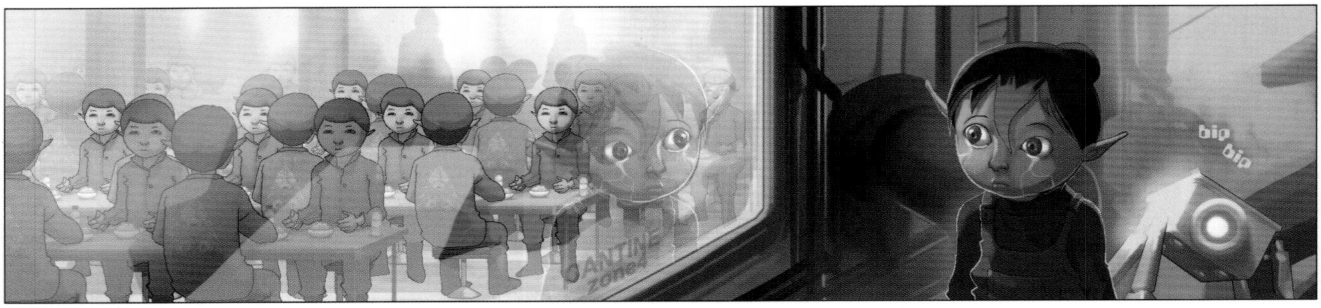
bip
bip

We beg you...

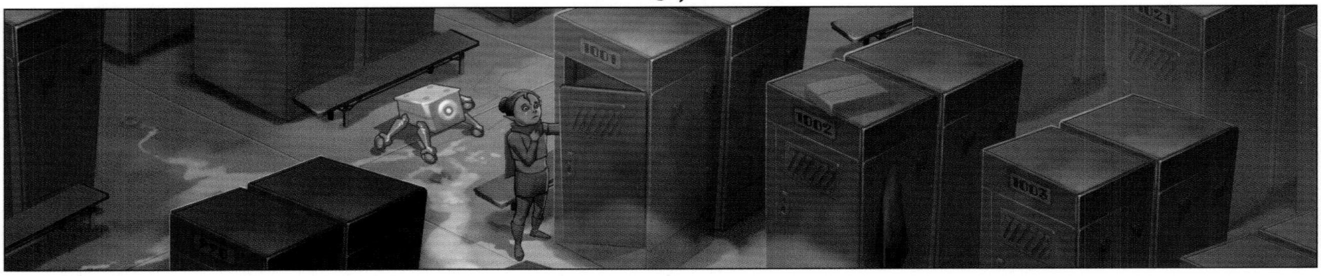
1001
1002
1003

turn your merciful gaze upon us.

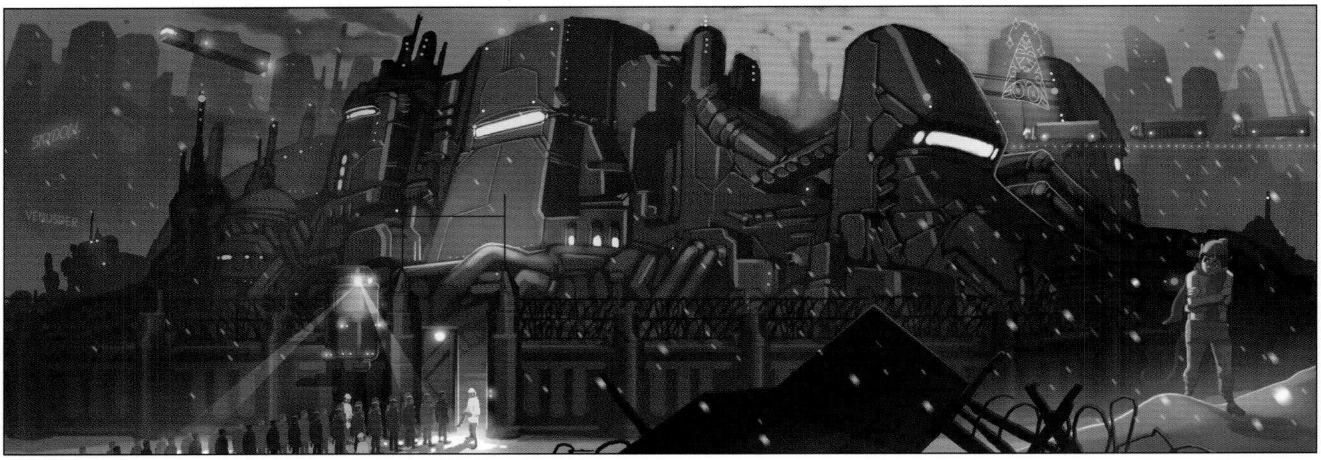

You who never strayed from baptismal innocence,

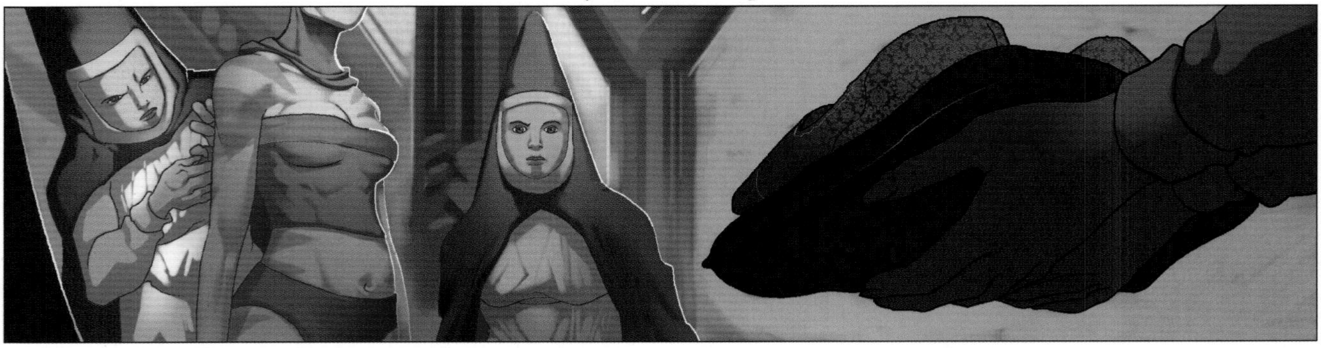

who fights so hard out of charity for the souls burdened by suffering...

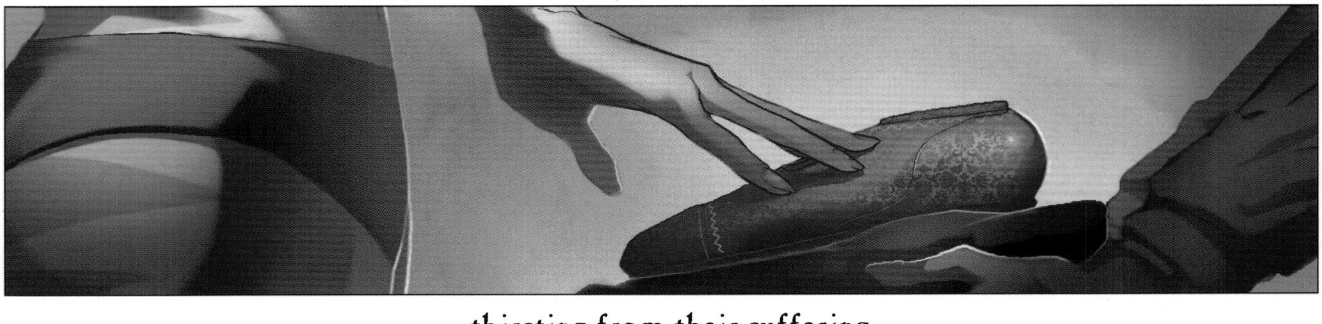

...thirsting from their suffering.

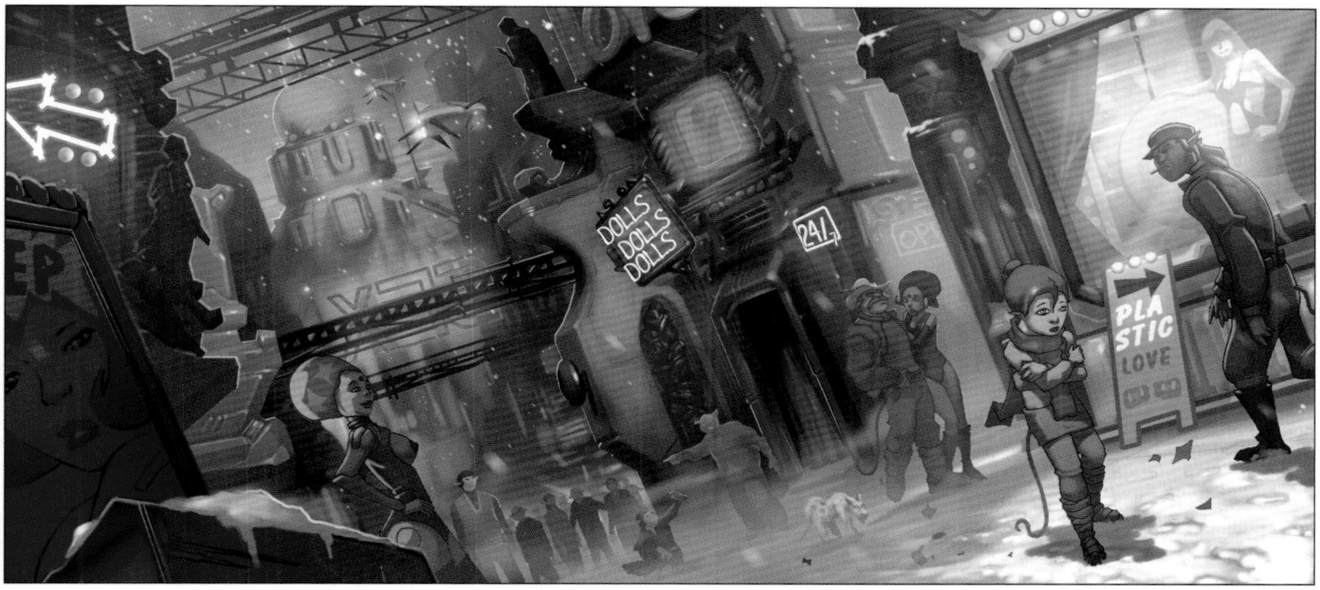
DOLLS
DOLLS
DOLLS
PLA
STIC
LOVE

We send you our faithful prayer for your grace, of which we have so much need.

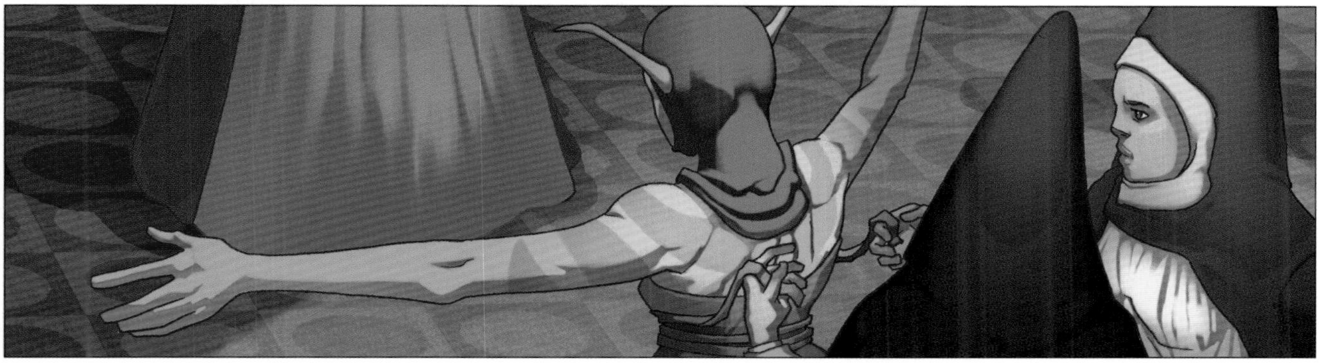

Oh, immaculate virgin,

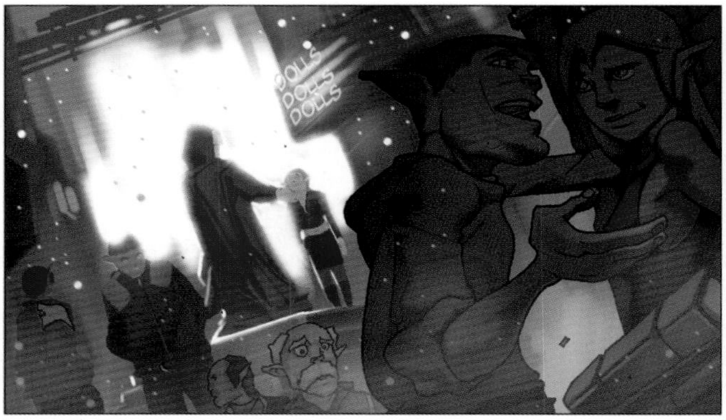
DOLLS
DOLLS
DOLLS

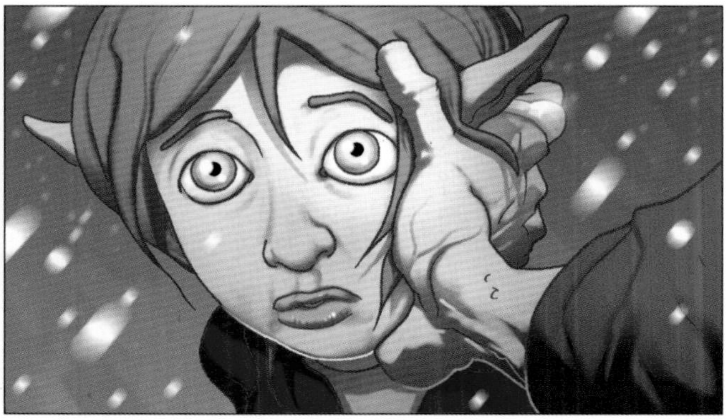

deign your benevolent gaze upon me.

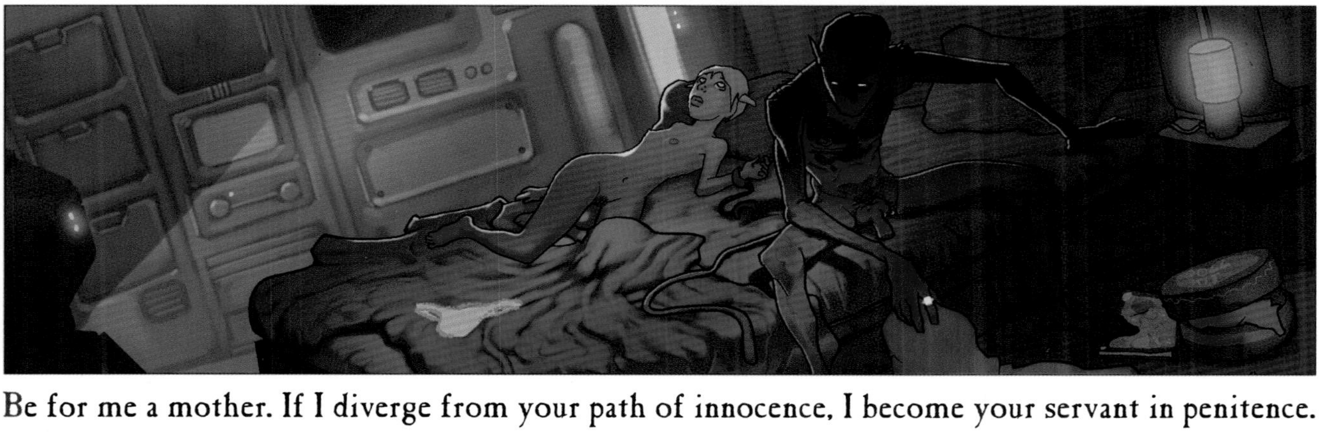

Be for me a mother. If I diverge from your path of innocence, I become your servant in penitence.

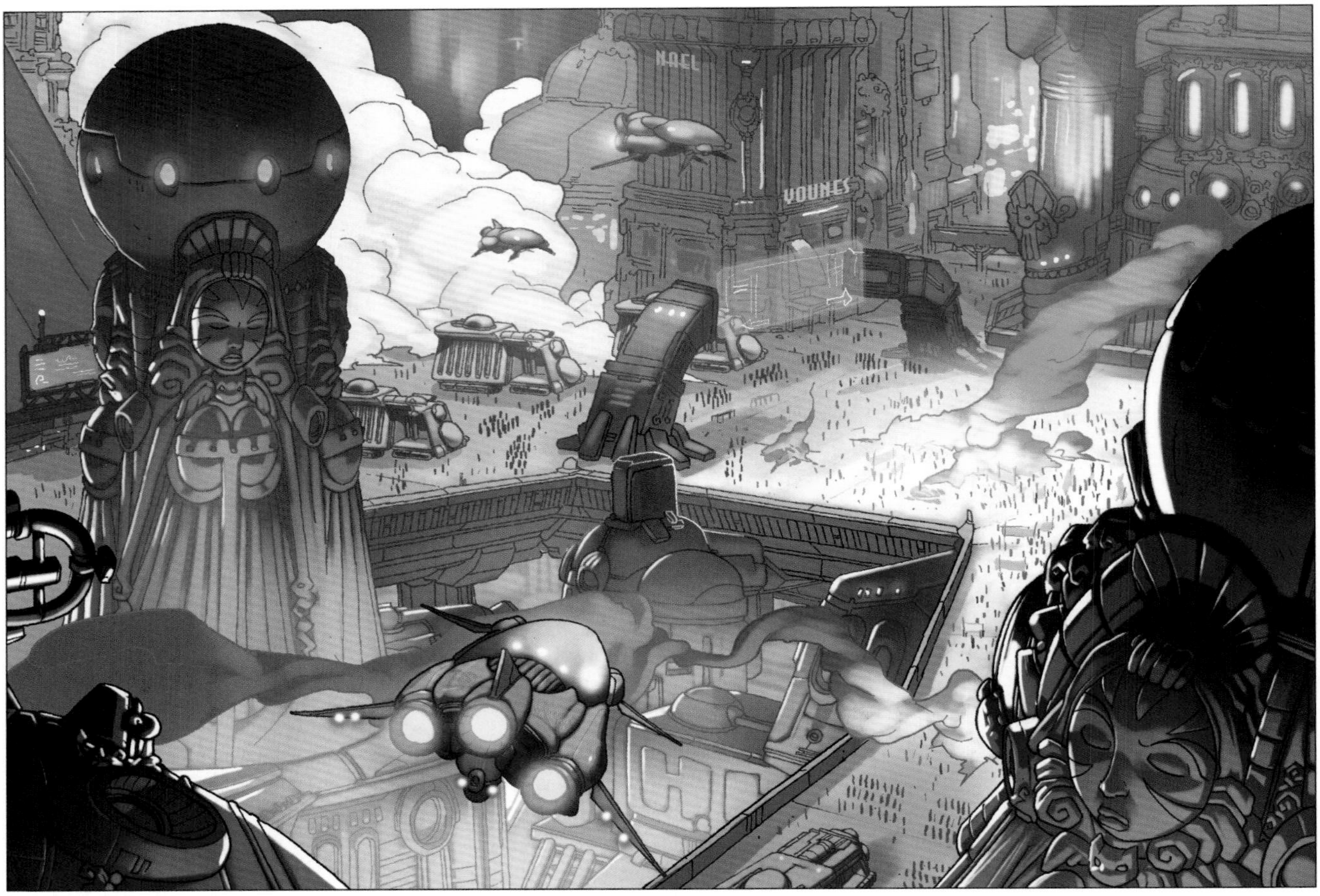

Shine your divine light upon those still blind to your path, guide these poor sinners.

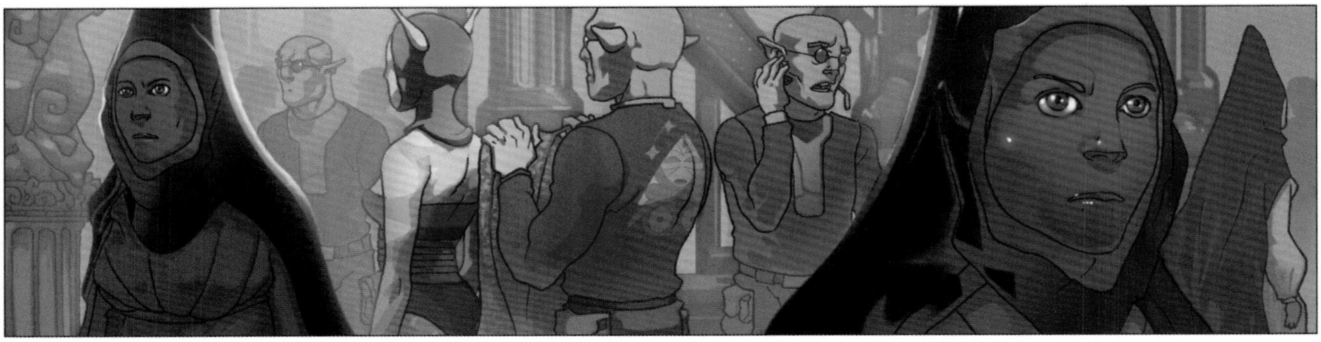

I throw myself at your feet, tears fill my eyes and I weep.

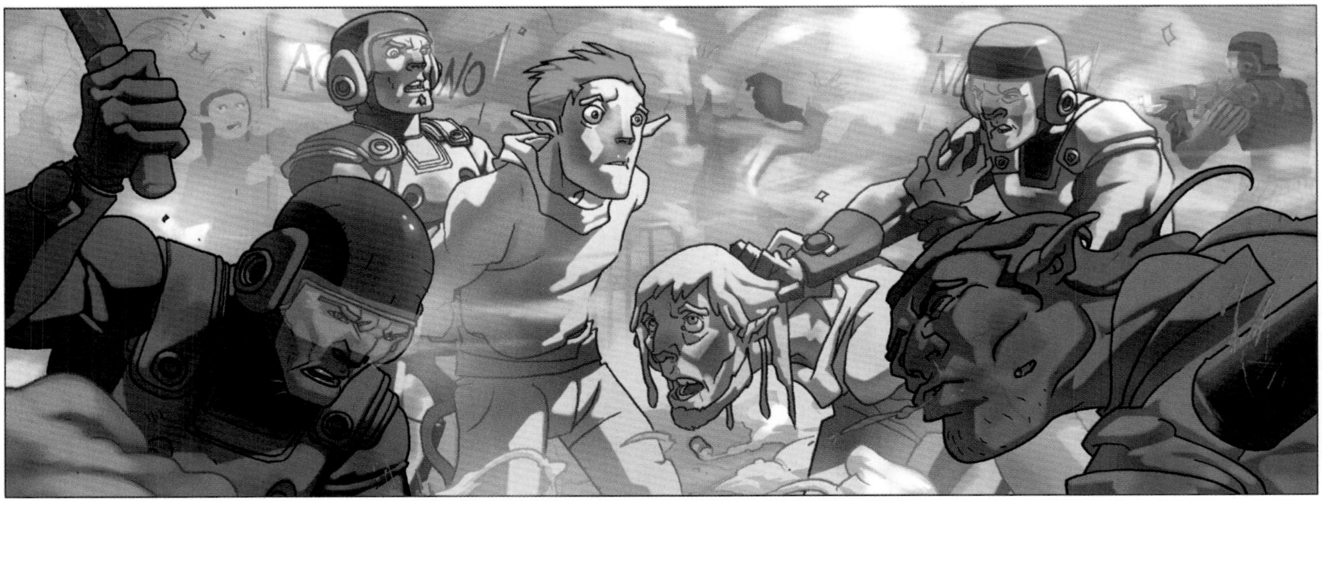

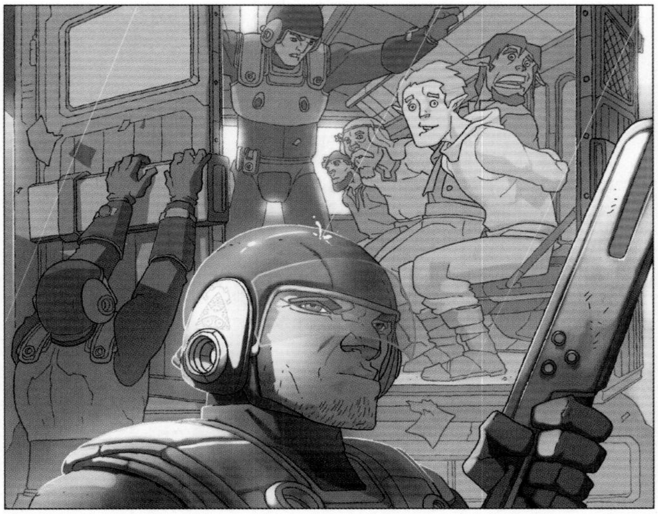

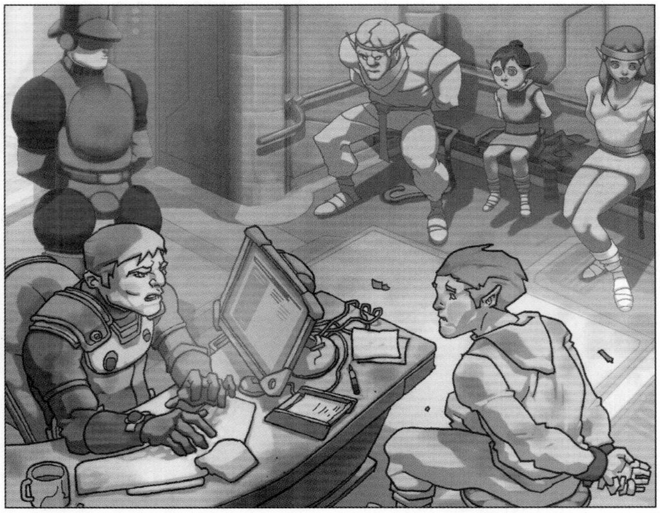

Give unto us the strength to confess our sins.

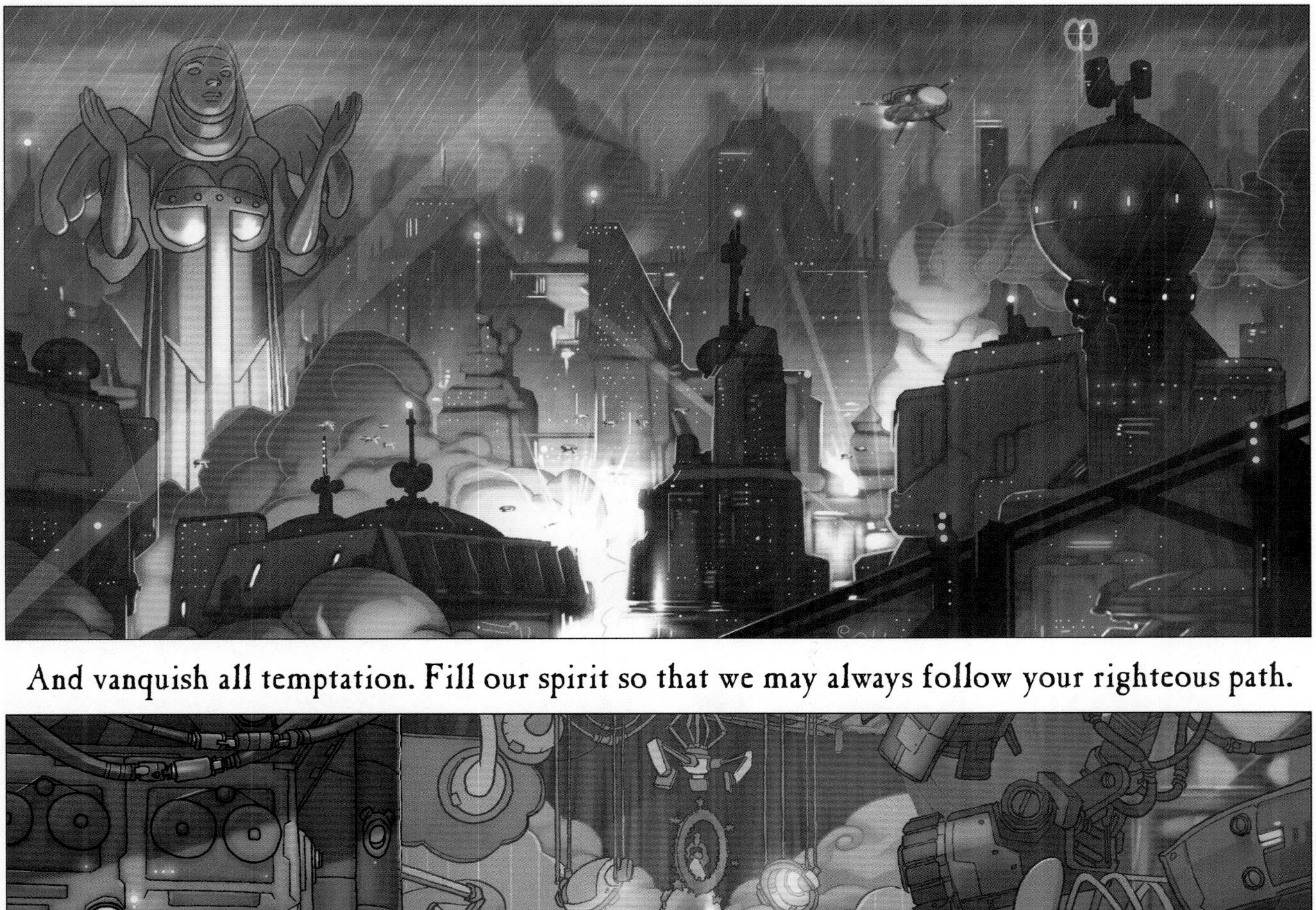

And vanquish all temptation. Fill our spirit so that we may always follow your righteous path.

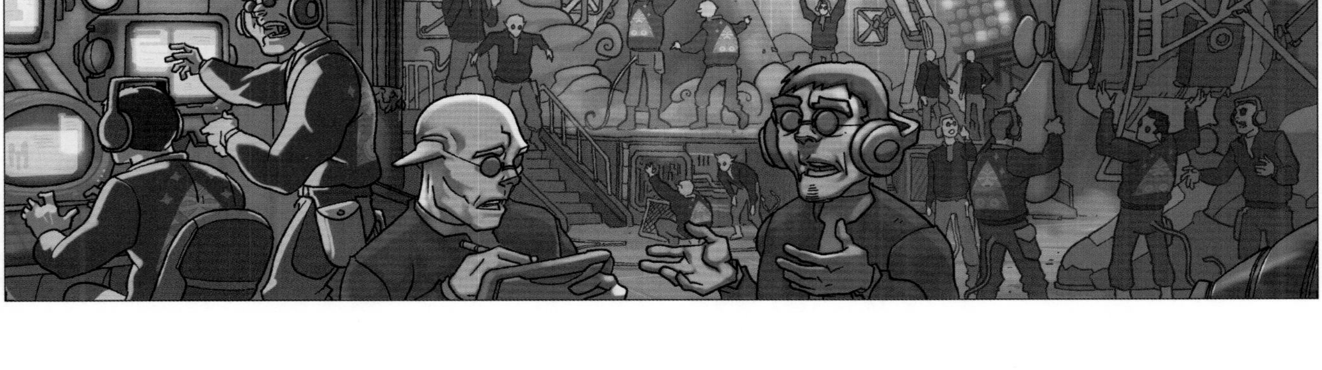

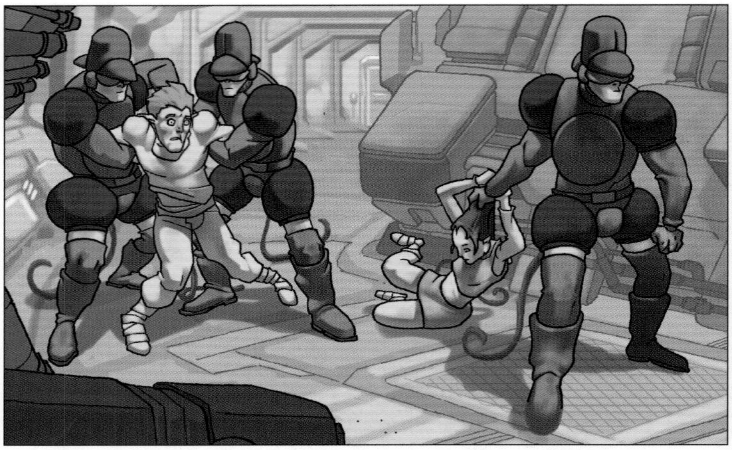

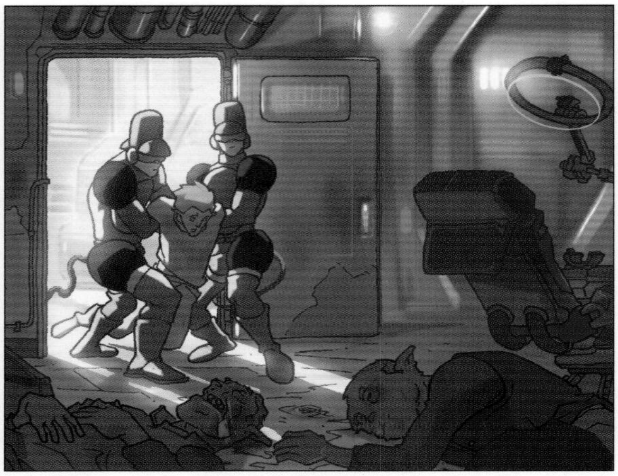

Oh, you, who see us wailing and crying...

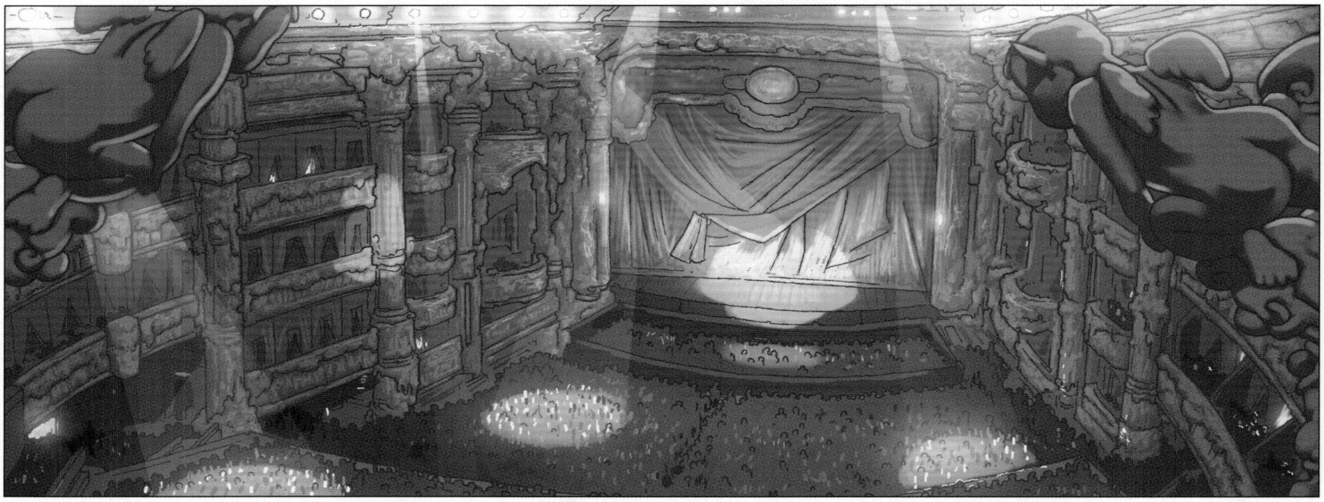

keep us in our resolve as we face the pitfalls of destiny...

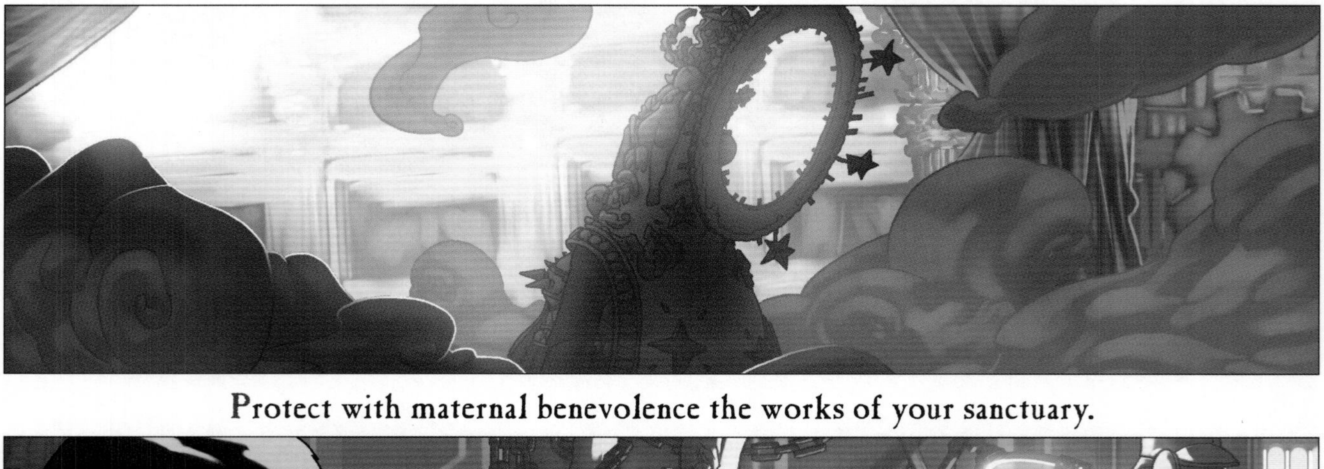

Protect with maternal benevolence the works of your sanctuary.

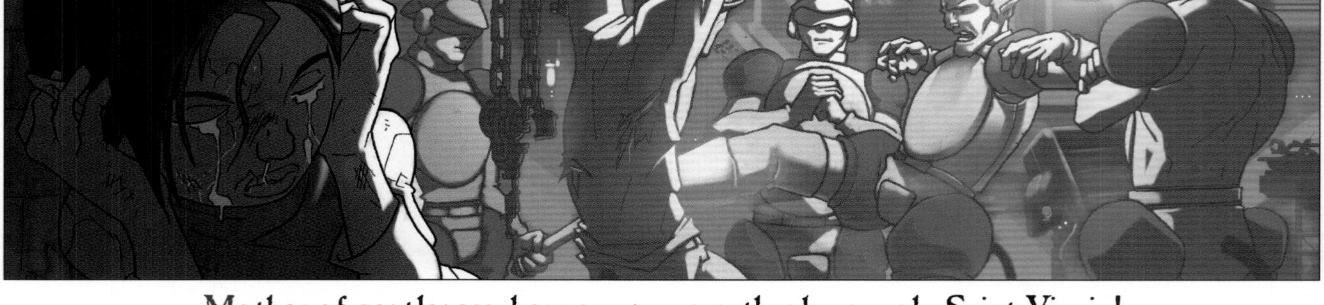

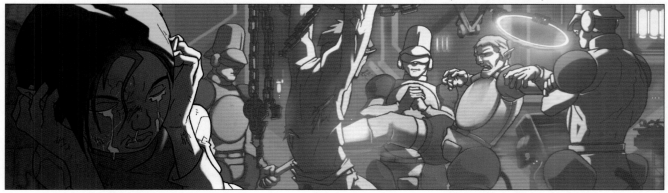

Mother of gentleness, hear our prayers; thank you, oh, Saint Virgin!

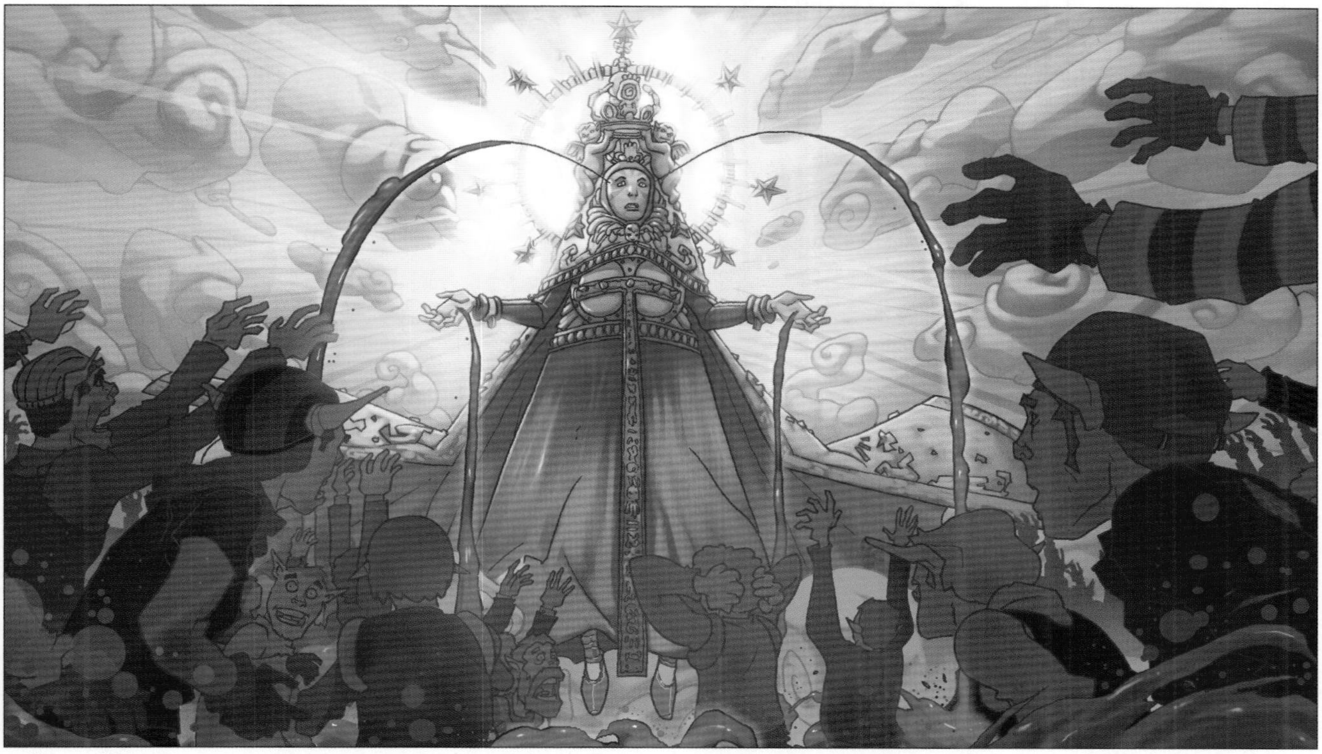

You, the source and giver and divine grace, allow us, your children, to praise you for eternity...

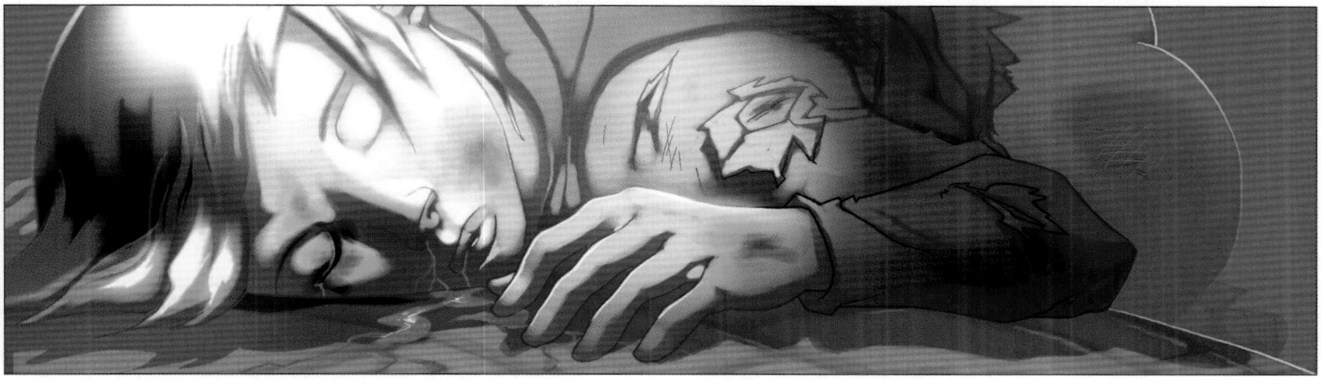

Oh, sweet Virgin Ludovic, burn in our hearts your Divine Love for all our lives,

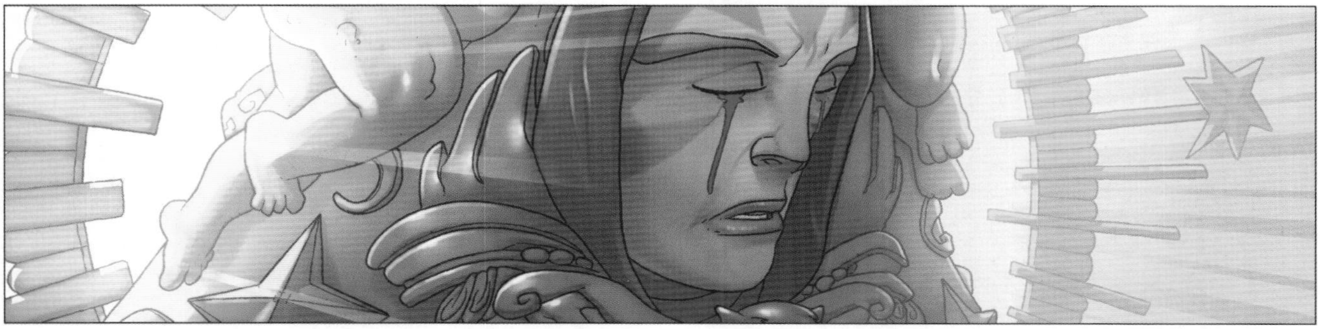

So that our joy may endure in Heaven.

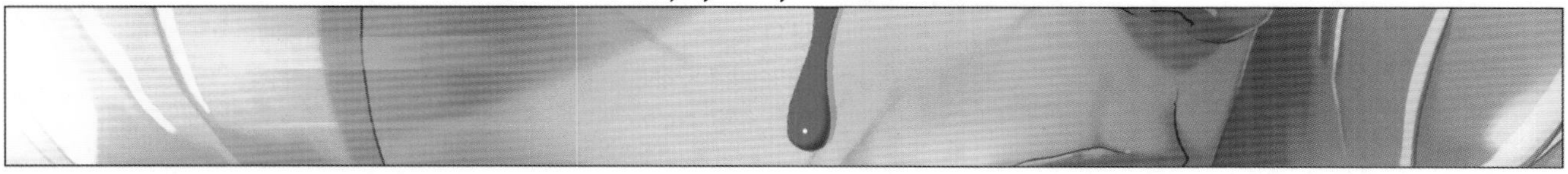

Amen.

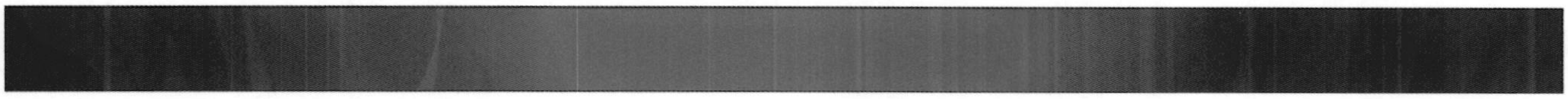

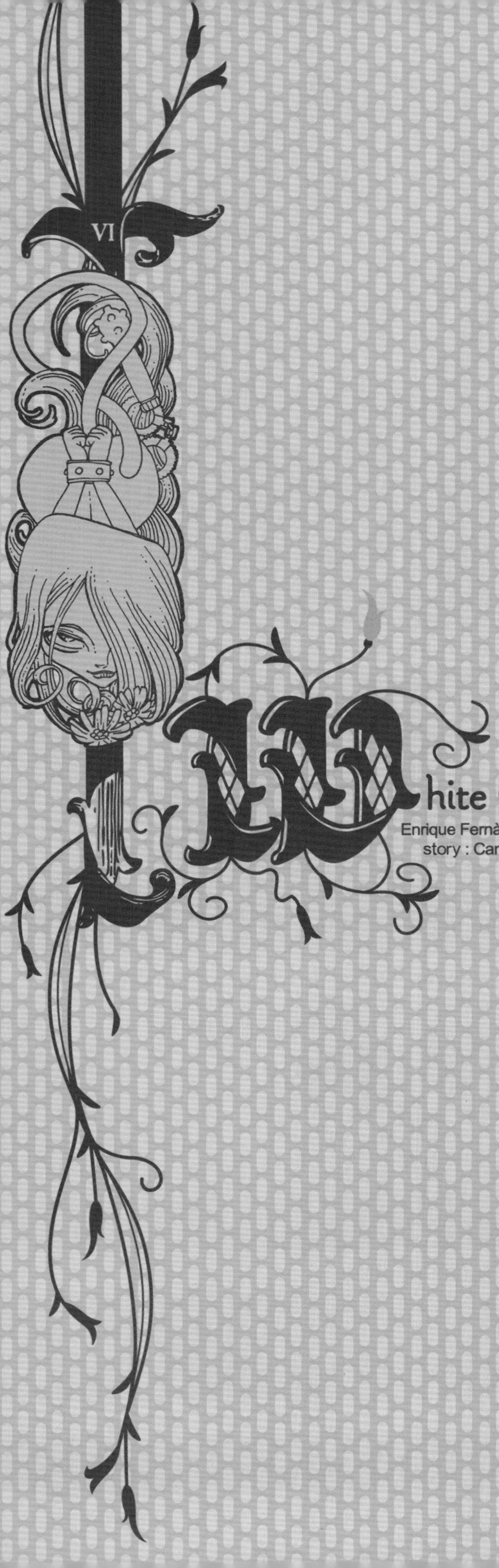
VI

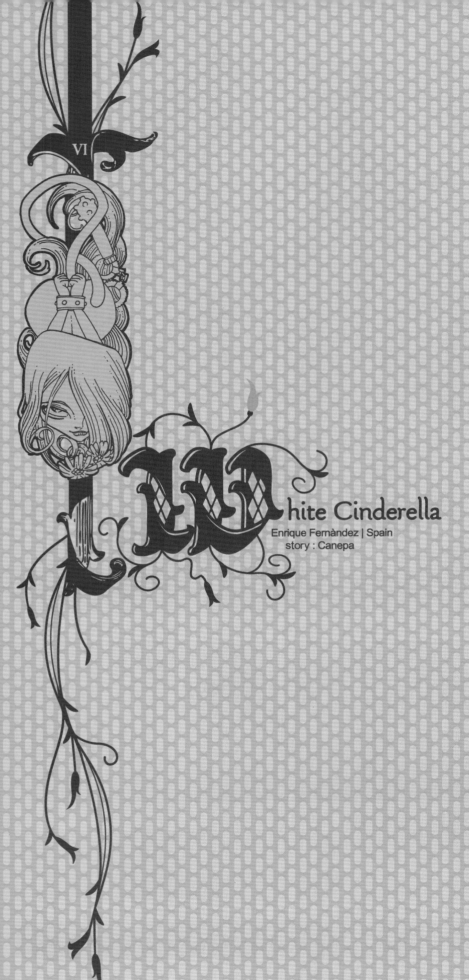

White Cinderella

Enrique Fernàndez | Spain
story : Canepa

"Cut the toe off; when you are queen you will
have no more need to go on foot."

The Brothers Grimm

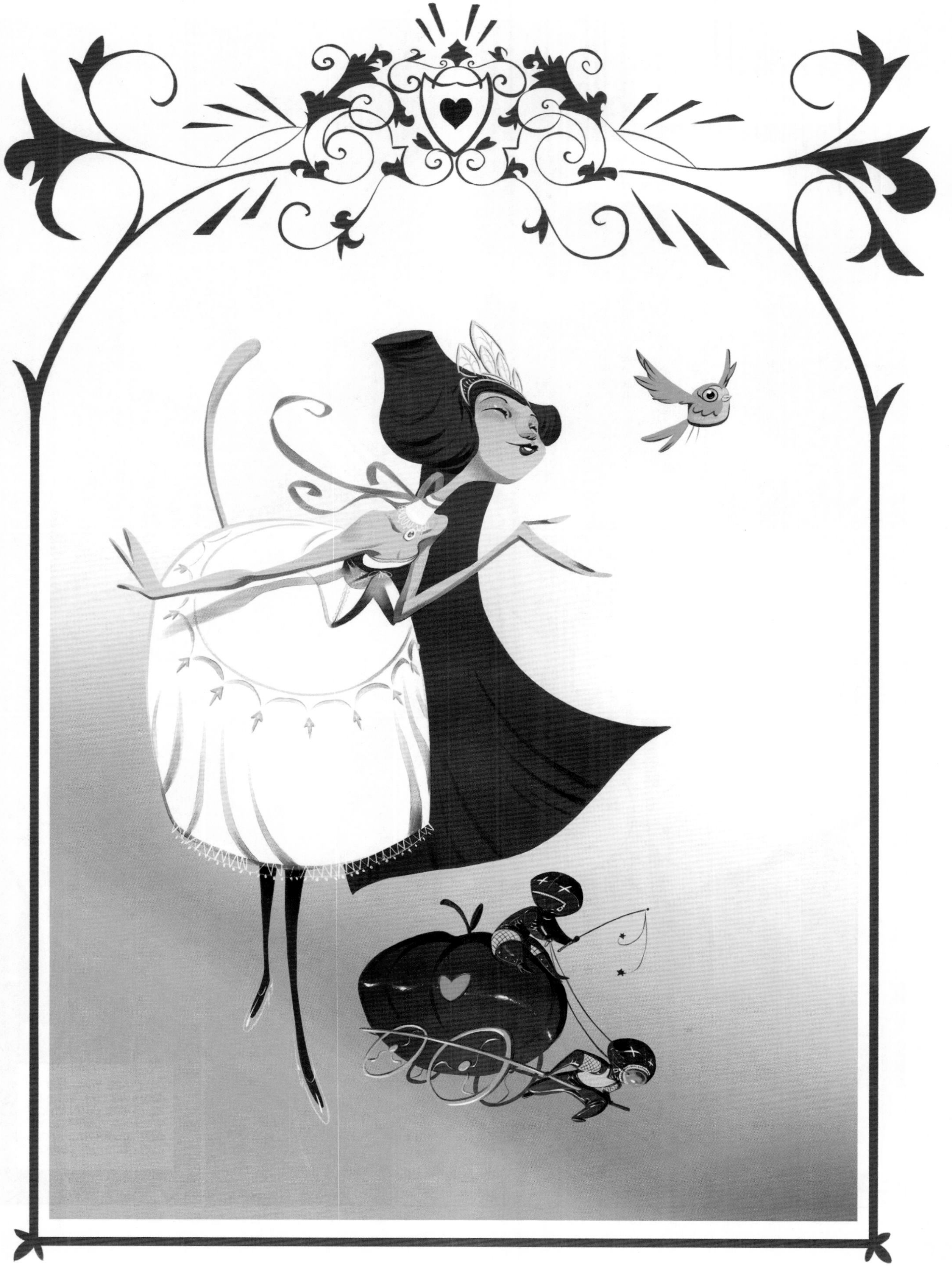

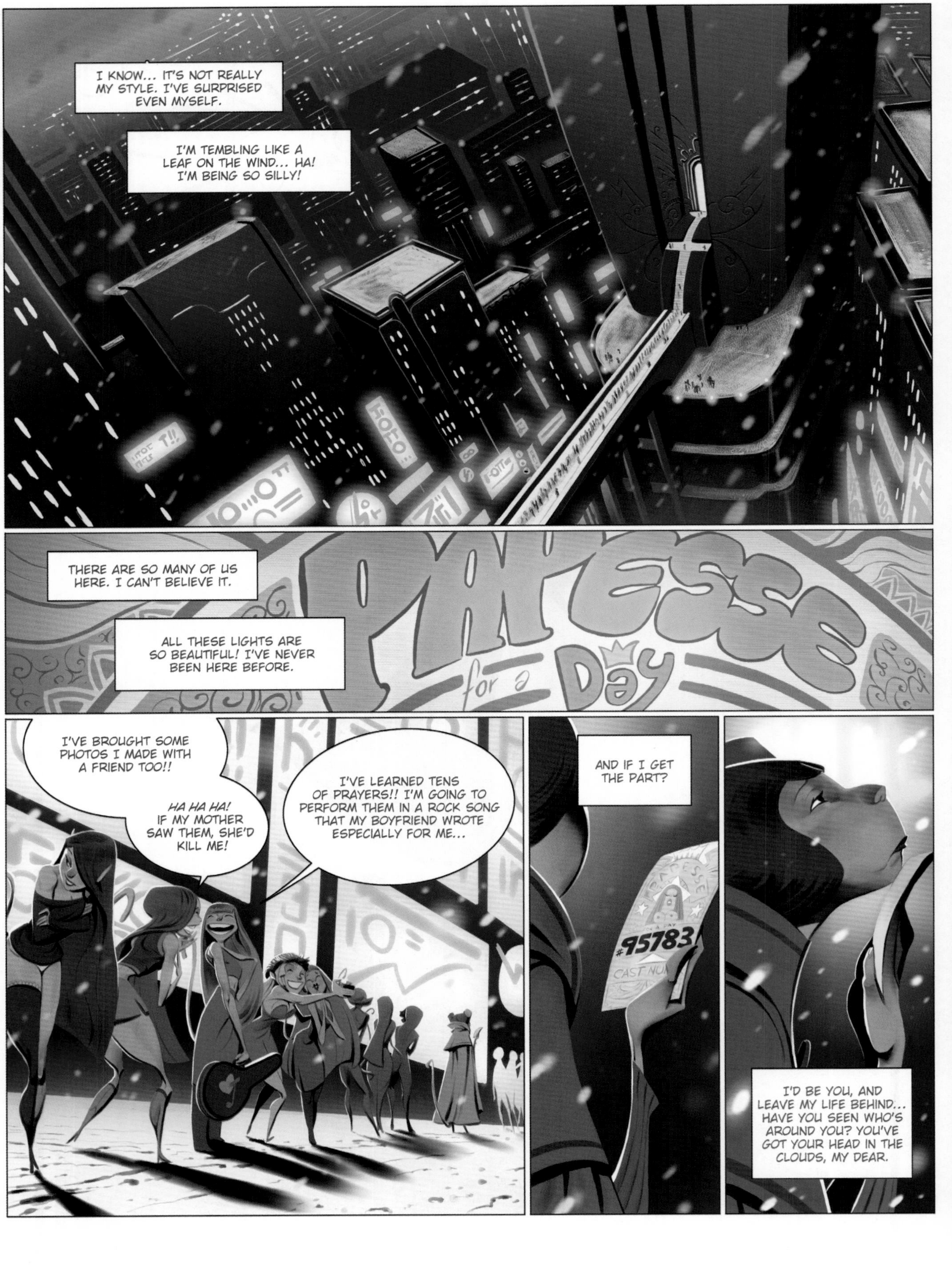
I KNOW... IT'S NOT REALLY MY STYLE. I'VE SURPRISED EVEN MYSELF.
I'M TEMBLING LIKE A LEAF ON THE WIND... HA! I'M BEING SO SILLY!
THERE ARE SO MANY OF US HERE. I CAN'T BELIEVE IT.
ALL THESE LIGHTS ARE SO BEAUTIFUL! I'VE NEVER BEEN HERE BEFORE.
for a Day
I'VE BROUGHT SOME PHOTOS I MADE WITH A FRIEND TOO!!
HA HA HA! IF MY MOTHER SAW THEM, SHE'D KILL ME!
I'VE LEARNED TENS OF PRAYERS!! I'M GOING TO PERFORM THEM IN A ROCK SONG THAT MY BOYFRIEND WROTE ESPECIALLY FOR ME...
AND IF I GET THE PART?
#95783
I'D BE YOU, AND LEAVE MY LIFE BEHIND... HAVE YOU SEEN WHO'S AROUND YOU? YOU'VE GOT YOUR HEAD IN THE CLOUDS, MY DEAR.

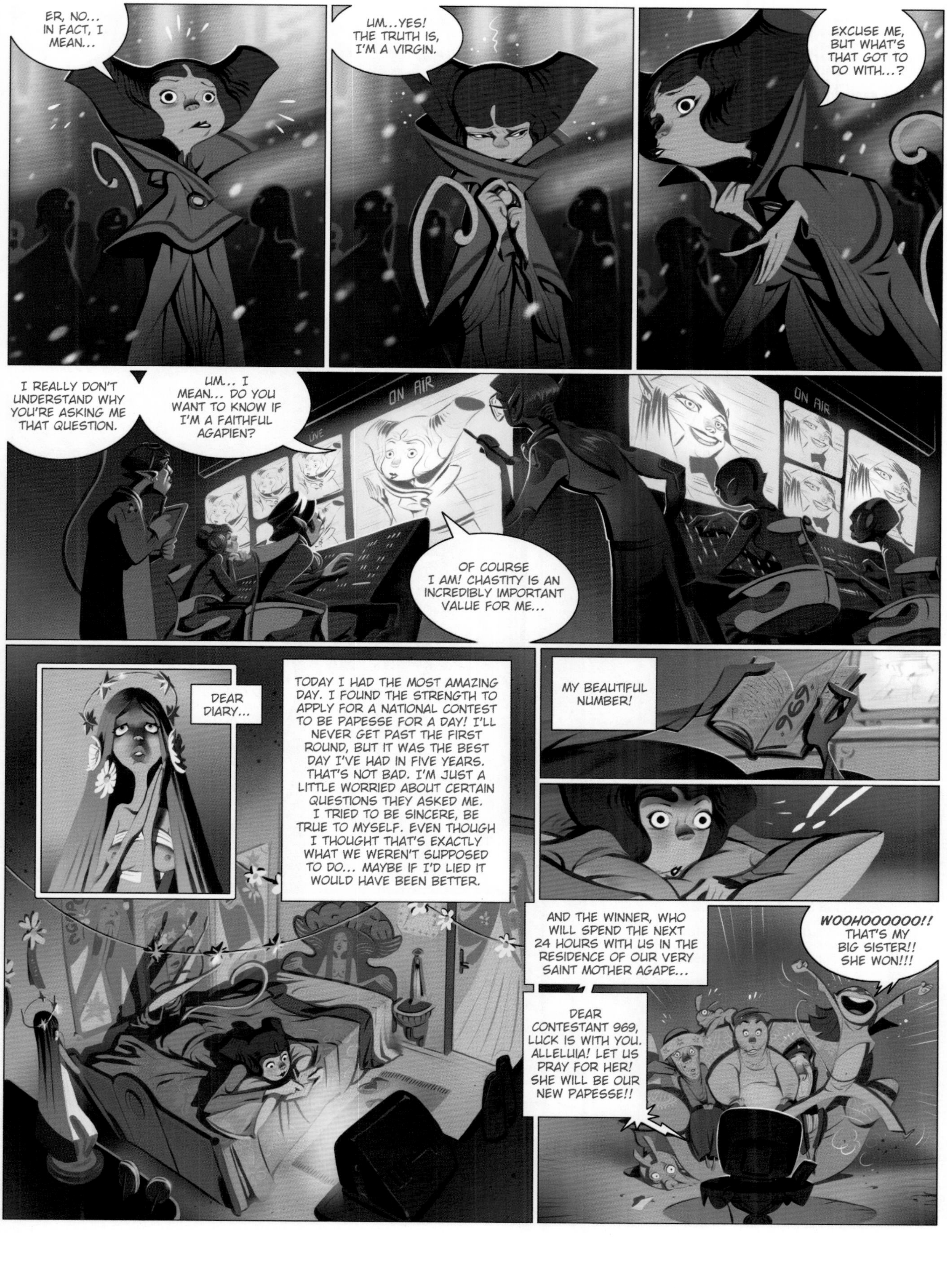
ER, NO... IN FACT, I MEAN...
UM...YES! THE TRUTH IS, I'M A VIRGIN.
EXCUSE ME, BUT WHAT'S THAT GOT TO DO WITH...?
I REALLY DON'T UNDERSTAND WHY YOU'RE ASKING ME THAT QUESTION.
UM... I MEAN... DO YOU WANT TO KNOW IF I'M A FAITHFUL AGAPIEN?
ON AIR
LIVE
ON AIR
OF COURSE I AM! CHASTITY IS AN INCREDIBLY IMPORTANT VALUE FOR ME...
DEAR DIARY...
TODAY I HAD THE MOST AMAZING DAY. I FOUND THE STRENGTH TO APPLY FOR A NATIONAL CONTEST TO BE PAPESSE FOR A DAY! I'LL NEVER GET PAST THE FIRST ROUND, BUT IT WAS THE BEST DAY I'VE HAD IN FIVE YEARS. THAT'S NOT BAD. I'M JUST A LITTLE WORRIED ABOUT CERTAIN QUESTIONS THEY ASKED ME. I TRIED TO BE SINCERE, BE TRUE TO MYSELF. EVEN THOUGH I THOUGHT THAT'S EXACTLY WHAT WE WEREN'T SUPPOSED TO DO... MAYBE IF I'D LIED IT WOULD HAVE BEEN BETTER.
MY BEAUTIFUL NUMBER!
969
AND THE WINNER, WHO WILL SPEND THE NEXT 24 HOURS WITH US IN THE RESIDENCE OF OUR VERY SAINT MOTHER AGAPE...
DEAR CONTESTANT 969, LUCK IS WITH YOU. ALLELUIA! LET US PRAY FOR HER! SHE WILL BE OUR NEW PAPESSE!!
WOOHOOOOOOO!! THAT'S MY BIG SISTER!! SHE WON!!!

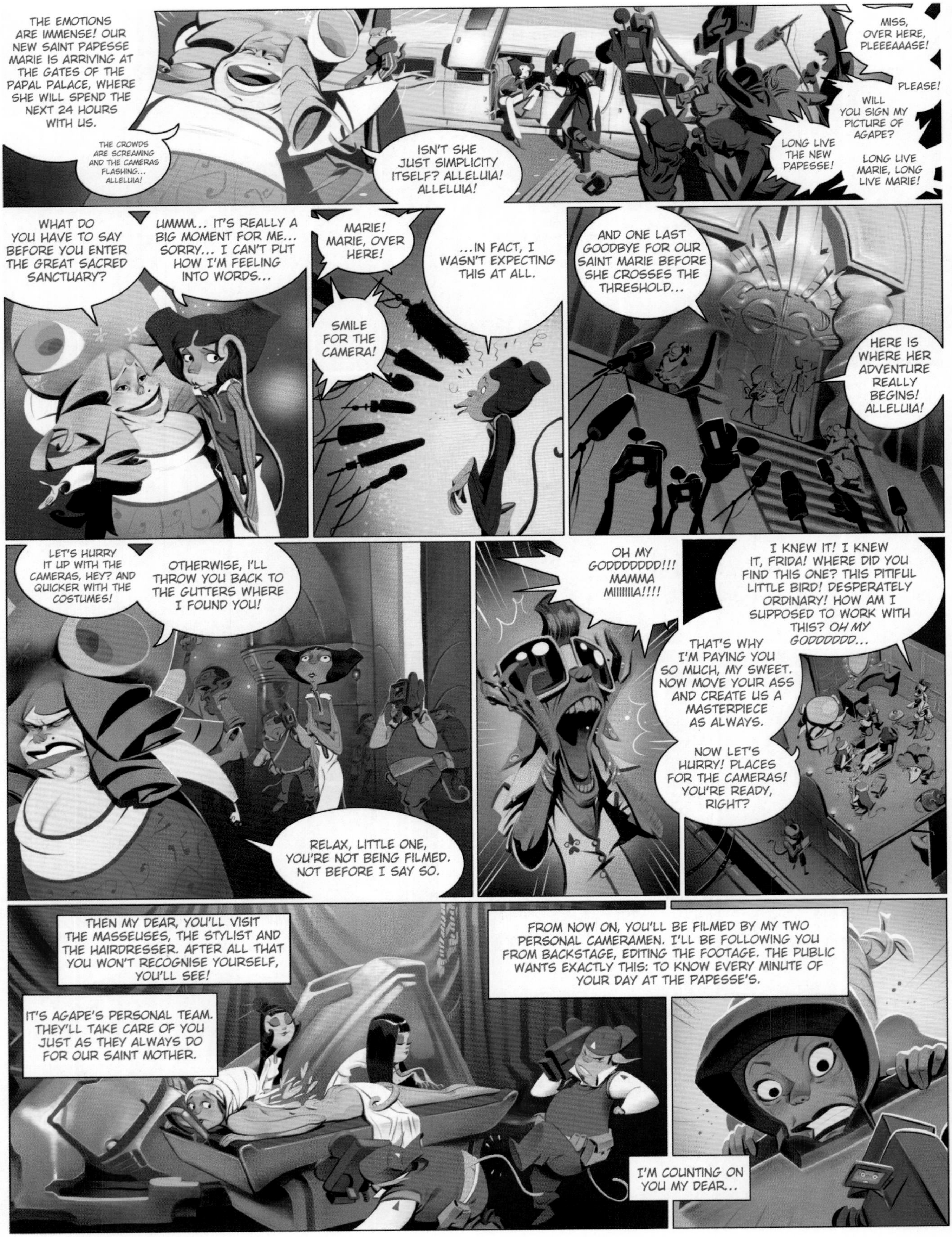
THE EMOTIONS ARE IMMENSE! OUR NEW SAINT PAPESSE MARIE IS ARRIVING AT THE GATES OF THE PAPAL PALACE, WHERE SHE WILL SPEND THE NEXT 24 HOURS WITH US.
THE CROWDS ARE SCREAMING AND THE CAMERAS FLASHING... ALLELUIA!
ISN'T SHE JUST SIMPLICITY ITSELF? ALLELUIA! ALLELUIA!
MISS, OVER HERE, PLEEEAAAASE!
PLEASE!
WILL YOU SIGN MY PICTURE OF AGAPE?
LONG LIVE THE NEW PAPESSE!
LONG LIVE MARIE, LONG LIVE MARIE!
WHAT DO YOU HAVE TO SAY BEFORE YOU ENTER THE GREAT SACRED SANCTUARY?
UMMM... IT'S REALLY A BIG MOMENT FOR ME... SORRY... I CAN'T PUT HOW I'M FEELING INTO WORDS...
MARIE! MARIE, OVER HERE!
...IN FACT, I WASN'T EXPECTING THIS AT ALL.
SMILE FOR THE CAMERA!
AND ONE LAST GOODBYE FOR OUR SAINT MARIE BEFORE SHE CROSSES THE THRESHOLD...
HERE IS WHERE HER ADVENTURE REALLY BEGINS! ALLELUIA!
LET'S HURRY IT UP WITH THE CAMERAS, HEY? AND QUICKER WITH THE COSTUMES!
OTHERWISE, I'LL THROW YOU BACK TO THE GUTTERS WHERE I FOUND YOU!
RELAX, LITTLE ONE, YOU'RE NOT BEING FILMED. NOT BEFORE I SAY SO.
OH MY GODDDDDDD!!! MAMMA MIIIIIIA!!!!
I KNEW IT! I KNEW IT, FRIDA! WHERE DID YOU FIND THIS ONE? THIS PITIFUL LITTLE BIRD! DESPERATELY ORDINARY! HOW AM I SUPPOSED TO WORK WITH THIS? OH MY GODDDDDD...
THAT'S WHY I'M PAYING YOU SO MUCH, MY SWEET. NOW MOVE YOUR ASS AND CREATE US A MASTERPIECE AS ALWAYS.
NOW LET'S HURRY! PLACES FOR THE CAMERAS! YOU'RE READY, RIGHT?
THEN MY DEAR, YOU'LL VISIT THE MASSEUSES, THE STYLIST AND THE HAIRDRESSER. AFTER ALL THAT YOU WON'T RECOGNISE YOURSELF, YOU'LL SEE!
IT'S AGAPE'S PERSONAL TEAM. THEY'LL TAKE CARE OF YOU JUST AS THEY ALWAYS DO FOR OUR SAINT MOTHER.
FROM NOW ON, YOU'LL BE FILMED BY MY TWO PERSONAL CAMERAMEN. I'LL BE FOLLOWING YOU FROM BACKSTAGE, EDITING THE FOOTAGE. THE PUBLIC WANTS EXACTLY THIS: TO KNOW EVERY MINUTE OF YOUR DAY AT THE PAPESSE'S.
I'M COUNTING ON YOU MY DEAR...

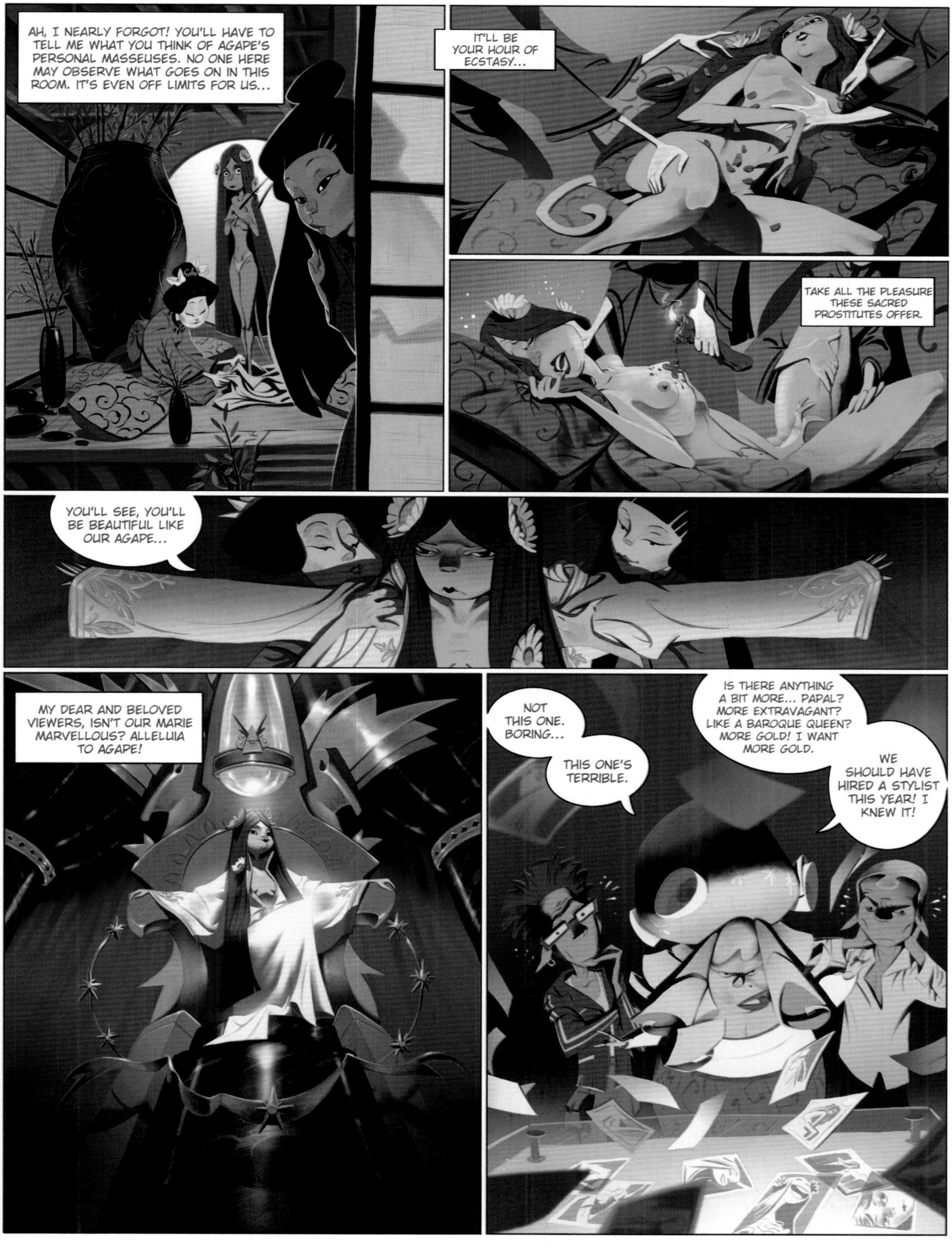
AH, I NEARLY FORGOT! YOU'LL HAVE TO TELL ME WHAT YOU THINK OF AGAPE'S PERSONAL MASSEUSES. NO ONE HERE MAY OBSERVE WHAT GOES ON IN THIS ROOM. IT'S EVEN OFF LIMITS FOR US...
IT'LL BE YOUR HOUR OF ECSTASY...
TAKE ALL THE PLEASURE THESE SACRED PROSTITUTES OFFER.
YOU'LL SEE, YOU'LL BE BEAUTIFUL LIKE OUR AGAPE...
MY DEAR AND BELOVED VIEWERS, ISN'T OUR MARIE MARVELLOUS? ALLELUIA TO AGAPE!
NOT THIS ONE. BORING...
THIS ONE'S TERRIBLE.
IS THERE ANYTHING A BIT MORE... PAPAL? MORE EXTRAVAGANT? LIKE A BAROQUE QUEEN? MORE GOLD! I WANT MORE GOLD.
WE SHOULD HAVE HIRED A STYLIST THIS YEAR! I KNEW IT!

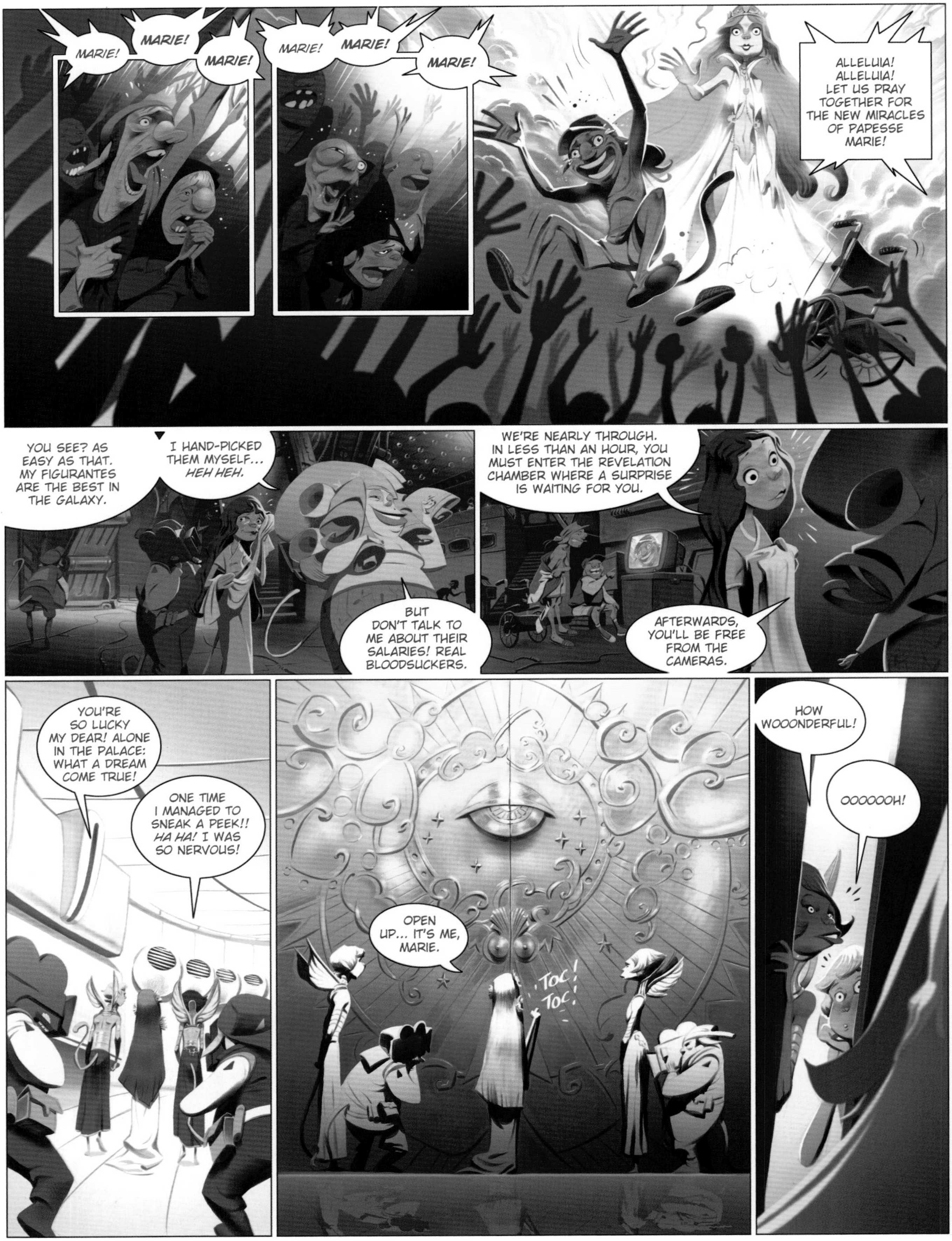
MARIE!
MARIE!
MARIE!
MARIE!
MARIE!
MARIE!
ALLELUIA! ALLELUIA! LET US PRAY TOGETHER FOR THE NEW MIRACLES OF PAPESSE MARIE!
YOU SEE? AS EASY AS THAT. MY FIGURANTES ARE THE BEST IN THE GALAXY.
I HAND-PICKED THEM MYSELF... HEH HEH.
BUT DON'T TALK TO ME ABOUT THEIR SALARIES! REAL BLOODSUCKERS.
WE'RE NEARLY THROUGH. IN LESS THAN AN HOUR, YOU MUST ENTER THE REVELATION CHAMBER WHERE A SURPRISE IS WAITING FOR YOU.
AFTERWARDS, YOU'LL BE FREE FROM THE CAMERAS.
YOU'RE SO LUCKY MY DEAR! ALONE IN THE PALACE: WHAT A DREAM COME TRUE!
ONE TIME I MANAGED TO SNEAK A PEEK!! HA HA! I WAS SO NERVOUS!
OPEN UP... IT'S ME, MARIE.
TOC! TOC!
HOW WOOONDERFUL!
OOOOOOH!

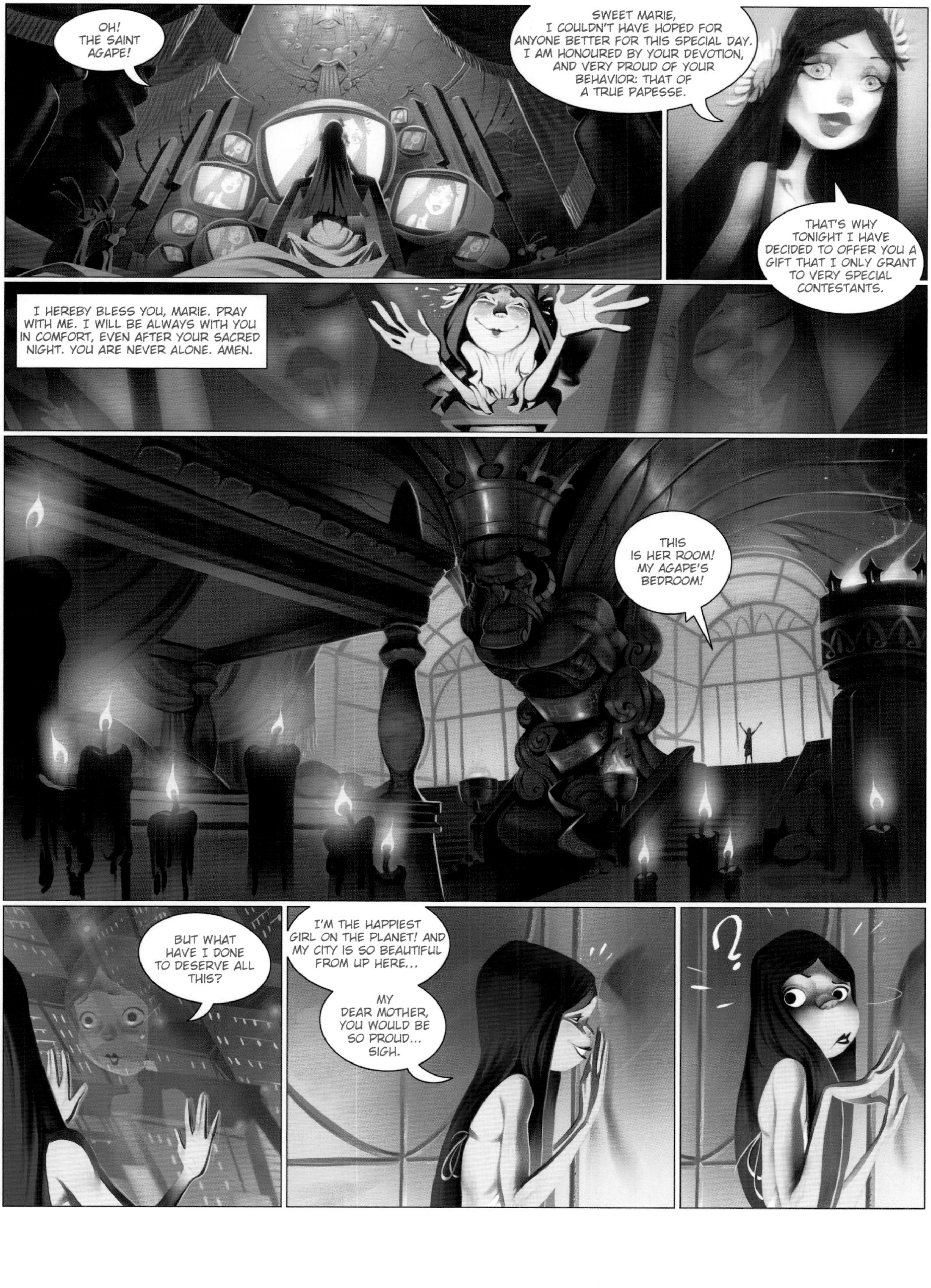

OH! THE SAINT AGAPE!
SWEET MARIE, I COULDN'T HAVE HOPED FOR ANYONE BETTER FOR THIS SPECIAL DAY. I AM HONOURED BY YOUR DEVOTION, AND VERY PROUD OF YOUR BEHAVIOR: THAT OF A TRUE PAPESSE.
THAT'S WHY TONIGHT I HAVE DECIDED TO OFFER YOU A GIFT THAT I ONLY GRANT TO VERY SPECIAL CONTESTANTS.
I HEREBY BLESS YOU, MARIE. PRAY WITH ME. I WILL BE ALWAYS WITH YOU IN COMFORT, EVEN AFTER YOUR SACRED NIGHT. YOU ARE NEVER ALONE. AMEN.
THIS IS HER ROOM! MY AGAPE'S BEDROOM!
BUT WHAT HAVE I DONE TO DESERVE ALL THIS?
I'M THE HAPPIEST GIRL ON THE PLANET! AND MY CITY IS SO BEAUTIFUL FROM UP HERE...
MY DEAR MOTHER, YOU WOULD BE SO PROUD... SIGH.
?

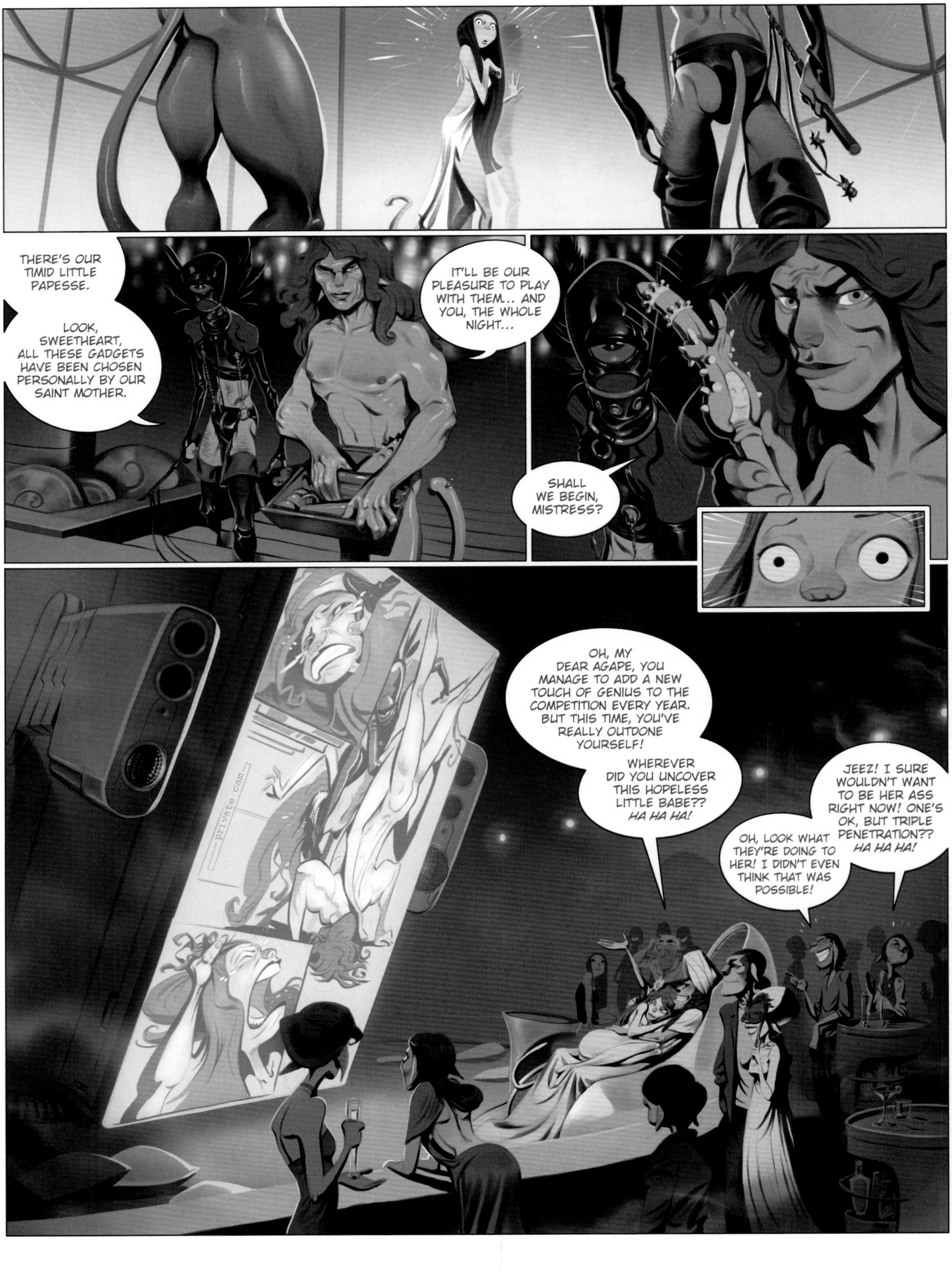
THERE'S OUR TIMID LITTLE PAPESSE.
LOOK, SWEETHEART, ALL THESE GADGETS HAVE BEEN CHOSEN PERSONALLY BY OUR SAINT MOTHER.
IT'LL BE OUR PLEASURE TO PLAY WITH THEM... AND YOU, THE WHOLE NIGHT...
SHALL WE BEGIN, MISTRESS?
OH, MY DEAR AGAPE, YOU MANAGE TO ADD A NEW TOUCH OF GENIUS TO THE COMPETITION EVERY YEAR. BUT THIS TIME, YOU'VE REALLY OUTDONE YOURSELF!
WHEREVER DID YOU UNCOVER THIS HOPELESS LITTLE BABE?? *HA HA HA!*
OH, LOOK WHAT THEY'RE DOING TO HER! I DIDN'T EVEN THINK THAT WAS POSSIBLE!
JEEZ! I SURE WOULDN'T WANT TO BE HER ASS RIGHT NOW! ONE'S OK, BUT TRIPLE PENETRATION?? *HA HA HA!*

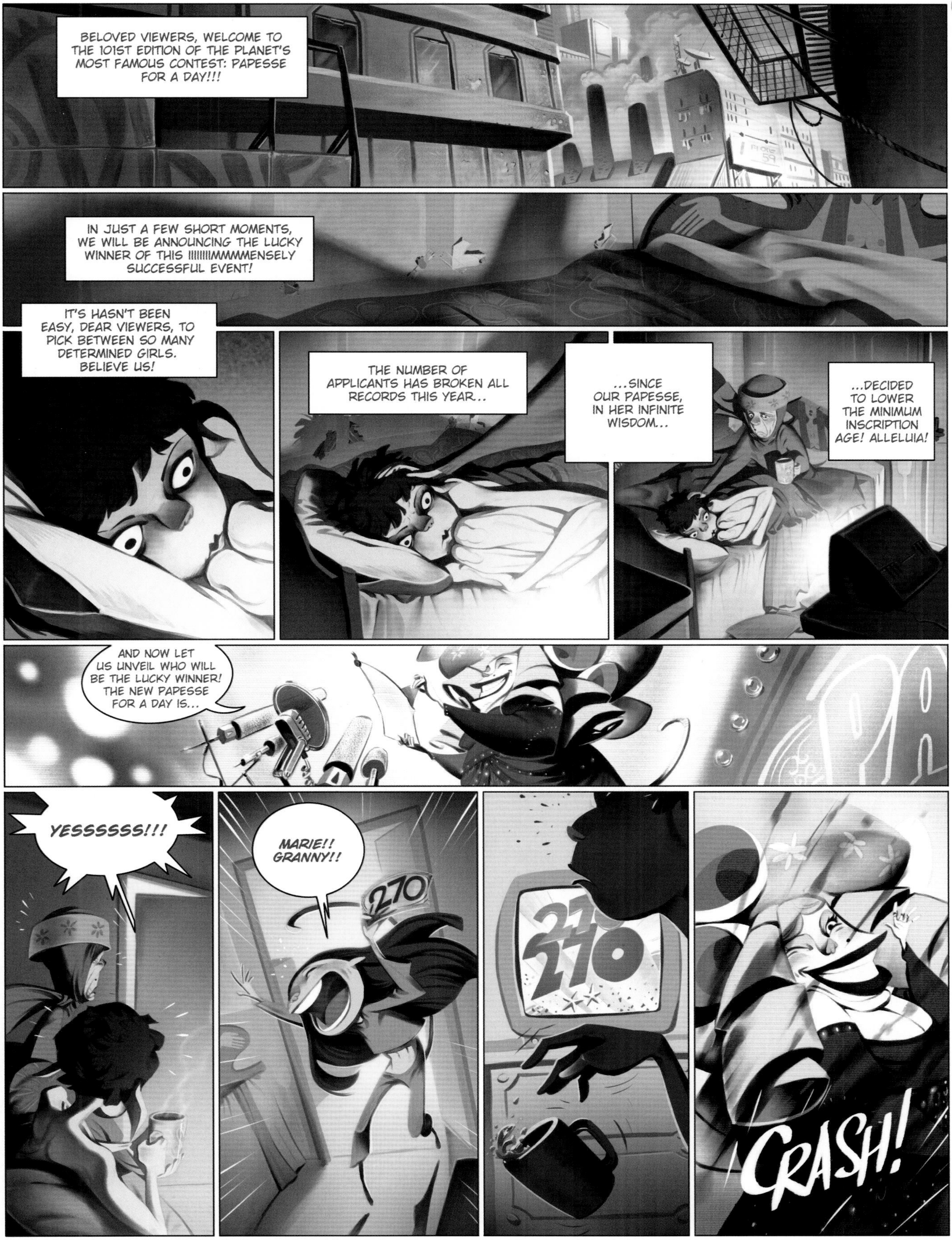
BELOVED VIEWERS, WELCOME TO THE 101ST EDITION OF THE PLANET'S MOST FAMOUS CONTEST: PAPESSE FOR A DAY!!!
IN JUST A FEW SHORT MOMENTS, WE WILL BE ANNOUNCING THE LUCKY WINNER OF THIS IIIIIIIIMMMMENSELY SUCCESSFUL EVENT!
IT'S HASN'T BEEN EASY, DEAR VIEWERS, TO PICK BETWEEN SO MANY DETERMINED GIRLS. BELIEVE US!
THE NUMBER OF APPLICANTS HAS BROKEN ALL RECORDS THIS YEAR...
...SINCE OUR PAPESSE, IN HER INFINITE WISDOM...
...DECIDED TO LOWER THE MINIMUM INSCRIPTION AGE! ALLELUIA!
AND NOW LET US UNVEIL WHO WILL BE THE LUCKY WINNER! THE NEW PAPESSE FOR A DAY IS...
YESSSSSS!!!
MARIE!! GRANNY!!
270
270
CRASH!

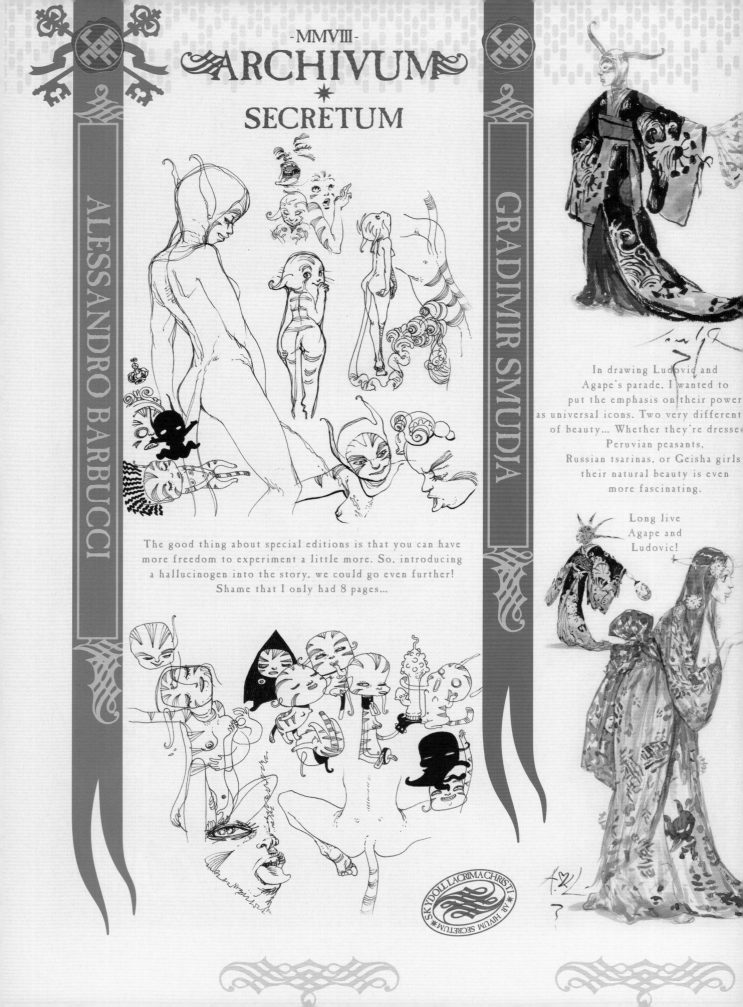

-MMVIII-

ARCHIVUM

SECRETUM

ALESSANDRO BARBUCCI

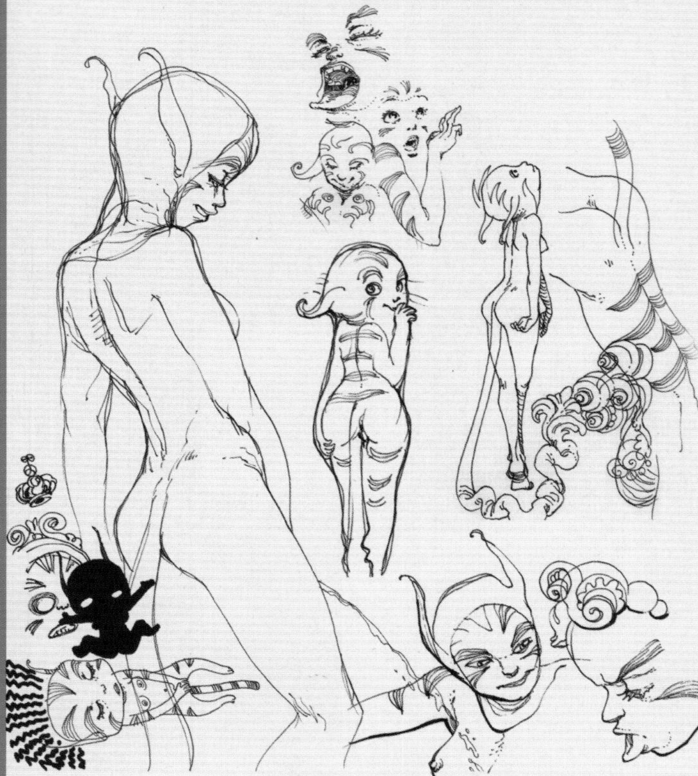

The good thing about special editions is that you can have more freedom to experiment a little more. So, introducing a hallucinogen into the story, we could go even further! Shame that I only had 8 pages...

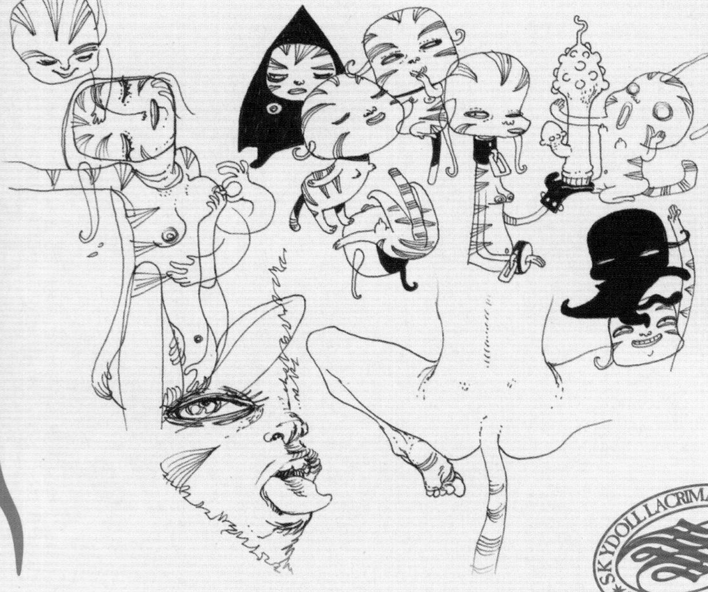

GRADIMIR SMUDIA

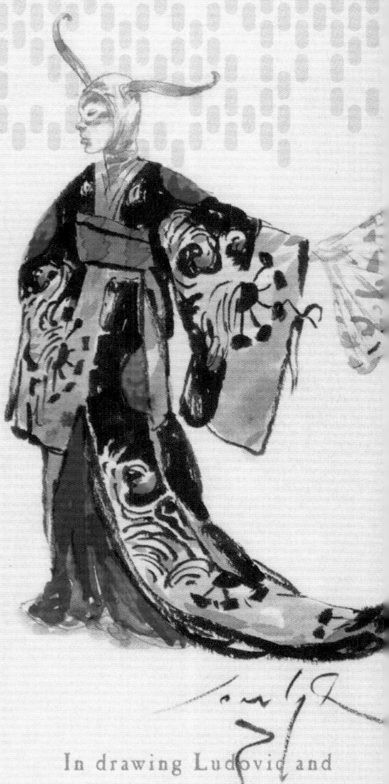

In drawing Ludovic and Agape's parade, I wanted to put the emphasis on their power as universal icons. Two very different of beauty... Whether they're dresse Peruvian peasants, Russian tsarinas, or Geisha girls their natural beauty is even more fascinating.

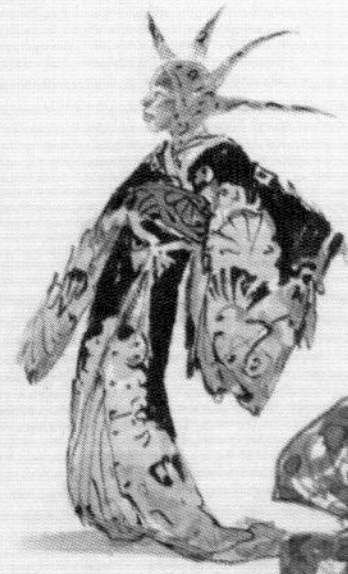

Long live Agape and Ludovic!

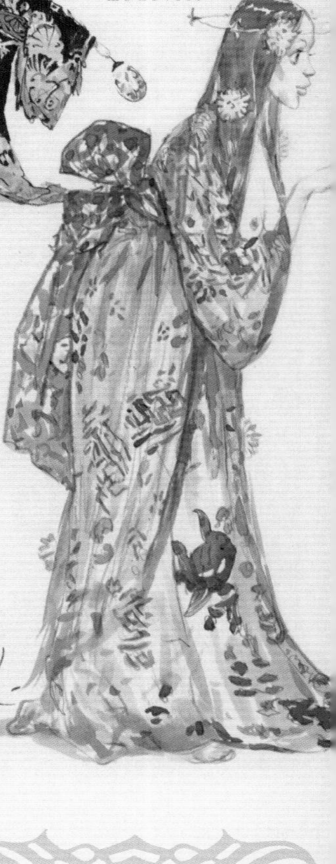

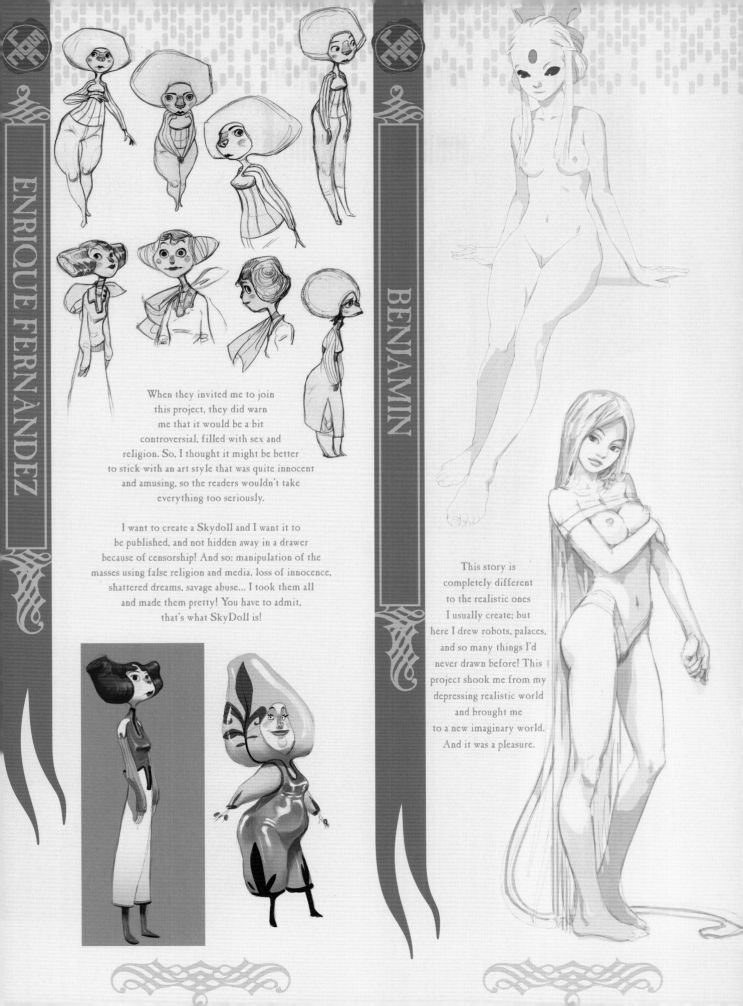

ENRIQUE FERNÀNDEZ

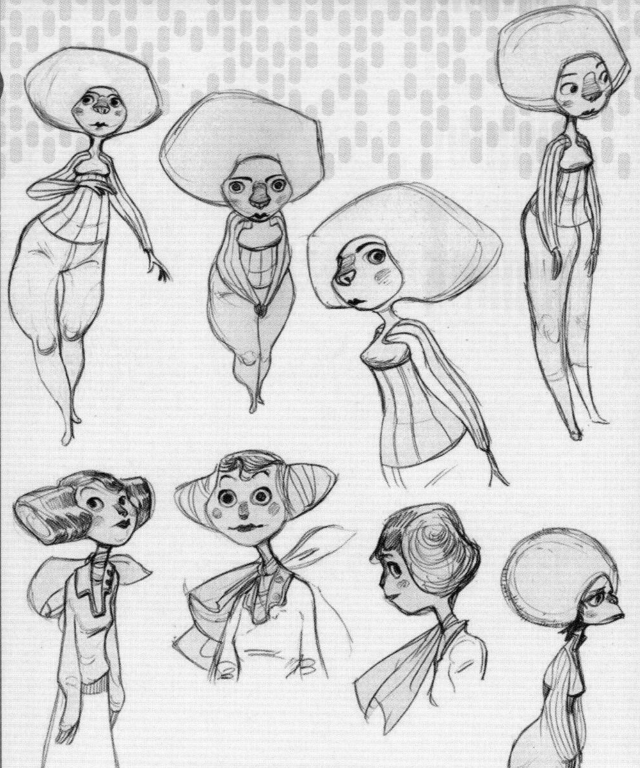

When they invited me to join this project, they did warn me that it would be a bit controversial, filled with sex and religion. So, I thought it might be better to stick with an art style that was quite innocent and amusing, so the readers wouldn't take everything too seriously.

I want to create a Skydoll and I want it to be published, and not hidden away in a drawer because of censorship! And so: manipulation of the masses using false religion and media, loss of innocence, shattered dreams, savage abuse... I took them all and made them pretty! You have to admit, that's what SkyDoll is!

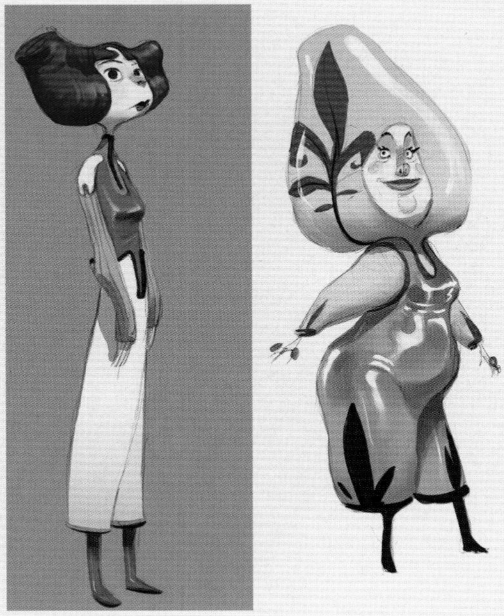

BENJAMIN

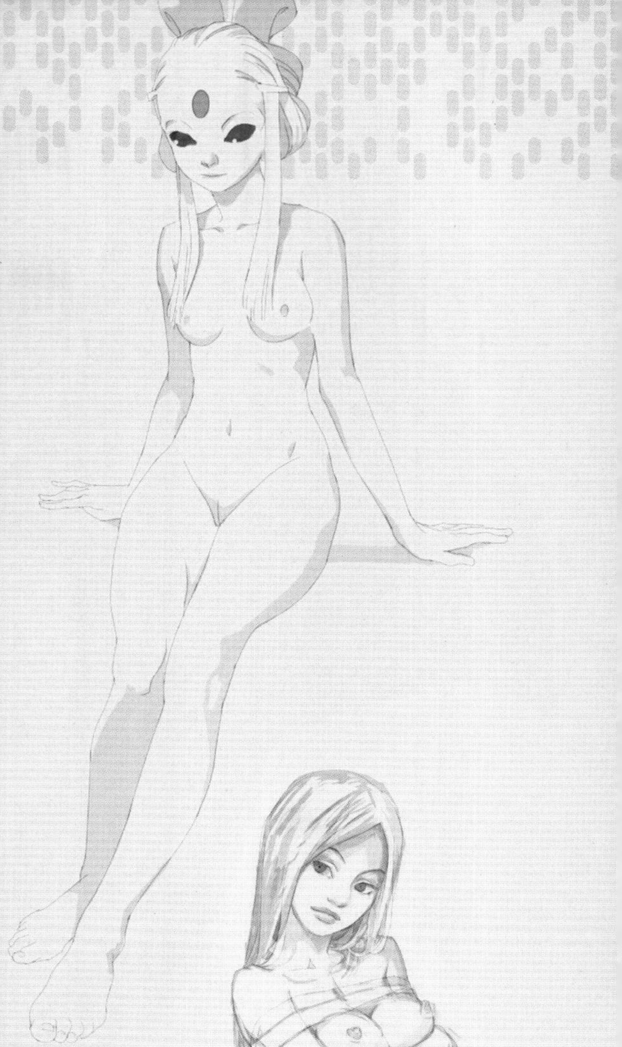

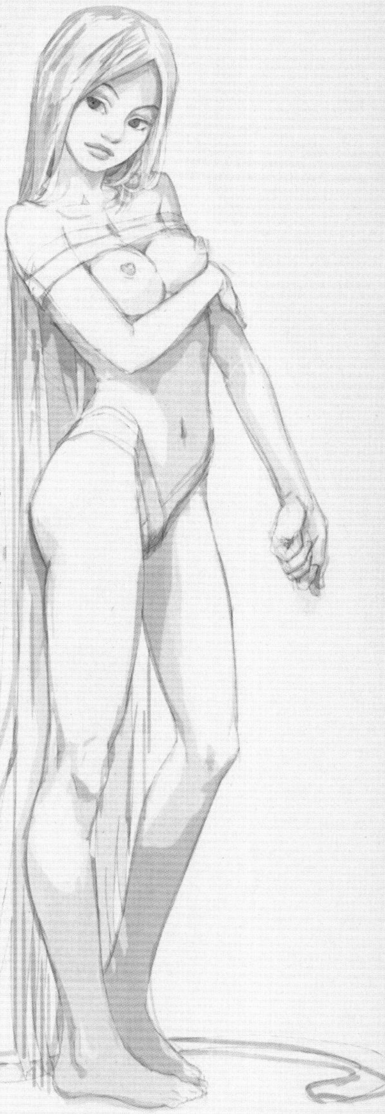

This story is completely different to the realistic ones I usually create; but here I drew robots, palaces, and so many things I'd never drawn before! This project shook me from my depressing realistic world and brought me to a new imaginary world. And it was a pleasure.

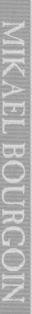

AFIF KHALED

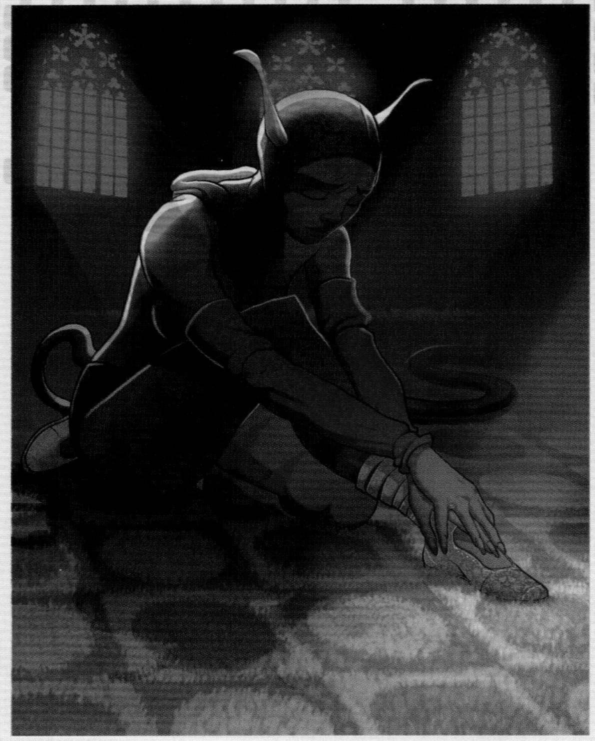

First and foremost, as a fan of Alessandro and Barbara's work, collaborating on Skydoll really was a great time for me.

It was a real pleasure to be able to delve into this universe and reimagine the references.

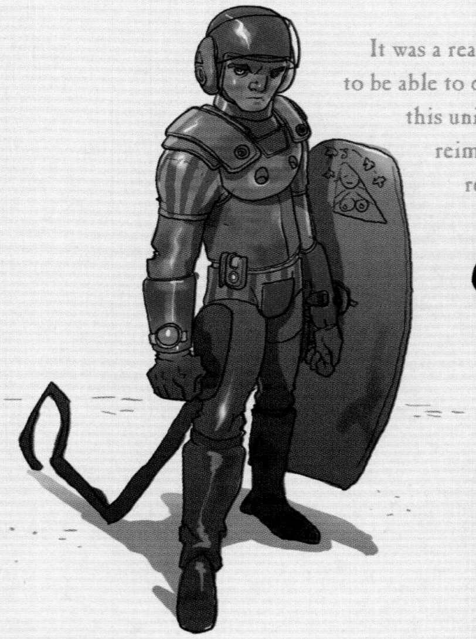

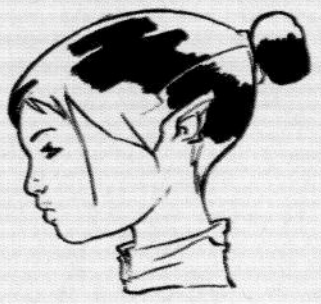

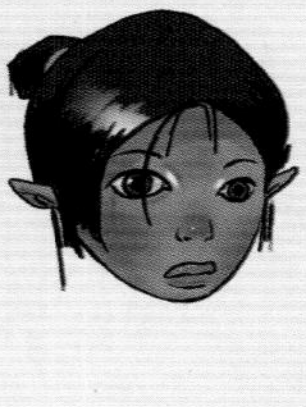

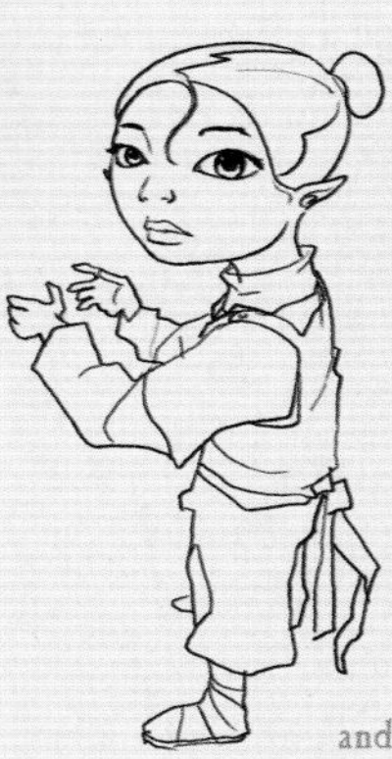

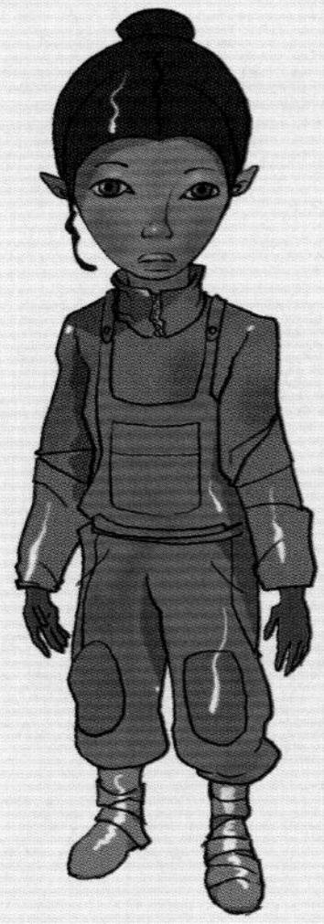

I worked on my pages as if it were a cartoon: characters and backgrounds designed, inked and colored exclusively digitally.

MIKAEL BOURGOIN

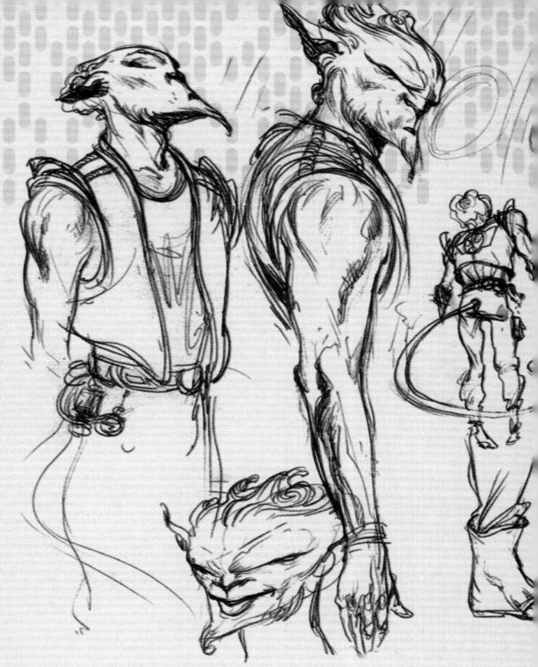

You must tread carefully when entering another's universe, t ensure that you give your own take on the characters while preserving their essence. This world is also something very different from anything I've worked on before. As someone w often errs toward dark stories, it was a real breath of fresh air work on such a 'bright' piece as this.

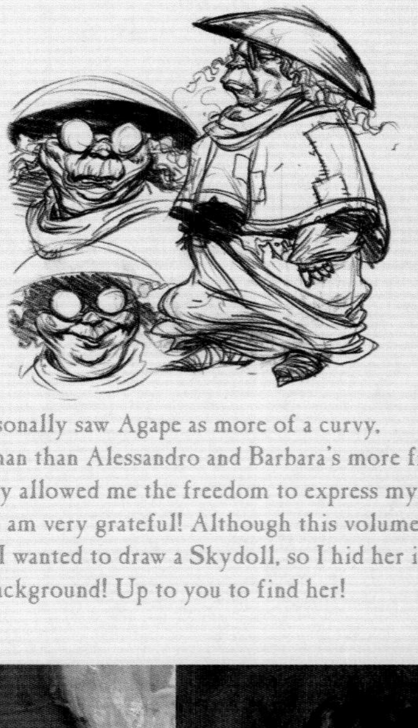

I personally saw Agape as more of a curvy, sensual woman than Alessandro and Barbara's more frail version. They allowed me the freedom to express myself and for that I am very grateful! Although this volume was about Agape, I wanted to draw a Skydoll, so I hid her in the background! Up to you to find her!

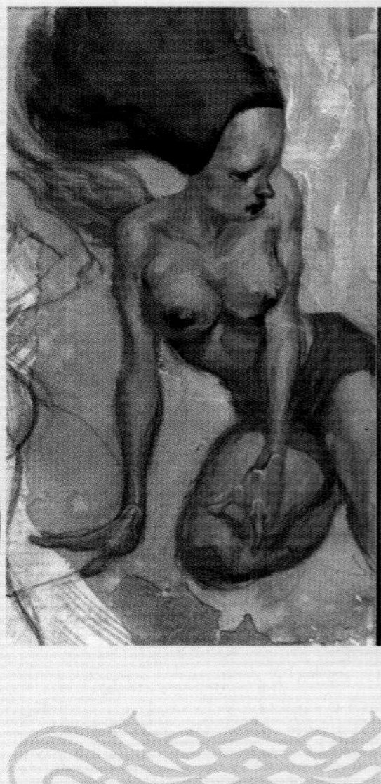

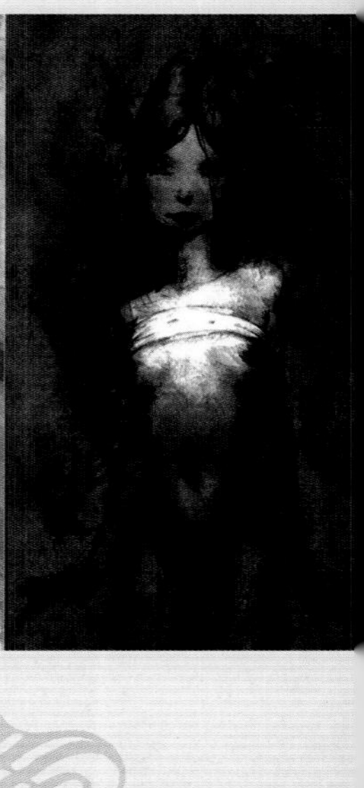

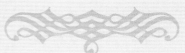

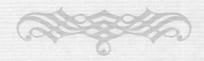

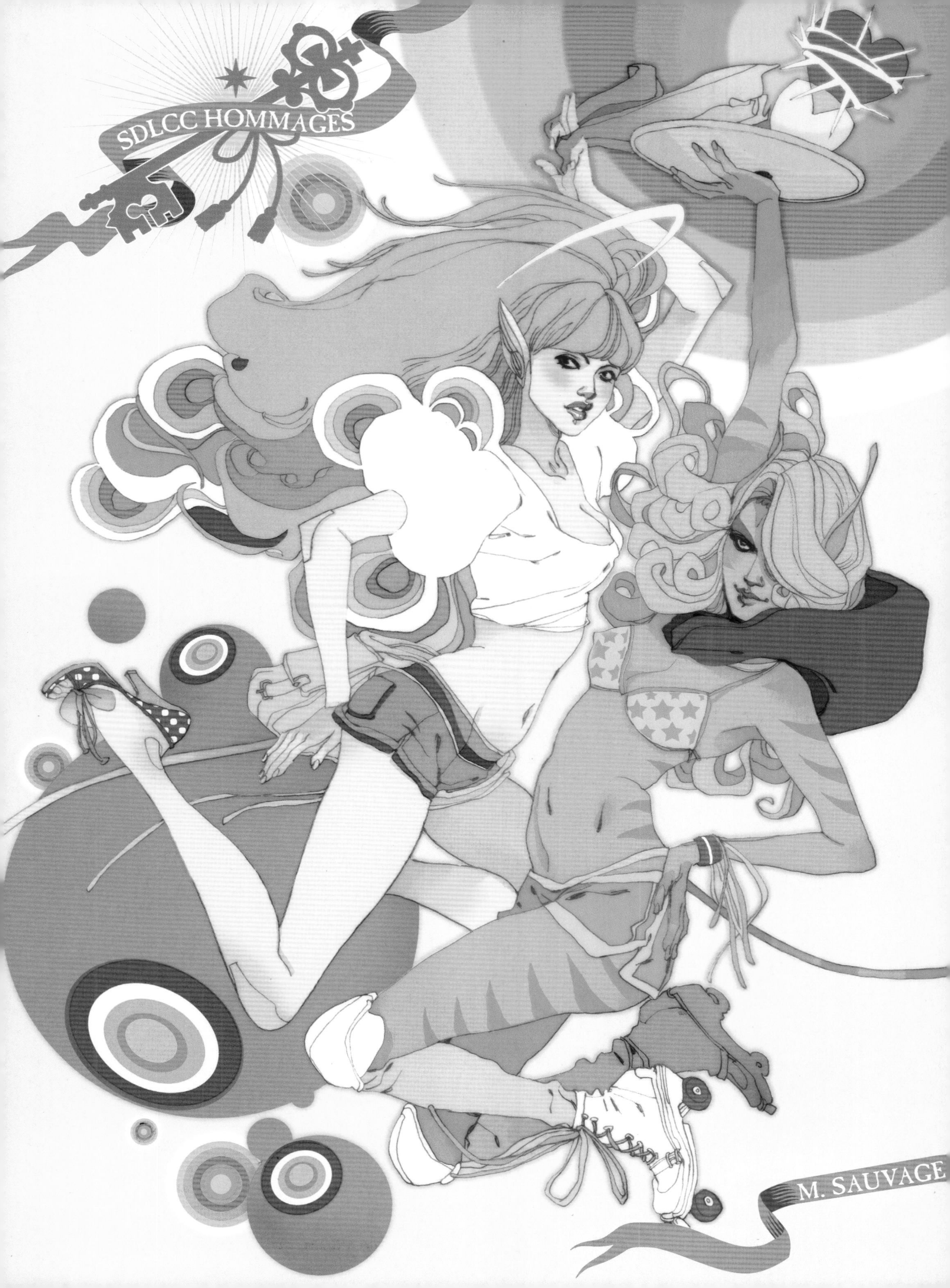
SDLCC HOMMAGES
M. SAUVAGE

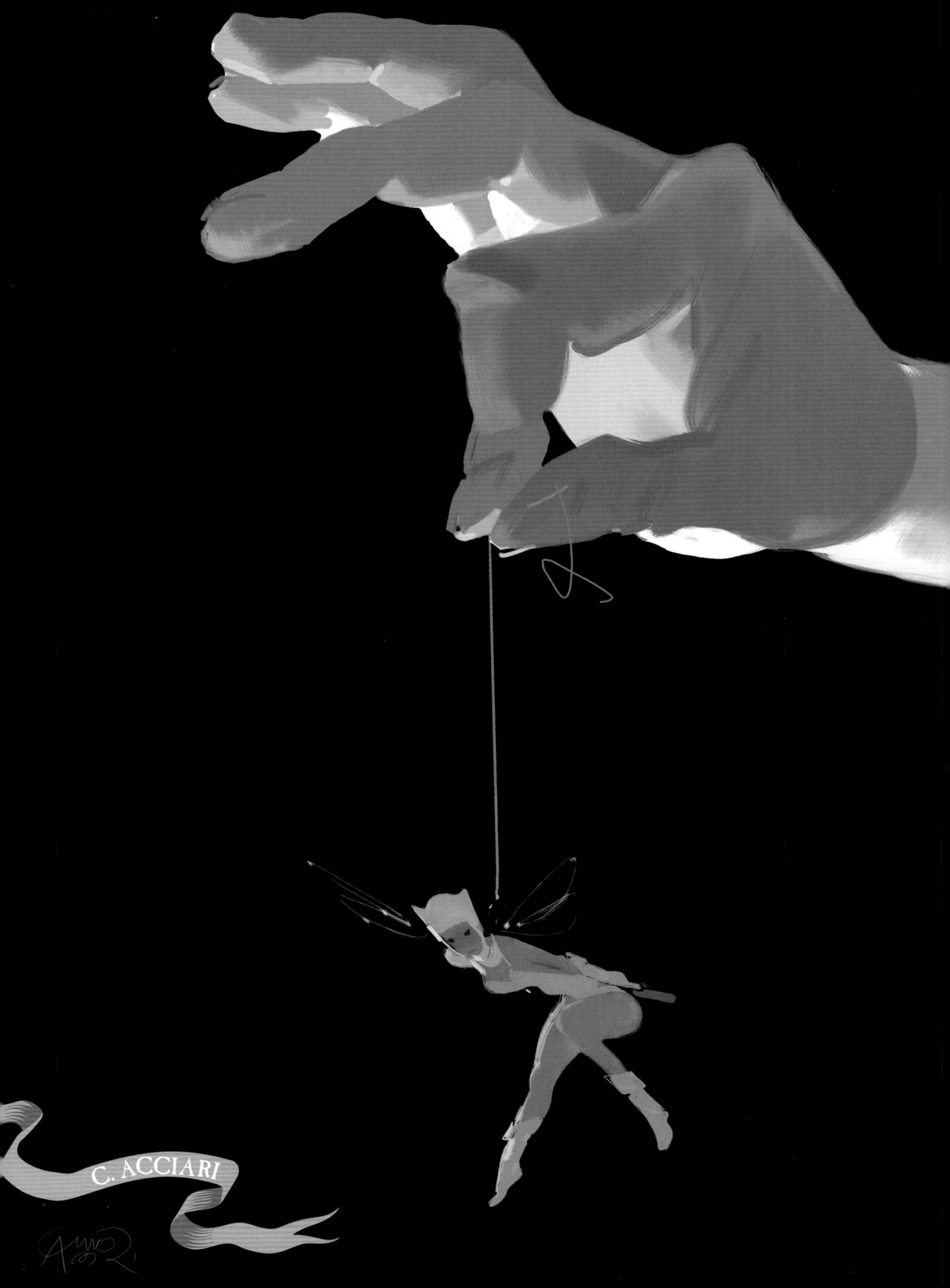
C. ACCIARI

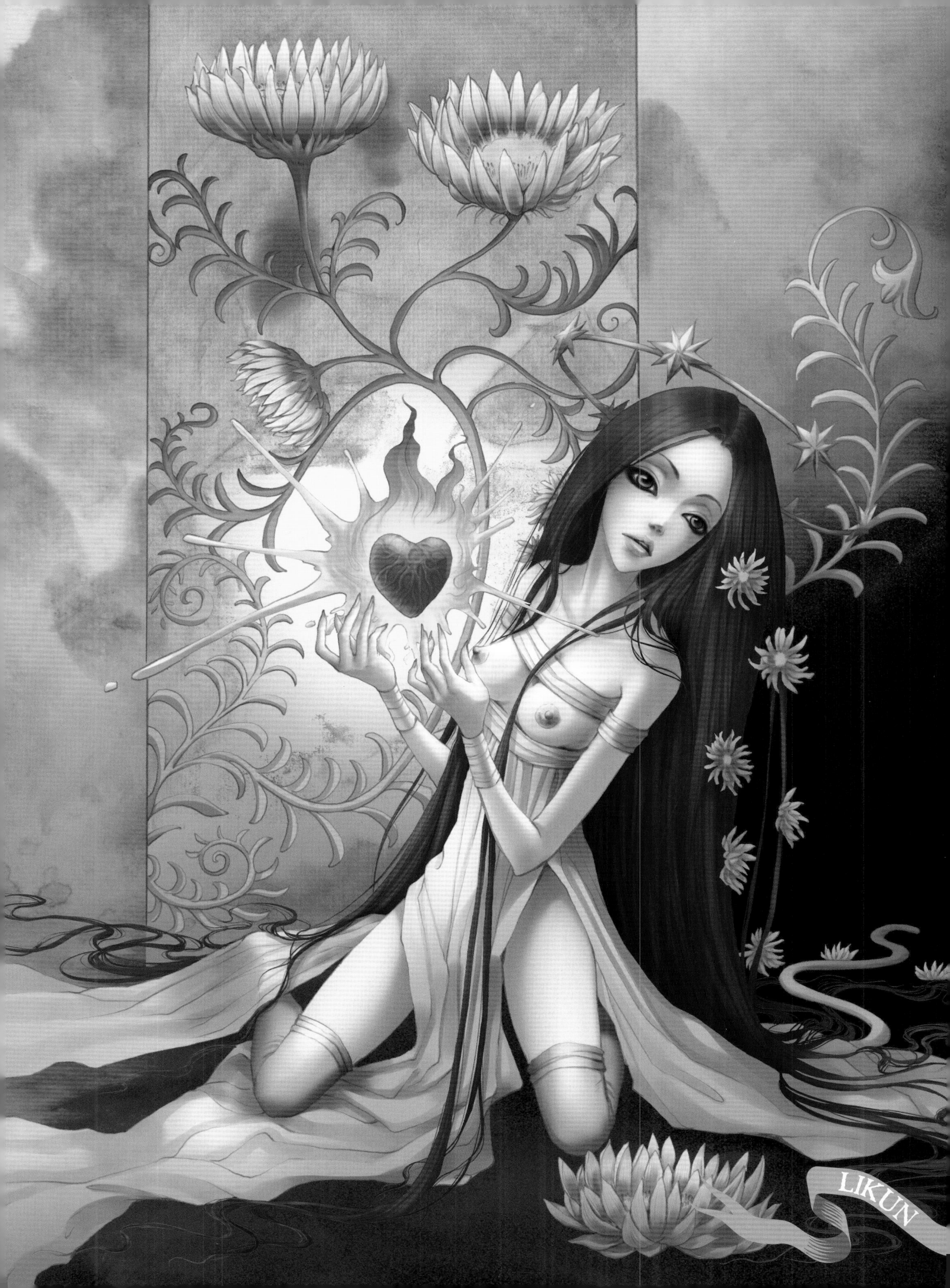
LIKUN

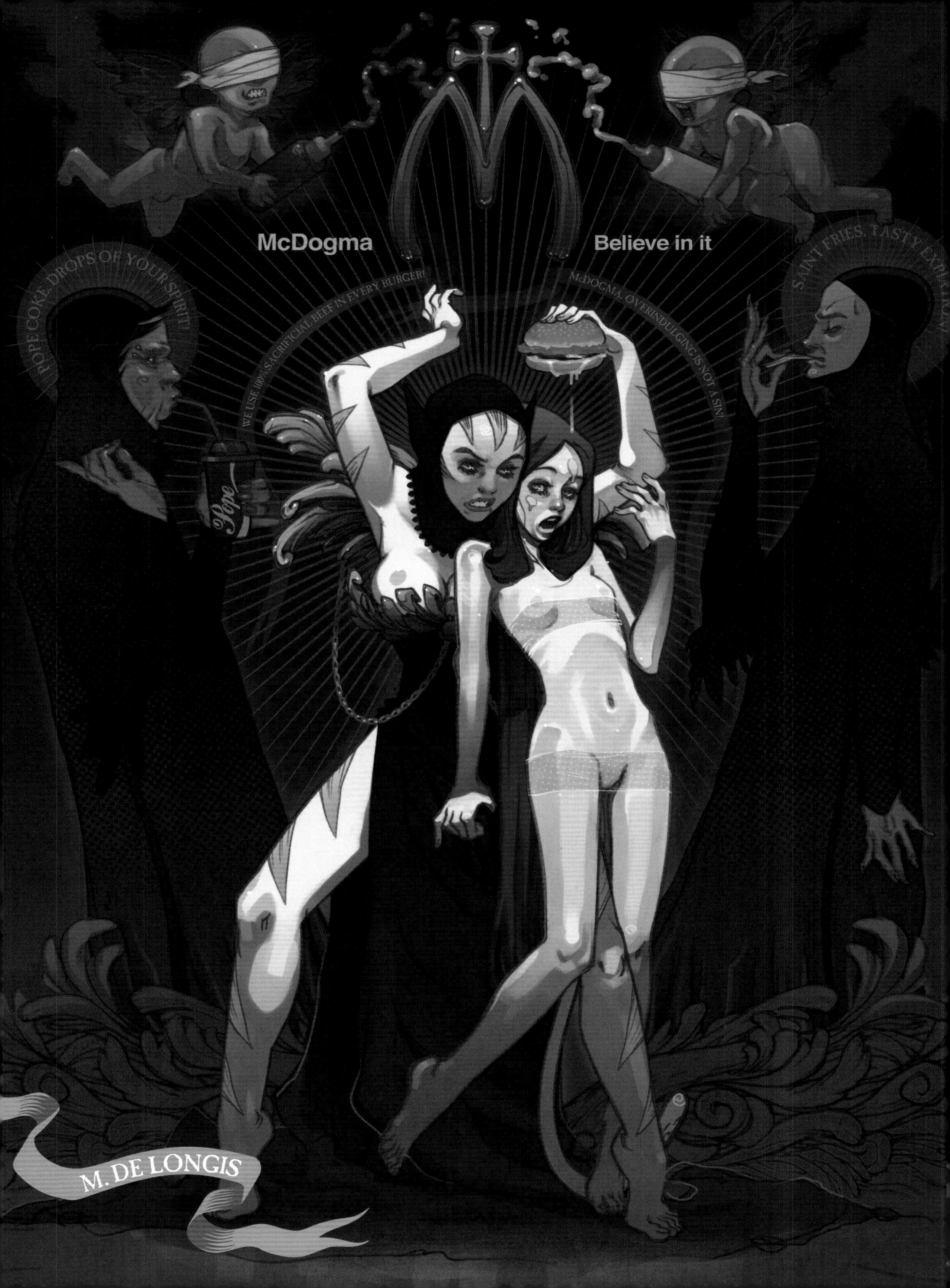
McDogma
Believe in it
POPE COKE. DROPS OF YOUR SPIRIT!
WE USE 100% SACRIFICIAL BEEF IN EVERY BURGER!
McDOGMA. OVERINDULGING IS NOT A SIN!
SAINT FRIES, TASTY
Pope
M. DE LONGIS

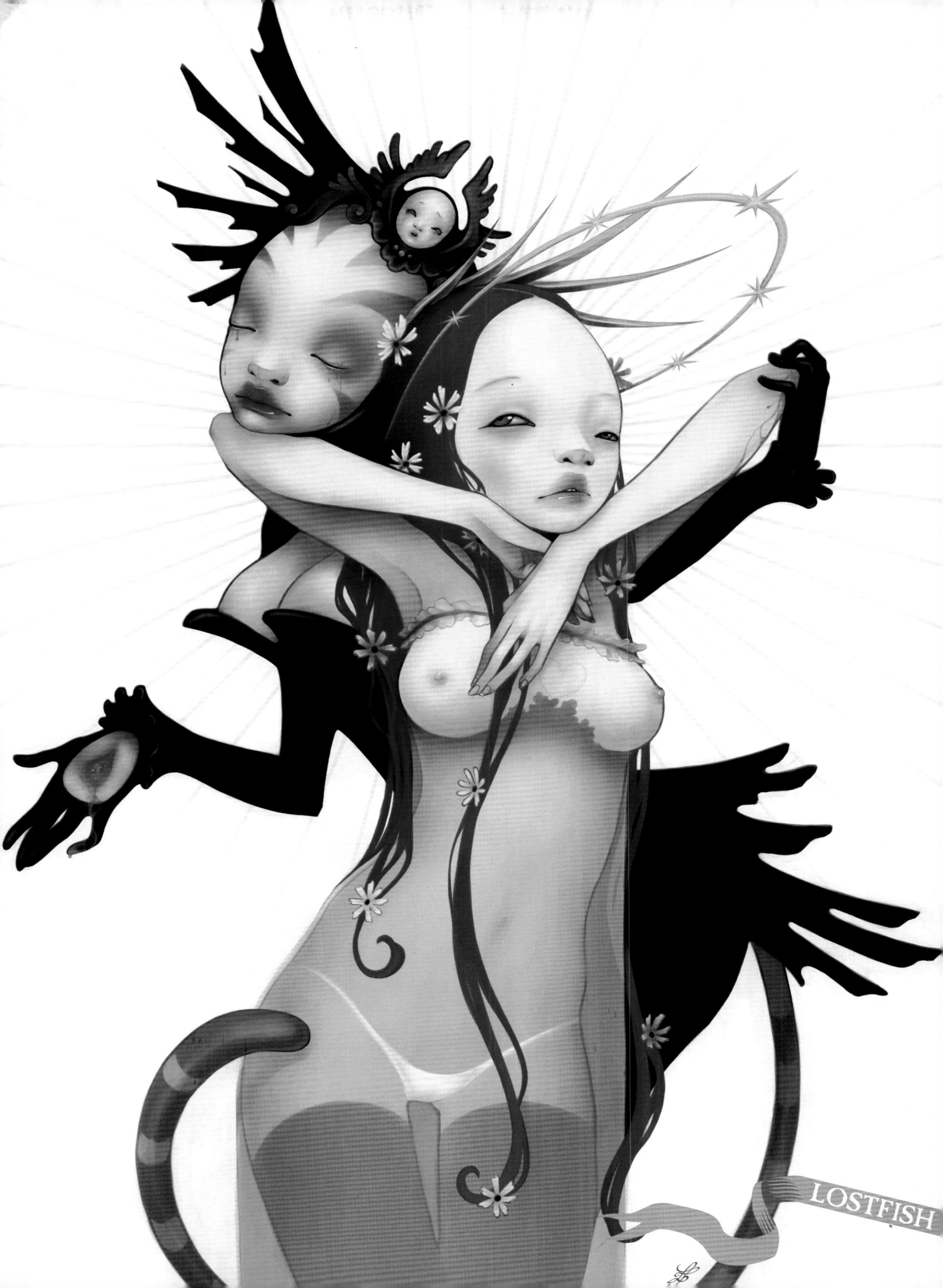
LOSTFISH

For Younes and Nael.
Afif

And, as always, thank you to all the friends and colleagues who have made this so much fun.
This album of Sky Doll is for you.
Barbara

I am grateful to Alessandro and Barbara,
for giving me the chance to work on this album with such excellent artists .
I also want to thank my friends Li Ming and Yan Teng for their help with translation.
Ben

For all my crazy wednesday lunch friends.
Enrique

Thank you to Alessandro and Barbara for allowing me to work with them.
It was a great pleasure. I loved drawing Agape. It was all I hoped for!
Mikael

For the Sky Doll fans, for the passion, encouragement, and patience.
Alessandro

SKY Doll Spaceship:
Volume coordinated by | Jean Wacquet, Alessandro Barbucci & Barbara Canepa
Graphic Design | Alessandro Barbucci, Barbara Canepa & Matteo De Longis
Designer | Matteo De Longis
Cover & Title Page | Alessandro Barbucci & Barbara Canepa

SKY Doll Lacrima Christi:
Volume coordinated by | Jean Wacquet, Alessandro Barbucci & Barbara Canepa
Graphic Design | Alessandro Barbucci, Barbara Canepa & Matteo De Longis
Designer | Studio Soleil
Cover & Title Page | Alessandro Barbucci & Barbara Canepa
Hommages | LostFish, Claudio Acciari, Marguerite Sauvage, Likun, Matteo De Longis

Collection Editor
Lizzie Kaye

Collection Designer
Andrew Leung

Senior Editor
Andrew James

Titan Comics Editorial
Tom Williams, Jessica Burton, Amoona Soahin

Production Manager
Obi Onuora

Production Supervisors
Jackie Flook,
Maria Pearson

Production Assistant
Peter James

Art Director
Oz Browne

Senior Sales Manager
Steve Tothill

Direct Sales & Marketing Manager
Ricky Claydon

Senior Marketing & Press Executive
Owen Johnson

Publishing Manager
Darryl Tothill

Publishing Director
Chris Teather

Operations Director
Leigh Baulch

Executive Director
Vivian Cheung

Publisher
Nick Landau

SKY DOLL: Spaceship Collection
ISBN: 9781782767374

Collects SKY DOLL: Spaceship & SKY DOLL: Lacrima Christi

Published by Titan Comics. A division of Titan Publishing Group Ltd. 144 Southwark St, London, SE1 0UP

SKY DOLL and all contents are copyright © EDITIONS SOLEIL / BARBUCCI / CANEPA / DE LONGIS / BOURGOIN / BENJAMIN/ FERNANDEZ / SMUDJA / CHAN / ACCIARI / BENGAL / RIFF REB'S / KHALED

10 9 8 7 6 5 4 3 2 1

Printed in China. Titan Comics. TC0919

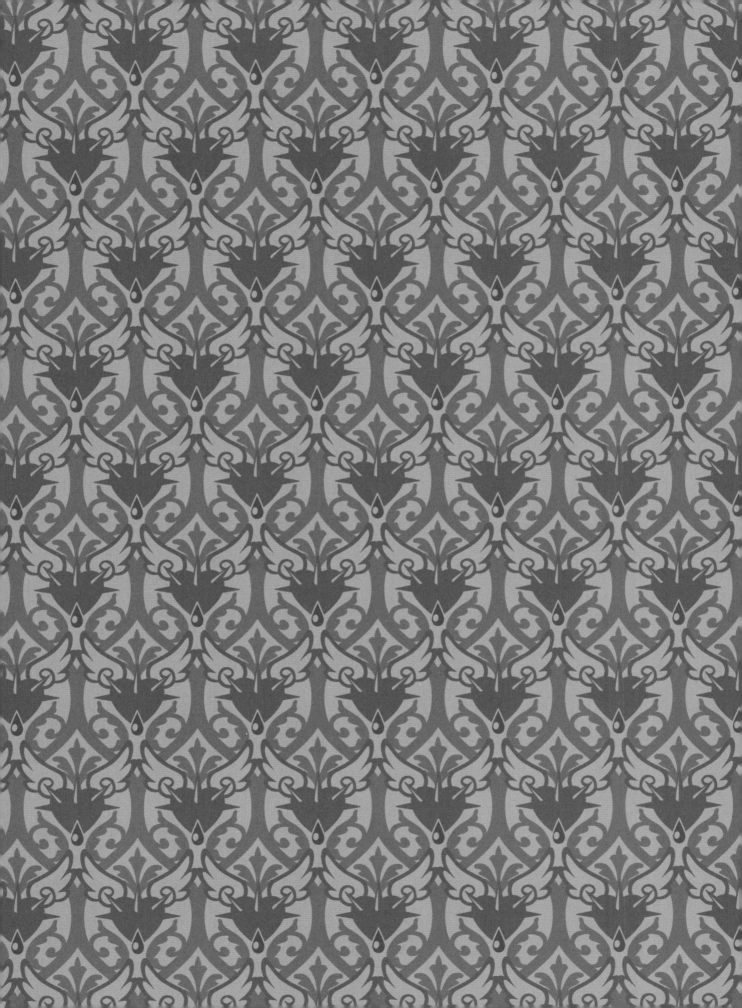